William Blake Odgers

The Principles of Pleading in Civil Actions under the Judicature Acts

William Blake Odgers

The Principles of Pleading in Civil Actions under the Judicature Acts

ISBN/EAN: 9783337402181

Printed in Europe, USA, Canada, Australia, Japan

Cover: Foto ©Suzi / pixelio.de

More available books at **www.hansebooks.com**

THE

PRINCIPLES OF PLEADING

IN

CIVIL ACTIONS

UNDER THE

JUDICATURE ACTS.

BY

W. BLAKE ODGERS, M.A., LL.D.,
LATE SCHOLAR AND LAW STUDENT OF TRINITY HALL, CAMBRIDGE,
OF THE MIDDLE TEMPLE AND THE WESTERN CIRCUIT, BARRISTER-AT-LAW,
Author of "A Digest of the Law of Libel and Slander."

LONDON:

STEVENS AND SONS, LIMITED,
119 & 120, CHANCERY LANE,
Law Publishers and Booksellers.

1892.

PREFACE.

The system of pleading introduced by the Judicature Acts is in theory the best and wisest, and indeed the only sensible, system of pleading in civil actions. Each party in turn is required to state the material facts on which he relies; he must also deal specifically with the facts alleged by his opponent, admitting or denying each of them in detail; and thus the matters really in dispute are speedily ascertained and defined. Some such preliminary process is essential before the trial.

How is it, then, that it is the fashion to decry our modern pleadings, to treat them as waste-paper, and to deplore the loss of the ancient method with its counts and pleas known by fantastic names, half Latin and half Norman-French? There are many reasons why the new system has not yet met with the success which it deserves. It has hitherto been worked mainly by men educated under the former practice. The modern system has never been so thoroughly taught to the younger generation of pleaders. Moreover, the reform was not, in one or two instances, sufficiently thorough. Some antiquated fragments of the old procedure remain (such as the plea of Not Guilty by Statute) which destroy the symmetry of the modern rules. There is yet another reason why our present system of pleading does not work so well as it should. Each party in turn ought to admit clearly or to deny expressly each fact alleged by his opponent. But counsel cannot do this, unless he is fully instructed as to the actual facts. The solicitor cannot fully instruct counsel as to the facts without thoroughly getting up the case; and the taxing master always discourages his doing so at this early stage. The amount allowed for Instructions for Defence and Reply is wholly inadequate to recompense the solicitor for the time and labour involved in properly instructing counsel how to plead. Hence admissions which ought to be made are not made.

It is in the hope of removing one cause of this want of success that I have written this Book on the principles of our present system of pleading. I have embodied in it notes made from time to time for the use of my own pupils. The rules of law are stated in large type; explanations, historical matter, and practical hints are given in smaller type, but larger than that used for the Illustrations. These have often been drawn from the older reports. It is to the sixteenth and seventeenth centuries that we must turn for a clear exposition of the rules of pleading at common law; and it was only in those days that the rules of pleading were rigorously and inflexibly enforced. Now, our regard for "the merits" overrides our respect for nice questions of pleading, though such questions still largely affect costs. But while the old law is freely referred to, all relevant decisions since 1875 will be found cited under their appropriate headings.

I am indebted to my friend and former pupil, Mr. M. STEWART PRICHARD, of the Inner Temple, for the full and convenient Index which he has prepared, and also for his kindness in revising the proof-sheets.

W. B. O.

4, ELM COURT, TEMPLE, E.C.
December 1891.

TABLE OF CONTENTS.

	PAGE
TABLE OF CASES CITED	xi—xxviii
TABLE OF STATUTES CITED	xxix, xxx
TABLE OF RULES AND ORDERS CITED	xxxi, xxxii

CHAPTER I.

THE FUNCTION OF PLEADINGS	1—6
The Object of Pleadings	1
History of Pleading	3
Nature of Pleadings	5

CHAPTER II.

MATERIAL FACTS	7—41
Fundamental Rule	7
Pleadings must state Facts and not Law	8
Ambiguity of previous system of Pleading	11
Pleadings must state Material Facts only	15
Jumping before you come to the Stile	20
Conditions Precedent	24
Matters affecting Damages	26
Pleadings must state Facts and not Evidence	31
How to plead Material Facts	36

CHAPTER III.

	PAGE
CERTAINTY	42—62
Degree of Certainty required	42
Certainty of Time	44
Certainty of Place	45
Certainty of Title	46
Pleading Authority	56
Imputations of Misconduct	59
Uncertainty	61

CHAPTER IV.

ANSWERING YOUR OPPONENT'S PLEADING	63—92
Different Ways of Answering Opponent's Pleading . .	63
I. Objections in Point of Law	71
II. Traverses	74
Facts not denied, admitted . . .	75
Specific Denials	79
Evasive Denials	81
III. Matters in Confession and Avoidance . .	89

CHAPTER V.

ATTACKING YOUR OPPONENT'S PLEADING	93—105
Application to strike out Opponent's Pleading . . .	94
Objection in Point of Law	95
Application to amend Opponent's Pleading . . .	96
Summons for Particulars	97

CHAPTER VI.

INDORSEMENT ON WRIT	106—115
Special Indorsement	107
in actions for the Recovery of Land .	111
General Indorsement	113
Indorsement for an Account	114

CHAPTER VII.

	PAGE
STATEMENT OF CLAIM	116—129
Old Forms of Action	116
Joinder of Causes of Action	118
Matters of Inducement	120
Statement of Claim in Tort	ib.
Statement of Claim in Contract	121
Damages	125
Relief	126
Venue	128

CHAPTER VIII.

DEFENCE	130—159
General Character of Defence	130
Pleading to Damages	133
Plea of Not Guilty by Statute	134
Plea of Possession	135
Special Defences	136
Set-off and Counter-claim	148
Third Parties	150
Severing Defences	151
Time	152
Precedents of Defences	154

CHAPTER IX.

REPLY, ETC.	160—171
Reply when there is a Counter-claim	160
Joinder of Issue	161
Departure	164
New Assignment	167
Rejoinder	169
Trial without Pleadings	170

CHAPTER X.

	PAGE
INTERROGATORIES	172—188
Object of Interrogatories	172
What Interrogatories are admissible	173
Setting aside Interrogatories	179
Answering Interrogatories	180
Objections to Answer	182
Precedents of Interrogatories and Objections to Answer	184

CHAPTER XI.

ADVICE ON EVIDENCE	189—201
Burden of Proof	190
Witnesses	191
Documentary Evidence	192
Secondary Evidence	194
Mode and Place of Trial	198
Precedents of Advices on Evidence	199

APPENDIX.

PLEADING RULES	203—221

INDEX	223—260

TABLE OF CASES CITED.

A.

Abl—Att PAGE

Abley *v.* Dale, 10 C. B. 62; 20 L. J. C. P. 33; 1 L. M. & P. 626; 14 Jur. 1069 - - - - - - - 59

Abrath *v.* North Eastern Rail. Co., 11 Q. B. D. 440; 52 L. J. Q. B. 620; 32 W. R. 50; 49 L. T. 618; 11 App. Cas. 247; 55 L. J. Q. B. 457; 55 L. T. 63 - - - - - - - 200

Adams *v.* Batley, 18 Q. B. D. 625; 56 L. J. Q. B. 393; 35 W. R. 437; 56 L. T. 770 - - - - - - - 178

Adams *v.* Kelly, Ry. & Moo. 157 - - - - - - 194

Aldis *v.* Mason, 11 C. B. 132; 20 L. J. C. P. 193 - - - 84

Alexander *v.* North Eastern Rail. Co., 6 B. & S. 340; 34 L. J. Q. B. 152; 11 Jur. N. S. 619; 13 W. R. 651 - - - - 163

Allhusen *v.* Labouchere, 3 Q. B. D. 654; 47 L. J. Ch. 819; 27 W. R. 12; 39 L. T. 207 - - - - - - - 174, 179

Alsager *v.* Currie, 11 M. & W. 14 - - - - 30, 84

Anderson *v.* Hamilton, 2 Brod. & B. 156, n.; 4 Moore, 593, n.; 8 Price, 244, n. - - - - - - - 195

Andrews *v.* Marris, 1 Q. B. 3 - - - - - - 58

Anon., 3 Dyer, 253 b. - - - - - - - 166

Anon., 2 Salk. 519 - - - - - - - 57

Anon., Style, 392 - - - - - - - 18

Anon., 2 Vent. 196 - - - - - - - 75

Anon., W. N. (1875) p. 220 - - - - - - 110

Anstice, *Re*, 54 L. J. Ch. 1104; 33 W. R. 557; 52 L. T. 572 - - 60

Argent *v.* Durrant, 8 T. R. 403 - - - - - 92

Armory *v.* Delamirie, 1 Sm. L. C. (9th ed.) 385 - - - 23, 47

Ash *v.* Dawnay, 8 Ex. 237; 22 L. J. Ex. 59 - - - - 169

Ashby *v.* White, 1 Sm. L. C. (9th ed.) 268 - - - - 18

Ashley *v.* Taylor, 37 L. T. 522; 38 L. T. 44 - - - - 176

Aston *v.* Hurwitz, 41 L. T. 521 - - - - - - 110

Atherley *v.* Harvey, 2 Q. B. D. 524; 46 L. J. Q. B. 518; 25 W. R. 727; 36 L. T. 551 - - - - - - - 180

Attorney-General *v.* Gaskill, 20 Ch. D. 519; 51 L. J. Ch. 870; 30 W. R. 558; 46 L. T. 180 - - - - - - 175

Att—Boy PAGE
Attorney-General v. Gauntlett, 3 Y. & J. 93 - - - - 48
Attorney-General v. Mellor, Hardr. 459 - - - - - 55
Auberie v. James, Vent. 70; 1 Sid. 444; 2 Keb. 623 - - - 85
Augustinus v. Nerinckx, 16 Ch. D. 13; 29 W. R. 225; 43 L. T. 458 - - - - - - - - 44, 99

B.

Bagot v. Easton, 7 Ch. D. 1; 47 L. J. Ch. 225; 26 W. R. 66; 37 L. T. 369 - - - - - - - - 119
Bainbridge v. Lax, 9 Q. B. 819; 16 L. J. Q. B. 85 - - - 138
Baines v. Bromley, 6 Q. B. D. 691; 50 L. J. Q. B. 465; 29 W. R. 706; 44 L. T. 915 - - - - - - - 150
Baker v. Farmer (not reported) - - - - - - 166
Barker v. Braham, 3 Wils. 368 - - - - - 58
Barnes v. Prudlin vel Bruddel, 1 Sid. 396; Ventr. 4; 1 Lev. 261; 2 Keb. 451 - - - - - - - 125
Barry v. Barclay, 15 C. B. N. S. 849 - - - - 192
Basan v. Arnold, 6 M. & W. 559 - - - - - 84
Beak v. Tyrrell, Carth. 31 - - - - - - 59
Beatson v. Skene, 5 H. & N. 838; 29 L. J. Ex. 430; 6 Jur. N. S. 780; 2 L. T. 378 - - - - - - - 194
Belk v. Broadbent, 3 T. R. 183 - - - - - 57
Belt v. Lawes, 51 L. J. Q. B. 359 - - - - 18, 69
Benbow v. Low, 13 Ch. D. 553; 49 L. J. Ch. 259; 28 W. R. 384; 42 L. T. 14 - - - - - - - - 161
Bennion v. Davison, 3 M. & W. 179; 1 Horn. & H. 46 - - 75
Berdan v. Greenwood, 3 Ex. D. 251; 47 L. J. Ex. 628; 26 W. R. 962; 39 L. T. 223 - - - - - - - 130
Berryman v. Wise, 4 T. R. 366 - - - - - 191
Bickers v. Speight, 22 Q. B. D. 7; 58 L. J. Q. B. 42; 37 W. R. 139- 111
Birch v. Bellamy, 12 Mod. 540 - - - - 23, 57
Birch v. Mather, 22 Ch. D. 629; 52 L. J. Ch. 292; 31 W. R. 362 - 176
Blackie v. Osmaston, 28 Ch. D. 119; 54 L. J. Ch. 473; 33 W. R. 158; 52 L. T. 6 - - - - - - - - 44, 99
Bolckow, Vaughan & Co. v. Fisher and others, 10 Q. B. D. 161; 52 L. J. Q. B. 12; 31 W. R. 235; 47 L. T. 724 - - - 181
Bonner v. Walker, Cro. Eliz. 524 - - - - - 51
Boone v. Mitchell, 1 B. & C. 18 - - - - - 122
Bovey's (Sir Ralph) Case, Vent. 217 - - - - 20, 21
Bowman v. Rostron, 2 A. & E. 295, n. - - - 69, 141
Boyce v. Whitaker, 1 Doug. 97 - - - - - 10
Boyle v. Wiseman, 10 Ex. 647; 24 L. J. Ex. 160; 24 L. T. O. S. 274 195

Boyle v. Wiseman, 11 Ex. 360; 24 L. J. Ex. 284; 25 L. T. O. S. 203   196
Bradbury v. Cooper, 12 Q. B. D. 94; 53 L. J. Q. B. 558; 32 W. R. 32; 48 J. P. 198 - - - - - - - - - 102
Bradshaw's (Robert) Case, 9 Rep. 60, b. - - - - 33, 55
Braunstein v. Lewis, 64 L. T. 265 - - - - - 19
Brembridge v. Latimer, 12 W. R. 878; 10 L. T. 816 - - - 144
Breslauer v. Barwick, 24 W. R. 901; 36 L. T. 52 - - - 166
Bridgwater v. Bythway, 3 Lev. 113 - - - - - 20
Brinsmead v. Harrison, L. R. 7 C. P. 547; 41 L. J. C. P. 190; 20 W. R. 784; 27 L. T. 99 - - - - - - - 140
Briton Medical, &c., Life Association v. Britannia Fire Association, 59 L. T. 888 - - - - - - 18, 99, 102
Britton v. Cole, 1 Salk. 408; Carth. 443; 1 Ld. Raym. 305; 3 Ld. Raym. 145 - - - - - - - - 20, 58
Brook v. Brook, 12 P. D. 19; 56 L. J. P. 108; 35 W. R. 351; 57 L. T. 425 - - - - - - - - 16, 40
Brooking v. Maudslay, 55 L. T. 343; 6 Asp. M. C. 13 - - 97
Brown v. Murray, 4 D. & R. 830 - - - - - - 191
Brown v. Wootton, Cro. Jac. 73; Yelv. 67; Moo. 762 - - 140
Brown's Case, 4 Rep. 22, b. - - - - - - - 53
Bruce v. Nicolopulo, 11 Ex. 129; 24 L. J. Ex. 321 - - - 195
Buchanan v. Taylor, W. N. (1876) p. 73; Bitt. 131; 20 Sol. J. 298; 60 L. T. Notes, 268 - - - - - - - 177
Buckley v. Rice Thomas, Plow. 118 - - - - - 104
Burton v. Plummer, 2 A. & E. 341; 4 N. & M. 315 - - 197
Burton v. Webb, 8 T. R. 459 - - - - - - - 98
Butts v. Bilke, 4 Price, 240 - - - - - - 141
Byrd v. Nunn, 5 Ch. D. 781; 7 Ch. D. 284; 47 L. J. Ch. 1; 25 W. R. 749; 26 W. R. 101; 37 L. T. 90, 585 - - 16, 43, 80, 88, 132
Byrne v. Brown, 22 Q. B. D. 657; 58 L. J. Q. B. 410; 60 L. T. 651- 151

C.

Cannell v. Curtis, 2 Bing. N. C. 228; 2 Scott, 379 - - - 191
Cargill v. Bower, 10 Ch. D. 502; 47 L. J. Ch. 649; 26 W. R. 716; 38 L. T. 779 - - - - - - - - 128
Carr v. Duckett, 5 H. & N. 783; 29 L. J. Ex. 468 - - - 144
Carr v. Wallachian Petroleum Co., L. R. 1 C. P. 636; 35 L. J. C. P. 314; L. R. 2 C. P. 468; 36 L. J. C. P. 236; 15 W. R. 874; 16 L. T. 460 - - - - - - - - - - 122
Carter v. Jones, 6 C. & P. 64; 1 M. & R. 281 - - 78, 191
Casey v. Hellyer, 17 Q. B. D. 97; 55 L. J. Q. B. 207; 34 W. R. 337; 54 L. T. 103 - - - - - - - - - 111

Cat—Dav PAGE

Catherwood v. Chabaud, 1 B. & C. 150; 2 D. & R. 271 - - 190
Cave v. Torre, 32 W. R. 324; 54 L. T. 87, 515; 2 Times L. R. 355, 405 - - - - - - - 92, 104
Chalie v. Belshaw, 6 Bing. 529; 4 Moo. & P. 275 - - 23
Cheasley v. Barnes, 10 East, 73 - - - - 58, 169
Christie v. Christie, L. R. 8 Ch. 499; 42 L. J. Ch. 544; 21 W. R. 493; 28 L. T. 607 - - - - - - 97
Clark v. Hougham, 2 B. & C. 149; 3 D. & R. 322 - - 91, 163
Clarke v. Berger, 36 W. R. 809 - - - - - 109
Coates v. Croyle, 4 Times L. R. 735 - - - - 99
Colborne v. Stockdale, 1 Stra. 493 - - - 75, 83
Colebourne v. Colebourne, 1 Ch. D. 690; 45 L. J. Ch. 749; 24 W. R. 235 - - - - - - - - 127
Collett v. Bailiffs of Shrewsbury, 2 Leo. 34 - - - 61
Collett v. Dickinson, 26 W. R. 403 - - - - 166
Collett and another v. Lord Keith, 2 East, 260 - - 58, 59
Collette v. Goode, 7 Ch. D. 842; 47 L. J. Ch. 370; 38 L. T. 504 - 43, 88
Collins v. Carnegie, 1 A. & E. 695; 3 N. & M. 703 - - 189
Cooke v. Hughes, R. & M. 112 - - - - 193
Cooper v. Blackmore and others, 2 Times L. R. 746 - - 175
Copley v. Jackson, W. N. (1884) p. 39 - - - - 133
Cornwallis v. Savery, 2 Burr. 772; 2 Ld. Ken. 492 - - 98
Cromwell's (The Lord) Case, 4 Rep. 12 - - - 96
Cuddington v. Wilkins, Hob. 67, 81; 2 Hawk. P. C. c. 37, s. 48 - 163
Cudlip v. Rundle, Carth. 202 - - - - 29, 50, 55
Cuthbertson v. Irving, 4 H. & N. 742; 6 H. & N. 135; 28 L. J. Ex. 306; 29 L. J. Ex. 485; 5 Jur. N. S. 740; 6 Jur. N. S. 1211; 8 W. R. 704; 3 L. T. 335 - - - - 51, 52, 54
Cutler v. Southern, 1 Wms. Saund. 116 - - - 17, 166

D.

Dalrymple v. Leslie, 8 Q. B. D. 5; 51 L. J. Q. B. 61; 30 W. R. 105; 45 L. T. 478 - - - - - 177, 182
Darley Main Colliery Co. v. Mitchell, 11 App. Cas. 127; 55 L. J. Q. B. 529; 54 L. T. 882 - - - - - 140
Daubuz and others v. Lavington, 13 Q. B. D. 347; 53 L. J. Q. B. 283; 32 W. R. 772; 51 L. T. 206; W. N. (1884) p. 95 - - 112
Davies v. Williams, 10 Q. B. 725; 16 L. J. Q. B. 369 - - 201
Davis v. James, 26 Ch. D. 778; 53 L. J. Ch. 523; 32 W. R. 406; 50 L. T. 115 - - - - - - - 53
Davy v. Garrett and others, 7 Ch. D. 473; 47 L. J. Ch. 218; 26 W. R. 225; 38 L. T. 77 - - - - - 34, 97

Daw—Eve

Dawkins v. Lord Penrhyn, 6 Ch. D. 318 ; 4 App. Cas. 51 ; 48 L. J.
Ch. 304 ; 27 W. R. 173 ; 39 L. T. 583 - - - - 137
Dawkins v. Lord Rokeby, L. R. 8 Q. B. 255 ; 42 L. J. Q. B. 63 ; 21
W. R. 544 ; 4 F. & F. 806 ; 28 L. T. 134 ; L. R. 7 H. L. 744 ; 45
L. J. Q. B. 8 ; 23 W. R. 931 ; 33 L. T. 196 - - - - 195
Dawson v. Wrench, 3 Ex. 359 ; 18 L. J. Ex. 229 ; 6 D. & L. 474 - 84
Day v. Brownrigg, 10 Ch. D. 294 ; 48 L. J. Ch. 173 ; 27 W. R. 217 ;
39 L. T. 553 - - - - - - - - 9
De Medina v. Norman, 9 M. & W. 820 ; 2 Dowl. N. S. 239 - - 84
Denham v. Stephenson, 1 Salk. 355 - - - - - - 56
Derisley v. Custance, 4 T. R. 75 - - - - - 55, 56
Dews v. Riley, 11 C. B. 434 ; 20 L. J. C. P. 264 ; 15 Jur. 1159 - 58
Digby v. Alexander, 8 Bing. 416 - - - - 34, 141
Dobson v. Blackmore, 9 Q. B. 991 ; 16 L. J. Q. B. 233 ; 11 Jur. 556 - 18
Doe v. Wright, 10 A. & E. 763 ; 2 P. & D. 672 - - - 52, 91
Doe d. Devine v. Wilson, 10 Moo. P. C. 502, 530 - - - 193
Doe d. Mudd v. Suckermore, 5 A. & E. 703 - - - - 193
Doe d. Winnall v. Broad, 2 Man. & Gr. 523 - - - - 101
Doraston v. Payne, 2 Sm. L. C. (9th ed.) 154 ; 2 H. Bl. 530 - - 49
Dowman's Case, 9 Rep. 9, b - - - - - - 31
Duckworth v. McClelland, 2 L. R. Ir. 527 - - - - 166
Dudlow v. Watchorn, 16 East, 39 - - - - - 11
Dumsday v. Hughes, 3 Bos. & Pul. 453 - - - - 14, 53
Duncan v. Thwaites, 3 B. & C. 556 ; 5 D. & R. 447 - - 92, 144

E.

Eade and another v. Jacobs, 3 Ex. D. 335 ; 47 L. J. Ex. 74 ; 26 W.
R. 159 ; 37 L. T. 621 - - - - - 44, 176
Eagleton v. Kingston, 8 Ves. 473 - - - - - 193
Earp v. Henderson, 3 Ch. D. 254 ; 45 L. J. Ch. 738 ; 34 L. T. 844 - 165
Eaton v. Southby, Willes, 131 - - - - - 34, 45
Edelston v. Russell, 57 L. T. 927 - - - - 103
Eden v. Turtle, 10 M. & W. 635 - - - - - - 84
Edevain v. Cohen, 41 Ch. D. 563 ; 43 Ch. D. 187 ; 38 W. R. 8, 177 ;
61 L. T. 168 ; 62 L. T. 17- - - - - - 141
Edison Swan Co. v. Holland, 33 Ch. D. 497 ; 56 L. J. Ch. 124 ; 35
W. R. 178 ; 55 L. T. 587 ; 41 Ch. D. 28 ; 58 L. J. Ch. 525 ; 37 W.
R. 699 ; 61 L. T. 32 - - - - - - - 151
Egerton v. Anderson, W. N. (1884) p. 95 - - - - 153
Elliott v. Hardy, 3 Bing. 61 ; 10 Moore, 347 - - - - 45
Evelyn v. Evelyn, 28 W. R. 531 ; 42 L. T. 248 - - - 14

F.

Fal—Glo

Falck *v.* Axtholm, 24 Q. B. D. 174; 59 L. J. Q. B. 161; 38 W. R. 196 - - - - - - - - 105
Farrell *v.* Coogan, 12 L. R. Ir. 14 - - - - 9, 121
Fenwick *v.* Laycock, 1 Q. B. 414; 1 G. & D. 27 - - - 91
Field *v.* Bennett, 2 Times L. R. 91, 122 - - - - 180
Fisher *v.* Owen, 8 Ch. D. 645; 47 L. J. Ch. 477, 681; 26 W. R. 417, 581; 38 L. T. 252, 577 - - - 96, 179, 180
Fisher *v.* Pimbley, 11 East, 188 - - - - - 11
Fitzgerald *v.* Campbell, 18 Ir. Jur. 153; 15 L. T. 74 - - 92
Fitzgibbon *v.* Greer, Ir. R. 9 C. L. 294 - - - - 177
Forsyth *v.* Bristowe, 8 Ex. 347, 716; 22 L. J. Ex. 70, 255; 17 Jur. 46, 675 - - - - - - - 14, 98, 162
Foulger *v.* Newcomb, L. R. 2 Ex. 327; 36 L. J. Ex. 169; 15 W. R. 1181; 16 L. T. 595 - - - - - - 121
Frankum *v.* Lord Falmouth, 2 A. & E. 452; 4 N. & M. 330; 1 H. & W. 1 - - - - - - - 9, 90
Freeman *v.* Cooke, 2 Ex. 654; 18 L. J. Ex. 114; 12 Jur. 777 - 141
Freshney *v.* Wells, 26 L. J. Ex. 228 - - - - - 62
Fryer *v.* Gathercole, 4 Ex. 262; 18 L. J. Ex. 389; 13 Jur. 542 - 193
Fulmerston *v.* Steward, Plowd. 102 - - - - 167

G.

G. *v.* H., W. N. (1883) p. 233 - - - 117, 153
Gale *v.* Lewis, 9 Q. B. 730; 16 L. J. Q. B. 119; 11 Jur. 780 - - 75
Gale *v.* Reed, 8 East, 80 - - - - - - 98
Gallwey *v.* Marshall, 9 Ex. 300; 23 L. J. Ex. 78; 2 C. L. R. 399 19, 81
Garrells *v.* Alexander, 4 Esp. 37 - - - - - 192
Gay *v.* Labouchere, 4 Q. B. D. 206; 48 L. J. Q. B. 279; 27 W. R. 413 - - - - - - - 176, 179
Gebruder Naf *v.* Ploton, 25 Q. B. D. 13; 59 L. J. Q. B. 371; 38 W. R. 566; 63 L. T. 328 - - - - - 138
Gee *v.* Bell, 35 Ch. D. 160; 56 L. J. Ch. 718; 35 W. R. 805; 56 L. T. 305 - - - - - - - 113
Gibbons *v.* Norman, 2 Times L. R. 676 - - - - 104
Gibbs *v.* Guild, 8 Q. B. D. 296; 9 Q. B. D. 59; 51 L. J. Q. B. 228, 313; 30 W. R. 407, 591; 46 L. T. 135, 248 - - - 163
Gibson *v.* Evans, 23 Q. B. D. 384; 58 L. J. Q. B. 612; 61 L. T. 388 - 187
Gilbert *v.* Parker, 2 Salk. 629 - - - - - 51
Gill *v.* Woodfin, 25 Ch. D. 707; 53 L. J. Ch. 617; 32 W. R. 393; 50 L. T. 490 - - - - - - - 153
Glover *v.* Dixon and another, 9 Ex. 158; 23 L. J. Ex. 12 - - 162

God—Har

Godden v. Corsten, 5 C. P. D. 17; 49 L. J. C. P. 112; 28 W. R. 305; 41 L. T. 527 - - - - - - 43, 99
Goram v. Sweeting, 2 Wms. Saund. 205 - - - - - 84
Gourand v. Fitzgerald, 37 W. R. 55, 265 - - - 102, 103
Gourley v. Plimsoll, L. R. 8 C. P. 362; 42 L. J. C. P. 121; 21 W. R. 683; 28 L. T. 598 - - - - - - 177
Graves v. Terry, 9 Q. B. D. 170; 51 L. J. Q. B. 464; 30 W. R. 748 - 153
Green v. Sevin, 13 Ch. D. 589; 41 L. T. 724 - - - - 161
Greenhow v. Ilsley, Willes, 619 - - - - - 19
Griffith and others v. Curtis & Harvey (not reported) - - - 61
Griffiths v. Eyles, 1 Bos. & Pul. 413 - - - - - 82
Griffiths v. London & St. Katharine Docks Co., 13 Q. B. D. 259; 53 L. J. Q. B. 504; 33 W. R. 35; 51 L. T. 533 - - - - 17
Griffiths v. Ystradyfodwg School Board, 24 Q. B. D. 307; 59 L. J. Q. B. 116; 38 W. R. 425; 62 L. T. 151 - - - - 145
Gwatkin v. Bird, 52 L. J. Q. B. 263 - - - - - 128
Gwynne v. Burnell, 6 Bing. N. C. 453; 7 C. & F. 572; 2 Scott, N. R. 711 - - - - - - - - 85

H.

Hall v. Brice, 3 Times L. R. 344 - - - - - 176
Hall v. Eve, 4 Ch. D. 341; 46 L. J. Ch. 145; 25 W. R. 177; 35 L. T. 926 - - - - - 20, 162, 164, 165, 170
Hall v. Hollander, 4 B. & C. 660; 7 D. & R. 133 - - - 201
Hall v. L. & N. W. Rail. Co., 35 L. T. 848 - - - - 182
Hall v. Tapper, 3 B. & Ad. 655 - - - - - 19
Hall v. Truman, 29 Ch. D. 307; 54 L. J. Ch. 717; 52 L. T. 586 - 178
Hammond v. Bussey, 20 Q. B. D. 79; 57 L. J. Q. B. 58 - - 151
Hammond v. Schofield, (1891) 1 Q. B. 453; 60 L. J. Q. B. 539 - - 140
Hancock v. De Nicoville, W. N. (1875) p. 230 - - - 166
Hamner v. Flight, 24 W. R. 346; 35 L. T. 127 - - - - 116
Harbord v. Monk, 38 L. T. 411 - - - - - 60
Harding v. Holmes, 1 Wils. 122 - - - - - 11
Hardwick, The, 9 P. D. 32; 53 L. J. P. 23; 32 W. R. 598; 50 L. T. 128 - - - - - - - - 40
Harris v. Butler, 2 M. & W. 539; M. & H. 117; 1 Jur. 608 - - 201
Harris v. Gamble, 6 Ch. D. 748; 46 L. J. Ch. 768 - - - 76
Harris v. Jenkins, 22 Ch. D. 481; 52 L. J. Ch. 437; 31 W. R. 137; 47 L. T. 570 - - - - - - 13, 45, 121
Harris v. Mantle, 3 T. R. 307 - - - - 88, 101, 124
Harris v. Warre, 4 C. P. D. 125; 48 L. J. C. P. 310; 27 W. R. 461; 40 L. T. 429 - - - - - - - 16, 121

Har—I'An

	PAGE
Hartley v. Hindmarsh, L. R. 1 C. P. 553; 35 L. J. M. C. 255; 12 Jur. N. S. 502; 14 W. R. 862; 13 L. T. 795 - - -	196
Hawkings v. Billhead, Cro. Car. 404 - - - - -	137
Hawkins v. Eckles, 2 Bos. & Pul. 359 - - - -	49
Hayes v. Keene, 12 C. B. 233; 21 L. J. C. P. 204; 16 Jur. 976 - -	59
Head v. Baldrey, 6 A. & E. 459; 2 N. & P. 217; W. W. & D. 464 -	123
Heap v. Marris, 2 Q. B. D. 630; 46 L. J. Q. B. 761 - - 31,	131
Heath v. Durant, 12 M. & W. 438; 13 L. J. Ex. 95; 1 D. & L. 571; 8 Jur. 131 - - - - - - - -	16
Hedges v. Chapman, 2 Bing. 523 - - - - -	152
Hedges v. Tagg, L. R. 7 Ex. 283; 41 L. J. Ex. 169; 20 W. R. 976 -	201
Hendry v. Turner, 32 Ch. D. 355; 55 L. J. Ch. 562; 34 W. R. 513; 54 L. T. 292 - - - - - - -	128
Hendy v. Stephenson, 10 East, 60 - - - - -	53
Hennessy v. Wright (No. 2), 24 Q. B. D. 445, n. ; 36 W. R. 879; 4 Times L. R. 511 - - - - - - -	187
Herring v. Bischoffsheim, W. N. (1876) p. 77 - - -	17
Hewitt v. Macquire, 7 Ex. 80; 21 L. J. Ex. 30 - - -	89
Hey v. Moorhouse, 6 Bing. N. C. 52; 8 Scott, 156 - - -	138
Heydon v. Thompson, 1 A. & E. 210; 3 N. & M. 319 - -	169
Hicks v. Faulkner, 8 Q. B. D. 167; 51 L. J. Q. B. 268; 30 W. R. 545; 46 L. T. 127 - - - - - - -	200
Hill v. Allen, 2 M. & W. 283; 5 Dowl. 471; M. & H. 37; 1 Jur. 44 -	60
Hobbs v. Hudson, 25 Q. B. D. 232; 38 W. R. 682; 63 L. T. 215 -	178
Hobbs v. Wayet, 36 Ch. D. 256; 56 L. J. Ch. 819; 36 W. R. 73; 57 L. T. 225 - - - - - - - -	128
Hobson v. Monks, W. N. (1884) p. 8 - - - -	153
Home v. Bentinck, 2 Brod. & B. 130; 4 Moore, 563 - - -	195
Horsefall v. Testar, 7 Taunt. 385; 1 Moore, 89 - - 16,	123
Horton v. McMurtry, 5 H. & N. 667; 29 L. J. Ex. 260; 8 W. R. 285 - - - - - - - - 61,	70
Hotham v. East India Company, 1 T. R. 638; 1 Dougl. 272 - 22,	26
Houston v. Sligo, 29 Ch. D. 448; 52 L. T. 96 - - -	140
Howarth v. Brown, 1 H. & C. 694; 32 L. J. Ex. 99; 11 W. R. 270; 7 L. T. 638 - - - - - - - -	139
Huggins v. Wiseman, Carth. 110 - - - - -	33
Hurdman v. N. E. Rail. Co., 3 C. P. D. 168; 47 L. J. C. P. 368; 26 W. R. 489; 38 L. T. 339 - - - - - -	9
Hyde v. Graham, 1 H. & C. 593; 32 L. J. Ex. 27 - - -	152

I.

I'Anson v. Stuart, 1 T. R. 748; 2 Sm. L. C. (5th ed.) 63 - -	61

J.

Jac—Kno   PAGE

Jackson v. Kelly, 12 Ir. L. T. 136 - - - - - 110
James v. Page, 85 L. T. Newspaper, 157 - - - - 161
James v. Radnor County Council, 6 Times L. R. 240 - 62, 98, 104
James v. Smith, (1891) 1 Ch. 384 ; 63 L. T. 524 - - 42, 92, 137
Johns v. James, 13 Ch. D. 370 - - - - - - 176
Johns v. Whitley, 3 Wils. 65 - - - - - - 53
Johnson v. Hudson and Morgan, 7 A. & E. 233, n. ; 1 H. & W. 680 - 194
Jones v. Broadhurst, 9 C. B. 173 - - - - - - 138
Jones v. Jones, 22 Q. B. D. 425 ; 58 L. J. Q. B. 178 ; 37 W. R. 479 ;
   60 L. T. 421 - - - - - - - 178
Jones v. Mackie, L. R. 3 Ex. 1 ; 37 L. J. Ex. 1 ; 16 W. R. 109 ; 17
   L. T. 151 - - - - - - - - 148
Jones v. Monte Video Gas Co., 5 Q. B. D. 556 ; 49 L. J. Q. B. 627 ;
   28 W. R. 758 ; 42 L. T. 639 - - - - - - 178
Jones v. Powell, 5 B. & C. 647 ; 8 D. & R. 416 - - - - 19
Jones v. Richards, 15 Q. B. D. 439 ; 1 Times L. R. 660 - 175, 183
Jones v. Turner, W. N. (1875) p. 239 - - - - - 34
Jubb v. Ellis, 15 L. J. Q. B. 94 ; 3 D. & L. 364 ; 9 Jur. 1057 - 169

K.

Kelly v. Briggs, 85 L. T. Newspaper, 78 - - - - 99
Kemp v. Goldberg, 36 Ch. D. 505 ; 36 W. R. 278 ; 56 L. T. 736 - 44, 100
Kempe v. Gibbon, 9 Q. B. 609 ; 16 L. J. Q. B. 120 ; 11 Jur. 299 - 163
Kendall v. Hamilton, 4 App. Cas. 504 ; 48 L. J. C. P. 705 ; 28 W. R.
   97 ; 41 L. T. 418 - - - - - - - 142
Kennane v. Mackey, 24 L. R. Ir. 495 - - - - 153
Kennett v. Mundy (not reported) - - - - - 81
Kepp v. Wiggett, 6 C. B. 280 ; 17 L. J. C. P. 295 ; 12 Jur. 831 - 82
King v. Hoare, 13 M. & W. 494 ; 14 L. J. Ex. 29 ; 2 D. & L. 382 - 140
King v. Norman, 4 C. B. 884 ; 17 L. J. C. P. 23 ; 11 Jur. 824 - - 75
Kingdon v. Kirk, 37 Ch. D. 141 ; 57 L. J. Ch. 328 ; 36 W. R. 430 ;
   58 L. T. 383 - - - - - - - 113
Kirby v. Simpson, 3 Dowl. 791 - - - - - - 152
Knight v. Abbott, 10 Q. B. D. 11 ; 52 L. J. Q. B. 131 ; 31 W. R.
   505 ; 49 L. T. 94 - - - - - - - 109
Knight v. Engle, 61 L. T. 780 - - - - - 98, 99
Knowles v. Roberts, 38 Ch. D. 263 ; 58 L. T. 259 - - 94, 97
Knowlman v. Bluett, L. R. 9 Ex. 1, 307 ; 43 L. J. Ex. 29, 151 ; 22
   W. R. 77, 758 ; 29 L. T. 462 - - - - - - 127

L.

Lab—Mac PAGE
Labouchere *v.* Shaw, 41 J. P. 788 - - - - - 174
Lafone *v.* Smith, 4 H. & N. 158; 5 Jur. N. S. 127 - - - 148
Lamb *v.* Mills, 4 Mod. 377 - - - - - - 57
Lamb *v.* Munster, 10 Q. B. D. 110; 52 L. J. Q. B. 46; 31 W. R. 117; 47 L. T. 442 - - - - - - - 183
Lane *v.* Alexander, Yelv. 122 - - - - 30, 84
Lawrance *v.* Lord Norreys, 15 App. Cas. 210; 59 L. J. Ch. 681; 38 W. R. 753; 62 L. T. 706; 6 Times L. R. 285 - - 61, 143, 163
Lee Conservancy Board *v.* Button, 12 Ch. D. 383; 41 L. T. 500 - 77
Leech *v.* Widsley, Ventr. 54; 1 Lev. 283 - - - - 133
Legh *v.* Lillie, 6 H. & N. 165; 30 L. J. Ex. 25 - - - 124
Leitch *v.* Abbott, 31 Ch. D. 374; 55 L. J. Ch. 460; 34 W. R. 506; 54 L. T. 258; 50 J. P. 441 - - - - - - 102
Leke's (Sir Francis) Case, 3 Dyer, 365; 2 Wms. Saund. 206 a, n. (22) 29
Leslie *v.* Clifford, 50 L. T. 590 - - - - - - 114
Lethbridge *v.* Cronk, 44 L. J. C. P. 381; 23 W. R. 703; 33 L. T. 171 - 178
Leyfield's Case, 10 Rep. 91 a; 3 Salk. 273 - - - - 90
Leyman *v.* Latimer, 3 Ex. D. 15, 352; 46 L. J. Ex. 765; 47 L. J. Ex. 470; 25 W. R. 751; 26 W. R. 305; 37 L. T. 360, 819; 14 Cox, C. C. 51 - - - - - - 143, 163
Lillie *v.* Price, 5 A. & E. 645; 1 N. & P. 16; 5 Dowl. 432; 2 H. & W. 381 - - - - - - - - 144
Lisle's (Lord) Case, cited 9 Rep. 25, a - - - - 13
Lloyd *v.* Byrne, 22 L. R. Ir. 269 - - - - - - 109
London & North Western Rail. Co. *v.* Lee, 7 Times L. R. 603 - 100
Lowden *v.* Goodrick, Peake, 46 - - - - - - 126
Loweth *v.* Smith, 12 M. & W. 582; 14 L. J. Ex. 5 - - - 169
Lumb *v.* Beaumont, 49 L. T. 772 - - - - 27, 34
Lush *v.* Russell, 5 Ex. 203; 19 L. J. Ex. 214; 1 L. M. & P. 369; 7 D. & L. 228; 14 Jur. 435 - - - - - 9, 70, 90
Lynn's (Mayor of) Case, 10 Rep. 122, b - - - - 118

M.

M'Cauley *v.* Thorpe, 1 Chitt. 685; 5 Madd. 19 - - - 191
M'Cawley *v.* Campbell, 4 L. R. Ir. 410 - - - - 110
McColla *v.* Jones, 4 Times L. R. 12 - - - - - 176
McCorquodale *v.* Bell, W. N. (1876) p. 39; Bitt. 111; 20 Sol. J. 260; 60 L. T. Notes, 232 - - - - - - - 178
MacDougall *v.* Knight, 25 Q. B. D. 1; 38 W. R. 553; 63 L. T. 43; 6 Times L. R. 276 - - - - - - - 94

Mac—Mor

MacDougall v. Knight and another (not reported) - - - 72
Mackay v. Manchester Press Co., 54 J. P. 22; 6 Times L. R. 16 - 147, 159
M'Pherson v. Daniels, 10 B. & C. 263; 5 M. & R. 251 - - 92
Maddison v. Alderson, 8 App. Cas. 467; 52 L. J. Q. B. 737; 31 W. R.
  820; 49 L. T. 303; 47 J. P. 821 - - - - - 163
Malone v. Fitzgerald, 18 L. R. Ir. 187 - - - - 180
Manchester (Mayor, &c., of) v. Williams, (1891) 1 Q. B. 94; 60 L. J.
  Q. B. 23; 54 J. P. 712 - - - - - - - 72
Manvell v. Thomson, 2 C. & P. 303 - - - - - 201
Marriott v. Chamberlain, 17 Q. B. D. 154; 55 L. J. Q. B. 448; 34
  W. R. 783; 54 L. T. 714 - - - 175, 176, 182
Marsh v. Bulteel, 5 B. & Ald. 507 - - - - - 120
Martin v. Smith, 4 Bing. N. C. 436; 6 Scott, 268; 6 Dowl. 639; 1
  Arn. 194; 9 Jur. 376 - - - - - - - 91
Martin v. Treacher, 16 Q. B. D. 507; 55 L. J. Q. B. 209; 34 W. R.
  315; 54 L. T. 7 - - - - - - - - 178
Mary's Case, 9 Rep. 113; Co. Litt. 56, a - - - - 18
Maunder v. Venn, M. & M. 323 - - - - - 201
Mayor v. Collins, 24 Q. B. D. 361; 59 L. J. Q. B. 199; 38 W. R.
  349; 62 L. T. 326 - - - - - - - 178
Mercer v. Whall, 5 Q. B. 447; 14 L. J. Q. B. 267 - - 78, 191
Mercier v. Cotton, 1 Q. B. D. 442; 46 L. J. Q. B. 184; 24 W. R. 566;
  35 L. T. 79 - - - - - - - - - 179
Middleton v. Price, 2 Stra. 1184; 1 Wils. 17 - - - - 58
Millar v. Harper, 38 Ch. D. 110; 57 L. J. Ch. 1091; 36 W. R. 454;
  58 L. T. 698 - - - - - - - - 103
Miller v. David, L. R. 9 C. P. 118; 43 L. J. C. P. 84; 22 W. R. 332;
  30 L. T. 58 - - - - - - - - - 121
Millington v. Loring, 6 Q. B. D. 190; 50 L. J. Q. B. 214; 29 W. R.
  207; 43 L. T. 657; 45 J. P. 268 - - - 26, 27, 97
Mints v. Bethil, Cro. Eliz. 749 - - - - - 86
Mitchell v. Tarbutt and others, 5 T. R. 649 - - - 142
Monkman v. Shepherdson, 11 A. & E. 411 - - - 169
Moor v. Roberts, 3 C. B. N. S. 671; 26 L. J. C. P. 246 - - 177
Moore v. Boulcott, 1 Bing. N. C. 323 - - - - 84
Moravia v. Sloper, Willes, 30 - - - - - 58
Morgan, Re, Owen v. Morgan, 35 Ch. D. 492; 56 L. J. Ch. 603; 35
  W. R. 705; 56 L. T. 503 - - - - - 96, 130
Morgan v. Man, 1 Sid. 180; Sir T. Raym. 94 - - - 11
Morrell v. Martin, 3 M. & Gr. 581; 4 Scott, N. R. 300 - - 58
Morris v. Edwards, 15 App. Cas. 309; 60 L. J. Q. B. 292; 63
  L. T. 26 - - - - - - - - - 178
Morse v. James, Willes, 122 - - - - - 58, 59
Mortimer v. M'Callan, 6 M. & W. 58; 4 Jur. 172 - - 195

Mos—Pen

PAGE

Mostyn v. West Mostyn Coal and Iron Co., Limited, 1 C. P. D. 145;
45 L. J. C. P. 401; 24 W. R. 401; 34 L. T. 325 - - - 131
Munster v. Cox, 1 Times L. R. 542 - - - - - 140
Mure v. Kaye, 4 Taunt. 34 - - - - - - 60
Myn v. Cole, Cro. Jac. 87 - - - - - - 85
Mynours v. Turke & Yorke, 1 Dyer, 66, b - - - - 87

N.

Newell v. National Provincial Bank, 1 C. P. D. 496; 45 L. J. C. P.
285; 24 W. R. 458; 34 L. T. 533 - - - - - 150
Newport Dry Dock Co. v. Paynter, 34 Ch. D. 88; 56 L. J. Ch. 1021;
55 L. T. 711 - - - - - - - - 60
Newton v. Chaplin, 10 C. B. 356; 19 L. J. C. P. 374; 14 Jur. 1121 - 195
Nurton v. Dickson, 5 H. & N. 637; 29 L. J. Ex. 337; 6 Jur. N. S.
708; 8 W. R. 530 - - - - - - - 91

O.

Oakley v. Davis, 16 East, 82 - - - - - - 169
Oglethorp v. Hyde, Cro. Eliz. 233 - - - - - 82
O'Keefe v. Cardinal Cullen, Ir. R. 7 C. L. 319 - - - 144
Orient Steam Navigation Co. v. Ocean Marine Insurance Co., 34 W.
R. 442 - - - - - - - - - 104
Osborne v. Rogers, 1 Wms. Saund. 267 - - - 30, 84
Owen v. Morgan, Re Morgan, 35 Ch. D. 492; 56 L. J. Ch. 603; 35
W. R. 705; 56 L. T. 503 - - - - - 96, 130

P.

Painter v. Wallis, The Times for Nov. 5th, 1878 - - - 110
Palmer v. Gooden, 8 M. & W. 890; 1 Dowl. N. S. 673 - - - 84
Pankhurst v. Hamilton, 2 Times L. R. 682 - - - 174, 177
Pankhurst v. Wighton & Co., 2 Times L. R. 745 - - - 174
Paraire v. Loibl, 49 L. J. C. P. 481; 43 L. T. 427 - - 104, 146
Paris v. Levy, 2 F. & F. 71 - - - - - - 195
Parnell v. Walter and another, 24 Q. B. D. 441; 59 L. J. Q. B. 125;
38 W. R. 270; 62 L. T. 75; 54 J. P. 311 - - 103, 175, 187
Parton, In re, Townsend v. Parton, 30 W. R. 287; 45 L. T. 755 - 9, 41
Partridge v. Strange, Plow. 84 - - - - - - 10
Penrhyn (Lord) v. The Licensed Victuallers' Mirror, 7 Times L. R. 1 158

Peppiatt and Wife v. Smith, 3 H. & C. 129; 33 L. J. Ex. 239; 11 L. T. 139 - - - - - - - - - 174
Peters v. Edwards, 3 Times L. R. 423 - - - - - 190
Pettit v. Addington, Peake, 62 - - - - - 126
Phelan v. Shanks, 18 Ir. L. T. 13 - - - - - 110
Philipps v. Philipps, 4 Q. B. D. 127; 48 L. J. Q. B. 135; 27 W. R. 436; 39 L. T. 556 - - - - 32, 33, 42, 52, 99, 135
Phillips v. Harris, W. N. (1876) p. 54 - - - - - 108
Phillips v. Im Thurn, 18 C. B. N. S. 400 - - - - 141
Phillips v. Routh, L. R. 7 C. P. 287; 41 L. J. C. P. 111; 20 W. R. 630; 26 L. T. 845 - - - - - - - - 180
Pilley v. Robinson, 20 Q. B. D. 155; 57 L. J. Q. B. 54; 36 W. R. 269; 58 L. T. 110 - - - - - - - - 143
Pinhorn v. Souster, 8 Ex. 138; 22 L. J. Ex. 18 - - - - 53
Platt v. Hill, 1 Lord Raym. 381 - - - - - - 10
Playfair v. Musgrove, 14 M. & W. 239; 15 L. J. Ex. 26; 3 D. & L. 72; 9 Jur. 783 - - - - - - - - - 169
Porter v. Izat, 1 M. & W. 381; 1 Tyr. & G. 639 - - - 134
Potts v. Sparrow, 1 Bing. N. C. 594 - - - - - 91
Powers v. Cook, 1 Ld. Raym. 63; 1 Salk. 298 - - - 22
Praed v. Duchess of Cumberland, 4 T. R. 585; 2 H. Bl. 280; 2 Wms. Saund. 190, n. (d) - - - - - - - - 11
Pratt v. Groome, 15 East, 235 - - - - - - 169
Priddle and Napper's Case, 11 Rep. 8 - - - - - 68
Priest v. Uppleby, In re Salmon, 42 Ch. D. 351; 38 W. R. 150; 61 L. T. 146; 5 Times L. R. 479 - - - - - 151
Procter v. Raikes and another, 3 Times L. R. 229 - - 183
Procter v. Smiles, 55 L. J. Q. B. 467, 527 - - - - 183
Procter v. Tyler, 3 Times L. R. 282 - - - - - 192
Property Investment County of Scotland v. Lucas & Son (not reported) 124
Pugh v. Griffith, 7 A. & E. 827; 3 N. & P. 187 - - - 169
Pullin v. Nicholas, 1 Lev. 83 - - - - - - 86
Pybus v. Scudamore, Arn. 464 - - - - - - 199
Pyster v. Hemling, Cro. Jac. 103 - - - - - - 53

R.

Raikes v. Todd, 8 A. & E. 846; 1 P. & D. 138; 1 W. W. & H. 619 - 16
Rasbotham v. Shropshire Union Railways and Canal Co., 24 Ch. D. 110; 53 L. J. Ch. 327; 32 W. R. 117; 48 L. T. 902 - 180, 182
Rees v. Watts, 11 Ex. 410; 25 L. J. Ex. 30; 1 Jur. N. S. 1023 - 149
Reeves v. Butcher, (1891) 2 Q. B. 509; 60 L. J. Q. B. 619 - - 44
Reichel v. Magrath, 14 App. Cas. 665; 59 L. J. Q. B. 159; 54 J. P. 196 - - - - - - - - - - 94

R. v. Aickles, 1 Leach, 330 - - - - - - 195
R. v. Boucher, 1 F. & F. 486 - - - - - - 195
R. v. Chester (Bishop of), 2 Salk. 560 - - - - 75
R. v. Chillesford, 4 B. & C. 94 - - - - - - 201
R. v. Cooke, 2 B. & C. 871; 4 D. & R. 592 - - - 14
R. v. Dendy, 1 E. & B. 829; 22 L. J. Q. B. 247; 17 Jur. 970 - - 29
R. v. Eccles, 3 Dougl. 337 - - - - - - 33
R. v. Llanfaethly, 2 E. & B. 940; 23 L. J. M. C. 33; 17 Jur. 1123 - 195
R. v. Lyme Regis, 1 Doug. 148 - - - - - - 10
R. v. Slaney, 5 C. & P. 213 - - - - - - 193
R. v. Watson, 2 Stark. 116 - - - - - - 194
Richards v. Hodges, 2 Wms. Saund. 84 - - - - 86
Richardson v. Mayor of Orford, 2 H. Bl. 182; 1 Anst. 231 - - 68
Riddell v. Earl of Strathmore, 3 Times L. R. 329 - - 14, 61, 163
Rider v. Smith, 3 T. R. 766 - - - - - - 55
Rist v. Faux, 4 B. & S. 409; 32 L. J. Q. B. 386; 10 Jur. N. S. 202;
   11 W. R. 918; 8 L. T. 737 - - - - - - 201
Roakes v. Manser, 1 C. B. 531; 14 L. J. C. P. 199 - - - 82
Roberts v. Jones; Willey v. Gt. N. Rail. Co., (1891) 2 Q. B. 194; 60
   L. J. Q. B. 441 - - - - - - - 199
Roberts v. Mariett, 2 Wms. Saund. 188 - - - - 165
Roberts v. Owen, 54 J. P. 295; 6 Times L. R. 172 - - 98, 104
Roe v. Lord, 2 Bl. Rep. 1099 - - - - - - 14, 53
Rose v. Groves, 5 M. & Gr. 613; 12 L. J. C. P. 251; 6 Scott, N. R.
   645; 1 D. & L. 61; 7 Jur. 951 - - - - - 18, 126
Roselle v. Buchanan, 16 Q. B. D. 656; 55 L. J. Q. B. 376; 34 W. R.
   488; 2 Times L. R. 367 - - - - - 44, 102
Rouse v. Bardin, 1 H. Bl. 351 - - - - - - 45
Rowland v. Veale, Cowp. 18 - - - - - - 57, 59
Rubery v. Grant, L. R. 13 Eq. 443; 42 L. J. Ch. 19; 26 L. T. 538 - 97
Rumley v. Winn, 22 Q. B. D. 265; 58 L. J. Q. B. 128; 37 W. R.
   285; 60 L. T. 32 - - - - - - - 160
Runnacles v. Mesquita, 1 Q. B. D. 416; 45 L. J. Q. B. 407; 24 W. R.
   553 - - - - - - - - - 108
Rutter v. Tregent, 12 Ch. D. 758; 48 L. J. Ch. 791; 27 W. R. 902;
   41 L. T. 16 - - - - - - - - 76
Ryan v. Clark, 14 Q. B. 65; 18 L. J. Q. B. 267; 7 D. & L. 8; 13
   Jur. 1000 - - - - - - - 52, 91

S.

Sachs v. Speilman, 37 Ch. D. 295; 57 L. J. Ch. 658; 36 W. R. 498;
   58 L. T. 102 - - - - - - - 99, 103
Salmon, In re, Priest v. Uppleby, 42 Ch. D. 351; 38 W. R. 150; 61
   L. T. 146; 5 Times L. R. 479 - - - - - 151

Sal—Ste

	PAGE
Salt *v.* Cooper, 16 Ch. D. 544; 50 L. J. Ch. 529; 29 W. R. 553; 43 L. T. 682	128
Scilly *v.* Dally, 2 Salk. 562	53
Scott *v.* Sampson, 8 Q. B. D. 491; 51 L. J. Q. B. 380; 30 W. R. 541; 46 L. T. 412	27, 197
Seear *v.* Lawson, 15 Ch. D. 426; 16 Ch. D. 121; 49 L. J. Bk. 69; 50 L. J. Ch. 139; 28 W. R. 929; 29 W. R. 109; 42 L. T. 893; 43 L. T. 716	24, 53
Seligmann *v.* Young, W. N. (1884) p. 93	44
Serrao *v.* Noel, 15 Q. B. D. 549	140
Seymour's Case, 10 Rep. 98	50
Sharland *v.* Leifchild, 4 C. B. 529; 16 L. J. C. P. 217; 5 D. & L. 139; 11 Jur. 523	16, 87
Sheahan *v.* Ahearne, Ir. R. 9 C. L. 412	121
Sheehan *v.* Gt. E. Rail. Co., 16 Ch. D. 59; 50 L. J. Ch. 68; 29 W. R. 69; 43 L. T. 432	142
Shephcard's Case, Cro. Car. 190	53
Shorland *v.* Govett, 5 B. & C. 485; 8 D. & R. 257	58
Shortal *v.* Farrell, Ir. R. 3 C. L. 506	109
Shrapnel *v.* Laing, 20 Q. B. D. 334; 57 L. J. Q. B. 195; 36 W. R. 297; 58 L. T. 705	150
Shum *v.* Farrington, 1 Bos. & Pul. 640	98
Simmonds *v.* Dunne, Ir. R. 5 C. L. 358	10, 144
Simmons *v* Lillystone, 8 Ex. 431; 22 L. J. Ex. 217	45
Smith *v.* British Insurance Co., W. N. (1883) p. 232	32
Smith *v.* Edwardes, 22 Q. B. D. 10; 58 L. J. Q. B. 227; 37 W. R. 112; 60 L. T. 10	109
Smith *v.* Feverell, 2 Mod. 6; 1 Freem. 190	19, 57
Smith *v.* Pritchard, 8 C. B. 565; 19 L. J. C. P. 53; 14 Jur. 224	59
Smith *v.* Scott, 6 C. B. N. S. 771; 28 L. J. C. P. 325; 8 Jur. N. S. 1356	54
Smith *v.* Thomas, 2 Bing. N. C. 372; 1 Hodges, 355; 4 Dowl. 333	134
Smith *v.* West, W. N. (1876) p. 55	31
Smith *v.* Wilson, 5 C. P. D. 25; 49 L. J. C. P. 96; 28 W. R. 57; 41 L. T. 433	110
Southern Counties Bank *v.* Farquhar, 34 Sol. J. 182	111
Spackman *v.* Gibney (not reported)	144
Spedding *v.* Fitzpatrick, 38 Ch. D. 410; 58 L. J. Ch. 139; 37 W. R. 20; 59 L. T. 492	13, 97, 98
Stace *v.* Griffith, L. R. 2 P. C. 420; 6 Moore, P. C. C. N. S. 18; 20 L. T. 197	195
Stannard *v.* Vestry of St. Giles, 20 Ch. D. 190; 51 L. J. Ch. 629; 30 W. R. 693; 46 L. T. 243	17, 128
Stein *v.* Tabor, 31 L. T. 444	177
Stephenson *v.* Weir, 4 L. R. Ir. 369	108

Sto—Uth

	PAGE
Stoate *v.* Row, 14 C. B. N. S. 209; 32 L. J. C. P. 160; 11 W. R. 595	52
Stokes *v.* Grant, 4 C. P. D. 25; 27 W. R. 397; 40 L. T. 36	68, 72, 73
Stowell *v.* Lord Zouch, Plow. 376	21
Stubbs *v.* Lainson, 1 M. & W. 728; 2 Gale, 122; 5 Dowl. 162	84
Sutcliffe *v.* James, 27 W. R. 750; 40 L. T. 875	131
Sutton *v.* Clarke, 6 Taunt. 29; 1 Marsh. 429	142
Syms *v.* Chaplin, 5 A. & E. 634; 1 N. & P. 129; 2 H. & W. 411	19

T.

Taylor, *In re*, Turpin *v.* Pain, 44 Ch. D. 128; 59 L. J. Ch. 803; 38 W. R. 422; 62 L. T. 754	114
Tenny d. Gibbs *v.* Moody, 3 Bing. 3; 10 Moore, 252	104
Tetley *v.* Easton, 18 C. B. 643; 25 L. J. C. P. 293	178
Tetley *v.* Griffith, 36 W. R. 96; 57 L. T. 673	19
Thomas *v.* Morgan, 2 C. M. & R. 496; 4 Dowl. 223; 1 Gale, 172; 5 Tyr. 1085	17
Thomson *v.* Birkley, 31 W. R. 230; 47 L. T. 700	98, 99, 100
Thorp *v.* Holdsworth, 3 Ch. D. 637; 45 L. J. Ch. 406	42, 76, 77, 86
Thriscutt *v.* Martin, 3 Ex. 454; 18 L. J. Ex. 271; 6 D. & L. 489	54
Thurman *v.* Wild, 11 A. & E. 453; 3 P. & D. 489	85, 138
Tildesley *v.* Harper, 7 Ch. D. 403; 10 Ch. D. 393; 47 L. J. Ch. 263; 48 L. J. Ch. 495; 26 W. R. 263; 27 W. R. 249; 38 L. T. 60; 39 L. T. 552	83, 85
Toke *v.* Andrews, 8 Q. B. D. 428; 51 L. J. Q. B. 281; 30 W. R. 659	161
Torrence *v.* Gibbins, 5 Q. B. 297; 13 L. J. Q. B. 36; D. & M. 226; 7 Jur. 1158	80
Townsend *v.* Parton, *In re* Parton, 30 W. R. 287; 45 L. T. 755	9, 41
Trower *v.* Chadwick, 3 Bing. N. C. 334; 3 Scott, 699; 2 Hodges, 267	68
Tucker *v.* Lawson, 2 Times L. R. 593	174
Turner *v.* Lamb, 14 M. & W. 412	44
Turner *v.* Meryweather, 7 C. B. 251; 18 L. J. C. P. 155; 19 L. J. C. P. 10; 13 Jur. 683	191
Turpin *v.* Pain, *In re* Taylor, 44 Ch. D. 128; 59 L. J. Ch. 803; 38 W. R. 422; 62 L. T. 754	114
Turquand *v.* Fearon, 40 L. T. 543	98

U.

Ungley *v.* Ungley, 4 Ch. D. 73; 5 Ch. D. 887; 46 L. J. Ch. 189, 854; 25 W. R. 39, 733; 35 L. T. 619; 37 L. T. 52	163
Union Bank of London *v.* Manby, 13 Ch. D. 239; 49 L. J. Ch. 106; 28 W. R. 23; 42 L. T. 393	174
Uther *v.* Rich, 10 A. & E. 784; 2 P. & D. 579	91

Vea—Win

Veale v. Warner, 1 Wms. Saund. 325 - - - - - 141
Vere v. Goldsborough, 1 Bing. N. C. 353; 1 Scott, 265 - - 92
Vere v. Smith, 2 Lev. 5; Ventr. 121 - - - - - 167
Vessey v. Pike, 3 C. & P. 512 - - - - - 28
Victors v. Davies, 12 M. & W. 758; 13 L. J. Ex. 241; 1 D. & L. 984 - - - - - - - - - 22

W.

Wakelin v. L. & S. W. Rail. Co., 12 App. Cas. 41; 56 L. J. Q. B. 229; 35 W. R. 141; 55 L. T. 709 - - - - - 90
Walker v. Brogden, 17 C. B. N. S. 571 - - - - 199
Walker v. Hicks, 3 Q. B. D. 8; 47 L. J. Q. B. 27; 26 W. R. 113; 37 L. T. 529 - - - - - - - 110
Wallingford v. Mutual Society, 5 App. Cas. 685; 50 L. J. Q. B. 49; 29 W. R. 81; 43 L. T. 258 - - - - - 143
Wallis v. Smith, 51 L. J. Ch. 577; 46 L. T. 473 - - 24, 53
Walsingham's Case, Plowd. 564 - - - - - - 21
Ward v. Sinfield, 49 L. J. C. P. 696; 43 L. T. 253 - - - 196
Werderman v. Société Générale, &c., 19 Ch. D. 246; 30 W. R. 33; 45 L. T. 514 - - - - - - - - 142
West v. Baxendale, 9 C. B. 141; 19 L. J. C. P. 149 - - 42
Westacott v. Bevan and another, (1891) 1 Q. B. 774; 60 L. J. Q. B. 536; 65 L. T. 263 - - - - - - - 150
Westwood v. Cowne, 1 Stark. 172 - - - - - 125
Wheatcroft v. Mousley, 11 C. B. 677 - - - - - 198
Whelan v. Kelly, 14 L. R. Ir. 387 - - - - - 108
White v. Gt. W. Rail. Co., 2 C. B. N. S. 7; 26 L. J. C. P. 158 - 116, 123
Whyte v. Ahrens, 26 Ch. D. 717; 54 L. J. Ch. 145; 32 W. R. 649; 50 L. T. 344 - - - - - - - 102
Wigglesworth v. Dallison, 1 Sm. L. C. (9th ed.), 569 - - 16
Wilby v. Henman, 2 Cr. & M. 658; 4 Tyr. 957 - - - 190
Willey v. Gt. N. Rail. Co., Roberts v. Jones, (1891) 2 Q. B. 194; 60 L. J. Q. B. 441 - - - - - - - - 199
Williams v. Bryant, 5 M. & W. 447; 7 Dowl. 502 - - 118
Williams v. Wilcox, 8 A. & E. 314; 3 N. & P. 606; 1 W. W. & H. 477 - - - - - - - - 121, 196
Williamson v. L. & N. W. Rail. Co., 12 Ch. D. 787; 49 L. J. Ch. 559; 27 W. R. 724 - - - - - - - 164
Wilson v. Hodges, 2 East, 312 - - - - - 190
Wilton v. Brignell, W. N. (1875) p. 239; 1 Charley, 105; Bitt. 56; 20 Sol. J. 121; 60 L. T. Notes, 104 - - - - 174
Wingard v. Cox, W. N. (1876) p. 106; Bitt. 144; 20 Sol. J. 341; 60 L. T. Notes, 304 - - - - - - 102

Wol—Yor

Wolverhampton New Waterworks Co. v. Hawksford, 5 C. B. N. S. 703; 28 L. J. C. P. 198 - - - - - - 177
Wood v. Budden, Hob. 119 - - - - - - 29
Wood v. Cox, 4 Times L. R. 550 - - - - - 27
Wood v. Earl of Durham, 21 Q. B. D. 501; 57 L. J. Q. B. 547; 37 W. R. 222; 59 L. T. 142 - - - - - - 27
Wood v. Hawkshead, Yelv. 13 - - - - - - 167
Worth v. Terrington, 13 M. & W. 781; 14 L. J. Ex. 133 - - 169

Y.

York v. Stowers, W. N. (1883) p. 174 - - - - 114

TABLE OF STATUTES CITED.

	PAGE
31 Hen. VIII. c. 13	166
32 Hen. VIII. c. 34	53
7 Jac. I. c. 5	134
21 Jac. I. c. 4, s. 4	134
c. 12, s. 5	134
c. 16, s. 3 (Statute of Limitations)	12, 44, 61, 66, 90, 136, 137, 162, 163, 190, 206
29 Car. II. c. 3 (Statute of Frauds)	12, 66, 91, 136, 162, 163, 206
ss. 4, 7	92, 137
8 & 9 Will. III. c. 11	146, 212
4 & 5 Anne, c. 16	162
2 Geo. II. c. 22	149
11 Geo. II. c. 19, s. 21	134
s. 22	56
14 Geo. III. c. 48, s. 2	156
11 Geo. IV. & 1 Will. IV. c. 68	19
2 & 3 Will. IV. c. 71	47, 48
3 & 4 Will. IV. c. 27	116
s. 34	137
c. 42	14
ss. 3, 5	163
5 & 6 Vict. c. 45 (Copyright Act)	87
8 & 9 Vict. c. 75 (Lord Campbell's Act), s. 2	148, 190
11 & 12 Vict. c. 44, s. 17	134
15 & 16 Vict. c. 76 (Common Law Procedure Act, 1852)	5
s. 49	15
s. 50	71
s. 57	25
s. 67	92
s. 87	169
Schedule B, 46, 47	47
55—57	169

	PAGE
17 & 18 Vict. c. 125 (Common Law Procedure Act, 1854), s. 24	196
s. 25	196
s. 27	193
24 & 25 Vict. c. 96 (Larceny Act), s. 113	134
c. 97 (Malicious Injuries to Property Act), s. 71	134
c. 99, s. 33	134
28 & 29 Vict. c. 18, s. 6	196
34 & 35 Vict. c. 112 (Prevention of Crimes Act, 1871), s. 18	196
36 & 37 Vict. c. 48 (Railway and Canal Traffic Act, 1873)	100
c. 66 (Judicature Act, 1873)	5, 9, 11, 41, 77, 96, 122, 140, 144, 170, 178, 180
s. 24, sub-s. 1	127
sub-s. 2	131
s. 25, sub-s. 6	24, 53
37 & 38 Vict. c. 57 (Real Property Limitation Act, 1874)	137
44 & 45 Vict. c. 41 (Conveyancing Act, 1881), s. 14	24
45 & 46 Vict. c. 43 (Bills of Sale Act)	14, 21
c. 61 (Bills of Exchange Act, 1882), s. 48	17
51 & 52 Vict. c. 25 (Railway and Canal Traffic Act, 1888), s. 33, sub-s. 3	100
c. 64 (Law of Libel Amendment Act, 1888)	174
52 & 53 Vict. c. 49 (Arbitration Act, 1889), s. 1	119
s. 14	114

TABLE OF RULES AND ORDERS CITED.

PAGE

Order III. r. 4...113.
    r. 6...10, 106, 107, 109, 110, 111, 117, 132, 207, 209.
    r. 8...106, 114.
Order XI....67.
Order XII. r. 30...67.
Order XIII. r. 11...118.
    r. 12...118, 142, 208.
Order XIV....107, 109, 110, 147, 153, 210, 214.
Order XV. r. 1...114.
Order XVI. r. 1...119.
    r. 5...119.
    r. 6...119.
    r. 9...142.
    r. 37...142.
    r. 48...151.
    r. 49...151.
    r. 50...151.
    r. 51...151.
    r. 52...151.
    r. 53...151.
    r. 54...151.
Order XIX....76, 203.
    r. 1...203.
    r. 2...39, 203.
    r. 3...148, 203.
    r. 4...7, 15, 26, 40, 198, 204.
    r. 5...39, 204.
    r. 6...41, 43, 60, 204.
    r. 7...97, 204.
    r. 8...105, 153, 204.
    r. 9...204.
    r. 10...205.
    r. 11...5, 205.
    r. 12...93, 134, 205.
    r. 13...74, 131, 205.

PAGE

Order XIX. r. 14...24, 40, 122, 137, 167, 205.
    r. 15...11, 91, 136, 162, 170, 205.
    r. 16...136, 164, 165, 206.
    r. 17...74, 79, 85, 131, 161, 206.
    r. 18...144, 161, 206.
    r. 19...74, 81, 84, 85, 131, 132, 206.
    r. 20...11, 136, 206.
    r. 21...16, 40, 122, 206.
    r. 22...34, 207.
    r. 23...34, 207.
    r. 24...35, 207.
    r. 25...22, 40, 191, 207.
    r. 26...6, 93, 207.
    r. 27...6, 52, 61, 96, 130, 207.
Order XX....203, 207.
    r. 1...107, 110, 117, 207.
    r. 4...109, 113, 118, 208.
    r. 5...129, 208.
    r. 6...126, 208.
    r. 7...119, 130, 209.
    r. 8...35, 209.
Order XXI....203, 209.
    r. 1...10, 132, 209.
    r. 2...10, 132, 209.
    r. 3...10, 132, 209.
    r. 4...27, 40, 74, 133, 209.
    r. 5...81, 209.
    r. 6...152, 210.
    r. 7...113, 210.
    r. 8...153, 210.
    r. 9...78, 136, 210.
    r. 10...149, 210.
    r. 11...151, 210.

Order XXI. r. 12...151, 210.
    r. 13...151, 211.
    r. 14...151, 211.
    r. 15...151, 211.
    r. 16...149, 211.
    r. 17...149, 211.
    r. 19...134, 211.
    r. 20...67, 142, 211.
    r. 21...48, 135, 211.
Order XXII....212.
    r. 1...146, 147, 148, 212.
    r. 2...146, 212.
    r. 3...144, 212.
    r. 4...145, 212.
    r. 5...146, 212.
    r. 6...212.
    r. 7...145, 213.
    r. 8...214.
    r. 9...160, 214.
    r. 10...214.
    r. 11...147, 214.
Order XXIII....203, 214.
    r. 1...160, 214.
    r. 2...170, 214.
    r. 3...170, 215.
    r. 4...160, 215.
    r. 5...170, 215.
    r. 6...168, 215.
Order XXIV....215.
    r. 1...139, 160, 215.
    r. 2...139, 160, 215.
    r. 3...139, 215.
Order XXV....94, 95, 216.
    r. 1...71, 216.
    r. 2...71, 72, 96, 216.
    r. 3...71, 72, 216.
    r. 4...94, 216.
    r. 5...128, 216.
Order XXVI....118.
Order XXVII....216.
    r. 13...162, 170, 215, 216.
Order XXVIII....216.
    r. 1...127, 216.
    r. 2...109, 117, 152, 217, 218.
    r. 3...152, 217, 218.
    r. 4...217.
    r. 5...217.

Order XXVIII. r. 6...217.
    r. 7...217.
    r. 8...218.
    r. 9...218.
    r. 10...218.
    r. 11...218.
    r. 12...218.
    r. 13...218.
Order XXIX. r. 1...118.
Order XXXI....218.
    r. 1...172, 174, 218.
    r. 2...219.
    r. 3...219.
    r. 4...219.
    r. 5...219.
    r. 6...182, 219.
    r. 7...179, 219.
    r. 8...220.
    r. 9...220.
    r. 10...220.
    r. 11...220.
    r. 15...79.
    r. 26...220.
    r. 27...220.
Order XXXII. r. 2...192.
    r. 6...78.
Order XXXIII. r. 1...171.
    r. 2...171.
Order XXXIV. r. 1...171.
    r. 2...171.
    r. 9...170.
Order XXXVI....221.
    r. 1...46.
    r. 7...198.
    r. 30...5.
    r. 37...27, 28, 175, 197, 198, 221.
    r. 58...118.
Order XXXVII. r. 5...192.
Order L. r. 8...138.
Order LII. r. 1...145.
Order LXIV. r. 7...152, 153.
    r. 8...160, 170.
Order LXX....221.
    r. 1...221.
    r. 2...93, 221.
Order LXXII....221.
    r. 2...41, 170, 221.

PRINCIPLES OF PLEADING.

Chapter I.

THE FUNCTION OF PLEADINGS.

Before judge and jury are asked to decide any matter which is in controversy between litigants, it is desirable, and indeed necessary, that the subject for their decision should be clearly ascertained. Otherwise the parties may go to great expense in order to be able to prove at the trial facts which their opponents will at once concede. Moreover, it is necessary to ascertain the nature of the controversy in order to determine the most appropriate mode of trial. It may turn out to be a pure point of law, which should be decided by a judge or by the Court; it may involve a lengthy investigation of complicated accounts, in which case the action should be at once referred to a special or official referee; or it may be a question proper for a jury. In any event, before the trial comes on, it is in every way desirable that the parties should know exactly what they are fighting about. The only satisfactory method of attaining this object is to make each party state his own case and answer that of his opponent. Such statements and the replies to them are called the *pleadings*.

The plaintiff naturally begins; he delivers a *Statement of Claim*. The defendant then puts in his *Defence*, which, besides answering the plaintiff's claim, may also set up a *Counterclaim*.

The plaintiff then *replies*, and the defendant *rejoins*. It is very seldom that any further pleadings are necessary, though formerly there were *surrejoinders*, *rebutters*, and *surrebutters*.

These pleadings are so conducted as always to evolve some questions either of fact or law, asserted by one party and denied by the other, and which they mutually accept as the matters which they wish to have decided. The questions thus evolved are called the *issues*. It is the peculiarity of our English system of pleading that the litigants arrive at an issue by the effect of their own allegations, and without any interference or process of selection by the Court or any of its officers, prior to the trial of the action.

These issues are produced by the interchange of alternate pleadings, each of which in its turn must either admit or deny the facts alleged in the last-preceding pleading, besides alleging additional facts where necessary. The points mutually admitted are thus extracted and distinguished from those in controversy; other matters, though disputed, may prove to be immaterial to the real question at issue; and thus the litigation is narrowed down to one or two matters which are clearly defined beforehand, and both parties are saved much trouble and expense in preparing their evidence for the trial.

The function of pleadings, then, is to ascertain with precision where the parties differ and where they agree, in what points the case relied upon on the one side is inconsistent with that of the other; and thus to arrive at certain definite and material issues which both parties accept as the matters on which they desire a judicial decision. To attain this object it is necessary that the pleadings should be conducted according to certain rules, which it is my endeavour to state and explain in the following pages. The main object of these rules is to compel each party to state clearly and intelligibly the material facts on which he relies, omitting everything immaterial, and then to insist on his opponent frankly admitting or explicitly denying every material matter alleged against him; by which method they must speedily arrive at an issue.

This method of arriving at an issue by alternate allegations has been practised in England from the earliest times. It is apparently as ancient as any portion of our law of procedure. It certainly existed in substantially the same form in the reign of Henry II. The phrase itself, "issue," occurs at the very commencement of the Year Books, *i. e.*, in the first year of Edward II.; and the distinction between an *issue en ley* and an *issue en fet* is equally ancient. (See the Year Book, 3 Edw. II. 59.) And prior even to the reign of Edward II. the production of an issue had been not only the constant effect but the professed aim and object of pleading.

At first the pleadings were oral. The parties actually appeared in open court, and a *virâ voce* altercation took place in the presence of the judges. These oral pleadings were conducted either by the party himself or his pleader (called *narrator* or *advocatus*); and it seems that the rule was then already established that none but a professional advocate could be a pleader in any cause not his own. It was the office of the judges to superintend, or "moderate," the oral contention thus conducted before them. (See Reeves' History of the English Law, vol. ii. p. 344.) In doing this, their general aim was to compel the pleaders so to manage their alternate allegations, as at length to arrive at some specific point or matter affirmed on the one side, and denied on the other, and which they both agreed was the question requiring decision. When this result was attained, the parties were said to be *at issue—ad exitum*—at the end of their pleading. And so strict were the judges in those days, that they allowed only one issue in respect of each cause of action; if a defendant had two defences to the same claim he had to elect between them; it was only in the present reign that the parties were allowed to raise more than a single issue, either of law or fact. Hence the question for decision came itself to be called *the issue*.

During this parol altercation one of the officers of the Court was busy writing on a parchment roll an official report of the allegations of the parties and of the acts of the Court itself during the progress of the pleading. This was called *the Record*. As the suit proceeded, similar entries were made from time to time, each successive entry being called a *continuance*, and, when complete, the roll was preserved "as a perpetual intrinsic and exclusively admissible testimony of all the judicial transactions" which it purported to record.

It is not known, I believe, when the system of oral pleading fell into disuse; but it gradually became the practice for each pleader in turn to borrow the parchment roll, and enter his statements thereon himself. Later (probably in the reign of Edward IV.), the plan was adopted of drawing up the pleadings in the first instance on paper, and interchanging them between the parties in that form; then, later on, after an issue had been arrived at, they were transcribed on to a parchment roll. This was called, "*entering the proceedings on the record*." But though the practice of oral pleading was abandoned, the ancient method of alternate allegation continued. In order that the student may understand the reports of cases which turned on the old system of pleading, it may be as well to mention that what we now call a Statement of Claim was before 1875 called a *declaration;* a Defence was called a *plea* or *pleas;* and a Reply was called a *replication*. The names of the further pleadings remain unchanged. Each of the pleas had to be in itself a complete defence to the action. So, too, a declaration often contained more than one *count*, each of which stated a complete and separate cause of action, and would in fact by itself have been a good and valid declaration.

The principles on which pleadings were framed, and the rules which regulated them, continued substantially the same into this century. Their practical utility was, however, seriously impaired by the over-subtlety of the pleaders and by the excessive rigour with which the rules were applied; the merits of the case being entirely subordinated to technical questions of form. A determined effort was made to correct these defects by the provisions of the Common Law Procedure Acts, 1852—1860. In 1873, however, it was found necessary to adopt a more thorough method of reform; and the Judicature Act introduced into the new High Court of Justice the system of pleading which is still in force.

No entries now are made on any parchment roll; the pleadings are written or printed on paper and interchanged between the parties; the solicitor of one party delivers his pleading to the solicitor of the other party, or to the party himself, if he does not appear by a solicitor. This goes on till the pleadings are "closed." The cause is then entered for trial, for which purpose two copies of the complete pleadings are lodged with the officer of the Court. (Order XXXVI. r. 30.) And the copy which is marked with the stamp denoting the fee paid on entry is regarded as the record.

Every pleading should be marked on the face with the date of the day on which it is delivered, the reference to the letter and number of the action, the division to which the judge (if any) to whom the action is assigned belongs, the title of the action, and the description of the pleading, and indorsed with the name and place of business of the solicitor and agent (if any) delivering the same, or the name and address of the party delivering the same, if he does not act by a solicitor. (Order XIX. r. 11.) If it contain less than ten folios (every figure being counted as one word), it may be either printed or written or partly printed and partly written; if it contain ten folios or more, it must be printed. Every pleading must be divided into paragraphs, numbered consecutively. Dates, sums, and numbers should be expressed in figures, and not in words.

Signature of counsel is not necessary; but where pleadings have been settled by counsel or by a special pleader, they must be signed by him; and if not so settled, they must be signed by the solicitor or by the party if he sues or defends in person. No technical objection can now be raised to any pleading on the ground of any alleged want of form. (Order XIX. r. 26.) But "the Court or a judge may at any stage of the proceedings order to be struck out or amended any matter in any indorsement or pleading which may be unnecessary or scandalous, or which may tend to prejudice, embarrass, or delay the fair trial of the action." (Order XIX. r. 27.)

The allegations contained in every pleading must be—

   (i) Material.
   (ii) Certain.

The next two chapters are therefore devoted to Materiality and Certainty.

Chapter II.

MATERIAL FACTS.

Fundamental Rule.

The fundamental rule of our present system of pleading is this:—

Every pleading shall contain, and contain only, a statement in a summary form of the material facts on which the party pleading relies for his claim or defence, as the case may be, but not the evidence by which they are to be proved. (Order XIX. r. 4.)

This rule involves and requires four separate things:—

(i.) Every pleading must state facts and not law.

(ii.) It must state material facts and material facts only.

(iii.) It must state facts and not the evidence by which they are to be proved.

(iv.) It must state such facts in a summary form.

(i.) EVERY PLEADING MUST STATE FACTS AND NOT LAW.

Conclusions of law, or of mixed law and fact, are no longer to be pleaded. It is for the Court hereafter to declare the law arising upon the facts proved before it. A plaintiff must not aver "I am entitled to recover 100*l*. from the defendant," or "It was the defendant's duty to do so and so." He must state the facts which in his opinion give him that right, or impose on the defendant that liability or that duty, and the judge will decide, when those facts are proved, what are the legal rights and duties of the parties respectively. So, too, a defendant must state clearly the facts which in his opinion afford him a defence to the plaintiff's action, *e. g.*, that the goods were never delivered, or were never ordered, or that they were not equal to sample. He must not say merely "I do not owe the money"; he must allege facts which show he does not owe it. He may plead that even assuming every fact alleged in the Statement of Claim to have happened, the plaintiff has no cause of action against him. This is called "an objection in point of law," as to which see *post*, p. 71. But if he is not prepared to admit them all, he must deal with the facts alleged by his opponent, and deal with each of them clearly and explicitly. If he pleads that he never agreed as alleged, this will be taken to mean that he never in fact made any such contract—not that the contract is bad in law or not binding on him because he is an infant, or because he was induced to enter into it by fraud. All facts tending to show the insufficiency or illegality of any contract must be specially pleaded. To say "There never was any contract," is a different thing from saying "There was a contract, but I contend it is invalid." State the facts and prove them, and the judge will then decide the question of validity. The judges are bound to know the law, and they can apply it to the facts of the case for themselves without its being stated in the pleadings.

Illustrations.

It is bad pleading to allege merely that a right or a duty or a liability exists; the facts must be set out which give rise to such right or create such duty or liability. Hence, where the facts stated in the pleading afford no cause of action, the pleading will be held bad, in spite of any allegation to the effect that the act was "unlawful," or "wrongful," or "improper," or "done without any justification therefor or right so to do."

Day v. *Brownrigg*, 10 Ch. D. 294; 48 L. J. Ch. 173; 27 W. R. 217; 39 L. T. 553.

Hurdman v. *N. E. Rail. Co.*, 3 C. P. D. 168; 47 L. J. C. P. 368; 26 W. R. 489; 38 L. T. 339.

A Statement of Claim alleged that an intestate, "two days before his death, made a good and valid *donatio mortis causâ* to the plaintiff of the whole of his moneys standing on deposit to his account at the Ellesmere Savings Bank," but did not state any facts amounting to a *donatio mortis causâ*. It was struck out on the ground that the facts alleged in the Statement of Claim did not show a valid *donatio mortis causâ*.

Townsend v. *Parton, In re Parton*, 30 W. R. 287; 45 L. T. 755.

In an action to recover damages caused to the plaintiff's reversion in a dwelling-house by interference with an easement, it is not sufficient to allege in the Statement of Claim that the plaintiff is entitled to such easement; the plaintiff must show how he is so entitled, whether by grant, or prescription, or otherwise, and must set out the facts upon which he relies as entitling him to such easement.

Farrell v. *Coogan*, 12 L. R. Ir. 14.

In an action for diverting the water from the plaintiff's mill, before the Judicature Act, the defendant pleaded not guilty; and upon this the question arose, whether it put in issue the mere fact of the diversion of the water, or whether the defendant was entitled also to deny the plaintiff's right to the use of the stream as claimed. It was argued for the defendant that the word "wrongfully," as used in the declaration, was part of the substantive charge, and that the plea of not guilty therefore had the effect of denying the wrong so alleged; which made it competent to the defendant to show that the plaintiff had no such right to the stream as he claimed, for then the act of diversion could be no "wrong" to the plaintiff. But the Court decided, after conference with the other judges, that in cases like this the word "wrongfully" did not bring the title into issue, under a plea of not guilty; and that in the instance before them, the plea consequently denied nothing but the fact of diversion.

Frankum v. *Lord Falmouth*, 2 A. & E. 452.

Lush v. *Russell*, 5 Exch. 203; 19 L. J. Ex. 214.

If it be stated in pleading that an officer of a corporate body was removed for misconduct by the corporate body at large, it is unnecessary to aver that the power of removal was vested in such corporate body; because that is a power by law incidental to them, unless given by some charter, by-law, or other authority, to a select part only.

The King v. *Lyme Regis*, 1 Doug. 148.

It is unnecessary to state in a pleading the principles of the common law, or to set forth a public statute.

See *Boyce* v. *Whitaker*, 1 Doug. 97.

Partridge v. *Strange*, Plow. 84.

The case, however, of private Acts of Parliament is different: for these the Court does not officially notice; and therefore where a party has occasion to rely on an Act of this description, he must set forth such parts of it as are material.

See 1 Bl. Com. 85; *Platt* v. *Hill*, 1 Lord Raym. 381.

In actions for a debt or liquidated demand in money comprised in Order III. r. 6, a mere denial of the debt shall be inadmissible.

Order XXI. r. 1.

In actions upon bills of exchange, promissory notes, or cheques, a defence in denial must deny some matter of fact, *e. g.*, the drawing, making, endorsing, accepting, presenting, or notice of dishonour of the bill or note.

Order XXI. r. 2.

In actions comprised in Order III. r. 6, classes (a) and (b), a defence in denial must deny such matters of fact from which the liability of the defendant is alleged to arise, as are disputed; *e. g.*, in actions for goods bargained and sold, or sold and delivered, the defence must deny the order or contract, the delivery, or the amount claimed; in an action for money had and received, it must deny the receipt of the money, or the existence of those facts which are alleged to make such receipt by the defendant a receipt to the use of the plaintiff.

Order XXI. r. 3.

In an action of libel or slander, a defendant may not plead merely that "he published the words on a privileged occasion." He must set out the facts and circumstances on which he relies as creating the privilege, and then the judge will decide on the facts proved at the trial whether the occasion was or was not privileged.

Simmonds v. *Dunne*, Ir. R. 5 C. L. 358.

In an action of debt on a bond by which the defendant bound himself to duly perform an award when made, the defendant pleaded that the arbitrators never made any award. It turned out that the arbitrators had in fact duly made their award, but that it was bad in law, as it included matters not within the submission. It was urged that the defendant could not raise this legal objection, for by his plea he had alleged that there was no award, which meant no award in fact; whereas in fact an award had been made. The Court, however, held that the plea of no award meant no legal and valid award according to the submission, and that consequently it was open to the defendant to show that the award was not conformable to the submission, and therefore void in law.

Fisher v. *Pimbley*, 11 East, 188.

And see *Dudlow* v. *Watchorn*, 16 East, 39.

But this appears to have been contrary to some former decisions.

See *Morgan* v. *Man*, 1 Sid. 180; Sir T. Raym. 94.

Harding v. *Holmes*, 1 Wils. 122.

Praed v. *Duchess of Cumberland*, 4 T. R. 585; 2 Hen. Bl. 280; 2 Wms. Saund. 190, n. (*d*).

And it clearly is not permissible now. A plea of "no award" would certainly mean, in the present day, that no award at all had ever been made, not that an invalid one had been made.

See Order XIX. r. 15.

When a contract, promise, or agreement is alleged in any pleading, a bare denial of the same by the opposite party shall be construed only as a denial in fact of the express contract, promise, or agreement alleged, or of the matters of fact from which the same may be implied by law, and not as a denial of the legality or sufficiency in law of such contract, promise, or agreement, whether with reference to the Statute of Frauds or otherwise.

Order XIX. r. 20.

This is one of the greatest improvements introduced by the Judicature Act. Each party was, before 1875, bound to state with reasonable precision the points which he intended to raise; but this he generally did by stating, not the facts which he meant to prove, but the conclusion of law he sought to draw from them. The other side thus learnt that the party pleading meant to prove *some* set of facts which would sustain a given legal conclusion; but how he proposed to sustain that legal conclusion was not disclosed. For instance, this was a very common form of declaration: "The plaintiff sues the defendant for £——, money payable to the plaintiff by the defendant for money received by the defendant to the use of the plaintiff." That might cover any one of the following cases, and many more besides:—

(a) The defendant was the plaintiff's rent collector, and had received money for him as such.

(b) The plaintiff claimed to be entitled to an office which the defendant also claimed, and under colour of which the defendant had received fees, which the plaintiff considered should be handed over to himself.

(c) The plaintiff, a customer, had paid the defendant, a tradesman, the price of goods to be supplied, and the defendant had never supplied them.

(d) The plaintiff had paid a sum of money to the defendant by mistake, having taken him for another person of the same name or appearance.

Which set of facts would be proved at the trial could not be ascertained from the plaintiff's pleading. Moreover, there were often several alternative legal conclusions which could be drawn from the facts, any one of which would serve the plaintiff's turn; and therefore several "counts" were pleaded in the same declaration, giving various legal aspects of the same transaction, the evidence given in support of which at the trial would be identical.

So, again, with the defence. In an action for goods sold and delivered, the defendant was allowed to plead "the general issue," that he never was indebted as alleged. This is a conclusion of law, and at the trial it was open to him to give in evidence under this plea any one or more of several totally different defences, of which the following may serve as instances:—

(i) That he never ordered the goods.
(ii) That they never were delivered to him.
(iii) That they were not of the quality ordered.
(iv) That they were sold on a credit which had not expired at the time that the action was commenced.
(v) That there was no memorandum of the contract in writing sufficient to satisfy the Statute of Frauds.

But the defendant might not, under this plea, set up the Statute of Limitations, nor allege payment or a set-off, because each of these defences implies that the defendant *was once* indebted to the plaintiff as alleged. He might deny that any express contract of sale was ever made; he might deny all or any of the matters of fact from which such a contract would by law be implied; but he was not permitted to insist that the contract, though made in fact, was void in law. In short, the common law pleadings, where these conclusions of law came in, were more like algebraical symbols than allegations of fact. The plaintiff pleaded x, and the defendant answered y: no one knew for certain what x and y meant, but the initiated knew that they could only mean a or b, or c or d, and that they could not mean l or m or n. Now all such ambiguous formulæ are abolished, and the actual facts on which either party relies must be stated as briefly as possible in his pleading. Facts, and not fictions, not even legal fictions!

Whenever the same legal result can be attained in several different ways, it is not sufficient to aver merely that that result has been arrived at, but the facts must be stated showing how and by what means it was attained.

Illustrations.

In an action of debt on a bond conditioned to show on a certain day a sufficient discharge of an annuity, the defendant pleaded that on that day he did offer to show a sufficient discharge. And it was adjudged that the plea was insufficient; "for his plea ought to have alleged what manner of discharge he offered to show, viz., a release or other matter of discharge, upon which the Court might judge if it was sufficient or not; for the country shall not inquire of it, but it ought to be adjudged by the Court; which the judges cannot do, if the special matter be not showed to them."

Lord Lisle's case, cited 9 Rep. 25a.

It is not sufficient in an action upon a contract for the defendant to plead that "the contract is rescinded." This may mean that the parties met, and in express terms agreed to put an end to the contract; or it may mean that such an intention is to be collected from a long correspondence and a whole series of transactions; or it may mean that the plaintiff himself has broken the contract in such a way as to amount to actual repudiation. The defendant must show in what manner and by what means he contends that it was rescinded.

Where a party claims that the estate formerly held by A. is now vested in himself, he must state in his pleading the date and nature of the conveyance or other alienation, whether it was by deed, or by will, &c.

Com. Dig. Pleader (E. 23), (E. 24).

Plaintiff alleged that he had a right of way. It was held that he was bound to say in his Statement of Claim whether he claimed it by prescription or by grant.

Harris v. *Jenkins*, 22 Ch. D. 481; 52 L. J. Ch. 437; 31 W. R. 137; 47 L. T. 570.

Spedding v. *Fitzpatrick*, 38 Ch. D. 410; 58 L. J. Ch. 139; 37 W. R. 20; 59 L. T. 492.

It is not enough for a plaintiff to reply to a plea of the Statute of Limitations that "that statute does not apply," or that "the case has been taken out of the statute." "The 3 & 4 Will. IV. c. 42, provides three modes by which a specialty debt may be taken out of the operation of that statute; and it is a prejudice to a defendant to be compelled to come prepared to meet three different matters, when perhaps the plaintiff intends to rely on one only."

Per Parke, B., in *Forsyth* v. *Bristowe*, 8 Ex. at p. 350.

It is not sufficient to plead "the said bill of sale is void and of no effect in law." Facts must be stated showing its invalidity, *e.g.*, that it has not been registered, or is not in the form given in the schedule to the Bills of Sale Act.

It is not sufficient for a plaintiff to say, "under and by virtue of a certain deed I am entitled, &c.," for that is an inference of law. The limitations of the deed and all other facts upon which he proposes to rely as showing that he is so entitled must be stated.

Riddell v. *Earl of Strathmore*, 3 Times L. R. 329.

If a man claims to be a peer, he must state whether he is a peer by writ, or by patent, or by descent, or by prescription. For if he "claims to be a peer by writ he is not a peer until he has taken his seat. . . . If by patent, the title is complete as soon as the patent is sealed."

Per Bayley, J., in *The King* v. *Cooke*, 2 B. & C. at p. 874.

Where a party claims by inheritance, he must do more than merely state "I am the heir-at-law." He must show how he is heir, viz., as son or otherwise; and if he does not claim by immediate descent he must show the pedigree. For example, if he claims as nephew, he must show how he is nephew, whether brother's son or sister's son, and account for all who would be nearer in blood.

Dumsday v. *Hughes*, 3 Bos. & Pul. 453.

And see *Roe* v. *Lord*, 2 Bla. Rep. 1099, and the cases there cited.

The decision of Malins, V.-C., to the contrary in *Evelyn* v. *Evelyn*, 28 W. R. 531; 42 L. T. 248, is in conflict with all the earlier common law cases on the point, none of which were cited to the learned Vice-Chancellor. Hence it is of doubtful authority.

(ii.) EVERY PLEADING MUST STATE MATERIAL FACTS ONLY.

What facts are material? Every fact is material which is essential to the plaintiff's cause of action or to the defendant's defence—which they must prove or fail.

Facts which are not necessary to establish either a cause of action or the defence to it are not, speaking generally, "material" within the meaning of Order XIX. r. 4, and should, therefore, be omitted from the pleading.* "All statements which need not be proved shall be omitted." (Common Law Procedure Act, 1852, s. 49.)

It is obvious, then, that the question, whether a particular fact is or is not material, depends mainly on the special circumstances of the particular case. It is a question which it is not always easy to answer, and yet it is a very important one; the result of the case often depends on the ruling of the judge at the trial that it is or is not necessary that a particular fact should be proved. Sometimes it is material to allege and prove that the defendant had notice of some fact; at other times it is sufficient to aver that he did such an act, without inquiring into the state of his mind. In some cases the defendant's intention is material: in a few cases his motives. The pleader must apply his knowledge of the law, or, better still, his common-sense, to the facts stated in his instructions, and decide for himself which he must plead and which he may safely omit. Former precedents may afford him some assistance; and so will books like Roscoe's Nisi Prius. But in the end he must rely on his own judgment.

If after consideration you are still in serious doubt whether a particular fact is or is not material, the safer course is to plead it,

---

* See *post*, p. 26.

if you think you can prove it. For if you omit to plead it, and it is held to be material, you cannot give any evidence of that fact at the trial, unless the learned judge will give leave to amend, which will only be allowed upon terms, such as payment of costs, &c. (See *Byrd* v. *Nunn*, 5 Ch. D. 781 ; 7 Ch. D. 284 ; and *Brook* v. *Brook*, 12 P. D. 19 ; 56 L. J. P. 108 ; 35 W. R. 351 ; 57 L. T. 425.)

Illustrations.

Here is a Statement of Claim in which the most material allegation of all has been omitted :—

"The defendant instructed and employed the plaintiff to do certain work (specifying it). The plaintiff's charges for such work amounted to £——, which sum the defendant promised to pay to the plaintiff."

The consideration for any contract not under seal is always material, and should be correctly set out in the Statement of Claim, except in the case of negotiable instruments, where the consideration is presumed. If the contract be under seal, the consideration is immaterial.

Raikes v. *Todd*, 8 A. & E. 854 ; 1 P. & D. 138.

In an action against a bailee, it is always material to know whether he was to be paid for his services ; as this affects the degree of diligence which the law expects from him. But the amount of his remuneration is not material ; it is sufficient to aver that he was to warehouse or carry the goods " for reward."

As a rule, the precise wording of a document is not material, and it is sufficient to state briefly its effect.

Order XIX. r. 21.

But in an action of libel or slander the precise words complained of are material, and they must be set out *verbatim* in the Statement of Claim.

Harris v. *Warre*, 4 C. P. D. 125 ; 48 L. J. C. P. 310 ; 27 W. R. 461 ; 40 L. T. 429.

So, the precise wording of a covenant may be material if it be in an unusual form ; for a change of phrase may alter the legal effect of the clause.

Horsefall v. *Testar*, 7 Taunt. 385 ; 1 Moore, 89.

Where either party relies on any custom of the country or of the trade as enlarging or restricting the rights given him by the ordinary law of the land, such custom must be specially pleaded with all necessary detail.

See *Wigglesworth* v. *Dallison*, 1 Smith's L. C. (9th ed.) 569.

Where the parties expressly agree to limit the liability ordinarily imposed on either of them in contracts of the particular class, such limitation is material, and should be alleged by the party who first purports to set out the true contract.

Sharland v. *Leifchild*, 4 C. B. 529 ; 16 L. J. C. P. 217.
Heath v. *Durant*, 12 M. & W. 438 ; 13 L. J. Ex. 95.

Notice.

In an action on a bill of exchange against an indorser, the holder must allege notice of dishonour; in an action against the acceptor, he need not.

Bills of Exchange Act, 1882, s. 48.

In an action by a creditor against a surety, there is no need to allege that the creditor gave the surety notice that the principal debtor had not paid.

In an action for wrongfully keeping a dog accustomed to chase and kill cattle (or bite men), the plaintiff must show that the defendant knew at least one instance in which his dog had done this.

Thomas v. *Morgan*, 2 C. M. & R. 496; 4 Dowl. 223.

In an action for negligence brought by a servant against his master for injuries resulting from the unsafe state of the premises, the Statement of Claim must show not only that the master knew, but also that the servant did not know, that the premises were in a dangerous condition.

Griffiths v. *London and St. Katharine Docks Co.*, 13 Q. B. D. 259; 53 L. J. Q. B. 504; 33 W. R. 35; 51 L. T. 533.

Action on a bond conditioned to keep the plaintiffs harmless and indemnified from all suits, &c., of one Thomas Cook. The defendants pleaded that they had kept the plaintiffs harmless, &c. The plaintiffs replied that Cook sued them, and so the defendants had not kept them harmless, &c. The defendants rejoined that they had not any notice of the damnification. And the Court held that the rejoinder was bad, as the plaintiffs were not bound to give the defendants notice of Cook's action against them.

Cutler v. *Southern*, 1 Wms. Saund. 116.

Intention, &c.

Whenever an injunction is applied for, it is material to allege that the defendant threatens and intends to repeat the illegal act complained of.

Stannard v. *Vestry of St. Giles*, 20 Ch. D. at p. 195; 51 L. J. Ch. 629; 30 W. R. 693; 46 L. T. 243.

Where words of praise are spoken ironically, so as to convey a defamatory meaning, it must be averred that they were so intended and understood; else the Statement of Claim will disclose no cause of action.

In an action brought on a fraudulent prospectus, it is unnecessary for the plaintiff to state the *motives* which induced the defendants to issue it, or which led to the scheme of which it was a part; it is sufficient to state generally that the prospectus was, to the knowledge of the defendants, fraudulent.

Herring v. *Bischoffsheim*, W. N. (1876) p. 77.

Yet where collusion is alleged between A. and B., the fact that A.

knew the improper motives which actuated B. is material, and for this purpose those improper motives must be stated.

Briton Medical, &c. Life Association v. *Britannia Fire Association*, 59 L. T. 888.

Where defamatory words are published on an occasion which is not privileged, it is not necessary to aver that they were published maliciously. But if the occasion be privileged, then malice becomes material.

Anon., Style, 392.

Belt v. *Lawes*, 51 L. J. Q. B. 359.

Each party must state his whole case. He must plead all facts on which he intends to rely at the trial, otherwise he cannot strictly give any evidence of them at the trial. The Statement of Claim must disclose a good cause of action: the defendant must show a good defence thereto. Omit no averment which is essential to success. Do not plead half a defence and leave the rest to be inferred.

Illustrations.

By a lease dated March 2nd, 1879, the plaintiff demised a house to A. for the term of twenty-one years at the yearly rental of 120*l.*, payable quarterly. A. is dead; the defendant is living in the house; three quarters' rent is in arrear, for which the plaintiff has issued a writ. A Statement of Claim which disclosed those facts and nothing more would be bad; the plaintiff must show that defendant is assignee of the lease and liable on the covenant to pay the rent thereby reserved.

If a commoner sue for a nuisance to the common (*e.g.*, where the defendant has dug a pit in the common), he must aver that his enjoyment of his right of common has thereby been appreciably impaired (*per quod communiam suam in tam amplo modo habere non potuit*); as otherwise he has no cause of action.

Per Lord Holt, C. J., in *Ashby* v. *White*, 1 Sm. L. C. (9th ed.) at p. 296.

Mary's Case, 9 Rep. 113; Co. Litt. 56, a.

And see *Rose* v. *Groves*, 5 M. & G. 613; 12 L. J. C. P. 251.

Dobson v. *Blackmore*, 9 Q. B. 991; 16 L. J. Q. B. 233.

In an action of slander, if the words are actionable only by reason of their being spoken of the plaintiff in the way of his office, profession, or trade, the Statement of Claim must always contain an averment that the plaintiff actually held the office or carried on the profession or trade at the time when the words were spoken. And there should also be an averment that the words were spoken of the plaintiff with reference to such office, profession, or trade.

Gallwey v. *Marshall*, 9 Ex. 300; 23 L. J. Ex. 78; 2 C. L. R. 399.

In an action for specific performance of an agreement made by a married woman, the Statement of Claim contained no allegation that she had separate estate at the date of the contract. Motion for judgment refused. Leave to amend.

Tetley v. *Griffith*, 36 W. R. 96; 57 L. T. 673.

And see *Braunstein* v. *Lewis*, 64 L. T. 265.

In an action against a carrier for the loss of a parcel, the defendant cannot set up at the trial that the parcel was above 10*l.* in value, and that no notice of its value was given at the time of its being delivered, as required by 11 Geo. IV. & 1 Will. IV. c. 68, unless this defence has been specially pleaded. It is not sufficient merely to deny the contract alleged by the plaintiff.

Syms v. *Chaplin*, 5 A. & E. 634; 1 N. & P. 129.

Action of replevin for wrongful seizing of cattle. The defendant avowed taking them in the close in question for rent in arrear. The plaintiff pleaded in bar to this avowry that the cattle were not levant and couchant on the close in question. This was held a bad plea. For it is a general rule of law that all things upon the premises are distrainable for rent in arrear, and the levancy and couchancy of the cattle is immaterial, unless under special circumstances such as did not appear by the plea in bar to have existed in this case.

Jones v. *Powell*, 5 B. & C. 647; 8 D. & R. 416.

See also *Hall* v. *Tapper*, 3 B. & Ad. 655.

In an action brought by a commoner against a stranger for putting his cattle on the common, *per quod communiam in tam amplo modo habere non potuit*, the defendant pleaded a licence from the lord to put his cattle there, but he did not aver that there was sufficient common left for the commoners; this was held to be no good plea, for the lord had no right to give a stranger such licence unless there was enough common left for the commoners. It was urged that it was rather for the plaintiff to reply that there was not enough common left; but the Court held that the defendant was bound to plead all such facts as were necessary to make good the defence he had pleaded.

Smith v. *Feverell*, 2 Mod. 6; 1 Freem. 190.

Greenhow v. *Ilsley*, Willes, 619.

"Regularly whensoever a man doth anything by force of a warrant or authority, he must plead it."

Co. Litt. 283 a; *ibid.* 303 b.; 1 Wms. Saund. 298, n. (1).

Sometimes the whole point of the action turns on one minute allegation. Thus:—

In an action of trespass for assault and battery, the defendant pleaded that a judgment was recovered and execution issued thereupon against a third person, and that the plaintiff, to rescue that person's goods from the execution, assaulted the bailiffs, and that in aid of the bailiffs, and by their command, the defendant *molliter manus imposuit* upon the plaintiff, to prevent his rescue of the goods. It was held that it was unnecessary to aver any command of the bailiffs, for, even without their command, the defendant might lawfully interfere to prevent a rescue, which is a breach of the peace.

Bridgwater v. *Bythway*, 3 Lev. 113.

It is otherwise if not done to prevent a rescue; for in a case where the defendant justifies merely as assistant to, and by command of, a person executing legal process, the command is material, and must be alleged, as without it the defendant would be a mere volunteer, meddling in other people's business.

Britton v. *Cole*, 1 Salk. 409; Carth. 443.

Do not jump before you come to the Stile.

But the pleader need only allege facts which are material at the present stage of the action. It is sufficient that each pleading in turn should contain in itself a good *primâ facie* case, without reference to possible objections not yet urged.

It is not necessary to anticipate the answer of the adversary, which, according to Hale, C. J., is "like leaping before one comes to the stile." (*Sir Ralph Borey's Case*, Vent. 217.)

"It is no part of the Statement of Claim to anticipate the defence, and to state what the plaintiff would have to say in answer to it. That would be a return to the old inconvenient system of pleading in Chancery, which ought certainly not to be encouraged, when the plaintiff used to allege in his bill imaginary defences of the defendant, and make charges in reply to them." (*Per* James, L. J., in *Hall* v. *Eve*, 4 Ch. D. at p. 345.)

So, too, it is quite unnecessary for the defendant to excuse himself from matters of which he is not yet accused, or to plead to causes of action which do not appear in the Statement of Claim.

Illustrations.

In an action of account, it is sufficient for the plaintiff, in the first instance, to allege facts which show that the defendant is *prima facie* liable to account to the plaintiff for certain moneys. If the defendant in his Defence sets up that all accounts up to a certain date were settled between them, it will then be for the plaintiff to state in his Reply the facts which may entitle him to have such settled account re-opened. Such facts would be immaterial in the original Statement of Claim.

In pleading a devise of land, it is enough to state that A. was seised of the land in fee, and devised it by his last will in writing, without alleging that such devisor was of full age. For if the devisor were within age, it was for the other party to show this in his answer; and it need not be denied by anticipation.

Stowell v. Lord Zouch, Plow. 376.

So in a declaration of debt upon a bond, it is unnecessary to allege that the defendant was of full age when he executed the bond.

Walsingham's Case, Plowd. 564.

Sir Ralph Bovey's Case, Vent. 217.

It is bad pleading in a Statement of Claim for trespass and conversion of goods to continue thus:—"The defendant committed the alleged trespass and seized and carried away the said goods under colour of a pretended bill of sale alleged to have been given him by the plaintiff, whereby, &c. But the said bill of sale, if any, has never been registered, and is also void in law because it is not in conformity with the form in the schedule to the Bills of Sale Act, &c." This is jumping before you come to the stile. Leave the defendant to set up his bill of sale, if he thinks he can make anything of it; and plead its invalidity in your Reply. He may have some other perfectly good defence, and never plead the bill of sale at all.

In an action for a libel, it would be bad pleading for the plaintiff to state, "The defendant will contend that the said words are part of a fair and accurate report of a judicial proceeding; but such report was neither fair nor accurate." How do you know what the defendant will contend? Do not suggest defences to your opponent. There is no necessity for the plaintiff to mention the judicial proceeding or to state that the words form part of any report.

A charterparty contained a covenant "that no claim should be admitted or allowance made for short tonnage, unless such short tonnage were found and made to appear on the ship's arrival, on a survey to be taken by four shipwrights, to be indifferently chosen by both parties." In an action brought on this charterparty to recover for short tonnage, the plaintiff had a verdict; and the defendants moved in arrest of judgment that it had not been averred in the declaration that a survey was taken, and short tonnage made to appear. But the Court held that if such survey had not been taken, this was matter of defence which ought to have been shown by the defendants, and refused to arrest the judgment.

Hotham v. *East India Co.*, 1 T. R. 638; 1 Dougl. 272.

In an action brought against the defendant, as *executrix* of J. S., on a bond given by J. S. in his lifetime, she pleaded in abatement that J. S. died *intestate*, and that *administration* was granted to her. On demurrer, it was objected that the plea was insufficient; that it should have gone on to aver that she never meddled with the estate before administration was granted, because, if she so meddled, she thereby became at once an executrix *de son tort*, and as such would be properly sued as executrix, notwithstanding the subsequent grant of letters of administration. But the Court held the plea good in that respect. And Holt, C. J., said, "It is enough for her to show that the plaintiff's writ ought to abate; which she has done in showing that she is chargeable only by another name. Then, as to the traverse that she did not administer as executrix before the letters of administration were granted, it would be to traverse what is not alleged in the plaintiff's declaration; which would be against a rule of law, that a man shall never traverse that which the plaintiff has not alleged in his declaration."

Powers v. *Cook*, 1 Ld. Raym. 63; 1 Salk. 298.

"Neither party need, in any pleading, allege any matter of fact which the law presumes in his favour, or as to which the burden of proof lies on the other side." (Order XIX. r. 25.)

Illustrations.

A plaintiff need not, in his pleading, set out the consideration for which a bill of exchange was given him, when he sues only on the bill. It will be for the defendant to plead no consideration. It is otherwise when the plaintiff sues on the consideration as a substantive ground of claim; then, of course, he must allege it specifically.

Order XIX. r. 25.

In an action for goods sold and delivered, it is unnecessary, in addition to the allegation that the plaintiff sold and delivered them to the defendant, to state that they were goods of the plaintiff; for a buyer who has accepted and enjoyed the goods cannot dispute the title of the seller.

Bull. N. P. 139.

In a claim for money lent, it is unnecessary to aver that the money was lent by the plaintiff to the defendant *at his request;* for no man lends money unasked.

Victors v. *Davies*, 12 M. & W. 758; 13 L. J. Ex. 241.

Where the plaintiff is or was in possession of any land or chattel, it is sufficient against a wrongdoer to aver possession only, and the plaintiff need not set out his title. *Omnia presumuntur contra spoliatorem.*
Armory v. *Delamirie*, 1 Sm. L. C. (9th ed.) 385.

Whenever the rule of law applicable to the case has an exception to it (as it generally has), all facts are material which tend to take the case out of the rule and bring it within the exception. And so are all facts which tend to take the case out of the exception and keep it within the rule.

Whenever there is a conflict between law and equity on any relevant point, all facts are material which tend either to raise or oust the equity.

Whenever the right claimed or the defence raised is the creature of statute, being unknown to the common law, every fact must be alleged necessary to bring the case within the statute.

Where the right claimed or the defence raised existed at common law, but the common law applicable to the case has been materially altered in its substance by statute, all facts are material which tend to take the case out of the rule at common law and bring it within the statute. And so are all facts which tend to show that the statute does not apply to the particular case.

But where the right claimed or the defence raised existed at common law, and the subsequent statute has not affected its validity, but merely introduced regulations as to the mode of its exercise or performance, the statute does not affect the form of pleading. It is sufficient to allege whatever was sufficient before the statute. (See 1 Wms. Saund. 211, n. (2), 276, n. (2); *Birch* v. *Bellamy*, 12 Mod. 540; *Chalie* v. *Belshaw*, 6 Bing. 529.)

Illustrations.

At common law the assignee of a debt could not sue at all; in equity he could sue if he joined the assignor as a co-plaintiff. Now by the

Judicature Act, s. 25, sub-s. 6, he can sue alone if the debt be absolutely assigned to him by writing under the hand of the assignor, and express notice in writing of such assignment has been given to the debtor. The Statement of Claim of such an assignee suing alone must expressly allege—
  (a) an absolute assignment
  (b) in writing; and
  (c) notice of such assignment
  (d) given in writing to the debtor.
For without these averments the case is not brought within the statute, and the plaintiff has no right of action.
  Seear v. *Lawson*, 15 Ch. D. 426; 16 Ch. D. 121; 49 L. J. Bk. 69; 50 L. J. Ch. 139; 28 W. R. 929; 29 W. R. 109; 42 L. T. 893; 43 L. T. 716.
  Wallis v. *Smith*, 51 L. J. Ch. 577; 46 L. T. 473.
By sect. 14 of the Conveyancing Act, 1881, a landlord cannot eject a tenant for breach of covenant to repair without serving on him, a reasonable time before the writ is issued, a notice in writing specifying the repairs that are needed and other matters. Need a landlord suing for recovery of possession allege in his Statement of Claim that he did give such a notice a reasonable time before action? No: for he has a perfectly good right of entry without it; the statute merely regulates his exercise of that right; in other words, it imposes a fresh condition precedent to his right of action. His due performance of the requirements of the statute will therefore be presumed until the defendant pleads that he never was served with any such notice.

A plaintiff need not show in his Statement of Claim that the Statute of Frauds has been complied with. It is for the defendant to plead that it was not.

Conditions Precedent.

Neither party need allege the performance of any condition precedent. The party who desires to contest the performance or occurrence of any condition precedent must raise the point specifically in his pleading. "Subject thereto, an averment of the performance or occurrence of all conditions precedent necessary for the case of the plaintiff or defendant shall be implied in his pleading." (Order XIX. r. 14.)

Note the wording of this rule. It does not say such an averment is immaterial; only that it shall be implied. There is a reason for this. Although it is not any longer necessary for a plaintiff to plead the due performance of all conditions precedent to his right of action, yet the burden of proving due performance is still on him, if the defendant specially plead non-performance. In former days it was essential for a plaintiff to set out in his declaration every condition precedent to his right and to aver the due performance of it with all particularity. Then came the Common Law Procedure Act, 1852, s. 57 of which provided: "it shall be lawful for the plaintiff or defendant in any action to aver performance of conditions precedent generally, and the opposite party shall not deny such averment generally, but shall specify in his pleading the condition or conditions precedent the performance of which he intends to contest." And now a general averment of the due performance of all conditions precedent is implied in every pleading.

But what is a condition precedent? and how does it differ from the material facts which must be pleaded?

Where everything has happened which would at common law *primâ facie* entitle a man to a certain sum of money, or vest in him a certain right of action; and yet in this particular case there is something further to be done, or something more must happen before he is entitled to sue, either by reason of the provisions of some statute, or because the parties have expressly so agreed; this something more is called a condition precedent. It is not of the essence of such a cause of action; but it has been made essential. It is an additional formality superimposed on what otherwise would have been valid. Hence the plaintiff can make out a perfectly good Statement of Claim without any reference to it; and it is for the defendant to raise the point if he thinks the plaintiff has not performed all that is required of him. If neither party refer to the condition, it will probably be because it has been duly complied with; anyhow its due performance will in that event be presumed.

Illustration.

A. agrees to build a house for B., according to a specification in writing, for 3,000*l*. A. has built the house according to the specification. But by the agreement to which such specification is scheduled, he agreed that payment should only be made upon the architect's certificate that so much is due. Obtaining and presenting such a certificate is, therefore, a condition precedent to his right to receive the 3,000*l*. But he can draft a Statement of Claim showing a good *primâ facie* right to the 3,000*l*., without mentioning any certificate. It will be for the defendant to plead that the architect has never certified that the amount is due.

Hudson on Building Contracts, p. 265.

And see *Hotham* v. *East India Company*, 1 T. R. 638, *ante*, p. 22.

Matters affecting Damages.

A "material fact" has been defined (*ante*, p. 15) as a fact which is essential to the plaintiff's cause of action or to the defendant's defence. But there are many facts which are not material on the main issue whether plaintiff ought to succeed or not, and which yet will be proved and discussed at the trial, because they affect the amount of *damages* which he will be entitled to recover. Such facts are called "matters in aggravation of damages," or "matters in mitigation of damages." How far is it right for the plaintiff and the defendant respectively to state such facts in their pleading?

The law on this point is not clear; but the better opinion is (in spite of the decision in *Millington* v. *Loring*, 6 Q. B. D. 190) that matters which merely tend to increase or diminish the amount of damages and which do not concern the right of action are strictly not "material facts" within the meaning of Order XIX. r. 4, and therefore ought not to be pleaded. However, the law on the point being somewhat unsettled, a convenient but illogical practice has grown up at Chambers, which allows either party to plead or not to plead such facts, according to his pleasure. If you wish to interrogate about them, it is as well to plead them.

I call this new practice illogical, because material facts, and material facts only, *may* be pleaded; and each party *must* plead *all* material facts on which he intends to rely. There is no intermediate class possible of facts which are so far material that you *may* plead them if you like, and yet *not* so material that you are obliged to plead them.

The difficulty is caused mainly by the decision in *Millington* v. *Loring*. The learned judges there appeared to assume that any fact which it would be open to either party to prove at the trial was a material fact within the rules of pleading. Moreover, the application made to them was to strike certain matters out of the Statement of Claim, and this they refused to do. They did not expressly decide that such matters could not have been given in evidence at the trial, unless they had been pleaded; though that is surely the logical result of holding that they were material facts. Pearson, J., followed *Millington* v. *Loring* in *Lumb* v. *Beaumont*, 49 L. T. 772. Then, again, in *Scott* v. *Sampson* (8 Q. B. D. 491; 51 L. J. Q. B. 380; 30 W. R. 541; 46 L. T. 412), the Divisional Court apparently decided that a defendant must always plead facts in mitigation of damages in his Defence. But that was an action of libel, and since that decision a new rule has been made, Order XXXVI. r. 37, requiring a defendant in any action of libel or slander, who has not pleaded a justification, to give particulars of such matters seven days at least before the trial; thus clearly implying that such a defendant was in no way bound to set out in his pleading the facts on which he proposes to rely in mitigation of damages.

It is impossible to draw any clear distinction between matters in aggravation and matters in mitigation of damages in this respect. If the former are material facts, the latter must be so too. The new rule (Order XXI. r. 4) does not create any such distinction; all it says is this: "No denial or defence shall be necessary as to damages claimed or their amount, but they shall be deemed to be put in issue in all cases, unless expressly admitted." This surely means no more than that a defendant need not plead to the concluding paragraphs of the Statement of Claim in which the plaintiff alleges his damage, special or general. It has no bearing on matters which the defendant proposes to allege for the first time in mitigation of damages. That being so, I think matters in aggravation and matters in mitigation of damages must be subject to precisely the same rule. It would seem to follow that the decisions—*Wood* v. *Earl of Durham*, 21 Q. B. D. 501; 57 L. J. Q. B. 547; and *Wood* v. *Cox*, 4 Times L. R. 550—practically overrule the decision of the Divisional Court in *Millington* v. *Loring*. If so, neither matters in aggravation nor matters in mitigation of damages are material facts, and if so they ought not to be pleaded.

At the same time there seems no sufficient ground for striking out such matters, if they be pleaded. It can scarcely be said that such a method of pleading embarrasses the plaintiff, for it gives him notice what will be the defendant's case at the trial. Hence, if such matters are pleaded, as a rule no objection is made. Hence has arisen the practice which I have described as convenient though illogical.

There is, however, one exception. In an action of libel or slander the defendant may, in mitigation of damages, by a special plea, justify part of the words, provided such part is distinct and severable from the rest. The plea must distinctly identify the portion justified. (*Vessey* v. *Pike*, 3 C. & P. 512.) Without such a plea the defendant could give no evidence that any portion of his words was true, not even though he had given a notice under Order XXXVI. r. 37.

In early days, when the Courts were very strict, they punished either party who pleaded immaterial facts in this way: If his opponent pleaded to such immaterial facts, and issue was joined thereon, they compelled the party who had alleged such facts to prove them literally, although they were immaterial; otherwise he failed in his action. He had himself raised this issue, so he must prove it or take the consequences.

Illustrations.

Action for trespass to a close of pasture containing eight acres in the township of Tollard Royal. Defence that the defendant had the right to use an ancient chase of deer which extended itself as well in and through the said eight acres of pasture, as in and through the said township of Tollard Royal; and justified the trespasses as committed in using the said chase. The plaintiff traversed that the said chase extended itself as well to the eight acres as to the whole town; and the jury, at the trial, found in the very words of the issue that the said chase did not extend as well to the whole town as to the eight acres. It was then moved, in arrest of judgment, "that this issue and verdict were faulty; because, if the chase did extend to the eight acres only, it was enough for the defendant; and therefore the finding of the jury, that it did not extend as well to the whole town as to the eight acres, did not conclude against the defendant's right in the eight acres, which was only in question. But it was answered by the Court that there was no fault in the issue, much less in the verdict (which was according to the issue); but the fault was in the defendant's plea; for he puts in his plea more than he needed,

viz., the whole town, to his own disadvantage. And so judgment was given for the plaintiff."
Wood v. *Budden*, Hob. 119.

Again, in an action on the case, the plaintiff alleged in his declaration that he demised a house to the defendant for seven years, and that during the term the defendant so negligently kept his fire that the house was burnt down; and the defendant having pleaded *non demisit modo et forma*, it appeared in evidence that the plaintiff had demised to the defendant several tenements, of which the house in question was one, but that with respect to this house it was, by an exception in the lease, demised at will only. The Court held that though the plaintiff might have declared against the defendant as tenant at will only, and the action would have lain, yet having stated a demise for seven years, he was bound to prove a demise for seven years, and that proof of a lease at will was a variance, and one in substance, not in form only; and on the ground of such variance, judgment was given for the defendant. [Now, the words "for seven years" would be rejected as surplusage.]

Cudlip v. *Rundle*, Carth. 202.

The plaintiff pleaded that he was seised in his demesne as of fee of B. close; that Sir F. L. was bound to repair the fence between B. close and the place in which, &c.; and that the cattle escaped through a defect of that fence. The defendant pleaded that the plaintiff was not seised in his demesne, as of fee, of B. close; and the Court was of opinion that it was a good traverse; for though a less estate than a seisin in fee would have been sufficient to sustain the plaintiff's case, yet as the plaintiff, who should best know what estate he had, had pleaded a seisin in fee, his adversary was entitled to traverse the title so laid, and the plaintiff must prove a seisin in fee at the trial.

Sir Francis Leke's Case, 3 Dyer, 365; 2 Wms. Saund. 206 a., n. (22).
The Queen v. *Dendy*, 1 E. & B. 829; 22 L. J. Q. B. 247.

Subsequently, however, the Courts adopted a far better method of preventing the parties from raising immaterial issues. They declared that "immaterial allegations were not traversable," *i.e.*, neither party was allowed to plead to any immaterial matter in his opponent's pleading, but must treat it as surplusage, and leave it alone. Thus, no issue could be raised on it; and the party pleading it was no longer bound to prove it at the trial.

Illustrations.

Where the plaintiff in his replication pleaded that the Queen, at a manor court held on such a day, by I. S., her steward, and by copy of court roll, &c., granted certain land to the plaintiff's lessor, and the defendant rejoined that the Queen had not, at a manor court held on such a day, by I. S., her steward, granted the land to the lessor, the Court held that the rejoinder was ill; "for the jury are thereby bound to find a copy on such a day, and by such a steward; which ought not to be."

Lane v. *Alexander*, Yelv. 122.

In an action of assumpsit brought to recover compensation for the plaintiff's service as a hired servant, the plaintiff alleged that he served the defendant from 21st March 1647 to 1st November 1664. To this the defendant pleaded that the plaintiff had not served until the 1st November 1664. This was a bad plea; for the plaintiff in such an action is entitled to compensation *pro tanto* for any period of service; hence it was obviously no answer to say that he did not serve the whole time alleged, and the plea, as it stood, raised an immaterial issue.

Osborne v. *Rogers*, 1 Wms. Saund. 267.

And see *Alsager* v. *Currie*, 11 M. & W. 14.

So where the condition of a bond was that the obligor should serve the obligee half a year, and in an action of debt on the bond the defendant pleaded that he had served him half a year at D., in the county of K., and the plaintiff replied that he had not served him half a year at D., in the county of K.; this was adjudged to be a bad traverse, as involving the place, which was immaterial.

Doctrina Placitandi, 360.

And now the Courts never compel either party to prove at the trial more than the substance of his pleading, even though his opponent may have expressly traversed some immaterial averment contained in it.

(iii.) EVERY PLEADING MUST STATE FACTS, AND NOT THE EVIDENCE BY WHICH THEY ARE TO BE PROVED.

Facts should be alleged as facts. It is not necessary to state in the pleadings circumstances which merely tend to establish the facts in issue.

The fact in issue between the parties is the *factum probandum*, the fact to be proved, and therefore the fact to be alleged. It is unnecessary to tell the other side how it is proposed to prove that fact; such matters are merely evidence, *facta probantia*; facts by means of which one proves the fact in issue. Such facts will be *relevant* at the trial, but they are not *material facts* for pleading purposes.

This was always a clear rule of the common law. "Evidence shall never be pleaded, because it tends to prove matter in fact, and therefore the matter in fact shall be pleaded." (*Dowman's Case*, 9 Rep. 9 b.)

In Chancery, however, this rule was never observed: the pleadings there were lengthy narratives which sometimes became intolerably prolix. They stated the evidence on which the party proposed to rely in full detail, with copious extracts from the material documents, and a great deal of interesting family history. They were, in fact, more like lengthy affidavits than modern pleadings.

This was to some extent due to the nature of the matters with which equity Courts had to deal, for even now an equitable defence or reply is pleaded in the Queen's Bench Division somewhat more in detail than is usual in the case of ordinary legal defences or replies. (See *Heap* v. *Marris*, 2 Q. B. D. 630; 46 L. J. Q. B. 761.) Moreover, it is not always easy to decide what are the facts to be proved, and what is only evidence of those facts. The question is often to some extent one of degree. "There are many cases in which facts and evidence are so mixed up as to be almost indistinguishable." (*Smith* v. *West*, W. N. (1876) p. 55.) But in most cases the line is sharp and clear between the fact in issue and the evidence by which that fact would be proved. "The difference, although not so easy to express, is perfectly easy to understand." (*Per* Brett, M. R., in *Philipps* v. *Philipps*, 4 Q. B. D. at p. 133.)

Illustrations.

Action on a policy of assurance on the life of A. Defence that A. committed suicide, in which event the company, by the express terms of the policy, is not liable. The issue is, Did A. kill himself? The facts that he had for weeks been in a moody miserable state, that he bought a pistol the day before his death, that he was found shot, with that pistol in his hand, that on him was found a letter to his wife stating that he intended to kill himself, &c., these are all "evidentiary facts" which go to prove the fact in issue. None of these should therefore be pleaded. The Defence should merely state, "The said A. died by his own hand," or whatever are the exact words of the condition on the back of the policy.

It would be still worse pleading to aver in the Defence that the coroner had held an inquest on A.'s body, and the jury had returned a verdict of *felo de se*. For such a verdict would not be evidence either for or against the company, and such an allegation would be struck out as an attempt to prejudice the fair trial of the action.

See *Smith* v. *The British Insurance Co.*, W. N. (1883) p. 232.

Where the main question in an action is, Was the defendant partner with his father in the Lime Street business?, it would be bad pleading to allege that the defendant shared in the profits and contributed to the losses incurred in the business, or any other facts which tend to show that he was a partner. Plead merely, "The defendant throughout the year 1890 carried on business at No. 21, Lime Street, in partnership with his father, under the style or firm of 'Davis & Son.'"

If the only point in dispute be, Had A. authority to make this contract on behalf of the defendant? the plaintiff may plead either that "the defendant employed A. as his agent to make this contract on his behalf," or that "the defendant held A. out as having authority to make the said contract on his behalf." But he may not allege that "when A. made the contract he represented that he was the defendant's agent, and had authority from him to enter into the said contract on his behalf." And it is ridiculous to plead, as was once done, that A. "has all along been regarded by the lessor, the bankers, and the plaintiff himself, as the agent of the defendant."

If the plaintiff's case is that certain damage has happened to him in consequence of some wrongful act of the defendant's, it is not necessary to set out the facts which show the connection between the damage and the wrongful act. These are but evidence of the plaintiff's assertion that the damage which he has sustained was the consequence of the defendant's act. It is sufficient to allege the wrongful act in the Statement of Claim, and then to continue, " The plaintiff has thereby suffered, &c., and been put to great expense in, &c." (specifying the damages).

" If both the unlawful act and the consequence are stated, it is unnecessary to allege the means by which that act produced that consequence. . . . . The means are matter of evidence."

Per Lord Mansfield, C. J., and Buller, J., in *Rex* v. *Eccles*, 3 Dougl. at p. 337.

" Where the facts in a pedigree are facts to be relied upon as facts to establish the right or title, they must be set out ; but where the pedigree is the means of proving the facts relied on as facts by which the right or title is to be established, then the pedigree is evidence that need not be set out."

Per Brett, L. J., in *Philipps* v. *Philipps*, 4 Q. B. D. at p. 134; 48 L. J. Q. B. 135; 27 W. R. 436; 39 L. T. 556.

So, in an action of covenant the plaintiff declared that the defendant by indenture demised to him certain premises, with a covenant that he, the defendant, had full power and lawful authority to demise the same according to the form and effect of the said indenture ; and then the plaintiff assigned a breach that the defendant had not full power and lawful authority to demise the said premises, according to the form and effect of the said indenture. After verdict for the plaintiff it was assigned for error, that he had not in his declaration shown " what person had right, title, estate or interest in the lands demised, by which it might appear to the Court that the defendant had not full power and lawful authority to demise." But upon conference and debate amongst the justices it was resolved " that the assignment of the breach of covenant was good, for he has followed the words of the covenant negatively; " and to state what person had a better estate or interest than the defendant in the demised premises would be pleading evidence of the main allegation that the defendant had not full power and authority to demise.

Robert Bradshaw's Case, 9 Rep. 60, b.

So, in assumpsit for labour and medicines for curing the defendant of a distemper, the defendant pleaded infancy. The plaintiff replied that the action was brought for necessaries generally. It was objected to this replication, that the plaintiff had not assigned in certain how or in what manner the medicines were necessary; but it was adjudged that the replication in this general form was good.

Huggins v. *Wiseman*, Carth. 110.

There is a curious long plea in abatement which occupies eight pages of the report in which all manner of evidence is pleaded to show that the defendant was an earl and had been received as an earl, and had voted as an earl, &c., but it strangely enough nowhere contained "a distinct allegation of the thing to be proved, that the defendant *was* Earl of Stirling at the time of the writ." It was therefore struck out.

Digby v. *Alexander*, 8 Bing. 416, 430.

Where time has not been made of the essence of the contract it is sufficient to aver that the work was done or the event happened " within a reasonable time in that behalf." It is unnecessary to explain that the weather was bad or that the men struck work, or to state any other reason why it took so long : that is the evidence by which you are going to prove your assertion that the time in fact occupied was a reasonable period.

Eaton v. *Southby*, Willes, 131, *post*, p. 45.

Where the plaintiff pleaded that he had "been informed by the defendant" that, &c., the paragraph was struck out. This was stating the evidence by which he proposed at the trial to prove the fact in issue.

Jones v. *Turner*, W. N. (1875) p. 239.

A Statement of Claim set out in full a multitude of letters which were said to be material because they contained admissions. But the Court held that if that were so, still admissions were only evidence, and that facts and not evidence should alone be pleaded. The letters were accordingly struck out.

Dary v. *Garrett and Others*, 7 Ch. D. 473 ; 47 L. J. Ch. 218 ; 26 W. R. 225 ; 38 L. T. 77.

The plaintiff alleged that certain windows of his were ancient lights. The defendant pleaded that in another action the plaintiff had sworn they were not ancient. This allegation was struck out.

Lumb v. *Beaumont*, 49 L. T. 772.

Wherever it is material to allege malice, fraudulent intention, knowledge, or other condition of the mind of any person, it shall be sufficient to allege the same as a fact without setting out the circumstances from which the same is to be inferred.

Order XIX. r. 22.

Wherever it is material to allege notice to any person of any fact, matter, or thing, it shall be sufficient to allege such notice as a fact, unless the form or the precise terms of such notice, or the circumstances from which such notice is to be inferred, be material.

Order XIX. r. 23.

Whenever any contract or any relation between any persons is to be implied from a series of letters or conversations, or otherwise from a number of circumstances, it shall be sufficient to allege such contract or relation as a fact, and to refer generally to such letters, conversations, or circumstances without setting them out in detail. And if in such case the person so pleading desires to rely in the alternative upon more contracts or relations than one as to be implied from such circumstances, he may state the same in the alternative.

Order XIX. r. 24.

In every case in which the cause of action is a stated or settled account, the same shall be alleged with particulars, but in every case in which a statement of account is relied on by way of evidence or admission of any other cause of action which is pleaded, the same shall not be alleged in the pleadings.

Order XX. r. 8.

(iv.) EVERY PLEADING MUST STATE MATERIAL FACTS IN A SUMMARY FORM.

In the first place, material facts must be stated clearly and definitely. Be as concise as you can, provided you do not thereby become obscure. Pleadings are useless unless they state facts with precision. The names of persons and places, if material, must be accurately given. Avoid pronouns; it often is not clear whom you mean by "he." Repeat "the plaintiff," or "the said Johnson," whenever "he" would be ambiguous. Use relative pronouns as little as possible; when you do use them, see that each has its proper antecedent. Call things by their right names, so far as you can, but in any event always allude to the same thing by the same name. Keep to the same phraseology throughout the pleading. If you are suing on a document, or relying on an Act of Parliament, do not attempt to improve on the language of either (however strong the temptation may be, especially in the latter case). A change of phrase suggests a change of meaning.

Illustrations.

The plaintiff and defendant should not be mentioned by name in the body of a pleading. They should always be called "the plaintiff" and "the defendant," or, if more than one, "the male plaintiff," "the female plaintiff," "the defendant Smith," "the defendant Robinson," or, if both defendants bear the same surname, "the defendant Henry," "the defendant John."

The name of any other person, not a party to the suit, should be given in full, if known, the first time he is mentioned. Afterwards, he can be referred to by his surname only, as "the said Johnson."

It does not matter in the least whether you allude to the cottage claimed by the plaintiff as "the said cottage," or "the said house," or "the said messuage," or "the said premises." But whichever phrase you use the first time, should be used throughout the pleading.

It will lead to confusion if you refer to the same document sometimes as "the Indenture of May 20th 1879," sometimes as "the said lease," and sometimes as "the agreement between the parties." In fact, it is technically wrong to call a contract under seal an agreement.

Land was limited so as to pass from A. to B. on A.'s becoming bankrupt. B. claimed the land, and pleaded that A. had become *insolvent*. In olden time, this would have been bad on special demurrer.

A policy of life assurance by its express terms becomes void "if the assured shall die by his own hand." Do not plead that "the assured killed himself," or that he "committed suicide." Plead in the very words of the policy, "the assured died by his own hand."

A policy of life assurance contained a condition that satisfactory proof of the title of the claimant, and of the age and death of the assured, must be given to the directors. The company is now sued on the policy, and relies on the fact that this condition has not been complied with. Set out the condition, and then aver that "no satisfactory proof of the title of the plaintiff or of the age of the deceased has ever been given to the directors of the defendant company." Do not plead, as was once done, that "no evidence satisfactory to the directors of the defendant company, either of the date of the birth of the assured, or of the plaintiff's right to receive the sum assured, has ever been afforded or supplied by the plaintiff, though he has been often requested by the defendant company so to do." Such a change of phrase is unnecessary and confusing.

Facts should be alleged as facts. Use terse, short, curt, blunt sentences, all in the indicative mood. Be positive. Do not beat about the bush. Go straight to the point. If you mean to allege a particular fact, state it boldly, plainly, clearly, and concisely. Avoid all "ifs" and all introductory averments. Avoid all periphrasis, all circumlocution. A pleading is not the place for fine writing, but simply for hard, downright, business-like assertion.

Avoid, too, the passive voice: always use the most direct and straightforward construction, and that, as a rule, will be the active voice. It is simpler and clearer to say, "He repaid the money on June 24th 1891," than to say, "The money was repaid by him on that date."

Above all, avoid participial phrases; never say that the defendant, being so-and-so, did something. Make two sentences of it; say that he was so-and-so, and then that he did something. Avoid all clauses that are introduced by "being" or "having." If a fact is material, it should be stated as a positive fact, and in a separate sentence.

Then, again, it always conduces to clearness to observe the strict order of time. In any case not of the simplest, dates are always of the greatest importance; and the only way to tell a long or complicated story clearly and intelligibly is to keep to strict chronological order.

Illustrations.

It is wholly unnecessary to plead:

"The defendant says that he does not admit that the goods referred to in paragraph 3 of the Statement of Claim, and therein alleged to have been delivered by the plaintiff to the defendant, or any of them, were in fact so delivered, and he puts the plaintiff to the proof of such delivery."

Omit all preamble, and plunge at once *in medias res*. Plead simply—

"The plaintiff never delivered any of the said goods to the defendant."

Here is a badly drawn Statement of Claim:—

"The defendant is indebted to the plaintiff, as executor of Lavinia Jones, deceased, in the sum of 231*l*. 5*s*. 10*d*., being the balance still owing of a sum of 700*l*. advanced to the defendant by the said Lavinia Jones in her lifetime, repayable on demand, with interest at 5 per cent. per annum."

It is all one sentence, and the facts are stated in inverse order of date. Surely the following is clearer:—

"1. Lavinia Jones, deceased, on May 15th 1882 lent the defendant 700*l*. He agreed to repay her this sum on demand, with interest at the rate of 5 per cent. per annum.

"2. During her lifetime he regularly paid her interest at the said rate when and as it became due. He also repaid her 468*l*. 14*s*. 2*d*. towards the principal.

"3. Lavinia Jones died on December 21st 1889, having by her last will appointed the plaintiff her executor.

"4. The plaintiff, as such executor, claims the balance, 231*l*. 5*s*. 10*d*., with interest thereon at the said rate from December 21st 1889 till payment."

Form No. 5 in sect. v. of App. C. to the Rules of the Supreme Court of 1883 appears to me to offend against the rule just laid down. It begins as follows:—

"The plaintiff has suffered damage by breach of contract by bill of lading of goods shipped by the plaintiff, signed by the master of the ship *Mary*, as the defendant's agent, dated the 1st of January 1882."

Here there are three distinct allegations depending on participles, and it appears to be left to implication that the defendant is the owner of the ship. Would it not be far better to allege:—

"1. On January 1st 1882 the plaintiff caused 200 quarters of wheat to be shipped on board the ship *Mary*, at Bilbao.

"2. The master of the said ship received the same to be carried to London upon the terms stated in a bill of lading, then signed by the said master, of which the following clauses are material. [*Here state the clauses sued on.*]

"3. The defendant is the owner of the said ship, and the said bill of lading was signed by the said master as agent for the defendant, and with his authority.

"4. [*As in paragraph 2 of the said Form.*]"

This, then, is the *first* essential of good pleading—to be *clear*. The next is to be *brief*. The new rules repeatedly insist on the necessity of brevity.

The fundamental rule cited at the head of this chapter requires that "every pleading shall contain and contain only a statement in a summary form of the material facts on which the party pleading relies."

"Such statements shall be as brief as the nature of the case will admit, and the taxing officer in adjusting the costs of the action shall, at the instance of any party, or may without any request, inquire into any unnecessary prolixity, and order the costs occasioned by such prolixity to be borne by the party chargeable with the same." (Order XIX. r. 2.)

"The forms in Appendices C., D., and E., when applicable, and where they are not applicable, forms of the like character as near as may be, shall be used for all pleadings, and where such forms are applicable and sufficient, any longer forms shall be deemed prolix, and the costs occasioned by such prolixity shall be disallowed to or borne by the party so using the same, as the case may be." (Order XIX. r. 5.)

Yet, as we have seen (*ante*, p. 18), each party must state his whole case; he cannot, strictly, prove at the trial any material fact which is not alleged in his pleading. (*Per* Sir J. Hannen, in *The Hardwick*, 9 P. D. 32; 53 L. J. P. 23; and see *Brook* v. *Brook*, 12 P. D. 19; 56 L. J. P. 108.) How, then, is the necessary brevity to be attained?

In two ways:—

I. By omitting every unnecessary allegation.

II. By omitting all unnecessary detail when alleging material facts.

I. It is bad pleading to insert a single unnecessary allegation.

Illustrations.

Neither party should cite public Acts of Parliament, or state in his pleading the propositions of law which he proposes to urge upon the Court.

Neither party may plead the evidence by which he proposes to prove the facts on which he relies.

Order XIX. r. 4.

Neither party need, in any pleading, allege any matter of fact which the law presumes in his favour, or as to which the burden of proof lies upon the other side.

Order XIX. r. 25.

Neither party need allege the performance of any condition precedent; such an averment is now implied in every pleading.

Order XIX. r. 14.

Neither party need set out the whole or any part of any document, unless its precise words are material. It is sufficient to state its effect as briefly as possible.

Order XIX. r. 21.

It is not necessary for any defendant to plead any denial or defence as to damages claimed or their amount; they shall be deemed to be put in issue in all cases, unless expressly admitted.

Order XXI. r. 4.

It is unnecessary for either party to plead any matter which merely affects costs.

It is unnecessary for either party to plead to his opponent's prayer or claim, or to his particulars, or to any matter introduced by a *videlicet*. He need only deal with the allegations contained in the body of the preceding pleading.

It is unnecessary for either party to plead to any matter of law set out in his opponent's pleading. This may be treated as mere surplusage.

It is not necessary for either party to plead any fact which is not yet material to his case; though he may reasonably suppose that it may become material at a later stage of the pleading.

II. When pleading material facts all unnecessary details should be omitted.

A certain amount of detail is essential to ensure clearness and precision. "Although pleadings must now be concise, they must also be precise." (*Per* Kay, J., in *Townsend* v. *Parton*, 30 W. R. 287; 45 L. T. 756.) Indeed Order XIX. r. 6, expressly requires that in all cases "in which particulars may be necessary beyond such as are exemplified in the forms aforesaid, particulars (with dates and items, if necessary) shall be stated in the pleading;" unless the particulars be of debt, expenses, or damages, and exceed three folios, when they must be delivered separately. But this rule does not state when such particulars are necessary, or what degree of particularity is expected of the pleader. Nor does any other rule give us this information. Hence, by virtue of Order LXXII. r. 2, the former procedure and practice applies, though it is necessarily qualified to some extent by the important alterations made by the Judicature Act. Under the old system of pleading there was much learning on this matter of "certainty," as it was called; and so much of it as appears likely to be of use to beginners in the art of pleading under the present system will be found in the next chapter.

Chapter III.

CERTAINTY.

Material Facts must be alleged with Certainty.

THE object of pleadings is to ascertain definitely what is the question at issue between the parties; and this object can only be attained when each party states his case with precision. If vague and general statements were allowed nothing would be defined; the issue would be "enlarged" as it is called, and neither party would know when the case came on for trial what was the real point to be discussed and decided. (*Per* Jessel, M. R., in *Thorp* v. *Holdsworth*, 3 Ch. D. at p. 639.) On the other hand, a party who pleads with unnecessary particularity may thereby fetter his hand at the trial (as in *James* v. *Smith*, (1891) 1 Ch. 384), and impose on himself an increased burden of proof at the trial (as in *West* v. *Baxendale*, 9 C. B. 141).

The amount of detail necessary to ensure precision naturally varies with the nature of each case. The only general rule that can be laid down is this—that there must be particularity sufficient to apprise the Court and the other party of the exact nature of the question to be tried. "What particulars are to be stated must depend on the facts of each case. But in my opinion it is absolutely essential that the pleading, not to be embarrassing to the defendants, should state those facts which will put the defendants on their guard, and tell them what they will have to meet when the case comes on for trial." (*Per* Cotton, L. J., in *Philipps* v. *Philipps*, 4 Q. B. D. at p. 139.)

The pleader then must decide for himself how far it is necessary for him to set out items and to go into figures, how far details of time and place and other surrounding circumstances are necessary to make his pleading intelligible and precise. Experience will teach him this: even common sense without experience will help him much; for our law is rapidly degenerating into common sense!

Perhaps the best test is this: After you have drafted your pleading, banish your instructions from your mind for a moment, and imagine yourself a stranger coming fresh to the matter. Would your draft, read by itself, convey to his mind a clear conception of your client's case? If not, you must make your draft more definite: and this object will often be best attained by omitting half of it. Length does not conduce to perspicuity. Half a dozen neat, short sentences, each clear in itself, will tell your story best.

And note this distinction. If you omit a material fact altogether from your pleading, this slip may lose the case for your client, as in *Collette* v. *Goode*, 7 Ch. D. 842; and *Byrd* v. *Nunn*, 5 Ch. D. 781; 7 Ch. D. 284. If you plead the fact, but with insufficient detail, the worse that can happen is that your opponent may obtain an order for particulars, the costs of which will probably be costs in the cause.

Illustrations.

Where the plaintiff claims a specific sum of money as the total amount due to him on an account containing many items, the plaintiff must give particulars showing how that figure is arrived at. Such particulars should be stated in the pleading if they do not exceed three folios; if they exceed three folios, this fact should be stated in the pleading, and particulars must be delivered separately, or a reference made to some bill or account already delivered.

Order XIX. r. 6.

So if a plaintiff merely gives credit in his Statement of Claim for a lump sum, and claims to recover the balance, the defendant is entitled to particulars, with dates and items, of the amounts credited. For without these he cannot tell whether it is necessary for him to plead payment or set-off, or to counterclaim for the sums which he has paid the plaintiff.

Godden v. *Corsten*, 5 C. P. D. 17; 49 L. J. C. P. 112; 28 W. R. 305; 41 L. T. 527.

Similarly, a mortgagee in possession who admits that he had received certain sums on account must give particulars of such payments.

Kemp v. *Goldberg*, 36 Ch. D. 505; 36 W. R. 278; 56 L. T. 736.

But if a general account is claimed, and the Court sees that such an account must be taken, then no such particulars need be given.

Augustinus v. *Nerincks*, 16 Ch. D. 13; 29 W. R. 225; 43 L. T. 458.

Blackie v. *Osmaston*, 28 Ch. D. 119; 54 L. J. Ch. 473; 33 W. R. 158; 52 L. T. 6.

Where an agreement is alleged its date should be given; it should also, as a rule, be stated whether it was made verbally or in writing, and if in writing whether under seal. But a party who alleges a verbal agreement will not be ordered to state in whose presence it was made, as this would be compelling him to name his witnesses.

Eade v. *Jacobs*, 3 Ex. D. 335; 47 L. J. Ex. 74; 26 W. R. 159; 37 L. T. 621.

In an action for false and fraudulent misrepresentation the Statement of Claim should state whether the alleged representations were oral or in writing, and when and where each of them was made.

Seligmann v. *Young*, W. N. (1884) p. 93.

In an action of libel or slander the plaintiff must state when, where, and to whom each publication complained of was made.

Roselle v. *Buchanan*, 16 Q. B. D. 656; 55 L. J. Q. B. 376; 34 W. R. 488; 2 Times L. R. 367.

Damages.

No particulars will be required of general damage; for this the law presumes in the plaintiff's favour. But special damage must be alleged with sufficient particularity to inform the defendant of the nature and extent of the loss sustained. And the plaintiff will not be allowed to give evidence of any special damage which is not claimed explicitly; for the defendant cannot be supposed to have anticipated, or to be aware of such damage.

Time.

In an action brought by a lessor against a lessee during the continuance of the term for breach of a covenant to repair, the Statement of Claim must state the time which the term still has to run.

Turner v. *Lamb*, 14 M. & W. 412.

Where the defendant has pleaded the Statute of Limitations, or any other defence of waiver by laches, dates are most material.

See App. D. sect. VI., Nuisance, 4.

Reeves v. *Butcher*, (1891) 2 Q. B. 509; 60 L. J. Q. B. 619.

If in trespass to land the defendant pleads that the *locus in quo* was his freehold, he must allege that it was his freehold "at the time of the alleged trespass"; otherwise the plea is insufficient.

Com. Dig. Pleader (E. 5).

As to duration of time, it is generally sufficient to aver that the work was done, or that some event happened "within a reasonable time in that behalf."

Action of replevin for seventy cocks of wheat which the defendant had distrained for rent in arrear while they were standing on a field called "Seven Acres," portion of the demised premises. The plaintiff pleaded that he suffered the wheat to grow till it was ripe and ready to be cut, and then cut it and suffered it "to lie on the said 'Seven Acres' until the same in the course of husbandry was fit to be carried away; and that while it was so lying the defendant, of his own wrong, took and distrained the same, under pretence of a distress, the said wheat not then being fit to be carried away according to the course of husbandry, &c." The defendant urged, among other objections to this plea, that it ought to have been particularly shown therein how long the wheat remained on the land after cutting, that the Court might judge whether it were a reasonable time or not. But the Court decided against the objection: "It is absurd to say that in the present case the Court must judge of the reasonableness; for if so, it ought to have been set forth in the plea not only how long the corn lay on the ground, but likewise what sort of weather there was during that time, and many other incidents which would be ridiculous to be inserted in a plea. We are of opinion, therefore, that this matter is sufficiently averred."

Eaton v. *Southby*, Willes, 131.
Elliott v. *Hardy*, 3 Bing. 61; 10 Moore, 347.

Place.

In an action for the recovery of land the property must be described with sufficient certainty to enable the sheriff to put the plaintiff in possession of it, if he succeed in the action.

In an action of trespass the plaintiff should describe the close on which the defendant trespassed so as to identify it.

In an action of replevin the *place* where the cattle or goods were distrained is material.

3 Chitty on Pleading (7th ed.) 291.

In alleging a right of way, the *termini* of the way should be stated.

Harris v. *Jenkins*, 22 Ch. D. 481; 52 L. J. Ch. 437; 31 W. R. 137; 47 L. T. 570.
Rouse v. *Bardin*, 1 H. Bl. 351.
Simmons v. *Lillystone*, 8 Exch. 431; 22 L. J. Ex. 217.

There was formerly a special reason for requiring that the *place* where the property claimed was situated, or where any wrongful act was committed, should be stated with great precision in the declaration, especially in *local* as distinguished from *transitory* actions. This was necessary in order to enable the sheriff to summon the jury from the proper venue. At first the jury was always summoned from the hundred where the facts happened; and when that was no longer necessary, *local* actions still had to be tried in the county in which the realty, &c., was situated. But in 1875 all local venues were abolished (Order XXXVI. r. 1). And now certainty of place is only necessary to give reasonable clearness and precision to the statement of facts.

Title.

Where either party claims to be the owner of any property, real or personal, or of any right or interest to, in, or over it, he must state his title to such property, right, or interest with all due particularity. "The pleadings must show title."

But very different degrees of particularity are necessary in different cases. In the first place, our law always respects possession. Possession is a physical fact, and an obvious one: it is wholly distinct from ownership, which is often a difficult question of law. The true owner of a field or of a chattel may be in possession of it, or he may not. Again, he may be rightfully out of possession, as where he has let it to a tenant or lent it to a friend; or he may be wrongfully out of possession, as where he has been evicted by a trespasser from the field, or where the chattel has been stolen.

A man may be said to be in possession of land or of a chattel whenever he has full and uncontrolled physical dominion over it. Thus, he is in possession of a house when he or his servants are living in it; if he or they are absent from it he would still be held to be in possession, if such absence was only temporary, and if he could return and re-enter at any moment, if he chose, without asking anyone's permission, and without any preliminary ceremony. But the moment anyone else enters into and remains on the premises, the former possessor is ousted: for two persons cannot be in possession of the same property at the same time (unless they be partners or joint occupiers).

1. *Where the person showing title is in possession, or was in possession at the date of the wrong complained of.*

As against a wrong-doer it is always sufficient to allege a merely possessory title. (*Armory* v. *Delamirie*, 1 Smith's Leading Cases (9th ed.) p. 385.) Thus, in trover, detinue, or trespass to goods it is sufficient to describe them as "the goods and chattels of the plaintiff"; in trespass to land it is sufficient to describe the *locus in quo* as the "close of the plaintiff," or to allege that "the plaintiff was lawfully possessed of a certain close," describing it. So, with respect to incorporeal hereditaments, it is sufficient to allege that the plaintiff was possessed of the corporeal thing in respect of which the right is claimed; *e. g.*, "the plaintiff was possessed of a certain messuage" (stating its name and situation), and that by reason thereof he was entitled to common of pasture, or to a right of way, &c.

Illustrations.

In an action of trespass it is sufficient to allege that the defendant broke and entered certain land of the plaintiff, called, &c. (describing it).

In an action of trover it is sufficient to say that the defendant converted to his own use the plaintiff's goods (specifying them).

In an action of detinue it is sufficient to allege that the defendant detained from the plaintiff his title-deeds of, &c. (describing the land).

In an action on a policy of assurance it may be alleged "that A., B., C. and D., or some or one of them, were or was interested," without averring the precise interest of each.

Reg.-Gen. H. T. 1853, (Pl.), r. 9, re-enacting Reg.-Gen. 4 Will. IV.

In an action for obstructing a right of way it is sufficient to allege that the plaintiff was possessed of a certain messuage, the occupier whereof had from time immemorial (*or* for so many years before suit) enjoyed as of right and without interruption a way from the said messuage across a certain close called Blackacre to a public highway, and back again from the said public highway over the said close to the said messuage, for themselves and their servants, on foot and with horses, cattle, and carriages at all times of the year.

See 2 & 3 Will. IV. c. 71, and C. L. P. Act, 1852, Sched. B. 46, 47.

As to pleading a prescriptive right at common law to an easement, or to any profit or benefit taken or arising out of land, see 2 Wms. Saunders, 401, a; *Attorney-General* v. *Gauntlett*, 3 Y. & J. 93; Bullen & Leake, 3rd ed. p. 713.

As to pleading a period of prescription under the Act, see sect. 5 of the 2 & 3 Will. IV. c. 71; and Bullen & Leake, 3rd ed. p. 711; 4th ed. part i. p. 365; part ii. p. 513.

A defendant who is in possession of land may rely on that fact and nothing else; he need not state what particular estate or interest he claims in the property. This privilege is preserved to him by the express words of Order XXI. r. 21: "No defendant in an action for the recovery of land who is in possession by himself or his tenant need plead his title, unless his defence depends on an equitable estate or right, or he claims relief upon any equitable ground against any right or title asserted by the plaintiff. But, except in the cases hereinbefore mentioned, it shall be sufficient to state by way of defence that he is so in possession, and it shall be taken to be implied in such statement that he denies, or does not admit, the allegations of fact contained in the plaintiff's Statement of Claim. He may nevertheless rely upon any ground of defence which he can prove except as hereinbefore mentioned."

A defendant who is in possession of a chattel is in a somewhat different position: he may, if he think fit, content himself with denying that the goods are the plaintiff's, and so put him to proof of his title. But if the defendant claims any right to the possession of the chattels apart from ownership, this should be specially pleaded; otherwise, as soon as the plaintiff proves his title, the right to the possession of his own property (which is always inherent in ownership) will at once attach and displace the defendant's *primâ facie* title. A plaintiff who has proved his title to the property is not a wrongdoer, and mere possession will not avail against him.

Illustrations.

In an action for the recovery of land, the defendant need not plead that the plaintiff's ancestor demised the land to the defendant for a term of years, or conveyed it to him by way of mortgage or sale. But he must plead that the plaintiff's ancestor *agreed* to demise, mortgage, or sell the property to the defendant; for this, in the absence of any formal document transferring the legal estate to the defendant, would be an equitable defence.

In an action for the recovery of a chattel, the defendant must plead specially that it was hired out to him for a definite period not yet expired, or lent to him for a purpose not yet accomplished, or pawned to him, or that he has a lien on it for warehouse rent, or any other lien. For such defences admit the plaintiff's title to the ownership of the goods, and should therefore be specially pleaded by way of confession and avoidance.

But neither in an action for the recovery of land nor of a chattel is it necessary to plead that the plaintiff's ancestor by his marriage settlement vested the property in certain trustees, not parties to the action, in whom the legal estate still remains. For that is a flaw in the plaintiff's case which it is always open to a defendant in possession to point out under a mere traverse of the plaintiff's title.

In an action of trespass for assault and battery, if the defendant justifies on the ground that the plaintiff wrongfully entered his house, and was making a disturbance there, and that the defendant gently removed him, the form of plea is that "the defendant was lawfully possessed of a certain dwelling-house, &c.; and being so possessed, the said plaintiff was unlawfully in the said dwelling-house," &c.; and it is not necessary for the defendant to show any title to the house, beyond this of mere possession.

3 Chitt. Pl. (7th ed.) 323.

So in an action of trespass* for seizing cattle, if the defendant justifies on the ground that the cattle were damage feasant on his close, it is not necessary for him to show any title to his close, except that of mere possession.

1 Wms. Saund. 221, n. (1), 346; 2 Wms. Saund. 285, n. (3); Bac. Ab. Trespass (5th ed.) 613.

It is sometimes said that the reason why it is sufficient to lay a possessory title in such cases is, that the title is matter of inducement only to the main subject of the plea. But this doctrine, if well examined,

---

* According to Buller, J., in *Doraston* v. *Payne* (2 H. Bl. 530; 2 Sm. L. C. 9th ed. 154), this general averment of a merely possessory title is not permissible, even against a wrongdoer, in an action of replevin. But if such an averment is sufficient in an action of trespass, I fail to see why it is not also sufficient in replevin. See Bullen & Leake, 2nd ed. at p. 659; 3rd ed. at p. 782. And also *Hawkins* v. *Eckles*, 2 Bos. & Pul. 359, 361, n. (*a*).

O.   E

resolves itself into the broader and more extensive rule given in the text, that possession is *primâ facie* seisin against a wrongdoer; and the plaintiff who has entered on a close in the possession of another against his will is deemed a wrongdoer till he pleads and establishes his title thereto.

Where it is sufficient to allege such a mere possessory title, it is a mistake to go into details.

See *Cudlip* v. *Rundle*, Carth. 202, *ante*, p. 29.

II. *Where the party pleading is out of possession and his opponent is in possession.*

Here, if the party pleading claims either to be the owner of the property or to possess a right to the immediate possession thereof, he must state his title clearly.

This is easy enough where the party pleading claims the absolute present fee simple. In that case he need say no more than that he "is seised in fee of the close or tenement" (describing it), or, in more antiquated language, that he "is seised in his demesne as of fee of and in a certain messuage," &c. He need not show the derivation or commencement of his estate; for if he were required to show from whom he derived his title, he might, on the same principle, be required to show from whom that person derived *his*, and so on *ad infinitum*.

There is, however, one exception to this rule: where in the same pleading it has already been alleged that the fee was in some other person from whom the party pleading claims. In such a case he must show how the fee passed from such other person to himself.

Illustrations.

If A. be seised in fee, it is sufficient to allege this simply, without showing when or how or from whom he derived it.
Co. Litt. 303 b.

Though A.'s fee was conditional on an event which has happened, or be determinable in a certain event which has not happened, he may allege a present absolute fee without qualification, and without showing its commencement.
Seymour's Case, 10 Rep. 98; Doctrina Placitandi, 287.

An averment that A. was seised in fee will be taken to mean that he was *solely* seised, in the absence of anything to the contrary.
Gilbert v. *Parker*, 2 Salk. 629.
Bonner v. *Walker*, Cro. Eliz. 524.
An action for the breach of a covenant, contained in a lease granted by J. S. to the defendant, was brought by the heir of J. S. after his death. The plaintiff having alleged that J. S. was seised in fee when he granted the lease, must proceed to show how the fee passed to himself, viz., by descent.
Cuthbertson v. *Irving*, 4 H. & N. 742; 6 H. & N. 135.

But where the party pleading has only an estate in tail, or for life, or for years, or any other *particular estate* (as distinct from an estate in fee simple), or where his estate in fee simple is not yet in possession, but is an estate in reversion or remainder, there such title must be fully and particularly alleged. The pleading should state:—

(i.) The *tenure* (if no other tenure be alleged it will be assumed to be free and common socage).

(ii.) The *quantity of estate*, whether an estate tail or for life, or *pur autre vie*, or widowhood, or merely a leasehold interest, and for what term.

(iii.) The period of enjoyment. (Dates are always most material in any case of disputed title; and the commencement of any particular estate must be shown.)

(iv.) The number of owners, if more than one, at any stage of the story, and whether joint tenants or tenants in common, or coparceners.

(v.) The manner of acquisition or devolution. The pleading must show who granted the plaintiff his estate in tail or for life, or who granted the lease which he now holds, and to whom. All the steps in the title must be given, and the general nature of the instrument must be stated: *e. g.*, whether the estate or interest vested by deed or will or on an intestacy.

There were formerly two cases in which a defendant was permitted to state his title in a more general way. In a plea to an action of trespass to land, and in an avowry in replevin (1 Wms. Saund. 347, d.,

n. (6)), if the defendant claimed an estate of freehold in the *locus in quo*, he was allowed to plead generally "that at the time of the alleged trespass, &c., the said close was the close, soil and freehold of the defendant." This was called the plea or avowry of *liberum tenementum*. But I do not think this would be allowed under the present rules; he would be compelled to state whether he claimed the fee simple or some lesser estate, and in the latter case to state when and how, and by whom, such estate was created. (See *Stoate* v. *Rew*, 14 C. B. N. S. 209; 32 L. J. C. P. 160.)

This allegation of a general freehold title was formerly sustained by proof of any estate of freehold—whether in fee, in tail, or for life only, and whether in possession, or expectant on the determination of a term of years. But it did not apply to the case of a freehold estate in remainder or reversion expectant on a particular estate of freehold, or of copyhold tenure. Where the close was the defendant's freehold, but the plaintiff was in possession under a lease for years, and the defendant pleaded *liberum tenementum*, it was held that the plaintiff must plead the lease for years specially in confession and avoidance in his reply. The existence of the lease was no ground for traversing the plea of *liberum tenementum*. (See 5 Hen. VII. 10 a, pl. 2; *Doe* v. *Wright*, 10 A. & E. 763; *Ryan* v. *Clark*, 14 Q. B. 65; 18 L. J. Q. B. 267; 7 D. & L. 8.)

Illustrations.

In an action for the recovery of land of which the plaintiff has never been in possession, the Statement of Claim must allege the nature of the deeds and documents upon which he relies in deducing his title from the person under whom he claims; and a general statement, that by assurances, wills, documents and Crown grants in the possession of the defendants, without further describing them, the plaintiff is entitled to the land, is embarrassing, and liable to be struck out under the Rules of the Supreme Court, Order XIX. r. 27.

Philipps v. *Philipps*, 4 Q. B. D. 127; 48 L. J. Q. B. 135; 27 W. R. 436; 39 L. T. 556.

If a lease be granted by J. S. to the defendant, and the plaintiff, claiming as assignee of the reversion, sue the lessee on the covenant therein contained for rent, he must precisely show the conveyances, or other transfers of title from J. S. to himself, whereby he became entitled to the reversion. To say generally that the reversion came to him by assignment will not be sufficient without circumstantially alleging all the mesne assignments.

1 Wms. Saund. 112, n. (1).

See *Cuthbertson* v. *Irving*, 4 Hurl. & N. 742.

A claim was struck out as embarrassing for not showing the devolution of an estate to the plaintiff, who sued as assignee of the reversion by virtue of 32 Hen. VIII. c. 34.

 Davis v. *James*, 26 Ch. D. 778; 53 L. J. Ch. 523; 32 W. R. 406; 50 L. T. 115.

Where a plaintiff claims as assignee of a debt originally contracted between the defendant and A., he must show in the body of his pleading how he derives his title; he must allege an assignment in writing, and that notice of such assignment was given to the defendant before action, otherwise this plaintiff would not be entitled to sue, at all events without joining A. as a co-plaintiff. (Jud. Act, 1873, s. 25, sub-s. 6.)

 Seear v. *Lawson*, 15 Ch. D. 426; 16 Ch. D. 121; 49 L. J. Bk. 69; 50 L. J. Ch. 139; 28 W. R. 929; 29 W. R. 109; 42 L. T. 893; 43 L. T. 716.

 Wallis v. *Smith*, 51 L. J. Ch. 577; 46 L. T. 473.

Where a party claims by inheritance as heir of J. S., he must show how he is heir; *e. g.*, he must state whether he was J. S.'s son, and account for his elder brothers, if there were any; if he was J. S.'s nephew this must be stated, and the pedigree pleaded sufficiently to show how he is nephew, and that he is heir.

 Dumsday v. *Hughes*, 3 Bos. & Pul. 453.

 Roe v. *Lord*, 2 Blackstone, 1099; and see *ante*, p. 14.

With respect to all particular estates, the general rule is that their commencement must be shown. If, therefore, a party sets up in his own favour an estate tail, an estate for life, a term of years, or a tenancy at will, he must show the derivation of that title from its commencement, that is, from the last seisin in fee simple; and if derived from alienation or conveyance, the substance and effect of such conveyance should be precisely set forth.

 Co. Lit. 303 b; see 1 Wms. Saund. 187, n. (1).

 Scilly v. *Dally*, 2 Salk. 562.

 Johns v. *Whitley*, 3 Wils. 72.

 Hendy v. *Stephenson*, 10 East, 60.

 Pinhorn v. *Souster*, 8 Exch. 138; 22 L. J. Ex. 18.

The commencement of a copyhold estate must be shown, even though it be copyhold of inheritance; for the fee simple is in the lord. But it is necessary to go back to the admittance of the last heir or surrenderee only; for his admittance is considered as in the nature of a grant from the lord, and may be so pleaded.

 Pyster v. *Hemling*, Cro. Jac. 103.

 Brown's Case, 4 Rep. 22 b.

 Shepheard's Case, Cro. Car. 190.

But where an estate has been already laid in another copyholder from whom the party pleading claims, and it becomes necessary, therefore, to show how the estate passed from one to the other, the conveyances between the copyhold tenants by surrender, and the admittance by the lord, &c., must then be set forth according to the fact.

See the forms, 2 Chitt. Pl. (7th ed.) 423.

Title by Estoppel.

There is one case where all this particularity is unnecessary. No title need be shown at all where the opposite party is *estopped* from denying the title.

Thus, if a lessor sue the original lessee, or anyone who has attorned tenant to the lessor, on the covenants of the lease, he need allege no title to the premises demised, because a tenant is estopped from denying his landlord's title. But the tenant is not bound to admit title to any extent greater than might authorise the lease. Hence if the action be brought not by the lessor himself, but by his heir, executor, or other representative or assignee, the title of the lessor must be alleged, in order to show that the reversion is now legally vested in the plaintiff in the character in which he sues. (See *Cuthbertson* v. *Irving*, 4 Hurl. & N. 742; 6 Hurl. & N. 135 (in error); *Thriscutt* v. *Martin*, 3 Exch. 454, and the judgment of Willes, J., in *Smith* v. *Scott*, 6 C. B. N. S. 771.) So if the plaintiff sue as heir, he must allege that the lessor was seised in fee, for the tenant is not bound to admit that his lessor was seised in fee; and unless he was so the plaintiff cannot claim as heir. The lessor may have been only a tenant for life, and a tenant is not estopped from saying that his landlord's title is determined.

Pleading Title in Another.

So far we have dealt with the case where the party pleading alleges title in himself. The same rules apply with equal strictness where the party pleading sets up title in some third person from whom he says he derived his authority to do the act complained of. For instance, where a servant exercises a right of way by his master's order, the right must be pleaded with the same particularity as if the master whose authority he pleads had been made a defendant.

Next, we must consider the case where a party alleges title in his adversary, with the object of making him liable in respect of the property, real or personal.

In this case it is not necessary to allege title more precisely than is sufficient to show a liability in the party charged, or to defeat his present claim. The reason of this difference is, that a party may be presumed to be ignorant of the particulars of his adversary's title, though he is bound to know his own. (See *Rider* v. *Smith*, 3 T. R. 766; *Derisley* v. *Custance*, 4 T. R. 77; *The Attorney-General* v. *Meller*, Hardr. 459.) "It lies more properly in the knowledge of the lessor what estate he himself has in the land which he demises than of the lessee who is a stranger to it." (*Robert Bradshaw's Case*, 9 Rep. 60, b, *ante*, p. 33; and see *Cudlip* v. *Rundle*, Carth. 202, *ante*, p. 29.)

In order to show a liability in the party charged, according to the rule here given, it is in most cases sufficient to allege that your adversary is in possession, and to prove that he has some present interest in chattels, or is in actual possession of land. But this form of pleading is *ex hypothesi* inapplicable if the interest he possesses be by way of reversion or remainder. In that event the party pleading must state his opponent's title in detail. Then, again, there are cases in which to charge a party with mere possession would not be sufficient to show his liability. Thus, if the defendant be sued as assignee of a term of years for arrears of rent due under a covenant in the lease creating that term, it is not sufficient to show that he is in possession of the property demised, but it must be further shown that he is in possession as assignee of the term. But even here the party pleading is not expected to plead all the details of the various assignments of the term; though he must show all the assignments of the reversion.

Illustrations.

In an action of debt, where the defendant is charged for rent as the assignee of the term after several mesne assignments, it is sufficient, after stating the original demise, to allege that "after making the said indenture, and during the term thereby granted, all the estate and interest of the said E. F." (the original lessee) "of and in the said demised premises, by assignment came to and vested in the said C. D.," without further showing the nature of the mesne assignments.

See 1 Wms. Saund. 112, n. (1).
Derisley v. *Custance*, 4 T. R. 77.
2 Chitt. Pl. (7th ed.) 396; Bullen & Leake's Preced. Pl. 2nd ed. p. 182.

Upon the same principle, if title be laid in an adversary by descent—as, for example, where an action of debt is brought against an heir on the bond of his ancestor—it is sufficient to charge him as an heir, without showing how he is heir, viz., as son or otherwise; though where a party seeks to entitle himself by inheritance, the mode of descent must be alleged, as we have seen, *ante*, p. 53.

Denham v. *Stephenson*, 1 Salk. 355.

In making avowry or cognizance in replevin upon distresses for rent, quit-rents, reliefs, heriots, or other services, the defendant is enabled by the provisions of 11 Geo. II. c. 19, s. 22, "to avow or make cognizance generally, that the plaintiff in replevin, or other tenant of the lands and tenements whereon such distress was made, enjoyed the same under a grant or demise, at such a certain rent, during the time wherein the rent distrained for was incurred, which rent was then and still remains due; or that the place where the distress was taken was parcel of such certain tenements held of such honour, lordship, or manor; for which tenements the rent, relief, heriot, or other service distrained for was at the time of such distress and still remains due, without further setting forth the grant, tenure, demise, or title of such landlord or landlords, lessor or lessors, owner or owners of such manor."

Pleading Authority.

Whenever the party pleading seeks to justify an act *primâ facie* unlawful, he must show his authority or excuse with precision. If he plead that he did it by the command of A., he must show that A. had legal right and title so to command. If he seeks to justify his act by virtue of any writ, warrant, precept, or other authority, he must set it forth particularly in his pleading. And he ought also to show that he has substantially pursued such authority.

Illustrations.

In an action brought by a commoner against a stranger for putting his cattle on the common, *per quod communium in tam amplo modo habere non potuit*, the defendant pleaded a licence from the lord to put his cattle there, but he did not aver that there was sufficient common left for the commoners. This was held to be no good plea; for the lord had no right to give a stranger such licence, unless there was enough common left for the commoners.

Smith v. *Feverell*, 2 Mod. 6; 1 Freeman, 190.

The defendant seized the plaintiff's mare on the wastes of the manor of B. The defendant justified his act under a by-law made by the lord of the manor and the homage at a lawful court, which by-law the plaintiff had broken. This offence was presented at the next court, and thereupon the defendant, being bailiff of the lord of the said manor, did take the mare for the forfeiture incurred by the plaintiff, &c. The Court held the plea bad, "for the bailiff cannot take a forfeiture *ex officio*. There must be a precept directed to him for that purpose, which he must show in pleading."

Lamb v. *Mills*, 4 Mod. 377.

With respect to acts valid at common law, but regulated as to the mode of performance by statute, it is sufficient to use such certainty of allegation as was sufficient before the statute.

Anon., 2 Salk. 519.

4 Hen. VII. 8; 1 Wms. Saund. 211, n. (2); 276, n. (2).

Birch v. *Bellamy*, 12 Mod. 540.

Where the defendant justifies under judicial process, it is not sufficient to allege generally that he committed the act in question by virtue of a certain writ or warrant directed to him; he must set it forth particularly in his plea. (1 Wms. Saund. 298, n. (8); Co. Litt. 303 b.) But on this subject there are some important distinctions as to the degree of particularity required in different cases.

1. It is not necessary that any person justifying under judicial process should set forth the cause of action in the original suit in which that process issued. (*Rowland* v. *Veale*, Cowp. 18; *Belk* v. *Broadbent*, 3 T. R. 183; 1 Wms. Saund. 92, n. (2).)

2. If the justification be by the officer executing the writ, he is required to plead such writ only, and not the judgment on which it was founded; for it is his duty to execute the writ, without inquiring about the validity or even the existence of the judgment. (*Andrews* v. *Marris*, 1 Q. B. 3; *Dews* v. *Riley*, 11 C. B. 434.) But if the justification be by a party to the suit, or by any stranger, except an officer, the judgment as well as the writ must be set forth. (*Per* Holt, C. J., in *Britton* v. *Cole*, Carth. 443; 1 Salk. 408; 1 Ld. Raym. 305.) In the report in Salkeld it is said that the Court "seemed to hold, that if one comes in aid of the officer, at his request, he may justify as the officer may do." See however *Morse* v. *James*, Willes, 122, and *Barker* v. *Braham*, 3 Wils. 368.

3. Where it is an officer who justifies, he must show that the writ was returned, if it was such as it was his duty to return. But in general a writ of execution need not be returned, and therefore no return of it need in general be alleged. (See *Middleton* v. *Price*, 2 Stra. 1184; 1 Wils. 17; *Cheasley* v. *Barnes*, 10 East, 73; *Shorland* v. *Gorett*, 5 B. & C. 485.)

4. Where it is necessary to plead the judgment, this may be done (if it was a judgment of a superior Court) without setting forth any of the previous proceedings in the suit. (Bullen & Leake's Prec. Pl. (2nd ed.) 648.)

5. Where the justification is founded on process issuing out of an inferior English Court, or, as it seems, a Court of foreign jurisdiction, the nature and extent of the jurisdiction of such Court ought to be set forth; and it ought to be shown that the cause of action arose within that jurisdiction, though a justification founded on process of any of the superior Courts need not contain such allegations. (See *Collett* v. *Lord Keith*, 2 East, 274; *Moravia* v. *Sloper*, Willes, 30; *Morrell* v. *Martin*, 3 M. & G. 581.)

6. And in pleading a judgment of inferior Courts, the previous proceedings are in some measure stated. But it is allow-

able to set them forth in general terms, thus—"that A. B. at a certain Court, &c., held at, &c., issued a plaint against C. D. for debt (or for damages for trespass, as the case may be) for a cause of action arising within the jurisdiction, and *thereupon such proceedings* were had (*taliter processum est*) that afterwards, &c., it was considered by the said Court that the said A. B. should recover against the said C. D. the sum of £——, &c." (1 Wms. Saund. 92, n. (2); see *Rowland* v. *Veale*, Cowp. 18; *Morse* v. *James*, Willes, 122.)

For precedents of pleas justifying under process from the County Courts, see *Smith* v. *Pritchard*, 8 C. B. 565; *Abley* v. *Dale*, 10 C. B. 62; *Hayes* v. *Keene*, 12 C. B. 233.

Illustrations.

A plea justifying the arrest and detention of a ship under a judgment *in rem* of a competent Court, having jurisdiction in Admiralty, must state what the charge was, and who were parties to it, and at whose instance the order was given, and at what time, and for what object, and whether the defendant was a party to the suit or acted as an officer of the Court.

Cullett and another v. *Lord Keith*, 2 East, 260.

In an action for trover for taking a ship, the defendant set up that the admiralty of a certain port in the East Indies had given sentence against the said ship as a prize. It was held that the plea ought to have shown some special cause for which the ship became a prize; and that the judge who gave sentence should have been named, and the Court described with sufficient certainty to identify it.

Beak v. *Tyrrell*, Carth. 31.

And for similar reasons it was enacted by a former pleading rule of 4 Will. IV., and again by r. 10 of the Practice Rules of Hilary Term, 1853, that in the margin of every plea of judgment recovered should always be stated the date of the judgment, and if it be in a Court of record, the number of the roll in which the proceedings are entered; in default of which the plaintiff was at liberty to sign judgment.

Charges of Misconduct.

Particularity is especially needed where the pleading contains an imputation on the character of your opponent; as then it is only right and fair that he should know definitely before the trial what is the charge which is made against him. Justice requires you to define the accusation you bring against anyone; and this is a very different thing from setting out the evidence by which you intend to establish it.

Illustrations.

In all cases in which the party pleading relies on any misrepresentation, fraud, breach of trust, wilful default, or undue influence, particulars (with dates and items, if necessary) shall be stated in the pleading.
Order XIX. r. 6.
The plaintiff alleged that the defendants had made false entries in certain books; he was ordered to give a list of the entries alleged to be false, and also to state generally the nature of his objections to them.
Newport Dry Dock Co. v. *Paynter* (C. A.), 34 Ch. D. 88; 56 L. J. Ch. 1021; 55 L. T. 711.
Harbord v. *Monk*, 38 L. T. 411.
The plaintiff alleged that the defendant had "in various ways misapplied rent and profits of leaseholds, which he had received on behalf of the plaintiff, and had committed breaches of trust." He was ordered to give particulars.
Re Anstice, 54 L. J. Ch. 1104; 33 W. R. 557; 52 L. T. 572.
In an action for the price of work and labour done, a defendant was formerly permitted, under a general plea of "never indebted," to prove at the trial that the plaintiff did the work so unskilfully that it was useless to the defendant. This was the proper way of pleading such a defence; and, indeed, if the defendant pleaded in any other way, his plea was struck out and the general issue substituted for it. (*Hill* v. *Allen*, 2 M. & W. 283.) But now such a defence must be expressly pleaded, and particulars will be ordered of the alleged defects, so as to give the plaintiff notice of the charge that is going to be made against him.

Particulars will be readily ordered of any alleged negligence or contributory negligence.

In an action for false imprisonment the defendants pleaded that they "had reasonable cause to suspect, and did suspect, that the plaintiff had forged" certain documents. This plea was held bad, because it did not show the *grounds* of their suspicion.
Mure v. *Kaye*, 4 Taunt. 34.
So in an action of defamation, where the defendant justifies, if the libel or slander consists of one specific charge, it is sufficient to allege generally that the words are true, and no further particulars will be ordered. But where a general charge of misconduct is made, and the defendant has justified, specific instances must be given either in the plea or in the par-

CHARGES OF MISCONDUCT.

ticulars; and these must be pleaded with sufficient particularity to inform the plaintiff precisely what are the facts to be tried, and what is the charge made against him.

P'Anson v. *Stuart*, 1 T. R. 748; 2 Smith's Leading Cases (5th ed.), p. 63.

Where the defendant justified an imprisonment of the plaintiff on the ground of a contempt committed *tam factis quam verbis*, the plea was adjudged to be bad, because it set forth the contempt in this general way without showing its nature more particularly.

Collett v. *The Bailiffs of Shrewsbury*, 2 Leo. 34.

Action for wrongful dismissal. Defence, that the plaintiff did not serve the defendant faithfully, as in the said agreement stipulated. *Per* Bramwell, B., "this is a plea in confession and avoidance, and bad as being too general."

Horton v. *McMurtry* (1860), 5 H. & N. at p. 671.

When the pleader seeks to avoid the Statute of Limitations by pleading concealed fraud, he must state his case with the utmost particularity, or the pleading may be struck out under Order XIX. r. 27, or under the inherent jurisdiction of the Court.

Riddell v. *Earl of Strathmore*, 3 Times L. R. 329.

Lawrance v. *Lord Norreys*, 15 App. Cas. 210; 59 L. J. Ch. 681; 38 W. R. 753; 62 L. T. 706; 6 Times L. R. 285.

The defendants charged the plaintiffs with "an attempt to mislead the public." North, J., ordered them to give particulars of the way in which they alleged the plaintiffs had attempted to mislead the public.

Griffith and others v. *Curtis and Harvey* (not reported).

Uncertainty.

I conclude with one practical observation. Counsel often cannot be as precise as they desire, because they cannot obtain definite information. The lay client is abroad, or there is some other reason. Well, where you cannot be exact, make too broad rather than too narrow an allegation. It is better to claim too much than too little. It is wiser to state your client's right too largely; as the greater includes the less. Either party will be allowed as a general rule to prove so much of his allegation as is necessary to support his case, although he has alleged more in his pleading; for, in the language of the old pleaders, "pleadings are construed *distributively*."

Illustrations.

If the plaintiff claims 500*l.*, he will be allowed to recover 100*l.* or 200*l.*; though where the items are divisible and arise out of separate facts, he ought to be made to pay the costs occasioned by his joining the items as to which he has failed.

This was not so in Roman law; there if a defendant could show that the plaintiff had claimed too much he won the action. The plaintiff had to recover the full sum he claimed or nothing at all; this was called the *exceptio pluris*. This system had advantages to recommend it; but such strictness would be impossible in these days.

In cases of unliquidated damages, be sure you claim enough, as the plaintiff cannot recover more than the sum claimed on his writ or Statement of Claim, even though the jury award him more. But the judge will sometimes in such circumstances amend the figure.

If a defendant pleads that he has paid the plaintiff his whole debt, he will be allowed to prove part payment as a defence *pro tanto*, and the plaintiff will recover judgment only for the balance.

If a defendant in an action for the conversion or detention of goods denies that any of the goods are the plaintiff's, he will be allowed to prove at the trial that some of them are not, though he may have to admit that the rest are, the plaintiff's.

Freshney v. *Wells*, 26 L. J. Ex. 228.

If a defendant chooses on his pleading to deny his liability in respect of every item in the plaintiff's claim, he cannot be compelled to give particulars stating which of them he really intends to dispute at the trial.

James v. *Radnor County Council*, 6 Times L. R. 240.

Chapter IV.

ANSWERING YOUR OPPONENT'S PLEADING.

So far we have dealt only with the statement by a party of his own case. But after the first pleading each party must do more than state his own case; he must deal with that already presented by his opponent.

Now there are only three ways in which a party who means to fight can deal with his opponent's pleading :—

(i.) He can deny the whole or some essential part of the averments of fact contained in it. This is called *traversing* your opponent's allegations.

(ii.) He can say, "Well, that is true so far as it goes; but it is only half the truth. Here are several other facts which are omitted from this pleading, and which will put a very different complexion on the case." Alleging such facts is called *pleading by way of confession and avoidance*, or, more shortly, *confessing and avoiding*; because the pleader seems to confess that his opponent's statement discloses a good *primâ facie* case; that it is on the face of it good in law and true in fact; and he then goes on to allege new facts by which he hopes to destroy the effect of the allegations to which he is pleading.

(iii.) He may take a point of law, and say, "Assuming every word contained in this statement to be true, still I say that it is bad in law; it discloses no cause of action" (or "no defence to my action," or "no answer to my plea," as the case may be). This was formerly called *demurring* (from the Latin *demorari*, or French *demorrer*, to "wait," or "stay"); because the party who demurred would not proceed with his pleading, but awaited the judgment of the Court whether any case was made out for him to answer. Now, a longer phrase has been introduced, for no apparent reason; and what was formerly a *demurrer* is now called "*an objection in point of law*," which is a short definition rather than a name. However, it exactly expresses what a demurrer was.

Every objection in point of law asserts or implies that the pleading objected to is insufficient on the face of it; hence it admits for the moment that the allegations contained in it are true. Thus, it may be said that a traverse denies, and an objection admits. But they are alike in this, that neither of them introduces any collateral matter; whereas a plea in confession and avoidance neither simply admits nor merely denies; it admits the facts alleged in the opponent's pleading, subject however to the new facts by which it seeks to displace them.

Formerly, the party pleading had to elect which of these three courses he would adopt; he could not both demur and plead, nor could he traverse any allegation to which he also pleaded by way of confession and avoidance. Now, however, he may adopt either or any of these methods; the same allegation may be traversed in point of fact, objected to as bad in law, and at the same time collateral matter may be pleaded to destroy its effect. Remember, however, that it is foolish to needlessly multiply the issues; as your client will probably have to pay the costs of those which he fails to prove, even though he has succeeded on the main issue.

This may be best explained by one or two instances:—

Statement of Claim.

Writ issued November 18th 1890.

1. On August 18th 1890 the defendant promised to pay the plaintiff the sum of 300*l.* on November 18th 1890.

2. The defendant did not pay the plaintiff the said sum of 300*l*., or any part thereof, on November 18th 1890 or at all.

And the plaintiff claims the said sum of 300*l*. with interest thereon at the rate of 5 per cent. per annum, from November 18th 1890 till payment or judgment."

To this badly-drafted claim the defendant may, if he likes, take three objections in point of law: he is not bound to state them in his pleading unless he likes. But he will probably also traverse the alleged agreement.

Defence.

1. The defendant never promised as alleged. (*Traverse.*)
2. The defendant will object that no consideration is shown for his alleged promise.
3. The defendant will object that no facts are disclosed which render any interest payable on the said sum of 300*l*.
4. The defendant will object that the writ was issued one day too soon.

But this is a technical kind of defence. Paragraph 1 is probably untrue; and there was probably also some consideration for the promise, if indeed it was not under seal, so that the plaintiff could amend his Statement of Claim and proceed. Paragraph 4 raises a more serious objection, but this can be got over by the plaintiff's discontinuing this action, paying the costs, and issuing a second writ. In the second action the defendant would probably be driven to confess and avoid.

Defence in Second Action.

1. The defendant admits that he promised to pay the plaintiff the said sum of 300*l*. on November 18th 1890; but he promised to do so on one condition only, viz.:—that the plaintiff had by that day built a house for the defendant according to a specification dated August 18th 1890.
2. The plaintiff did not by November 18th 1890 or any other day build a house for the defendant according to the said specification.

[We thus learn at last what is the real bone of contention between the parties.]

Take another instance:—

Statement of Claim.
(Indorsed on writ.)

1. The defendant agreed that if the plaintiff would supply goods to C. D., he would see the plaintiff paid therefor.

2. On the faith of this guarantee, the plaintiff supplied C. D. with the following goods, the price of which is 213*l.* 8*s.* 11*d.*
(Particulars.)
3. Yet the defendant has not paid the plaintiff the said price or any part thereof.
And the plaintiff claims 213*l.* 8*s.* 11*d.*

Defence.

1. The defendant never agreed as alleged.
2. There is no memorandum in writing of the alleged agreement sufficient to satisfy the Statute of Frauds.
3. The plaintiff discharged the defendant from all liability by giving time to the principal debtor, the said C. D.
4. By a deed dated January 13th 1889 made between the plaintiff and the defendant, the plaintiff released the cause of action on which he now sues.
5. Such cause of action, if any, did not accrue within six years, and the defendant will rely on the Statute of Limitations (21 Jac. 1. c. 16).

(*N.B.—Here the first paragraph traverses; the other four confess and avoid.*)

Reply.

1. The plaintiff joins issue with the defendant upon paragraphs 1, 2, and 3 of the Defence.

[*This is a compendious form of traverse which is permitted in a Reply or any subsequent pleading.*]

2. The plaintiff was induced to execute the said release by the fraud of the defendant. Particulars of such fraud are as follows :—(*State them.*)
3. The defendant on May 15th 1884 paid the plaintiff 123*l.* 10*s.*, being 100*l.* on account of the principal money, and 23*l.* 10*s.* on account of the interest then due; and the defendant thereby acknowledged that the debt now sued for remained unpaid and due to the plaintiff.

[*Paragraphs 2 and 3 respectively confess and avoid paragraphs 4 and 5 of the Defence.*]

Rejoinder.

The defendant joins issue with the plaintiff on paragraphs 2 and 3 of his Reply.

[*N.B.—He does not join issue on paragraph 1, because that is itself a joinder of issue.*]

Besides pleas by way of traverse and pleas by way of confession and avoidance, there were formerly also certain pleas which were called *dilatory pleas*, because they offered a merely formal objection to the proceedings, without presenting any substantial answer to the merits of the action. Such were—

(a) A plea to the jurisdiction, by which the defendant took exception to the jurisdiction of the Court to entertain the action. Such an objection is, of course, still possible. It is, however, very seldom met with in practice, owing to the stringent provisions of Order XI. and to the power given to a defendant to move under Order XII. r. 30.

(b) A plea in suspension of the action; a plea which shows some ground for not proceeding in the suit at the present period, and prays that the pleading may be stayed until that ground be removed. The number of these pleas was always small, and none of them were of ordinary occurrence in practice. Their place is now taken by a summons to stay proceedings, on the hearing of which the point is summarily decided.

(c) A plea in abatement; a plea which showed some reason for abating or quashing the Statement of Claim on the ground that it was improperly framed, without, at the same time, tending to deny the right of action itself: *e.g.*, the misnomer of a defendant, or the non-joinder of a necessary party. But now "no plea or defence shall be pleaded in abatement." (Order XXI. r. 20.) The defendant must himself correct the misnomer, and he may, if he thinks fit, take out a summons to have the missing plaintiff or defendant made a party.

In contradistinction to these dilatory pleas, traverses and pleas in confession and avoidance were called *peremptory* pleas or *pleas in bar*, because they barred or impugned the right of action altogether.

These three things—traverse, confession and avoidance, and objection in point of law—must be kept clear and distinct. The pleader may adopt any one or two or all three of these methods of pleading, so long as he makes it quite clear which he is adopting. The object of a traverse is merely to compel the opposite party to prove the substance of his allegation; to object to its sufficiency in point of law is not within the scope of a traverse. Hence, if either party desires to object to his opponent's pleading in point of law, he must do so clearly and distinctly and in the proper way. A traverse must not be taken upon matter of law. A plea which may be either a traverse or an objection is embarrassing and will be struck out. (*Stokes* v. *Grant*, 4 C. P. D. 25; 27 W. R. 397; 40 L. T. 36.)

Moreover, an objection in point of law can only be raised where the fault of which you desire to take advantage is apparent on the face of the pleading objected to. You cannot state new facts in your own pleading or on affidavit, and then contend that the result of the combination is to show that your opponent has no case. It is the province of a plea in confession and avoidance to state new facts which put your opponent out of court.

Illustrations.

Where, in an action for trespass for fishing in the plaintiff's fishery, the defendant pleaded that the *locus in quo* was an arm of the sea, in which every subject of the realm had the liberty and privilege of free fishing, and the plaintiff, in his replication, traversed that in the said arm of the sea every subject of the realm had the liberty and privilege of free fishing, this was held to be a traverse of a mere inference of *law*, and therefore bad.

Richardson v. *Mayor of Orford*, 2 H. Bl. 182.

So where, in an action for improperly removing a wall, the plaintiff alleged that it was the defendant's *duty* to have taken proper precautions in pulling it down so as not to injure an adjoining vault of the plaintiff's, and the defendant pleaded by way of traverse that it was not his duty to have taken any precaution, this plea was considered as open to the same objection.

Trower v. *Chadwick*, 3 Bing. N. C. 334; 3 Scott, 699.

If in a Statement of Claim facts be alleged "by reason whereof the plaintiff became seised, &c.," or "the defendant became liable, &c.," the defendant must not traverse, denying that "by reason thereof, &c." (or, if I may use phraseology now nearly obsolete, "a *virtute cujus* is not traversable"). For if he intend to question the facts from which the seisin or liability is deduced, he should traverse those facts and them only; if he disputes the legal inference drawn from the facts, then the proper course is for him to object; or he may do both if he keeps the two defences clear and distinct.

Priddle and Napper's Case, 11 Rep. 8, 10.

In an action of covenant, the plaintiff declared upon a deed reciting that he was the inventor of certain looms, and had given the defendants permission to use them, in consideration of which they were to pay him certain sums. The defendants, while admitting the recital, pleaded that the plaintiff was not the true inventor. The plaintiff, instead of demurring, took issue in fact on the plea. It was held, that in that state of the record the defendants were not estopped by the recital of the deed from proving that the plaintiff was not the true inventor. The plaintiff had in fact waived the point by his pleading.

Bowman v. *Rostron*, 2 A. & E. 295, n.

So, too, a traverse cannot be made to do the work of a plea in confession and avoidance. Its office is to contradict, not to excuse. Matter justifying an act must not be insinuated into a plea which denies the act. "All matters in confession and avoidance shall be pleaded specially." (Pleading Rules of Hilary Term, 1853, rr. 12, 17.)

As a general rule,* the burden lies on the party pleading to prove at the trial the facts which he has alleged by way of confession and avoidance; on his opponent to prove the facts which he has traversed. And he will not be allowed to shift the *onus* of proof by traversing when he should confess and avoid, even where his opponent has given him the opportunity by introducing an unnecessary averment into the preceding pleading.

Illustrations.

A Statement of Claim in libel or slander always alleges that "the defendant falsely and maliciously wrote [*or* 'spoke'] and published the words." Yet the defendant may not plead "the defendant never wrote [*or* 'spoke'] or published the said words falsely or maliciously or at all." For this, while apparently merely a denial of the fact of publication, is also an insinuation that the words are true, and that the occasion of publication is privileged. It is in fact a traverse and *two* pleas in confession and avoidance all rolled into one. It is for the plaintiff to prove the publication; for the defendant to prove truth or privilege.

Belt v. *Lawes*, 51 L. J. Q. B. 359.

So in an action against a master for the dismissal of his servant, the Statement of Claim will certainly allege that the defendant *wrongfully* dismissed the plaintiff from his employ. But the defendant ought not to traverse this allegation in its entirety. To plead that he never wrong-

---

* But see *post*, p. 190.

fully dismissed the plaintiff would be bad. He may traverse the fact of dismissal, but he must plead in confession and avoidance the particular misconduct which justified the plaintiff's dismissal, if he desire that the lawfulness as well as the fact of the dismissal should be in issue at the trial. It is for the plaintiff to prove the dismissal, and for the defendant to show that it was justified.

Lush v. *Russell*, 5 Exch. 203; 19 L. J. Ex. 214.

Horton v. *McMurtry*, 5 H. & N. 667; 29 L. J. Ex. 260; 8 W. R. 285.

I.—OBJECTIONS IN POINT OF LAW.

Either party may object to the pleading of the opposite party on the ground that such pleading does not set forth *a sufficient ground* of action, defence, or reply, as the case may be, but not on the ground of any imperfection, omission, or defect in *form* merely.* Such an objection can only be raised where the fault is apparent on the face of the pleading to which exception is taken.

Demurrers were abolished by rule 1 of Order XXV. But it was desirable, and indeed necessary, to preserve some form of objection in point of law, otherwise parties might incur great expense in trying questions of fact which, when decided, would not determine their rights. Hence rule 2 of the same Order enacts that, "Any party shall be entitled to raise by his pleadings any point of law, and any point so raised shall be disposed of by the judge who tries the cause at or after the trial, provided that by consent of the parties, or by order of the Court or a judge on the application of either party, the same may be set down for hearing and disposed of at any time before the trial." And rule 3 provides that, "If, in the opinion of the Court or a judge, the decision of such point of law substantially disposes of the whole action, or of any distinct cause

---

* *Special demurrers*, as they were called, *i.e.*, mere objections to the *form* of an opponent's pleading, were entirely abolished by the Common Law Procedure Act, 1852; the 50th section of which provided that "on such demurrer the Court shall proceed and give judgment according as the very right of the cause and matter in law shall appear unto them, without regarding any imperfection, omission, defect in, or lack of form."

of action therein, the Court or judge may thereupon dismiss the action or make such other order therein as may be just."

For the purposes of such an argument, the party objecting is taken to admit all the facts alleged in the opposite pleading. And the Court will, moreover, take the whole record into their consideration and give judgment for the party who, on the whole, appears to be entitled to it. Thus, a plaintiff who objects to a Defence may find himself called on to defend the sufficiency of his Statement of Claim; and, if unsuccessful, judgment will be given for the defendant.

No one is bound to take an objection in point of law; the rule cited above (Order XXV. r. 2) merely says that he shall be *entitled* to raise it by his pleading. He *must* raise it on his pleading if he desires to apply under the latter part of that rule to have the point of law set down for hearing, and disposed of *before the trial:* but at the trial he may urge any point of law he likes, whether raised on the pleadings or not. This was decided under the new rules by a Divisional Court (Day and Wills, JJ.) on June 10th, 1886, in the case of *MacDougall* v. *Knight and another* (not reported on this point). And it was also the law under the former system.* Having regard, however, to the words of Order XXV. r. 3, it is clearly worth while to raise on the pleadings any point of law which will substantially dispose of the whole action, as in *Mayor, &c. of Manchester* v. *Williams*, (1891) 1 Q. B. 94; 60 L. J. Q. B. 23.

Illustrations.

It is a common error to suppose that where a man who has made two wills at different times revokes the second, he thereby revives the first

---

* "If the defendant wants to avail himself of" his points of law "in a summary way, he must demur; but if he does not demur, he does not waive the objection, and may say at the trial that the claim is bad on the face of it." (*Per* Lindley, J., in *Stokes* v. *Grant*, 4 C. P. D. at p. 28; 27 W. R. 397; 40 L. T. 36.) And going still further back, read the advice given by Lord Coke, which is set out *post*, p. 95.

will. Suppose a plaintiff in that belief propounds the first will: the defendant would plead it was revoked by the execution of the second will: the plaintiff would reply that the second will was in its turn revoked. If the defendant joins issue on this, the cause would proceed to trial on an issue of fact which is wholly immaterial: for the revocation of the second will would not (without more) re-establish the first. Either the second will operates, or the testator has died intestate.

Where special damage is clearly essential to the plaintiff's cause of action, an objection can be taken which may dispose of the whole action, in the Form given in Appendix E., s. III., No. 2: "The defendant will object that the special damage stated is not sufficient in point of law to sustain this action." Similarly, if no special damage be alleged, the defendant may object " that the matters disclosed in the Statement of Claim are not actionable without proof of special damage, and that none is alleged."

An objection in point of law must be taken explicitly. An allegation which suggests insufficiency, but does not take the point clearly, is embarrassing, and liable to be struck out.

Stokes v. *Grant*, 4 C. P. D. 25; 27 W. R. 397; 40 L. T. 36.

II.—TRAVERSES.

A traverse is the express contradiction of an allegation of fact in an opponent's pleading; it is generally a contradiction in terms. It is, as a rule, framed in the negative; because the facts which it denies are, as a rule, alleged in the affirmative.

As to traverses, there are three fundamental rules, the object of which is to compel each party in his turn to admit frankly, or deny fully, each allegation of fact in the pleading of his opponent:—

I. EVERY ALLEGATION OF FACT IN ANY PLEADING, IF NOT DENIED SPECIFICALLY, OR BY NECESSARY IMPLICATION, OR STATED TO BE NOT ADMITTED IN THE PLEADING OF THE OPPOSITE PARTY, SHALL BE TAKEN TO BE ADMITTED, EXCEPT AS AGAINST AN INFANT, LUNATIC, OR PERSON OF UNSOUND MIND, NOT SO FOUND BY INQUISITION. (Order XIX. r. 13.)

II. EACH PARTY MUST DEAL SPECIFICALLY WITH EACH ALLEGATION OF FACT OF WHICH HE DOES NOT ADMIT THE TRUTH, EXCEPT DAMAGES.* (Order XIX. r. 17.)

III. WHEN A PARTY IN ANY PLEADING DENIES AN ALLEGATION OF FACT IN THE PREVIOUS PLEADING OF THE OPPOSITE PARTY, HE MUST NOT DO SO EVASIVELY, BUT ANSWER THE POINT OF SUBSTANCE. (Order XIX. r. 19.)

The object of these rules is to force the parties to a speedy and definite issue.

Note, first, that only allegations of fact must be denied. As we have just seen (*ante*, p. 67), a traverse must not be taken on any matter of law. Neither party need plead to his opponent's particulars, or to any matter in his pleading introduced by a

---

* No denial or defence is "necessary as to damages claimed, or their amount; but they shall be deemed to be put in issue in all cases, unless expressly admitted." (Order XXI. r. 4.)

videlicet; nor to the prayer or claim for relief at the end of his pleading. Neither should he traverse matter not alleged; he should be content to answer the case that is actually laid against him, not that which he thinks his opponent ought to have raised.

Illustrations.

Action against an administratrix founded on a promise made by the intestate. Defence: "The defendant (*i. e.*, the administratrix, not the intestate) never promised as alleged." This was held to be obviously immaterial and bad.

Anon., 2 Vent. 196.

Matters of law, or any other matters which are not fit subjects of traverse, are not taken to be admitted by pleading over.

See *The King* v. *The Bishop of Chester,* 2 Salk. 561.

Bennion v. *Davison,* 3 M. & W. 179.

Gale v. *Lewis,* 9 Q. B. 730; 16 L. J. Q. B. 119.

King v. *Norman,* 4 C. B. 884; 17 L. J. C. P. 23.

It is quite unnecessary to plead: "The particulars delivered by the plaintiff in pursuance of the order of Master ———, dated July 2nd, 1891, are insufficient to enable the defendant to check the prices of the items charged for." Plead boldly: "The defendant never agreed to pay the plaintiff the prices he has charged for the said work, labour, and materials. Such prices are unreasonable and exorbitant."

In an action of debt on a bond conditioned for the payment of 1,550*l.*, the defendant pleaded, that " part of the sum mentioned in the condition, to wit, 1,500*l.*, was won by gaming, contrary to the statute in such case made and provided;" and that the bond was consequently void. The plaintiff replied that the bond was given for a just debt, and denied that the 1,500*l.* was won by gaming as alleged. It was objected that the replication was ill, because it put the precise sum in issue, and tended to oblige the defendant to prove that the whole 1,500*l.* was won by gaming; whereas the statute avoids the bond, if any part of the consideration be on that account. The Court was of opinion that the material part of the plea was, that part of the money for which the bond was given was won by gaming; and that the words "to wit, 1,500*l.*," were only form, of which the replication ought not to have taken any notice.

Colborne v. *Stockdale,* 1 Str. 493.

I. *Every allegation of Fact not denied is admitted.*

The pleader must either admit or deny every material fact in the pleading of his opponent: and he must make it absolutely clear which facts he admits and which he denies. To ensure this, the rule provides that every allegation of fact which the pleader desires not to admit, must either be denied specifically or by necessary implication, or be stated in his pleading to be not admitted. As a rule, he should deny when the facts are necessarily within his client's own knowledge; other facts which happened *inter alios*, &c., he may refuse to admit. But he must be just as specific in not admitting as in denying (*per* Jessel, M. R., in *Thorp* v. *Holdsworth*, 3 Ch. D. at p. 640); in either case he must leave no uncertainty as to how much or how little he intends to admit.

What is meant by "necessary implication?" Where traversing one allegation necessarily and unmistakeably traverses another as well, the latter allegation is denied by necessary implication. But if there can possibly be any misconception about the matter, it is safer to expressly deny both.

There is no third or intermediary stage. If the judge does not find in the pleading a specific denial or a definite refusal to admit, there is an end of the matter; the fact stands admitted. It is in the power of the party either to admit or to deny each allegation in his opponent's plea, as he thinks fit. If he decides to deny it, he must do so clearly and explicitly. Any equivocal or ambiguous phrase will be construed into an admission of it.

Illustrations.

Claim for specific performance of a contract. Defence: "The defendant puts the plaintiffs to proof of the several allegations in their Statement of Claim." Held, that all the plaintiffs' allegations were admitted.

Harris and others v. *Gamble*, 6 Ch. D. 748; 46 L. J. Ch. 768.

Defence: "The defendants do not admit the correctness of" certain allegations in the Statement of Claim, "and require proof thereof." Held, an insufficient denial. The defendants were ordered to state in what respects they disputed these allegations.

Rutter v. *Tregent*, 12 Ch. D. 758; 48 L. J. Ch. 791; 27 W. R. 902; 41 L. T. 16.

Defence: "The terms of the arrangement were never definitely agreed upon as alleged." Held, that such a traverse was an evasive denial within the rules of Order XIX., and that it admitted that an agreement was in fact made as alleged. Jessel, M.R.: "The whole object of plead-

ings is to bring the parties to an issue, and the meaning of the rules of this Order is to prevent the issue being enlarged, which would prevent either party from knowing, when the cause came on for trial, what the real point to be discussed and decided was. . . . The defendant is bound to deny that any agreement or any terms of arrangement were ever come to, if that is what he means; if he does not mean that, he should say that there were no terms of arrangement come to, except the following terms, and then state what the terms were."
Thorp v. *Holdsworth*, 3 Ch. D. 637; 45 L. J. Ch. 406.

If I deny that the defendant was ever tenant to the plaintiff of certain premises, I deny by necessary implication that the plaintiff ever demised those premises to the defendant. But the converse does not hold. The plaintiff's ancestor may have demised the premises to the defendant's father for a long term which is still unexpired, and the defendant may now be tenant to the plaintiff.

The party pleading is entitled either to admit or deny, as he thinks fit. Hence there is no need for him to apologize for his denial, or to explain why he does not admit the allegation. For instance, it is quite unnecessary for him to plead: "The defendants do not know when the plaintiffs first published the photographs referred to in the second paragraph of the Statement of Claim, and therein alleged to be photographs representing, &c.; and therefore they do not admit that such photographs were first published and circulated by the plaintiffs in or about the month of October, 1889, as in the said paragraph alleged."

How much ought the party pleading to admit, and how much to deny? Clearly it is wrong to deny plain and acknowledged facts, or any fact which it is not to your client's interest to disprove. (*Per* Malins, V.-C., in *Lee Conservancy Board* v. *Button*, 12 Ch. D. 383.) It was intended by the framers of the Judicature Act that each party in his pleading should frankly admit every statement of fact which he does not intend to seriously dispute at the trial. But this intention has not been carried out. Counsel hesitate to make admissions unless they are expressly instructed to do so, which they very seldom are. Solicitors hesitate to instruct counsel to make admissions, because the facts have not yet been thoroughly sifted; they do not feel sure that they have got to the bottom of the case; and they fear something may turn up hereafter which may make them wish to recall the admission. You must be careful how you admit even introductory paragraphs, which may appear immaterial; they were not inserted without some purpose. Either party may at any stage of the case move for judgment on the admissions which have been made by the other side. (Order XXXII. r. 6.) Besides, it is sometimes desirable to deny a particular fact so as to compel your opponent to call as his witness a person whom you wish to cross-examine, or by whose evidence you hope to prove a particular fact essential to your case, and thus, perhaps, to be enabled to dispense with calling any witnesses, and so gain the right to the last word.

On the other hand, in actions for debts or liquidated damages, the defendant, by omitting to plead any denial or refusal to admit, and pleading affirmatively only, may gain the right to begin. Where however the action is brought for unliquidated damages, this consideration does not apply; for in that case the plaintiff is always entitled to begin, even though the burden of proof lies on the defendant. (*Carter* v. *Jones*, 6 C. & P. 64; 1 M. & R. 281; *Mercer* v. *Whall*, 5 Q. B. 447, 463; 14 L. J. Q. B. 267, 272.)

But as a rule each party should admit whatever facts can be proved against him without trouble. Moreover, it looks weak to deny everything in your opponent's pleading. It suggests that you have no substantial defence to it. And remember that by Order XXI. r. 9, "where the Court or a judge shall be of opinion that any allegations of fact denied or not admitted by the Defence ought to have been admitted, the Court or judge may make such order as shall be just with respect to any extra costs occasioned by their having been denied or not admitted." It is a pity that our judges make little or no use of this power.

There is one case in which it is shameful not to make a proper admission. If your opponent relies on a written document, he will either set out the words of the document in his pleading, or he will state shortly its effect. In the latter case, as your construction of the document will probably differ from his, it is quite legitimate to traverse his version of its effect. But if he sets out the actual words correctly, it is to my mind slovenly work to plead, as is so often done: "The defendant does not admit that the terms of the said indenture are sufficiently or correctly set forth in paragraph 4 of the Statement of Claim, and craves leave to refer to the original thereof at the trial for greater certainty as to its terms and effect." Why "crave leave" to do hereafter that which you have now an absolute right to do? "Every party to a cause shall be entitled at any time, by notice in writing, to give notice to any other party, in whose pleadings reference is made to any document, to produce such document for the inspection of the party giving such notice, or of his solicitor, and to permit him or them to take copies thereof." (Order XXXI. r. 15.) Obtain a copy of the document under this rule, if you have not one already, and see if its terms are or are not correctly stated by your opponent. If they are, admit that they are, adding such other portions as you yourself rely on. If they are not, then set them out correctly yourself, if you deem them material. I always suspect that the man who "craves leave" is perfectly familiar with the contents of the document all the time.

II. *Denials must be Specific.*

"It shall not be sufficient for a defendant in his Statement of Defence to deny generally the grounds alleged by the Statement of Claim, or for a plaintiff in his Reply to deny generally the grounds alleged in a Defence by way of counterclaim, but each party must deal specifically with each allegation of fact of which he does not admit the truth, except damages." (Order XIX. r. 17.) It is the duty of the party pleading to make it quite certain how much of his opponent's case he disputes. Yet he often unintentionally uses phrases which are ambiguous, or are capable of being misunderstood. Sometimes, in order to obey the rule and to deal specifically with every allegation of fact of which he does not admit the truth, it is necessary for him to place on the record two or more distinct traverses to one and the same allegation. To merely deny the allegation in terms will often be ambiguous.

Thus, if the defendant pleads: "The defendant never broke or entered the close of the plaintiff," the more obvious meaning of this allegation is that he never broke or entered the close which the plaintiff claims as his; but it may be that his case is that the close in question was not the plaintiff's. The words are capable of that meaning.

Hence, in Hilary Term, 1853, a rule was made that in an action of trespass to land, the defendant must specially deny the plaintiff's possession, or right to possession, of the land, and that a literal traverse of the declaration should be taken to deny merely that the defendant broke and entered that close.

Pleading Rules of Hilary Term, 1853, r. 19.

In any action of trover, detinue, or trespass to goods, the defendant was similarly required to specially deny that the goods were the plaintiff's property. A mere traverse of the conversion, detention, or trespass would be taken as denying merely the acts complained of.

Pleading Rules of Hilary Term, 1853, rr. 15, 20.

If, then, the defendant desires to raise both defences—to deny both the act complained of and the plaintiff's title to the land—he must put on the record two separate paragraphs, *e.g.*:—"1. The defendant never broke or entered the said close. 2. The said close is not the plaintiff's close."

Again, if the plaintiff alleges that "the said A. B. executed the said deed on behalf of the defendant, as his agent, acting under a power of attorney duly signed by the defendant," the defendant must not plead: "The defendant denies that the said A. B. executed the said deed on behalf of the defendant, as his agent under a power of attorney duly signed by the defendant." If he wishes to traverse the whole allegation he must plead:

"1. The said A. B. never executed the said deed.

2. The said A. B. never executed the said deed on behalf of the defendant, or as his agent.

3. The defendant never signed any such power of attorney as alleged, nor did A. B. ever act thereunder."

Otherwise it would not be clear how much of the plaintiff's allegation the defendant really denies.

See *Byrd* v. *Nunn*, 5 Ch. D. 781; 25 W. R. 749; 37 L. T. 90.

So, if the defendant says that he never seduced the plaintiff's daughter, this will be taken as a denial of the act of seduction merely. The defence that the girl seduced was not the plaintiff's servant must be specially pleaded.

Torrence v. *Gibbins*, 5 Q. B. 297; 13 L. J. Q. B. 36.

Whenever the cause of action depends on the plaintiff's holding a certain office, or carrying on a profession or trade, the defendant **must** always specially deny that he held that office, or carried on that profession or trade at date of writ.

Gallwey v. *Marshall*, 9 Ex. 300 ; 23 L. J. Ex. 78.

If either party wishes to deny the right of any other party to claim as executor, or as trustee, whether in bankruptcy or otherwise, or in any representative or other alleged capacity, or the alleged constitution of any partnership firm, he shall deny the same specifically.

Order XXI. r. 5.

III. *Denials must not be Evasive.*

"When a party in any pleading denies an allegation of fact in the previous pleading of the opposite party, he must not do so evasively, but answer the point of substance."

Or using the old phraseology, A TRAVERSE MUST BE NEITHER TOO LARGE NOR TOO NARROW. He must deny enough and not too much.

Illustrations.

"If it be alleged that he received a certain sum of money, it shall not be sufficient to deny that he received that particular amount, but he must deny that he received that sum or any part thereof, or else set out how much he received."

Order XIX. r. 19.

The plaintiff alleged that his agent, the defendant, had received rent from the plaintiff's tenants which he had not handed over to the plaintiff. Defence : "The defendant has handed over to the plaintiff all the rent which he has received from the plaintiff's tenants." This is a bad traverse, though it is in the very words of the claim. It is not clear whether the defendant has received all the rents or some or none. He must state whether he has received any, and, if any, how much rent, and what amount he handed over to the plaintiff, and when.

Kennett v. *Mundy*, Judge at Chambers (not reported).

To a Statement of Claim alleging that "the defendant in or about Michaelmas 1887 called upon several of the plaintiff's tenants at the premises Nos. 43, 45, and 47, Bayham Street, Camden Town, and spoke and published to them," a slander on the plaintiff's title, it is sufficient to plead, "The defendant never spoke or published the said words." For that answers the point of substance and the rest is denied by necessary implication.

Action against a sheriff for an escape. Defence that if any such escape was made, the prisoner voluntarily returned into custody before the defendant knew of the escape, &c. The Court refused to allow the plea to be so framed; for "he cannot plead hypothetically, that if there has been an escape, there has also been a return. He must either stand upon an averment that there has been no escape; or that there have been one, two, or ten escapes, after which the prisoner returned." It was an evasive denial, which was half an admission.

Griffiths v. *Eyles*, 1 Bos. & Pul. 413.

The condition of a bond obliged the defendants to see that L., a collector of property tax, duly performed certain duties of his office specified therein. The defendants pleaded that they had performed all things on their part to be performed. Such plea was held to be bad in substance, because (amongst other reasons) it averred general performance by the defendants, instead of showing how they had performed the condition.

Kepp v. *Wiggett*, 6 C. B. 280; 17 L. J. C. P. 295.

So in an action of debt on a bond conditioned for the payment of a sum of money and for the performance of covenants in an indenture, a plea of general performance was held ill; for the condition being to do several things, the defendant was bound to plead to each particularly by itself.

Roakes v. *Mauser*, 1 C. B. 531; 14 L. J. C. P. 199.

The defendant bound himself by a bond to perform all the covenants and other matters contained in a certain indenture, some of which are in the disjunctive or alternative form; so that the defendant engaged to do either one thing or another. Here also an allegation of general performance would be improper, and, indeed, altogether equivocal; the defendant must show which of the alternative acts he performed.

Oglethorp v. *Hyde*, Cro. Eliz. 233.

Do not traverse too literally. It is sufficient to answer the point of substance. A traverse may become evasive, if it follows too closely the precise language of the allegation traversed.

One instance of this deserves special attention. A traverse may be too large, by being taken in the *conjunctive* instead of the *disjunctive*, where it is not material that the allegation traversed should be proved conjunctively. In other words, when traversing, remember always to turn "and" into "or."

Illustrations.

In an action of debt on a bond conditioned for the payment of 1,550*l.*, the defendant pleaded that "part of the sum mentioned in the condition, to wit, 1,500*l.*, was won by gaming contrary to the statute," and that the bond was consequently void. The plaintiff replied, in the very words of the plea, that the 1,500*l.* was not won by gaming as alleged. It was objected that the replication was ill, because it put the precise sum in issue, and tended to oblige the defendant to prove that the whole 1,500*l.* was won by gaming; whereas he was entitled to succeed under the statute, if he could prove that any part of the consideration was on that account. The Court was of opinion that the material part of the plea was, that part of the money for which the bond was given was won by gaming; and that the words "to wit 1,500*l.*," were only form of which the replication ought not to have taken any notice. The proper replication would have been "No part of the sum mentioned in the condition was won by gaming." Now the plaintiff is allowed to merely join issue.

Colborne v. *Stockdale*, 1 Str. 493.

A Statement of Claim alleged that the defendant offered the plaintiff a bribe of 500*l.* The defendant pleaded "that he had never offered the plaintiff a bribe of 500*l.*," which would have been true if he had offered 400*l.* or any other sum instead of 500*l.* This was held to be a denial of the fact along with the circumstances stated in the Statement of Claim, and not a fair or substantial denial of the allegation of substance that there was a bribe. The defendant should have pleaded that he never offered a bribe of 500*l.* or any other sum.

Tildesley v. *Harper*, 7 Ch. D. 403; 47 L. J. Ch. 263; 26 W. R. 263; 38 L. T. 60; (C. A.) 10 Ch. D. 393; 48 L. J. Ch. 495; 27 W. R. 249; 39 L. T. 552.

Claim: "the defendants broke and entered the plaintiff's close and depastured the same with sheep and cattle." The proper traverse is "Neither defendant broke or entered the plaintiff's close or depastured the same with any sheep or cattle."

In an action of *assumpsit*, the plaintiff declared on a policy of insurance, and averred "that the ship insured did not arrive in safety; but that the said ship, tackle, apparel, ordnance, munition, artillery, boat, and other furniture were sunk and destroyed in the said voyage." The defendant pleaded, denying "that the said ship, tackle, apparel, ordnance, munition, artillery, boat, and other furniture were sunk and destroyed in the voyage, in manner and form as alleged." This traverse was adjudged to be bad; and it was held that the defendant ought to have denied disjunctively that the ship *or* tackle, &c., was sunk or destroyed; because in this action for damages the plaintiff would be entitled to recover compensation for any part of that which was the subject of insurance, and had been lost: whereas (it was said), if issue had been taken in the conjunctive form, in which the plea was pleaded, "and the defendant should

prove that only a cable or anchor arrived in safety, he would be acquitted of the whole."
  Goram v. *Sweeting*, 2 Wms. Saund. 205.
  Moore v. *Boulcott*, 1 Bing. N. C. 323.
  Stubbs v. *Lainson*, 1 M. & W. 728; 5 Dowl. 162.
See other instances of a traverse being too large—
  Basan v. *Arnold*, 6 M. & W. 559.
  De Medina v. *Norman*, 9 M. & W. 820; 2 Dowl. 239.
  Aldis v. *Mason*, 11 C. B. 132; 20 L. J. C. P. 193.
  Dawson v. *Wrench*, 3 Exch. 359; 18 L. J. Ex. 229.
As to traverses which have been held not too large, see—
  Palmer v. *Gooden*, 8 M. & W. 890; 1 Dowl. N. S. 673.
  Eden v. *Turtle*, 10 M. & W. 635.

"If an allegation is made with divers circumstances, it shall not be sufficient to deny it along with those circumstances." (Order XIX. r. 19.) The addition of the words "or at all" will generally cure this defect.

Illustrations.

The plaintiff pleaded that the Queen, at a manor court held on such a day by J. S., her steward, and by copy of court roll, &c., granted certain land to A. The defendant traversed this allegation *totidem verbis:* "that the Queen had not, at a manor court held on such a day by J. S., her steward, and by copy of court roll, granted any lands to A." The Court held that this was a bad traverse. "The Queen never granted as alleged" would have been sufficient.
  Lane v. *Alexander*, Yelv. 122.

In an action for wages, the plaintiff alleged that he had served the defendant as a hired servant from 21st March 1647 to 1st November 1664. To this the defendant pleaded, traversing that the plaintiff served until the 1st November 1664. This was a bad traverse; for as the plaintiff in such an action is entitled to be paid *pro tanto* for any period of service, it is obviously no answer to say that he did not serve the whole time alleged. The defendant must either deny the plaintiff ever served, or else state for how long he admits the plaintiff did serve.
  Osborne v. *Rogers*, 1 Wms. Saund. 267.
  And see *Alsager* v. *Currie*, 11 M. & W. 14.

So where the condition of a bond was that the obligor should serve the obligee half a year, and in an action of debt on the bond the defendant pleaded that he had served him half a year at D., in the county of K.; and the plaintiff replied, that he had not served him half a year at D., in

the county of K. This was adjudged to be a bad traverse, as involving the place, which was immaterial. The addition of the words "or anywhere else" or "or in any other place" would have made it a good traverse.
Doctrina Placitandi, 360.

Negative Pregnant.

A negative pregnant is such a form of negative expression as may imply or carry within it an affirmative proposition. It is therefore evasive and ambiguous, and to use it in traversing would be contrary both to rule 17 and to rule 19 of Order XIX.

Illustrations.

In an action of trespass the plaintiff claimed damages for the defendant's entering his house. The defendant pleaded that the plaintiff's daughter gave him license to do so; and that he entered by that license. The plaintiff replied that *he did not enter by her license.* This was considered as a *negative pregnant;* and it was held that the plaintiff should have traversed the entry by itself, or the license by itself, and not both together.

Myn v. *Cole*, Cro. Jac. 87.

It will be observed that this traverse might imply or carry within it that a license was given, though the defendant did not enter by that license. It is, therefore, in the language of pleading, said to be pregnant with the admission that a license was given. At the same time the license is not expressly admitted; and the effect therefore is to leave it in doubt whether the plaintiff means to deny the license or to deny that the defendant entered by virtue of that license. It is this ambiguity which constitutes the fault. (See *Thurman* v. *Wild*, 11 A. & E. 453; and *per* Parke, B., in *Gwynne* v. *Burnell*, 6 Bing. N. C. 530.)

Action for assault and battery, by a sailor against the master of his ship. The defendant justified, saying that he bade the plaintiff do some service in the ship, but the plaintiff refused; wherefore the defendant moderately chastised him. The plaintiff replied that the defendant did not moderately chastise him. And this traverse was held to be a negative pregnant: for while it apparently means to put in issue only the question of excess (admitting by implication the chastisement), it does not necessarily and distinctly make that admission; and is, therefore, ambiguous in its form.

Auberie v. *James*, Vent. 70; 1 Sid. 444; 2 Keb. 623.

And see *Tildesley* v. *Harper, ante,* p. 83.

There was, apparently, one instance in which such a form of traverse was permitted, and that was where a defendant denied an alleged breach of covenant in the very words of that covenant. Thus, in an action on a bond conditioned to perform the covenants in an indenture of lease, one of which covenants was that the defendant, the lessee, would not deliver possession to any but the lessor or such persons as should lawfully evict him, the defendant pleaded that he did not deliver the possession to any but such as lawfully evicted him. On demurrer to this plea, it was objected that the same was ill, and a negative pregnant; and that he ought to have said that such an one lawfully evicted him, to whom he delivered the possession, or that he did not deliver the possession to any; but the Court held the plea, as pursuing the words of the covenant, good (being in the negative), and that the plaintiff ought to have replied and assigned a breach, and therefore judgment was given against him.

Pullin v. *Nicholas*, 1 Lev. 83.
Mints v. *Bethil*, Cro. Eliz. 749.

But in the present day I think the defendant would be compelled to say plainly whether he ever was evicted, and, if so, when and by whom.

So where the defendant gave a bond, conditioned that he would "from time to time acquit, discharge, and save harmless, the churchwardens of the parish of P., and their successors, &c., from all manner of cost and charges, by reason of the birth and maintenance of" a certain child, he pleaded in his defence merely "that the churchwardens of the said parish, or their successors, &c., from the time of making the said bond, were not in any manner damnified by reason of the birth or maintenance of the said child." This was allowed, because it followed the exact words of the condition of the bond. But it is ambiguous; for it may mean either that the churchwardens never had to pay anything for the child, or that if they had had to pay, the defendant had recouped them. I think such a plea of *Non damnificatus* would not be allowed now, as it is really a negative pregnant.

See *Richards* v. *Hodges*, 2 Wms. Saund. 84.

How far should the pleader confine himself to merely traversing? Should he not, after denying his opponent's story, go on to add his own version of the matter?

This is sometimes a difficult question. The pleader must use his own discretion. It is sometimes most desirable to do so, in order to show clearly what is the real point in dispute.[*] If, for instance, a plaintiff in his Statement of Claim sets out or refers to certain clauses of a written contract on which he relies, the defendant should cer-

---

[*] See the judgment of Jessel, M. R., in *Thorp* v. *Holdsworth*, part of which is quoted *ante*, pp. 76, 77.

tainly set out or refer to other clauses, if any, which tell in his favour. Again, if the plaintiff gives his version of the effect of a written document, it will certainly tend to clear the matter up if the defendant, instead of merely denying the plaintiff's version, states also his own construction of the instrument. And in many cases it may be desirable for a defendant thus to definitely state what his exact contention is. But by so doing he necessarily somewhat limits his case at the trial. He has no longer the same free hand. And there is this further danger; that if the defendant, instead of merely denying, sets up an affirmative case as well, both judge and jury will expect him to prove his affirmative case, and are apt to find against him if he does not. The *onus* of proof is not really shifted by such a method of pleading. But if, when accused of a tort, the defendant pleads, " it was A. who did it, not I," it is only natural to treat this as an admission that either A. or the defendant did it, and it seems to follow that if the defendant cannot prove his assertion that A. did it, he must have done it himself.

Illustrations.

A purchaser sued his vendor for not delivering a proper abstract of title, and alleged that the sale was subject to a condition that the vendor should deliver an abstract, showing a good title, and that no such abstract had been delivered. The defendant would be entitled to plead that the contract between himself and the plaintiff really was that the defendant should deliver an abstract commencing with *a particular deed only*, and that he had done this.

Sharland v. *Leifchild*, 4 C. B. 529; 16 L. J. C. P. 217.

If the defendant's real case is that he was not guilty of any negligence himself, it is unwise for him to plead that there was contributory negligence on the part of the plaintiff.

Where the defendants were sued, as sheriffs of London, for allowing a debtor, Robinson, to escape, they pleaded that it was their predecessors in office who had allowed Robinson to escape. This was held a bad plea, because it neither traversed nor confessed the allegation that the defendants had allowed Robinson to escape. They should have merely denied the act attributed to themselves, and not have set up affirmatively that others were guilty of it.

Mynours v. *Turke and Yorke, Sheriffs of London*, 1 Dyer, 66, b.

Action for breach of copyright. The plaintiff alleged that his song had been duly registered according to the Copyright Act. The defendant pleaded, " the defendant denies that the said song has been duly registered; the date of the first publication thereof is not truly entered." Had he not added the latter clause he would have won the action; as it was, he failed. For it turned out at the trial that the date of publication was truly entered, but the name of the publisher was not. The Act required both to be truly stated; hence the song had not in fact been duly entered. But Fry, J., held that it was not open to the defendant to raise this point; the manner in which the defendant had pleaded was, in effect, "an admission that in every respect but that one which was mentioned, the registration was duly effected." And he refused leave to amend.

Collette v. *Goode*, 7 Ch. D. 842; 47 L. J. Ch. 370; 38 L. T. 504.

So where a plaintiff alleged that H. "agreed by writing under the hand of his agent thereunto lawfully authorized," the defendant pleaded that "H. never agreed by writing under the hand of any agent thereunto lawfully authorized," but added that "H. was of unsound mind, and therefore could not lawfully authorize any agent." It was held that H.'s unsoundness of mind was the only substantial issue raised; and that the defendant could not go into other matters showing that in fact H. never authorized any one to sign this agreement; because "the denial, being justified by a fact specifically alleged and no other, must be taken to refer to that fact alone."

Byrd v. *Nunn*, 5 Ch. D. 781; 25 W. R. 749; 37 L. T. 90; (C. A.) 7 Ch. D. 284; 47 L. J. Ch. 1; 26 W. R. 101; 37 L. T. 585.

Cf. *Harris* v. *Mantle*, 3 T. R. 307, *post*, p. 124.

III.—MATTERS IN CONFESSION AND AVOIDANCE.

The party pleading is often willing to admit that the facts alleged by his opponent are so far true, and that they make out a good *primâ facie* case or defence. But he desires to destroy the effect of these allegations either by showing some justification or excuse of the matter charged against him, or some discharge or release from it. A defendant, for instance, may seek to show on the one hand that the plaintiff never had any right of action, because the act charged was lawful; or on the other that though the plaintiff had once a right of action it is discharged or released by some matter subsequent. In either case, he confesses the truth of the allegation which he proposes to answer or avoid. Hence such defences are called *pleas in confession and avoidance*.

The effect of such admission, if it stand alone, is extremely strong; for it concludes the party making it, even though the jury should improperly go out of the issue, and find the contrary of what is thus confessed on the record. (*Hewitt* v. *Macquire*, 7 Exch. 80.) At the same time, the confession operates only to prevent the fact from being afterwards brought into question in the same suit; it is not conclusive as to the truth of that fact in any subsequent action between the same parties. And it will have no operation at all even in the same suit, if the party pleading also traverses the facts confessed, as he may do now.

Illustrations.

Action of assault. Defence that the defendant did the acts complained of in necessary self-defence. This is a plea in confession and avoidance; for it admits the assault while it justifies it.

Similarly in an action of libel a plea that the words are true or that they were published on a privileged occasion admits that the defendant has libelled the plaintiff, but justifies or excuses the act.

To plead that the defendant has a lien on certain goods admits that the goods are the plaintiff's, and that the defendant detains them from him.

In an action of trespass for breaking and entering the plaintiff's close, the defendant pleaded that the plaintiff demised the close to him for a term of years, by virtue whereof he entered and committed the supposed trespass. This was held to be a good plea in confession and avoidance, for it admitted the plaintiff's title subject to the effect of the demise.

Leyfield's Case, 10 Rep. 91 a; 3 Salk. 273.

The defence that there was contributory negligence on the part of the plaintiff must be specially pleaded. It admits that there was negligence on the part of the defendant which contributed to produce the injury which the plaintiff has sustained, but it shows matter which if proved bars any right of action.

Wakelin v. *L. & S. W. Ry. Co.*, 12 App. Cas. 41; 56 L. J. Q. B. 229; 35 W. R. 141; 55 L. T. 709.

On the other hand, pleas of tender, of payment or set-off, of waiver or accord and satisfaction, of laches or of the Statute of Limitations admit that the plaintiff once had a cause of action, but assert that it is now lost, suspended, or discharged.

And generally in any action of tort if the defendant admits the act complained of, but desires to show that it was not wrongful or no breach of duty, he must plead such justification specially by way of confession and avoidance.

Frankum v. *Lord Falmouth*, 2 A. & E. 452; 4 N. & M. 330.
Lush v. *Russell*, 5 Exch. 203; 19 L. J. Ex. 214.

All matter in confession and avoidance must be pleaded specially. (Pleading Rules of Hilary Term, 1853, rr. 12, 17.) The pleader must not attempt to insinuate it under an apparent traverse. (See *ante*, p. 69.)

The defendant or plaintiff, as the case may be, must raise by his pleading all matters which show the action or counter-claim not to be maintainable, or that the transaction is either void or voidable in point of law, and all such grounds of defence or reply, as the case may be, as if not raised would be likely to take the opposite party by surprise, or would raise issues of fact not arising out of the preceding pleadings, as, for instance, fraud, Statute of Limitations, release, payment, performance, facts showing illegality either by statute or common law, or Statute of Frauds. (Order XIX. r. 15.)

The pleader must be careful in all such cases not to confine himself to a mere traverse. At the same time he should not confess and avoid where a mere traverse is sufficient. For he will thereby introduce collateral matter which his client may have to prove instead of putting the plaintiff to proof of his allegations.

Illustrations.

Action of trespass. Defence that it was the defendant's own freehold. Joinder of issue. The plaintiff was not allowed to give evidence on this issue of a lease to himself from the defendant's ancestor, as that defence admitted that the freehold was in the defendant, which the plaintiff had expressly denied.

5 Hen. VII. 10 a., pl. 2.
Doe v. *Wright*, 10 A. & E. 763 ; 2 P. & D. 672.
Ryan v. *Clark*, 14 Q. B. 65 ; 18 L. J. Q. B. 267 ; 7 D. & L. 8.
And see *Clark* v. *Hougham*, 2 B. & Cr. 149 ; *post*, p. 163.

If a defendant merely pleads that "he never agreed as alleged," he cannot insist at the trial that though a contract was made as alleged it is invalid in point of law, for this must form the subject of a special allegation, showing the circumstances out of which the illegality is supposed to arise.

Martin v. *Smith*, 4 Bing. N. C. 436 ; 6 Dowl. 639.
Fenwick v. *Laycock*, 1 Q. B. 414 ; 1 G. & D. 27.
Nurton v. *Dickson*, 5 H. & N. 637 ; 29 L. J. Ex. 337.

This applies not only to the case where the claim is founded on an express promise of an illegal description, but also to cases where the action is based on an implied promise, and the services or considerations upon which the implication is supposed to arise were tainted with illegality.

Potts v. *Sparrow*, 1 Bing. N. C. 594.

Fraud must always be specially pleaded. In an action on a bill of exchange the defendant pleaded that the plaintiff was not a *bonâ fide* holder for value. It was held that he could not under that plea raise the question of his being privy to a fraud. The only question on such an issue will be, did he give value for the bill?

Uther v. *Rich*, 10 Ad. & E. 784 ; 2 P. & D. 579.

Action of trespass for breaking and entering plaintiff's close. Defence that J. S. was seised in fee of the close and demised it to the defendant for a term of years by virtue whereof he entered, which is the alleged trespass.

This was held a bad plea. A traverse denying that the close was the plaintiff's was all that was necessary.

Argent v. *Durrant*, 8 T. R. 403.

In confessing and avoiding, as in traversing, the plea must be neither too wide nor too narrow. It must be as broad and as long as the claim to which it is pleaded, and justify or excuse the whole of it; or if it be intended to apply to part only of the matter adversely alleged, it must be limited accordingly by a prefix "as to so much as alleges, &c.," or "as to paragraph 4 of the Statement of Claim." (See *Vere* v. *Goldsborough*, 1 Bing. N. C. 353; and the Common Law Procedure Act, 1852, s. 67.)

At the same time be careful not to make too wide an averment, whereby you will take on your shoulders an unnecessary burden, or too narrow an averment, which will fetter your hand at the trial.

Illustrations.

In an action for a slander in these words, " Woor says that M'Pherson is insolvent," it would be insufficient to plead that Woor had in fact said so; the defendant must allege and prove not merely what Woor said, but also that what he said was true.

M'Pherson v. *Daniels*, 10 B. & C. 263; 5 M. & R. 251.
Duncan v. *Thwaites*, 3 B. & C. 556; 5 D. & R. 447.

In a plea of privilege it is sufficient to aver that the defendant acted *bonâ fide* and without malice. Do not, therefore, allege that the defendant had just and reasonable grounds for believing the charges made against the plaintiff to be true. Such an averment runs dangerously near to a justification, and will either be struck out as immaterial (*Cave* v. *Torre*, 32 W. R. 324; 54 L. T. 87, 515), or particulars will be ordered of the grounds of such belief.

Fitzgerald v. *Campbell*, 18 Ir. Jur. 153; 15 L. T. 74.

In pleading the Statute of Frauds it is not necessary to plead any particular section. Where, however, the defendant had pleaded sect. 4, he was not allowed to amend or to avail himself of sect. 7.

James v. *Smith*, (1891) 1 Ch. 384; 63 L. T. 524.

CHAPTER V.

ATTACKING YOUR OPPONENT'S PLEADING.

THESE, then, are the leading rules of our present system of pleading. They are very clear, very simple, and very sensible. And, at the same time, they are very elastic. Pleadings are no longer cast all in one mould; there is full scope for individuality. No one is entitled to dictate to his opponent how he shall plead. "No technical objection shall be raised to any pleading on the ground of any alleged want of form" (Order XIX. r. 26). Moreover, "no application to set aside any proceeding for irregularity shall be allowed unless made within reasonable time, nor if the party applying has taken any fresh step after knowledge of the irregularity" (Order LXX. r. 2). Hence any *mere irregularity*, such as misjoinder of causes of action or pleading other defences with "not guilty by statute" in defiance of Order XIX. r. 12, will be cured by your opponent's pleading over. This is sometimes a comfort to a beginner. But experienced pleaders often break the *letter* of these rules for the sake of clearness or brevity. Thus, though it is in general unnecessary to allege matter of law, yet it is sometimes convenient to do so, and it may make the statements of fact more intelligible and show their connection *inter se*. This is, indeed, done in the statutory forms in Appendices C., D., and E. : *e.g.*, " The plaintiff is entitled to the possession of a farm and premises " (App. C., s. vii.). " The defendant is entitled to set-off " (App. D., s. iv., 5). There is no harm in this, if (as in both the cases referred to) the facts are also stated on which the proposition of law is based.

But what is a pleader to do when he is confronted by some flagrantly bad bit of pleading in flat violation of the rules? Even then, the best thing he can do as a rule is to leave it alone. But there are exceptions. As Bowen, L.J., says in *Knowles* v. *Roberts* (38 Ch. D. at p. 270; 58 L. T. at p. 262), " It seems to me that the rule that the Court is not to dictate to parties how they should frame their case, is one that ought always to be preserved sacred. But that rule is, of course, subject to this modification and limitation, that the parties must not offend against the rules of pleading which have been laid down by the law; and if a party introduces a pleading which is unnecessary, and it tends to prejudice, embarrass, and delay the trial of the action, it then becomes a pleading which is beyond his right."

Striking out your Opponent's Pleading.

The provisions of Order XXV. afford a prompt and summary method of disposing of groundless actions and of excluding immaterial issues. Under r. 4 of that Order a master at chambers has power to strike out any Statement of Claim which discloses no reasonable cause of action and to stay or dismiss any action which is shown by the pleadings to be frivolous and vexatious. And apart from all rules and orders the Court has inherent power to stay every action which is an abuse of its process. (See *Reichel* v. *Magrath*, 14 App. Cas. 665; 59 L. J. Q. B. 159; and *MacDougall* v. *Knight*, 25 Q. B. D. 1; 38 W. R. 553; 63 L. T. 43.) But these extreme powers are but rarely exercised, and it by no means follows that because you think your opponent's pleading discloses no cause of action or no defence to your claim, that you should at once take out a summons to have it struck out or amended.

Objection in point of Law.

Then, too, the same Order enables the defendant to raise by his pleading any point of law, and in a proper case to have it argued and disposed of before the trial.

Where the matter is one of first impression, or where for any other reason the law on the point is not clear, it may be very desirable to raise an objection and settle the point of law before incurring the expense of a trial with witnesses. But in ordinary cases it is generally more expedient to raise the objection on the pleading, not to apply to have it argued before the trial. The usual result of such an argument is that if the defendant succeeds, the plaintiff obtains leave, on paying the costs of the argument, to amend his Statement of Claim; and it is better for the defendant that the plaintiff should be driven to such amendment at the trial in the presence of the jury. Hence, as a rule, it is best not to apply to have any point of law argued before the trial, unless the objection is one which will dispose of the whole action, and which cannot be removed by any amendment which the plaintiff can truthfully make.

Clients are sometimes afraid that, by not taking out a summons, counsel throw away for ever one chance of success; that the objection, if not taken at once, cannot be taken afterwards. But this is not so. No doubt slight defects, such as slips of the pen, careless omissions, informal pleading, &c., may sometimes be aided by pleading over, and may still more often be cured by verdict. But it is never worth while in these days to incur the cost of a motion or summons over some purely formal defect. All matters of substance, as my Lord Coke says, " will be saved to you." You should always bear in mind the good advice which that great judge deduced as a moral from " the first cause that he ever moved in the King's Bench ":—

" When the matter, in fact, will clearly serve for your client, although your opinion is that the plaintiff has no cause of action, yet take heed you do not hazard the matter upon a demurrer, in which, upon the pleading and otherwise, more perhaps will arise

than you thought of; but first take advantage of the matters of
fact, and leave matters in law, which always arise upon the matters
in fact, *ad ultimum*, and never at first demur in law, when, after
trial of the matters in fact, the matters in law (as in this case
it was) will be saved to you" (*The Lord Cromwell's Case* (1581),
4 Rep. at p. 14). This advice, though more than three hundred years old, is as sound now as it was in the days of Queen
Elizabeth; in fact, owing to the liberal powers of amendment given
by the Judicature Acts, its efficacy has increased rather than
diminished. If, then, the facts are likely to prove in your favour,
you should not, as a rule, apply under Order XXV. r. 2; but if at
the trial you will be compelled to admit that you have no case on
the merits, then by all means take advantage of any point of law
you can.

Amending your Opponent's Pleading.

Again, by rule 27 of Order XIX. a Master at Chambers
may order to be struck out or amended any matter in any pleading which may be unnecessary or scandalous, or which may tend
to prejudice, embarrass, or delay the fair trial of the action.
But remember that "nothing can be scandalous which is relevant" (*per* Cotton, L. J., in *Fisher* v. *Owen*, 8 Ch. D. at
p. 653). The mere fact that an allegation is unnecessary is no
ground for striking it out; nor is a pleading embarrassing
merely because it contains allegations which are inconsistent or
stated in the alternative (*Re Morgan*, 35 Ch. D. 492; 56
L. J. Ch. 603).

Unless the defect is really seriously embarrassing, it is often
better policy to leave it unamended; you only strengthen your
opponent's position by reforming his pleading. But be careful
in drawing the Defence not to aid the defect in the claim in any
way; the less said about that part of the pleading the better.
Do not admit it; if need be, traverse it in so many words; but,
after such denial, avoid the whole topic, if possible, leaving the
plaintiff's counsel to explain it to the judge at the trial, if he can.

Illustrations.

" A defendant may claim *ex debito justitiæ* to have the plaintiff's case presented in an intelligible form, so that he may not be embarrassed in meeting it."

Per James, L. J., in *Davy* v. *Garrett,* 7 Ch. D. at p. 486; 47 L. J. Ch. 218; 26 W. R. 225; 38 L. T. 77.

In an action to enforce the compromise of a former action, the plaintiff will not be allowed to set out over again all the facts on which he relied before, so as to try the former action over again.

Knowles v. *Roberts,* 38 Ch. D. 263; 58 L. T. 259.

Allegations of dishonesty and outrageous conduct, &c., are not scandalous, if relevant to the issue.

Christie v. *Christie,* L. R. 8 Ch. 499; 42 L. J. Ch. 544; 21 W. R. 493; 28 L. T. 607.

Rubery v. *Grant,* L. R. 13 Eq. 443; 42 L. J. Ch. 19; 26 L. T. 538.

Millington v. *Loring,* 6 Q. B. D. 190; 50 L. J. Q. B. 214; 29 W. R. 207; 43 L. T. 657; 45 J. P. 268.

But where a plaintiff made allegations in his Statement of Claim of dishonest conduct against the defendant, but stated in his Reply that he sought no relief on that ground, the allegations were struck out as scandalous and embarrassing.

Brooking v. *Maudslay,* 55 L. T. 343; 6 Asp. M. C. 13.

Particulars.

But the most usual way of attacking your opponent's pleading is by taking out a summons for particulars.

"A further and better statement of the nature of the claim or defence, or further and better particulars of any matter stated in any pleading, notice, or written proceeding requiring particulars, may in all cases be ordered, upon such terms, as to costs and otherwise, as may be just." (Order XIX. r. 7.) If, then, either party considers that his opponent's pleading does not give him the information to which he is entitled, his remedy is to apply for further particulars under this order.

"The object of particulars is to enable the party asking for them to know what case he has to meet at the trial, and so to save unnecessary expense, and avoid allowing parties to be taken by surprise." (*Spedding* v. *Fitzpatrick,* 38 Ch. D. 413; 58 L. J. Ch. 139; 37 W. R. 20; 59 L. T. 492.) If your opponent has worded his pleading so vaguely that you cannot be sure what case he is going to make against you at the trial, it is worth while to take out a summons. Even though you think you can make a shrewd guess at his meaning, it is safer to pin him down to a definite story. Always ask for particulars of losses, expenses and other special damage, and for seven days further time to plead after such particulars are delivered. It is also most desirable to ascertain whether the plaintiff is relying on parol conversations or written documents as amounting to a misrepresentation or as establishing a contract.

Particulars are now ordered much more freely than in former days. Look at such cases as *Gale* v. *Reed*, 8 East, 80 ; *Shum* v. *Farrington*, 1 Bos. & Puller, 640 ; *Burton* v. *Webb*, 8 T. R. 459 ; *Cornwallis* v. *Savery*, 2 Burr. 772 ; and *Forsyth* v. *Bristowe*, 8 Exch. at p. 350. In each of these cases particulars giving the information asked for would now at once be ordered. "The old system of pleading at common law was to conceal as much as possible what was going to be proved at the trial." (*Per* Cotton, L.J., 38 Ch. D. 414.) Now we play with the cards on the table. Latterly, however, the Divisional Court has apparently considered that we have gone too far in that direction; and refused the particulars asked for in *Roberts* v. *Owen*, 6 Times L. R. 172 ; *James* v. *Radnor County Council*, 6 Times L. R. 240 ; *Thomson* v. *Birkley*, 31 W. R. 230 ; 47 L. T. 700 ; and *Knight* v. *Engle*, 61 L. T. 780.

Illustrations.

If an agreement is alleged generally (*e.g.*, " it was agreed between the plaintiff and the defendant that," &c.) particulars will be ordered of the alleged agreement, stating its date, and whether the same was verbal or in writing, in the latter case identifying the document.

Turquand v. *Fearon*, 40 L. T. 543.

Where it is alleged that " the defendant represented to the plaintiff," &c., an order will be made for similar particulars of the alleged misrepresentation.

So where the plaintiff alleged that certain directors had instigated the defendant to do something, Kay, J., held that the plaintiff ought to state whether the instigation alleged in paragraph 12 of the Amended Statement of Claim to have been made by the directors was verbal or in writing, and if verbal by whom it was made, and if in writing the date of such writing.

Briton Medical, &c. Association v. *Britannia Fire Association*, 59 L. T. 888.

Particulars of alleged adultery, specifying time and place of each act, were ordered in

Coates v. *Croyle*, 4 Times L. R. 735.

The defendant, in an action for seduction, applied, before Defence, for particulars of the alleged immoral intercourse. But the Divisional Court refused to make any order unless he made an affidavit that he had not seduced the girl.

Thomson v. *Birkley*, 31 W. R. 230; 47 L. T. 700, approved in *Sachs* v. *Speilman*, 37 Ch. D. at p. 304; 57 L. J. Ch. 658; 36 W. R. 498; 58 L. T. 102.

In a similar case, a Divisional Court declined to follow this decision, and ordered particulars.

Kelly v. *Briggs*, 85 L. T. Newspaper, 78.

But the principle of *Thomson* v. *Birkley* was followed in

Knight v. *Engle*, 61 L. T. 780.

Where a plaintiff claims a lump sum of money he must give particulars of the items of which it is composed.

Philipps v. *Philipps*, 4 Q. B. D. at p. 131; 48 L. J. Q. B. 135; 27 W. R. 436; 39 L. T. 556.

Where he gives the defendant credit for a lump sum, and sues for a balance, he must also give particulars of the items of which such credit is composed.

Godden v. *Corsten*, 5 C. P. D. 17; 49 L. J. C. P. 112; 28 W. R. 305; 41 L. T. 527.

Whenever the plaintiff claims a lump sum for carriage, warehouse rent, work and labour done, and money paid, he will be ordered to give the items composing such lump sum, and to distinguish which sums are charged for carriage, which for warehouse rent, which for work and labour, and which for money paid, and to state when and to whom each such payment was made.

Where, however, the plaintiff, instead of claiming a specific sum, asks on reasonable grounds that an account may be taken of the moneys due to him, no particulars will as a rule be ordered, the object of the action being to obtain the necessary information from the defendant.

Angustinus v. *Nerinckx*, 16 Ch. D. 13; 29 W. R. 225; 43 L. T. 458.

Blackie v. *Osmaston*, 28 Ch. D. 119; 54 L. J. Ch. 473; 33 W. R. 158; 52 L. T. 6.

Merely asking for an account will not prevent the Court ordering particulars, but if the Court sees that an account must be taken, it will not order particulars.

Kemp v. *Goldberg*, 36 Ch. D. 505 ; 36 W. R. 278 ; 56 L. T. 736.

Where a railway company sued a customer for the carriage of numerous consignments of iron, and for other charges connected therewith, the company was ordered in the first place to deliver particulars showing the price charged for each consignment. From these particulars, when delivered, it appeared that various consignments were charged at different rates, some less and some higher than the maximum rate allowed for carriage by the Railway and Canal Traffic Acts, 1873 and 1888. Thereupon the Divisional Court (Denman and Wills, JJ.), acting on the analogy of the provision contained in sub-sect. 3 of sect. 33 of the latter Act (51 & 52 Vict. c. 25), on June 23rd, 1891, ordered "that the plaintiffs do furnish further and better particulars as to each of the several specific rates mentioned in the particulars already delivered in the action, distinguishing the charges for conveyance from the terminal charges (if any), and from the dock charges (if any); and if any terminal charges or dock charges be included, specifying the nature and detail of the terminal charges or dock charges in respect of which they are made, and that such particulars be delivered within a month, and that there be no stay in the meantime." And this order was upheld in the Court of Appeal, Lindley and Fry, L.JJ. (July 30th, 1891).

London & North Western Rail. Co. v. *Lee*, 7 Times L. R. 603.

There is another advantage in obtaining particulars from your opponent. It limits the issue. He is bound by his particulars, and cannot at the trial (without special leave, which would only be granted on terms) go into any matters not fairly included therein.

Particulars thus "prevent surprise at the trial, and limit inquiry at the trial to matters set out in particulars. They tend to narrow issues, and ought to be encouraged." (*Per* Watkin Williams, J., in *Thomson* v. *Birkley*, 31 W. R. 230; 47 L. T. 700.)

Illustrations.

A landlord brought an action of ejectment against his tenant, and gave as particulars of the breaches of covenant on which he relied as a forfeiture :—"Selling hay and straw off the premises, removing manure, and non-cultivation." He was not allowed at the trial to give evidence that the defendant had mismanaged the farm by over-cropping, or by deviating from the usual rotation of crops. He was confined to the matters stated in his particulars.

Doe dem. Winnall v. *Broad,* 2 Man. & Gr. 523.

And see *Harris* v. *Mantle,* 3 T. R. 308, *post,* p. 124.

So, too, whenever any special damage is claimed, but not with sufficient detail, particulars will be ordered of the alleged damage, setting out the names of the customers who had ceased to deal with the plaintiff, &c. This is a very useful order, as, if plaintiff cannot give the names, he will be compelled to strike out the allegation of special damage; and the summons should ask that it be struck out if such particulars be not delivered. If he give the necessary particulars, he will be bound by them; he will not be allowed at the trial to give evidence of any special damage which is not claimed explicitly, either in his pleading or particulars. See *ante,* p. 44.

It is no objection to an application for particulars that the applicant must know the true facts of the case better than his opponent. He is entitled to know the outline of the case that his adversary is going to make against him, which may be something very different from the true facts of the case. His opponent may know more than he does; in any event it is well to bind him down to a definite story. Particulars will be ordered whenever the master is satisfied that without them the applicant cannot tell what is going to be proved against him at the trial.

Again, where the party applying is in other respects entitled to the particulars for which he asks, it is not a valid objection to his application that if the order be made it will compel the party giving them to name his witnesses, or otherwise to disclose or give some clue to his evidence. If the only object of the summons be to obtain particulars of the evidence on the other side, it should of course be dismissed as an improper application. But where the information asked for is clearly necessary to enable the applicant properly to prepare for trial, or in other respects the application is a proper one, the information must be given, even though it discloses the evidence on which the other party proposes to rely at the trial.

Illustrations.

A line can be drawn, though sometimes only with difficulty, between requiring a plaintiff to make a sufficient statement to prevent the defendant being taken by surprise at the trial, and requiring him to disclose the evidence on which he intends to rely. Thus, where the plaintiff alleged that the defendants "knew or ought to have known, and must be taken to have known, the improper motives which actuated the directors," and the defendants applied for particulars, stating what were the improper motives which actuated the directors, and how and in what manner were such motives known to the defendants, Kay, J., made an order for particulars of the alleged improper motives which actuated the directors, but declined to make the rest of the order asked for.

Briton Medical, &c. Association v. *Britannia Fire Association*, 59 L. T. 888.

It is now settled practice that in any action of libel* or slander, the defendant is entitled to particulars of the place where, the times when, and the persons to whom, the alleged slanders or libels were published, if such details are not given in the Statement of Claim.

Roselle v. *Buchanan*, 16 Q. B. D. 656; 55 L. J. Q. B. 376; 34 W. R. 488; extending the decision in

Bradbury v. *Cooper*, 12 Q. B. D. 94; 53 L. J. Q. B. 558; 32 W. R. 32; 48 J. P. 198.

Each publication is a separate cause of action, and the defendant is therefore entitled to this information, although the plaintiff may thus be compelled to name some of his witnesses.

But a person libelled in a newspaper cannot be expected to tell the proprietor the names of all who take his paper. That would be oppressive.

Nor can a plaintiff be compelled to give the names of the persons passing in the street at the time the alleged slander was uttered.

Wingard v. *Cox*, Weekly Notes (1876) p. 106; Bitt. 144; 20 Sol. J. 341; 60 L. T. Notes, 304.

In a proper case, a party who is ordered to give particulars is allowed to interrogate his opponent, and to obtain discovery of documents before giving them.

Whyte v. *Ahrens*, 26 Ch. D. 717; 54 L. J. Ch. 145; 32 W. R. 649; 50 L. T. 344.

Leitch v. *Abbott*, 31 Ch. D. 374; 55 L. J. Ch. 460; 34 W. R. 506; 54 L. T. 258; 50 J. P. 441.

---

* It is sometimes urged that this practice is confined to actions of slander, and does not apply in actions of libel. But I can see no ground for such a distinction, and I do not think the case of *Gourand* v. *Fitzgerald*, 37 W. R. 55, 265, affords any. All that the Court of Appeal decided was, that the application in that case was made too late.

"It is good practice and good sense that where the defendant knows the facts and the plaintiffs do not, the defendant should give discovery before the plaintiffs deliver particulars."
>   Per Bowen, L. J., in *Millar* v. *Harper*, 38 Ch. D. at p. 112; 57 L. J. Ch. 1091; 36 W. R. 454; 58 L. T. 698.
>   *Edelston* v. *Russell*, 57 L. T. 927.

It is no hardship on a party who has a good case to be ordered to give particulars. It is often a benefit to him, for it compels him to get his case up carefully in good time before the trial. It is also sometimes an advantage to have full particulars of his grievance, loss, expenses, &c. clearly stated in black and white, and laid before the judge with the pleadings.

At the same time, particulars will not be exacted where it would be oppressive or unreasonable to make such an order; as where the information is not in the possession of either party, or could only be obtained with great difficulty, or where the particulars are not applied for till the last moment. An order is often made for "the best particulars the plaintiff can give;" or that an approximate figure should be stated where the exact number is not essential, as in *Parnell* v. *Walter and another*, 24 Q. B. D. 441; 59 L. J. Q. B. 125.

Illustrations.

Application for particulars must be made with reasonable promptitude.
>   *Gourand* v. *Fitzgerald*, 37 W. R. 265.

But the mere fact that the defendant has already delivered his Defence is no waiver of his right to particulars of the allegations in the Statement of Claim.
>   *Sachs* v. *Speilman*, 37 Ch. D. 295; 57 L. J. Ch. 658; 36 W. R. 498; 58 L. T. 102.

The declaration alleged that the plaintiff was chosen and nominated a knight of the same county, &c. by the greater number of the forty-shilling freeholders present. It was objected that the plaintiff does not show the certainty of the number. But it was held that the declaration was "good enough, without showing the number of electors; for the election might be made by voices or hands, or by such other way wherein it is easy to tell who has the majority and yet very difficult to know the certain number of them." And it was laid down that, to put the plaintiff "to declare a certainty where he cannot by any possibility be presumed to

know or remember the certainty, is not reasonable nor requisite in our law."
Buckley v. *Rice Thomas*, Plow. 118.

Where the particulars were for non-payment of seven quarters' rent, and the evidence showed that only six quarters were in arrear, it was held that the variance was immaterial.
Tenny d. Gibbs v. *Moody*, 3 Bing. 3; 10 Moo. 252.

As a rule, particulars will only be ordered of an affirmative allegation. One cannot give particulars of a mere traverse or of a joinder of issue.

Illustrations.

In an action for malicious prosecution the plaintiff alleged that the defendant had prosecuted without any reasonable or probable cause. The defendant denied that he had prosecuted without reasonable or probable cause. The plaintiff applied for particulars of the defendant's reasonable and probable cause; but this application was refused. The Court did not see its way to order particulars of a traverse of the absence of something, without the help of an affidavit.
Roberts v. *Owen*, 6 Times L. R. 172; 54 J. P. 295.

If the allegation in the Defence had been drafted affirmatively, *e. g.*, "the defendant had reasonable and probable cause for prosecuting the plaintiff," an order for particulars would perhaps have been made.

Where the defendant on the face of his pleading disputes all the items of the plaintiff's claim, he cannot be made to give particulars of those he disputes. Where he alleges that all the prices charged by the plaintiff are unreasonable and excessive, he cannot be ordered to state to which items he objects.
James v *Radnor County Council*, 6 Times L. R. 240.

Where a defendant has paid money into Court generally to the whole of the plaintiff's claim, which consists of many items, he cannot be ordered to specify in respect of which items of the plaintiff's claim the payment into Court had been made. "It would be very unjust to make the defendant particularize how much he had paid into Court in respect of each item." *Per* Bramwell, L. J., in
Paraire v. *Loibl* (C. A.), 49 L. J. C. P. 481; 43 L. T. 427.

But see *Orient Steam Navigation Co.* v. *Ocean Marine Insurance Co.*, 34 W. R. 442.

Particulars will not be ordered of any immaterial allegation.
Care v. *Torre*, 32 W. R. 324; 54 L. T. 516.
Gibbons v. *Norman*, 2 Times L. R. 676.

"The party at whose instance particulars have been delivered under a judge's order shall, unless the order otherwise provides, have the same length of time for pleading after the delivery of the particulars that he had at the return of the summons. Save as in this rule provided, an order for particulars shall not, unless the order otherwise provides, operate as a stay of proceedings, or give any extension of time." (Order XIX. r. 8.) But this rule does not apply when a "peremptory" order has been made for the delivery of the pleading within a specified time. (*Falck* v. *Axthelm*, 24 Q. B. D. 174; 59 L. J. Q. B. 161; 38 W. R. 196.)

Chapter VI.

INDORSEMENT ON WRIT.

There are three kinds of indorsement:—

(i.) A special indorsement under Order III. r. 6 (which really is a Statement of Claim).
(ii.) A general indorsement.
(iii.) An indorsement for an account under Order III. r. 8.

And whenever any one of the parties sues, or is sued, in a representative capacity, the indorsement, whether special, general, or for an account, must state the fact, in the manner shown in Appendix A., Part III., s. 7. Take this for an example:—"The plaintiff A. B. sues as executor of C. D., deceased; the defendant M. N. is sued as the heir-at-law of C. D.; and the defendant X. Y. as the residuary devisee under the will of C. D."

(i.) SPECIAL INDORSEMENT.

The advantage of having a writ specially indorsed is threefold:—

(1.) That if the defendant does not appear to the writ, the plaintiff can at once, without any leave, sign final judgment for the full amount claimed, on filing an affidavit that the writ was properly served.

(2.) That if the defendant does appear to the writ, the plaintiff can take out a summons under Order XIV., and if the defendant fails to show that he has any defence, the master will give the plaintiff leave to sign final judgment; if the defendant shows only a very weak or shadowy defence, the master will order him to pay a sum of money into Court within so many days, as a proof of *bona fides*, otherwise judgment to be signed against him for that sum.

(3.) If no summons be taken out under Order XIV., or if on the hearing of such summons the defendant obtains leave to defend, then the defendant pleads at once to the special indorsement; no further Statement of Claim can be delivered (except by way of amendment under Order XX. r. 1).

Hence a plaintiff should, as a rule, specially indorse his writ whenever he can.

But the plaintiff can only indorse his writ specially in the six cases provided by Order III. r. 6, viz.:—Where he seeks only to recover a debt or liquidated demand in money payable by the defendant, with or without interest, arising:—

(a.) Upon a contract express or implied (as, for instance, on a bill of exchange, promissory note, or cheque, or other simple contract debt).

(b.) On a bond or contract under seal for payment of a liquidated amount of money.

(c.) On a statute where the sum sought to be recovered is a fixed sum of money, or in the nature of a debt, other than a penalty.

(d.) On a guaranty, whether under seal or not, where the claim against the principal debtor is in respect of a debt or liquidated demand only.

(e.) On a trust.

(f.) In actions for the recovery of land (with or without a claim for rent or mesne profits) by a landlord against a tenant whose term has expired or has been duly determined by a notice to quit, or against persons claiming under such tenant.

What is "a debt or liquidated demand in money payable by the defendant." These words are generally understood to include every "liquidated demand payable in money," although it may not be a "debt" in the strictest sense of that word.* (See *Runnacles* v. *Mesquita*, 1 Q. B. D. 416; 45 L. J. Q. B. 407; and *Phillips* v. *Harris*, W. Notes (1876) p. 54.) Where the price of goods sold and delivered is expressly agreed beforehand, or where the amount to be paid for a certain piece of work is fixed by a contract in writing, here there is a debt which is clearly within the rule. But supposing no price was fixed, and the plaintiff is to be paid whatever is usual in the trade, or such sum as the jury should think fair and reasonable ("*quantum meruit*"—such sum as he has earned—or "*quantum valebant*" such sum as the goods were worth) still the case is within the rule. (*Stephenson* v. *Weir*, 4 L. R. Ir. 369; *Whelan* v. *Kelly*, 14 L. R. Ir. 387.) This is clear from the very first precedent of a special indorsement given in Appendix C. section IV., an action on a butcher's bill, where it is improbable that the exact price to be paid for each joint was expressly fixed at the time it was ordered. But what is excluded by these words from the operation of the rule is an action for unliquidated damages, that is to say, an action in which the amount

---

* The old action of debt lay only for a sum certain.

to be recovered depends on all the circumstances of the case and on the conduct of the parties, and is fixed by opinion or conjecture. In such cases one cannot say positively beforehand whether the jury will award the plaintiff a farthing, or forty shillings, or a hundred pounds. But whenever the amount to which the plaintiff is entitled can be ascertained by calculation or fixed by any scale of charges or any other positive *data*, it is said to be *liquidated* or "made clear," and then the writ can be specially indorsed.

Illustrations.

A solicitor's bill is within the rule, although it is subject to taxation.
Smith v. *Edwardes*, 22 Q. B. D. 10; 58 L. J. Q. B. 227; 37 W. R. 112; 60 L. T. 10.
Shortal v. *Farrell*, Ir. R. 3 C. L. 506.

A writ may be specially indorsed with a claim for arrears of rent, but not for damages for breach of a covenant to repair.
Lloyd v. *Byrne*, 22 L. R. Ir. 269.
Clarke v. *Berger*, 36 W. R. 809.

Damages for wrongful dismissal are unliquidated; because the plaintiff may have obtained a better situation within a week of his dismissal.
And see *Knight* v. *Abbott*, 10 Q. B. D. 11; 52 L. J. Q. B. 131; 31 W. R. 505; 49 L. T. 94.

Again, the words of Order III., r. 6, are "where the plaintiff seeks *only* to recover a debt or liquidated demand in money." Hence, unless the *whole* of plaintiff's cause of action arises under one or other of these six heads, the writ cannot be specially indorsed. If the plaintiff has a cause of action which is within Order III., r. 6, and also other causes of action not within that rule, it will generally be found the best plan to begin by indorsing the writ specially with such claims only as are within it. Then apply under Order XIV., if the defendant appears. If the plaintiff succeeds under Order XIV., a fresh action can be brought for the other claims, with a writ generally indorsed. If he is unsuccessful in obtaining final judgment summarily, he can at once (before defendant delivers his Defence) put in an Amended Statement of Claim, embracing all his claims; which can be done without any leave or order, and without any amendment or re-service of the writ. (Order XXVIII., r. 2; Order XX., r. 4.)

If the writ be inadvertently indorsed with claims not within

Order III., r. 6, the master may, on an application under Order XIV., order the writ to be amended by striking them out; but in that case, the writ must be re-served before any order is made under Order XIV.; because that order is limited to cases "where the defendant appears to a writ of summons specially indorsed under Order III., r. 6." *Per* Wills and Charles, JJ., Aug. 12th, 1891.

A special indorsement is really a Statement of Claim, and should be so headed.

Hence, no other Statement of Claim can be delivered (except as an Amended Statement of Claim), even though defendant on appearing expressly demands one. (See Order XX., r. 1 (a).)

It must contain full particulars with dates and items sufficient to inform the defendant specifically what is the claim that is made against him, so that he may be able to make up his mind whether he will pay or fight. (*Walker and another* v. *Hicks*, 3 Q. B. D. 8; 47 L. J. Q. B. 27; *Smith* v. *Wilson* (C. A.), 5 C. P. D. 25; 49 L. J. C. P. 96; 28 W. R. 57; 41 L. T. 433.) It must also state all material facts necessary to constitute a complete cause of action. (See *ante*, p. 18.) But the more concisely such material facts are stated, the better.

Illustrations.

"The plaintiff's claim is for £——, balance of account for goods sold," is not a special indorsement, because no dates are given.

Painter v. *Wallis*, Times for Nov. 5th, 1878, overruling Lush, J., in *Anon.*, Weekly Notes (1875) at p. 220.

Jackson v. *Kelly*, 12 Ir. L. T. 136.

M'Cawley v. *Campbell*, 4 L. R. Ir. 410.

Phelan v. *Shanks*, 18 Ir. L. T. 13.

But this defect will be cured if the indorsement refers to some account already rendered which contains the necessary particulars.

Aston v. *Hurwitz*, 41 L. T. 521.

In any action on a bill of exchange or promissory note, full particulars of the amount and date of the negotiable instrument and of the parties thereto, must be given on the writ.

Walker and another v. *Hicks*, 3 Q. B. D. 8; 47 L. J. Q. B. 27; 26 W. R. 113; 37 L. T. 529.

An indorsement in an action of contract against a married woman must state that she had separate estate at the date of the contract. *Southern Counties Bank* v. *Farquhar*, 34 Sol. Journ. 182.

In an action by the assignee of a debt, the indorsement must allege an assignment in writing, and also notice in writing of such assignment.

See *Bickers* v. *Speight*, 22 Q. B. D. 7; 58 L. J. Q. B. 42; 37 W. R. 139.

Forms applicable to cases under heads A., B., C., D., and E., of Order III., r. 6, are given in Appendix C., sect. IV.; forms applicable to cases under head F., are given in sect. VII. of the same Appendix, and as to these, it must be remembered that Order III., r. 6, is confined to clear and simple cases where the relation of landlord and tenant is undisputed, *e.g.*, where the defendant has paid rent to the plaintiff, or has otherwise estopped himself from denying plaintiff's title. (*Casey* v. *Hellyer*, 17 Q. B. D. 97; 55 L. J. Q. B. 207.) I add three precedents.

STATEMENT OF CLAIM *to be indorsed on Writ in an Action for the Recovery of Land where the Term has expired.*

(a) *Where there is an Agreement in Writing.*

The plaintiff's claim is to recover possession of two plots of land situate at Waxham, in the parish and manor of Horsey, in the county of Norfolk, numbered 491 and 492 in the Tithe Apportionment Map, and containing in the whole about 5 acres, 1 rood, and 25 perches, which were demised by the plaintiff to the defendant by an agreement in writing bearing date the 17th of September, 1883, for a term which expired on the 27th day of May, 1884.

The plaintiff also claims mesne profits from the said 27th of May, 1884, till possession of the said plots of land is delivered up to him.

(b) *Tenancy at Will.*

1. The plaintiff's claim is to recover possession of certain premises situate in the parish of M., in the manor of N., in the county of S., and known as Hepthorp Farm, and for mesne profits from December 23rd, 1886.

2. The defendants were tenants at will to the plaintiff of the said premises; but the plaintiff on December 23rd, 1886, duly determined their tenancy and demanded possession of the said premises; yet the defendants refuse to deliver up possession thereof to the plaintiff.

STATEMENT OF CLAIM *to be indorsed on Writ in an Action for the Recovery of Land where the Tenancy has been duly determined by a proper Notice to Quit.*

1. The plaintiff's claim is to recover possession of certain premises known as Laurel Cottage, St. Anne's Churchyard, in the borough of Petersfield, in the county of Southampton.

2. The defendant occupied the said premises as a weekly tenant to the plaintiff on the terms that such tenancy should be determinable by a four weeks' notice to quit to be given by either party.

3. The plaintiff duly determined the said tenancy by serving on the defendant on October 7th, 1886, a notice to quit the said premises on the following 8th November, 1886; yet the defendant refuses to deliver up possession thereof to the plaintiff.

4. The plaintiff also claims the mesne profits of the said premises from the said 8th November, 1886, till possession be delivered up.

See another precedent in *Daubuz and others* v. *Lavington*, Weekly Notes (1884) p. 95; 13 Q. B. D. 347.

(ii.) GENERAL INDORSEMENTS

are seldom drawn by counsel. The exact wording of them only becomes important in case defendant does not appear; as if he does, a proper Statement of Claim will be delivered in due course stating everything in proper form. The indorsement on the writ, if general, in no way fetters or limits the future Statement of Claim. For by Order XX. r. 4, "whenever a Statement of Claim is delivered the plaintiff may therein alter, modify, or extend his claim without any amendment of the indorsement on the writ." But this rule does not apply where defendant has not appeared. (*Gee* v. *Bell*, 35 Ch. D. 160; 56 L. J. Ch. 718; *Kingdon* v. *Kirk*, 37 Ch. D. 141; 57 L. J. Ch. 328.) Hence, whenever there is any chance of judgment going by default, even a general indorsement must be carefully prepared.

Where the writ is only indorsed generally, the defendant, when entering appearance, usually requires the plaintiff to deliver a Statement of Claim. If he does not, he must, within ten days after appearance, plead to the substance of the claim stated in the indorsement as best he can. (Order XXI. r. 7.)

The writ is the proper place in which to state the character in which the parties sue or are sued. Where parties sue or are sued in a representative character, the indorsement on the writ must show the fact by specifically stating in what capacity they sue or are sued. (Order III. r. 4.) And this is so even when the writ is only indorsed generally; and the Statement of Claim in that case must correspond with the writ.

Here is a precedent of a general indorsement:—

The plaintiff's claim is for damages for wrongfully entering the plaintiff's land, known as Red Meadow, Whitchurch, in the county of Southampton; and for an injunction restraining the defendants, their servants, workmen, and agents, from entering on the plaintiff's said meadow, or from destroying or otherwise injuring the hedge or fence on the east side thereof, or from erecting or causing to be erected a wooden or other fence on the said east side thereof, or from in any way interfering with the plaintiff's use and enjoyment of the said meadow.

(iii.) INDORSEMENT FOR AN ACCOUNT.

In all cases of ordinary account, as a partnership, executorship, or ordinary trust account, the plaintiff may indorse a claim for such account on his writ. (Order III. r. 8.) In such a case, if the defendant fails to appear, an order for the account claimed will be forthwith made as of course; if he does appear, the order will nevertheless be made, unless the defendant shows that there is some preliminary question to be tried. (Order XV. r. 1.) The application for such order may be made at any time after the time for entering an appearance has expired.

The Queen's Bench Division has not the requisite machinery for taking complicated accounts. Where this has to be done, it is better to transfer the action to the Chancery Division. (*Leslie* v. *Clifford*, 50 L. T. 590.) But if the account is a simple one, it can be taken promptly and expeditiously in the Queen's Bench Division. (*York* v. *Stowers*, W. N. (1883) p. 174.) In either Division questions of account and actions involving the taking of accounts may be referred to a special or to an official referee under either sect. 13 or sect. 14 of the Arbitration Act, 1889. When that is done, the official referee is not bound to take the account in the strict way usually adopted before a Chief Clerk in Chancery Chambers: he may adopt that method if he thinks it convenient or any other method that, in his opinion, will best advance the ends of justice. (*In re Taylor; Turpin* v. *Pain*, 44 Ch. D. 128; 59 L. J. Ch. 803; 38 W. R. 422; 62 L. T. 754.)

INDORSEMENT FOR AN ACCOUNT, *under Order III. r. 8.*

"The plaintiffs' claim is for 932*l.*, monies had and received by the defendant as the plaintiffs' agent, on their behalf, and for their use; and also for an account of all monies had and received by the defendant as such agent, and for payment of the amount found due on taking such account."

Or thus:—

"The plaintiff's claim is as trustee in bankruptcy of one James Smith for 640*l*. 1*s*. 10½*d*., money payable by the defendant to the plaintiff for goods sold and delivered by the said J. S. to the defendant, and for money received by the defendant to the use of the said J. S., and for an account of all mutual dealings between the defendant and the said J. S. from May 3rd, 1877, up to the present time, and of all monies received by the defendant from the said J. S. between those dates, and for an order for the payment to the plaintiff of the amount found due to him on taking such account."

Chapter VII.

STATEMENT OF CLAIM.

A STATEMENT of Claim should state the material facts upon which the plaintiff relies and then claim the relief he desires. As "pleadings now are to be merely concise statements of the facts which the party pleading deems material to his case," it is unnecessary to particularise the form of action in which the relief would in former days have had to be sought. To state what form the plaintiff's right takes is to state a conclusion of law; the Court will draw the proper inference from the facts alleged. (*Hanmer* v. *Flight*, 24 W. R. 346; 35 L. T. 127.)

Forms of action are in fact abolished: it is now no longer necessary to state on the pleadings whether the plaintiff is suing in trespass or on the case, in detinue or in trover. This is a most important and most valuable alteration. Formerly, everything turned on the form of action in which the plaintiff elected to sue. If he sued on a money count and it turned out that there was a special contract, he was non-suited and had to pay the costs of the first action, before he could bring another on the special contract. (See *White* v. *The Gt. W. Rail. Co.*, 2 C. B. N. S. 7.) Again, if he sued in trespass and trespass did not lie, the plaintiff was non-suited, although trover or detinue would lie. In all the old reports, the form of action is always stated first in capitals. And the Court never decided that *no* action lay on such a set of facts; but only that the action did not lie in that form. There were seven different forms of *personal* actions: debt, covenant, assumpsit, detinue, trespass, trespass on the case, and replevin; there were three *real* actions: *

---

* The other real actions had been abolished by the 3 & 4 Will. IV. c. 27.

dower, writ of right of dower, and *quare impedit;* and one *mixed* action : ejectment. And in some cases, it was only by a costly process of elimination that a plaintiff could ascertain for certain what his proper remedy was.

This strictness had undoubted advantages. It taught barristers to be precise. And to this day it affords one of the best means of testing a point of law. Ask a lawyer of the old school whether an action would lie, if one guest at a shooting party shot another by accident through the hedge, there being no negligence on the part of either, and he will approach the question by asking himself, would trespass lie? or must the injured man sue in case? But it was clearly bad for the suitors, who deserve some consideration, and it has accordingly been abolished. Each party now states the facts on which he relies; and the Court will declare the law arising upon the facts pleaded.

"Where the writ is specially indorsed under Order III. r. 6, no further Statement of Claim shall be delivered, but the indorsement on the writ shall be deemed to be the Statement of Claim." (Order XX. r. 1 (a).) This is so although the defendant on entering an appearance demands a Statement of Claim. (*G.* v. *H.*, W. N. (1883) p. 233.) If the plaintiff desires in any way to add to or vary the statement indorsed on his writ, he must deliver an amended Statement of Claim, which he can do once without leave. (Order XXVIII. r. 2.)

Where, however, the writ is generally indorsed, a separate Statement of Claim is almost invariably delivered. If the defendant on entering appearance requires one, a Statement of Claim *must* be delivered and that within five weeks from the time when the plaintiff has notice of this requirement. If the defendant does not require one, still the plaintiff *may* deliver one, if he thinks fit, and he will generally be wise to do so; in which case, he must deliver it within six weeks after appearance has been entered.

"Whenever a Statement of Claim is delivered the plaintiff may therein alter, modify, or extend his claim without any amendment of the indorsement of the writ." (Order XX. r. 4.) But he may not add* new parties, though he may drop some of those named on the writ. Nor may he increase the total sum claimed on the writ, though he may re-adjust the items making up that amount. If any party to the action is improperly† or imperfectly named on the writ, the misnomer should be corrected in the Statement of Claim, by inserting the right name with a statement that the party misnamed had sued or been sued by the name in the writ, *e.g.*, "John William Smythe (sued as 'J. M. Smith')." The defendant can take no advantage of such an alteration; pleas in abatement for misnomer were abolished as long ago as 1834.

A plaintiff may include in his Statement of Claim any number of causes of action which *existed at the date of writ*, though not referred to therein. But Order XX. r. 4, does not entitle a plaintiff to claim any damages in his Statement of Claim in respect of a cause of action which has accrued *since* the date of writ. Damages accruing since writ from a cause of action vested in the plaintiff before writ can be recovered. (See Order XXXVI. r. 58.) But if plaintiff wishes to recover damages in respect of a new cause of action, which has vested

---

* To add fresh parties, an order under Order XIII. rr. 11, 12, must be obtained. But a Statement of Claim may narrow the scope of the writ. The plaintiff is not bound to continue the action against all the defendants named in the writ. He may drop some and proceed against the others without any order by merely not delivering his pleading to them. As, however, at the expiration of the time allowed for the delivery of the Statement of Claim, the defendants not proceeded against will certainly apply by summons under Order XXIX. r. 1, to have the action dismissed with costs as against them for want of prosecution, it is better to serve such defendants with a notice of discontinuance under Order XXVI. The Statements of Claim served on the other defendants, who are kept as parties to the action, must be identical in their contents.

† But where a defendant has executed a deed by a wrong name, it is right to sue him by the name in which he executed it. See *Williams* v. *Bryant*, 5 M. & W. 447; *Mayor of Lynn's Case*, 10 Rep. 122, b.

in him since the date of the writ, he must issue a second writ. He can then apply to have the two actions consolidated, if they can conveniently be tried together.

" Where the plaintiff seeks relief in respect of several distinct claims or causes of complaint founded upon separate and distinct grounds they shall be stated, as far as may be, separately and distinctly." (Order XX. r. 7.) Relief may be claimed against one or more defendants either solely, jointly, severally, or in the alternative. (Order XVI. rr. 1, 6; *Bagot* v. *Easton*, 7 Ch. D. 1 ; 47 L. J. Ch. 225.) It is not necessary that every defendant should be interested as to all the relief prayed for; or as to every cause of action included in the proceedings. (Order XVI. r. 5.) But the plaintiff will, of course, have to pay the costs of any defendant unnecessarily or improperly joined.

A plaintiff should always avail himself of all his causes of action, *e.g.*, his pleader should set out every covenant that there is any ground for believing broken ; and allege every available breach of each such covenant.

Illustrations.

A repairing lease generally contains three concurrent covenants as to repairs :
(a.) A general covenant to repair.
(b.) A covenant to repair on three months notice.
(c.) A covenant to paint the outside once in every three years, and the inside once in every seven years.

Each of these is distinct and severable from the others, and every breach of any one of them is a separate cause of action : therefore set out all three and allege that each is broken, as you may win on one, though you fail on the others.

By a deed of submission the defendant covenanted to perform the award when made and also to do nothing to prevent the arbitrators from making their award. The plaintiff sued on the award, alleging that the defendant had not performed the award in this, that he had not paid the sum awarded. The defendant pleaded that before the award was made he had by deed revoked the authority of the arbitrators. The Court held that the defendant was entitled thus to revoke their authority (as the law then stood; it is otherwise now : see sect. 1 of the Arbitration Act, 1889), and that the plea was an answer to the breach alleged and gave judgment for the defendant. But at the same time they pointed out that the defendant's conduct in thus revoking the authority of the arbitrators was a clear breach of the defendant's covenant not to prevent them from making their award, and that the plaintiff would have won the action if he had alleged that as a breach.

Marsh v. *Bulteel*, 5 Barn. & Ald. 507.

It is often desirable to commence a Statement of Claim with some introductory averments stating who the parties are, what business they carry on, how they are related or connected, and other surrounding circumstances leading up to the dispute. These are called *matters of inducement*, because they explain what follows, though they are in no way essential to the cause of action. A good pleader always reduces such prefatory statements to a minimum, and states them as concisely as possible. Next should come the essential portions of the claim, *i.e.*, the statement of the plaintiff's right which he alleges has been broken; and then the statement of the breach or wrong complained of. Then comes the allegation of damage, and last the claim for relief.

This order should always be followed in spite of the precedents set out in Appendix C. to the Rules of the Supreme Court of 1883. What can be more illogical than such a Statement of Claim as Appendix C., s. v., No. 10: "The plaintiff has suffered damage by breach of promise by the defendant to marry her on the —— day of ——." Here we have first the damage, then the breach, and last of all the promise. Surely this is "putting the cart before the horse."

Tort.

In an action of tort it is unnecessary to set out the right which has been violated in cases where that right is not peculiar to the plaintiff in any way, but is one possessed by every liege subject. Thus, in actions of libel, slander, false imprisonment, or assault, the claim is merely a statement of the breach. In other cases where the plaintiff claims a special right in himself (*e. g.*, an easement or copyright), the right must be stated with all due particularity. This is especially so in actions for the recovery of land. (See *ante*, p. 52.) And remember that it is not sufficient to allege in a pleading that a right or a duty, or a liability exists; but the facts must be stated which give rise to such right or create such duty or liability. (*Ante*, p. 9.)

Illustrations.

Where a plaintiff claims a right of way he must define the course of the path, state its termini, and show how the right vested in him, whether by prescription or grant.

Harris v. *Jenkins*, 22 Ch. D. 481; 52 L. J. Ch. 437; 31 W. R. 137; 47 L. T. 570.

Farrell v. *Coogan*, 12 L. R. Ir. 14.

But see *Williams* v. *Wilcox*, 8 A. & E. 314; 3 N. & P. 606.

In an action of libel or slander the precise words complained of are material, and they must be set out *verbatim* in the Statement of Claim.

Harris v. *Warre*, 4 C. P. D. 125; 48 L. J. C. P. 310; 27 W. R. 461; 40 L. T. 429.

In an action of slander, always aver, wherever there is any ground for doing so, that the words were spoken of the plaintiff in the way of his trade. This allegation won the demurrer for the plaintiff in *Foulger* v. *Newcomb* (L. R. 2 Ex. 327; 36 L. J. Ex. 169; 15 W. R. 1181; 16 L. T. 595); and had it been present it would probably have saved *Miller* v. *David*, L. R. 9 C. P. 118; 43 L. J. C. P. 84; 22 W. R. 332; 30 L. T. 58. Yet it does not always avail.

See *Shrahan* v. *Ahearne*, Ir. R. 9 C. L. 412.

A foundation should be laid for such an averment by alleging in paragraph 1 that "the plaintiff is a ——, carrying on business at ——, &c."

Contract.

Where the action is brought on a contract, the contract must first be alleged and then its breach. It should clearly appear whether the contract on which the plaintiff relies is express or implied; in the latter case the facts should be stated from which the plaintiff contends a contract should be implied. If the contract be by deed it should be so stated; if it be not by deed, then a consideration must be shown which must not be a past consideration.

Wherever the contract sued on is contained in a written instrument the pleader should shortly state what he conceives to be its legal effect; he should not set out the document itself *verbatim* unless the precise words of the document, or any part of them, are material. (Order XIX. r. 21.) It will be for the defendant, if he disputes the legal effect attributed to it by the plaintiff, to state his own version of the document, or, if he thinks fit, to set it out *verbatim* in the Defence, with an allegation that this is the contract referred to in the Statement of Claim.

The actual contract which was in force between the parties at the date of breach should be the one alleged. If there have at different times been different agreements between the parties, there is no need to go into ancient history. It is sufficient to state the modified contract as it stood when the plaintiff's right of action attached. There is no need to set out the original terms which have been dispensed with. (*Boone* v. *Mitchell*, 1 B. & C. 18; *Carr* v. *Wallachian Petroleum Co.*, L. R. 1 C. P. 636; 35 L. J. C. P. 314.) And contingencies need not be stated, if the events upon which they were contingent never happened; for so they do not affect the plaintiff's right or title.

It is no longer necessary for a plaintiff to allege generally the performance of all conditions precedent as was customary before the Judicature Act. Such an allegation is now implied in his pleading by Order XIX. r. 14. Where, however, the plaintiff is conscious that he has not performed a condition precedent, and has a good excuse for such non-performance, he should in his original pleading state the condition, the non-performance and the facts which afford him his excuse, *e.g.*, that the defendant prevented or discharged him from performing it. (See *post*, p. 167.)

If either the consideration or the promise is in the alternative, this should be stated according to the fact. If the promise or covenant sued on contains an exception or proviso qualifying the defendant's liability, such exception or proviso should be stated; for it would be incorrect to state the contract as an absolute one. But if the covenant or clause in the agreement is absolute in itself without any such exception or proviso, and without any reference to any such clause, it may be stated as an absolute contract; although there may be in a distinct part of the deed or instrument a proviso defeating or qualifying it in certain events. For such proviso is in the nature of a defeazance, and must be set up by the defendant if the facts permit. If, however, the subsequent clause is referred to by some such words as "except as hereinafter excepted," then strictly the exception or proviso ought to be set out in the Statement of Claim.

Illustrations.

The plaintiff sued the defendant for not repairing pursuant to the covenant in his lease, which the plaintiff stated as a covenant to "repair when and as need should require"; and issue was joined on a traverse of the deed alleged. The plaintiff, at the trial, produced the deed in proof, and it appeared that the covenant was to repair "when and as need should require, *and at farthest within three months after notice*"; the latter words having been omitted in the declaration. This was held to be a variance, because the additional words were material and qualified the legal effect of the contract.

Horsefall v. *Testar*, 7 Taunt. 385; 1 Moore, 89.

As to when a plaintiff should declare on a special contract, and when on a *quantum meruit* or an implied contract, see

Head v. *Baldrey*, 6 A. & E. 459; 2 N. & P. 217.

White v. *Gt. W. Ry. Co.*, 2 C. B. N. S. 7; 26 L. J. C. P. 158.

Where there are several covenants in the same deed, some of which are broken and some not, the plaintiff should, of course, omit all allusion to the covenants which he does not allege to have been broken. There is no need for him to set out the whole document. He should first of all set out all the covenants which he alleges have been broken in their order as they occur in the deed, and then allege separately the breach of each covenant in the same order. And in stating the breach he should follow the words of the covenant.

Breach.

The breach of contract, of which the plaintiff complains, must be alleged in the terms of the contract, or in words co-extensive with the effect or meaning of it. Be careful not to add particular breaches so as to narrow or exclude the general averment that the covenant has been broken. (See *Harris* v. *Mantle*, 3 T. R. 307.)

In averring a breach every "and" must be turned into "or." If the contract be to do more things than one, the plaintiff must either state expressly that the defendant had done none of them, or else set out precisely what and how much he has in fact done. And generally the rules as to traversing (*ante*, pp. 81—85) apply to pleading a breach.

Illustrations.

Action on a covenant. The breach was thus assigned: "that the defendant has not used a farm in an husbandlike manner, but on the contrary has committed waste." It was held that the plaintiff could not give any evidence of the defendant's using the farm in an unhusbandlike manner, if it do not amount to waste.

Harris v. *Mantle*, 3 T. R. 307.

This case was cited with approval by Mr. Baron Pollock, and acted on in the *Property Investment County of Scotland* v. *Lucas and Son*, on April 13th, 1886. The learned Baron said: "The case of *Harris* v. *Mantle* (3 T. R. 307) was decided by one of the greatest lawyers of the day in my early time, and although it sounds like a technical decision, it is one of the most sensible decisions ever made."

If the covenant or promise is in the alternative, the breach must allege that the defendant did not do either the one act or the other.

Legh v. *Lillie*, 6 H. & N. 165; 30 L. J. Ex. 25.

If the contract be to pay a sum of money, *e.g.*, 500*l.*, the breach alleged must be not merely that the defendant did not pay 500*l.*; the plaintiff must add the words "or any part thereof," or else state how much has been paid and give the defendant credit for that amount, claiming only the balance.

So, again, if the promise be to pay on a particular day, the plaintiff must not merely allege that the defendant has not paid the money on that day, he must add the words "or at all."

If the covenant be to deliver up certain boats and masts and nets and tackle on a certain day, the breach must be assigned that the defendant never delivered up any of the said boats or masts or nets or tackle.

Damages.

As to the allegation of damage, the distinction between special and general damages must be carefully observed. General damage is such as the law will presume to be the natural or probable consequence of the defendant's act. It arises by inference of law, and need not, therefore, be proved by evidence, and may be averred generally.

Special damage, on the other hand, is such a loss as the law will not presume to be the consequence of the defendant's act, but which depends in part, at least, on the special circumstances of the case. It must therefore be always explicitly claimed on the pleadings, and at the trial it must be proved by evidence both that the loss was incurred, and that it was the direct result of the defendant's conduct. A mere expectation or apprehension of loss is not sufficient, and no damages can be recovered unless they are either the natural and necessary consequences of the defendant's act, or such consequences as he in fact contemplated when he did it. All other damage is held "remote." In many cases, proof of special damage is essential to the right of action; in these the writ must not be issued till the special damage has accrued, and then it must be alleged with special care and exactness.

Matters in aggravation of damages may be pleaded in the Statement of Claim, as we have seen already, *ante*, p. 26.

Illustrations.

A plaintiff cannot prove that he has lost particular customers, unless he states their names, either in his pleading or particulars.

The plaintiff alleged that in consequence of the defendant's slander, she had "lost several suitors." This was held too general an allegation; for the names of the suitors, if there were any, could hardly have escaped the plaintiff's memory.

Barnes v. *Prudlin vel Bruddel*, 1 Sid. 396; Ventr. 4; 1 Lev. 261; 2 Keb. 451.

Where a plaintiff claimed generally for loss of his lodgers, he was not allowed to prove the loss of a particular lodger.

Westwood v. *Cowne*, 1 Stark. 172.

But where a plaintiff can prove a general loss of business or custom without having recourse to particular instances, he will be allowed to allege and prove this generally.

Rose v. *Groves*, 5 M. & Gr. 613; 12 L. J. C. P. 251.

In an action for an imprisonment, the plaintiff cannot prove as damage that he suffered in health, unless he charged it in the Statement of Claim.

Pettit v. *Addington*, Peake, 62.

Or that he was stinted of food in prison.

Lowden v. *Goodrick*, Peake, 46.

Claim for Relief.

"Every Statement of Claim shall state specifically the relief which the plaintiff claims, either simply or in the alternative, and it shall not be necessary to ask for general or other relief which may always be given, as the Court or a judge may think just, to the same extent as if it had been asked for." (Order XX. r. 6.)

Before this rule it was usual on the Chancery side to end every Statement of Claim thus:—

"(vi.) Such further or other relief as the nature of the case may require.

"(vii.) Costs."

But this was always unnecessary, and is now unusual.

On the common law side, the usual ending was, and is, "And the plaintiff claims £—— damages." Be sure to claim enough.

Where the plaintiff's claim can be ascertained exactly, the pleader should, of course, claim only the precise amount, with a sufficient margin for interest, if the plaintiff is entitled to any. But where he cannot be exact, it is wiser to make too large rather than too small a claim, for if the jury find a larger amount than the plaintiff claimed, that amount cannot be recovered without amending the writ, and such an amendment would only be allowed after verdict in an exceptional case. But the judge has power to make such an amendment, if he think fit.

(Order XXVIII. r. 1; and see *Knowlman* v. *Bluett*, L. R. 9 Ex. 1; 43 L. J. Ex. 29.)

But while the common law Courts could only compensate an injured plaintiff by awarding him damages, or ordering his goods or land to be restored to him, equity Courts, even where recognizing and enforcing exactly the same primary rights and liabilities as the common law Courts, applied different remedies to protect and enforce them. And much of the value of the Chancery system depended upon the efficiency of these remedies. Where the common law could award damages for a wrong when committed, equity could prevent its commission. Where law could give damages for a breach of contract, equity could enforce its specific performance. Where law could give damages for fraud or breach of faith, equity could declare the property affected by it to be held in trust for the injured party, in fact, to be his property. And now, by sub-sect. 1 of sect. 24 of the Judicature Act, 1873, " If any plaintiff or petitioner claims to be entitled to any equitable estate or right, or to relief upon any equitable ground against any deed, instrument, or contract, or against any right, title, or claim whatsoever, asserted by any defendant or respondent in such cause or matter, or to any relief founded upon a legal right, which heretofore could only have been given by a Court of equity, the said Courts respectively, and every judge thereof, shall give to such plaintiff or petitioner such and the same relief as ought to have been given by the Court of Chancery in a suit or proceeding for the same or the like purpose properly instituted before the passing of this Act." Hence, now every kind of equitable relief can be claimed in an action in the Queen's Bench Division. And even where it is not claimed, yet if the right to it appear incidentally in the course of the proceedings, the appropriate relief will be granted. Thus, a plaintiff is, in a proper case, entitled to a receiver, even though he has not asked for one on his writ or Statement of Claim. (*Colebourne* v. *Colebourne*, 1 Ch. D. 690, is overruled by

Jessel, M. R., in *Salt* v. *Cooper*, 16 Ch. D. 544; 50 L. J. Ch. 529; and see *Gwatkin* v. *Bird*, 52 L. J. Q. B. 263.)

Prior to October, 1883, a plaintiff could not bring an action merely in order to obtain a declaration of title in a case where the facts showed no right to any consequential relief. (See Wilson, Jud. Acts, 5th ed. p. 302.) But it is now provided by Order XXV. r. 5, that "No action or proceeding shall be open to objection, on the ground that a merely declaratory judgment or order is sought thereby, and the Court may make binding declarations of right, whether any consequential relief is or could be claimed or not." (See *Hendry* v. *Turner*, 32 Ch. D. 355; 55 L. J. Ch. 562; *Hobbs* v. *Wayet*, 36 Ch. D. 256; 56 L. J. Ch. 819.)

An injunction should be claimed whenever there is any reason to apprehend any repetition of the defendant's unlawful act. In such a case it must be averred that the defendant threatens and intends to repeat the unlawful act; it will not be sufficient to set out circumstances from which such an intention can be inferred. (*Stannard* v. *Vestry of St. Giles*, 20 Ch. D. at p. 195; 51 L. J. Ch. 629.)

Remember that a Statement of Claim supersedes the writ; hence, if some special form of relief be claimed on the writ, and not in the Statement of Claim, it will be taken that so much of the claim is abandoned. (*Cargill* v. *Bower*, 10 Ch. D. at p. 508; 47 L. J. Ch. 649; 26 W. R. 716; 38 L. T. 779.)

Venue.*

Lastly, some place of trial must be named, unless the plaintiff desires that the action be tried in Middlesex. "The Statement of Claim must in all cases in which it is proposed that the trial

---

* Formerly, every issue of fact had to be tried by a jury summoned from the place or neighbourhood where the facts occurred, or as it was then called, the *venue* or *visne* (*vicinetum*, neighbourhood). Now the word means merely the place where the action is to be tried.

should be elsewhere than in Middlesex, show the proposed place of trial." (Order XX. r. 5.)

The plaintiff's choice will be determined as a rule by considerations of economy and convenience; he will fix the trial in the place that best suits himself and his witnesses. But if the action be against a newspaper of wide circulation in the district, or if the defendant in any other way is popular or powerful in his own neighbourhood, the plaintiff should decide on Middlesex, where he is sure of an impartial jury. The defendant cannot obtain an order changing the venue, unless he can show that the plaintiff fixed the place of trial arbitrarily or capriciously, or else that there is an overwhelming preponderance of convenience in trying the action elsewhere.

Chapter VIII.

DEFENCE.

The defendant must state in his Defence every material fact on which he proposes to rely at the trial; he must deal specifically with every fact alleged in the Statement of Claim, either admitting or denying it; he may plead further facts in answer to those he admits; he may object to the whole pleading as insufficient in law, or he may rely on a set-off or counterclaim. All these separate grounds of defence must be stated, as far as may be, separately and distinctly, especially where they are founded upon separate and distinct facts. (Order XX. r. 7.)

Any number of defences may be pleaded together in the same action without leave, although they are obviously inconsistent. A defendant may "raise by his Statement of Defence, without leave, as many distinct and separate, and therefore inconsistent, defences as he may think proper, subject only to the provision contained in Order XIX. r. 27," as to striking out embarrassing matter. (*Per* Thesiger, L. J., in *Berdan* v. *Greenwood*, 3 Ex. D. 255; 47 L. J. Ex. 628; 26 W. R. 902; 39 L. T. 223.) And a Defence is not embarrassing merely because it contains inconsistent averments. (*Re Morgan* (C. A.), 35 Ch. D. 492; 56 L. J. Ch. 603; 35 W. R. 705; 56 L. T. 503.)

Equitable defences and counterclaims may now, of course, be pleaded in the Queen's Bench Division. "If any defendant claims to be entitled to any equitable estate or right, or to relief upon any equitable ground against any deed, instrument, or contract, or against any right, title, or claim asserted by any plaintiff or petitioner in such cause or matter, or alleges any ground of equitable defence to any claim of the plaintiff or petitioner in such cause or matter, the said Courts respectively, and every judge thereof, shall give to every equitable estate, right, or ground of relief so claimed, and to every equitable defence so alleged, such and the same effect by way of defence against the claim of such plaintiff or petitioner, as the Court of Chancery ought to have given if the same or the like matters had been relied on by way of defence in any suit or proceeding instituted in that Court for the same or the like purpose before the passing of this Act." (Judicature Act, 1873, s. 24, sub-s. 2. And see *Mostyn* v. *West Mostyn Coal and Iron Co., Limited*, 1 C. P. D. 145; 45 L. J. C. P. 401; 24 W. R. 401; 34 L. T. 325.) Equitable defences must be pleaded fully. (*Sutcliffe* v. *James*, 40 L. T. 875; *Heap* v. *Marris*, 2 Q. B. D. 630; 46 L. J. Q. B. 761.)

Denials must be specific.

"It shall not be sufficient for a defendant, in his Statement of Defence, to deny generally the grounds alleged by the Statement of Claim, but EACH PARTY MUST DEAL SPECIFICALLY WITH EACH ALLEGATION OF FACT OF WHICH HE DOES NOT ADMIT THE TRUTH, except damages." (Order XIX. r. 17.)

And in order that the pleader may fully understand what is meant by "dealing specifically," other rules are added.

"Every allegation of fact in any pleading, not being a petition or summons, if not denied specifically or by necessary implication, or stated to be not admitted in the pleading of the opposite party, shall be taken to be admitted." (Order XIX. r. 13.)

"When a party in any pleading denies an allegation of fact in the previous pleading of the opposite party, he must not do so evasively, but answer the point of substance." (Order XIX. r. 19.)

And instances are given:—

"In actions for a debt or liquidated demand in money, comprised in Order III. r. 6, a mere denial of the debt shall be inadmissible." (Order XXI. r. 1.)

"In actions upon bills of exchange, promissory notes, or cheques, a defence in denial must deny some matter of fact, *e.g.*, the drawing, making, endorsing, accepting, presenting, or notice of dishonour of the bill or note." (Order XXI. r. 2.)

"In actions comprised in Order III. r. 6, classes (a) and (b), a defence in denial must deny such matters of fact from which the liability of the defendant is alleged to arise as are disputed; *e. g.*, in actions for goods bargained and sold, or sold and delivered, the Defence must deny the order or contract, the delivery, or the amount claimed; in an action for money had and received, it must deny the receipt of the money or the existence of those facts which are alleged to make such receipt by the defendant a receipt to the use of the plaintiff." (Order XXI. r. 3.)

"If it be alleged that he received a certain sum of money, it shall not be sufficient to deny that he received that particular amount, but he must deny that he received that sum, or any part thereof, or else set out how much he received." (Order XIX. r. 19.)

"If an allegation is made with divers circumstances, it shall not be sufficient to deny it along with those circumstances." (*Ibid.*)

These rules were expressly intended to prevent a defendant's pleading the general issue, as it was called (see *ante*, p. 12), and to make him "take matter by matter, and traverse each of them separately." (*Per* Thesiger, L. J., in *Byrd* v. *Nunn*, 7 Ch. D. at p. 287.)

Illustrations.

Claim for work and labour done. The first paragraph of the Defence was a denial of any indebtedness whatever; the second paragraph pleaded payment; the third paragraph set up special contract under which the work was done. Paragraph 1 was held bad within the above rules. The defendant should have shown why he was not indebted. He was, however, allowed to amend by linking paragraphs 1 and 3 together, the plaintiff having costs in any event.

Copley v. *Jackson*, W. N. (1884) p. 39.

But in order to deny specifically, it is not necessary to write out every sentence in the Statement of Claim and traverse it in detail. It is sufficient to plead that "the defendant denies each of the allegations contained in paragraph 3." This will have the same effect as copying out the whole paragraph, and constantly inserting "not." But it will not do more than traverse the main allegation in each sentence in that paragraph. All matters, such as those referred to in pp. 80, 81, must still, of course, be specially pleaded.

There are, however, *three* exceptions to the rule that a defendant must deal specifically with every allegation of fact in the Statement of Claim which he does not admit. All three are legacies from the old procedure; the first is a very sensible and proper provision; but I fail to see any sufficient reason for the preservation of the other two exceptions.

(i.) *Do not Plead to Damages.*

"No denial or defence shall be necessary as to damages claimed or their amount; but they shall be deemed to be put in issue in all cases, unless expressly admitted." (Order XXI. r. 4.)

Observe that the rule distinctly says that no denial or defence is necessary as to damages claimed or their amount, hence it must surely apply to cases where damage is part of the cause of action, as well as those in which the action lies without proof of special damage, although I note that the learned authors of Bullen and Leake's Precedents of Pleadings hold the contrary opinion. (4th ed. Part II. at p. 349.)

Illustrations.

Action of trespass for chasing sheep, *per quod* the sheep died. It is not necessary to traverse expressly the dying of the sheep.

Leech v. *Widsley*, Vent. 54; 1 Lev. 283.

Action for not properly building a ship, according to covenant, whereby she was obliged to put back and was detained. A plea "to so much of the declaration as relates to the detaining," was held bad.
Porter v. *Izat*, 1 M. & W. 381; 1 Tyr. & G. 639.
And see *Smith* v. *Thomas*, 2 Bing. N. C. 378; 4 Dowl. 333.

(ii.) *Not Guilty by Statute.*

"Nothing in these rules contained shall affect the right of any defendant to plead 'Not guilty by statute.' And every defence of 'Not guilty by statute' shall have the same effect as a plea of 'Not guilty by statute' has heretofore had. But if the defendant so plead, he shall not plead any other defence to the same cause of action without the leave of the Court or a judge." (Order XIX. r. 12.)

"In every case in which a party shall plead the general issue, intending to give the special matter in evidence by virtue of an Act of Parliament, he shall insert in the margin of his pleading the words 'by statute,' together with the year of the reign in which the Act of Parliament on which he relies was passed, and also the chapter and section of such Act, and shall specify whether such Act is public or otherwise; otherwise such defence shall be taken not to have been pleaded by virtue of any Act of Parliament." (Order XXI. r. 19.)

The following are some of the more important cases in which this plea may be pleaded:—In all penal actions (21 Jac. I. c. 4, s. 4); in actions of trespass or on the case relating to distress for rent (11 Geo. II. c. 19, s. 21); in actions against justices of the peace or their assistants for anything done by them in the execution of their office (11 & 12 Vict. c. 44, s. 17); in actions against the bailiff of a city or town corporate, constable, churchwardens, or overseers of the poor and their deputies (7 Jac. I. c. 5; and 21 Jac. I. c. 12, s. 5); in respect of things done under the Larceny Act (24 & 25 Vict. c. 96, s. 113); or under the Malicious Injuries to Property Act (24 & 25 Vict. c. 97, s. 71); in respect of offences relating to the coin (24 & 25 Vict. c. 99, s. 33); and there are other statutes which will be found cited in Bullen & Leake (4th ed. pt. 2, pp. 433—435), conferring the same privilege on officers, county police, constables, &c., in respect of all acts done by them in the honest discharge of their official duties. It is quite right that these gentlemen should be protected in every way from vexatious actions. But why should they not be required either to admit or deny each allegation in the Statement of Claim, as everyone else is? As it is, they must do so the moment interrogatories are addressed to them.

(iii.) *Possession of Land.*

By Order XXI. r. 21, "No defendant in an action for the recovery of land who is in possession by himself or his tenant need plead his title unless his defence depends on an equitable estate or right, or he claims relief upon any equitable ground against any right or title asserted by the plaintiff. But, except in cases hereinbefore mentioned, it shall be sufficient to state by way of defence that he is so in possession, and it shall be taken to be implied in such statement that he denies, or does not admit, the allegations of fact contained in the plaintiff's Statement of Claim. He may, nevertheless, rely upon any ground of defence which he can prove except as hereinbefore mentioned."

The defendant in an action for the recovery of land is never bound to disclose his title or want of title. The plaintiff must recover on the strength of his own title, not on the weakness of his adversary's title. And no one would wish to disturb these settled rules of law. But it does not follow that the defendant should be permitted to put the plaintiff to unnecessary trouble and expense by implicitly denying, under colour of this plea of possession, well-known and indisputable facts. The plaintiff must set out his title in full detail, stating each separate link. (*Philipps* v. *Philipps*, 4 Q. B. D. 127.) Why should not the defendant be called on to admit, or to deny expressly, each of these allegations? He need not disclose his own title, but is it too much to ask him to admit, for instance, that J. S., some common ancestor, died in 1803? If he were made to admit or deny expressly each link in the plaintiff's chain of title, the issue would be narrowed down to one or two simple questions of fact, or perhaps to a mere point of law as to the construction of a deed or will, which could be taken direct to a Divisional Court in the shape of a special case. Some facts in any event would be admitted, for the defendant would have the fear of Order XXI. r. 9, before his eyes; and thus expense would be saved. Whereas this is what now takes place: the plaintiff delivers his claim, which invariably concludes with the statement that the defendant is in possession and refuses to deliver up possession to the plaintiff, &c. Then, for his sole defence, the defendant pleads the very thing which the plaintiff has already said against him, viz., that he is in possession. And on that the plaintiff must join issue, thus denying in his Reply the fact which he himself alleged in his claim, in flat defiance of rule 16 of Order XIX. And the parties eventually come into Court apparently to try as the sole issue in the action the one fact on which they are both agreed!

Special Defences.

"The defendant must raise by his pleading all matters which show the action not to be maintainable, or that the transaction is either void or voidable in point of law, and all such grounds of defence as if not raised would be likely to take the opposite party by surprise, or would raise issues of fact not arising out of the preceding pleadings, as, for instance, fraud, Statute of Limitations, release, payment, performance, facts showing illegality either by statute or common law, or Statute of Frauds." (Order XIX. r. 15.)

"When a contract, promise, or agreement is alleged in any pleading, a bare denial of the same by the opposite party shall be construed only as a denial in fact of the express contract, promise, or agreement alleged, or of the matters of fact from which the same may be implied by law, and not as a denial of the legality or sufficiency in law of such contract, promise, or agreement, whether with reference to the Statute of Frauds or otherwise." (Order XIX. r. 20.)

In all such cases the fresh facts on which the defence is based must be specially pleaded. The defendant must moreover distinctly specify in his pleading any condition precedent, the performance or occurrence of which he intends to contest;

otherwise the performance or occurrence of all conditions precedent necessary to establish the plaintiff's case will be admitted. (Order XIX. r. 14. See *ante*, p. 24.)

Plea of the Statute of Frauds.

"There is no memorandum in writing of the alleged contract sufficient to satisfy the Statute of Frauds." It is not necessary to plead any particular section, and it is wiser not to do so. For if you specify sect. 4, you will not be allowed to avail yourself of sect. 7, unless the judge will give you leave to amend, which he refused to do in *James* v. *Smith*, (1891) 1 Ch. 384; 63 L. T. 524.

Plea of the Statute of Limitations.

"The plaintiff's cause of action, if any, did not accrue within six years before this suit, and the defendant will rely on the Statute 21 Jac. I. c. 16, s. 3."

The objection that the action is brought too late must be raised by a special plea, even though it appear on the face of the Statement of Claim. This was decided as long ago as 1636. (*Hawkings* v. *Billhead*, Cro. Car. 404.)

It is otherwise, however, in an action for the recovery of land. There, if the defendant be in possession of the premises, he need not plead the Statute of Limitations at all; for it is not an equitable defence. If, however, he likes to plead the statute, he should do so in this form:—

"The plaintiff's alleged claim was and is barred by the Real Property Limitation Act, 1874, and the plaintiff's right and title (if any) to the land were extinguished by virtue of that Act and the 3 & 4 Will. IV. c. 27, s. 34." (See *Dawkins* v. *Lord Penrhyn*, 6 Ch. D. 323; 4 App. Cas. 59, 64.)

Payment.

A plea of payment should state that the payment relied on was made before action, and give the date and amount of each instalment, if money was paid on more than one occasion. There is no need, however, for a defendant to plead that he paid the plaintiff before action any sums for which credit is specifically given by the plaintiff in the Statement of Claim or in any particulars; because the plaintiff, in such cases, is considered as suing only for the balance claimed beyond the amount credited; and all pleas will be taken as addressed to such balance.

Accord and Satisfaction.

There must be both. Neither an accord without satisfaction, nor satisfaction without an accord, will constitute a defence. An accord and satisfaction made by a third party on the defendant's behalf, and accepted by the plaintiff in discharge, will be a bar to the action. (*Jones* v. *Broadhurst*, 9 C. B. 173.) As to accord and satisfaction made by one jointly liable with the defendant, see *Bainbridge* v. *Lax*, 9 Q. B. 819; *Thurman* v. *Wild*, 11 A. & E. 453; *Hey* v. *Moorhouse*, 6 Bing. N. C. 52.

Lien.

This defence must be specially pleaded, for it admits the plaintiff's property in the goods he seeks to recover, but states a good reason why he should, for the time, be deprived of the possession of them. It is thus a plea in confession and avoidance. Where it is pleaded, the master may order the goods to be given up to the plaintiff on his paying into Court, to abide the event of the action, the full sum claimed by the defendant as the amount of his lien, together with a further sum for interest and costs. (Order L. r. 8; and see *Gebruder Naf* v. *Ploton* (C. A.), 25 Q. B. D. 13; 59 L. J. Q. B. 371; 38 W. R. 566; 63 L. T. 328.)

Matter arising since Writ.

"Any ground of defence which has arisen after action brought but before the defendant has delivered his Defence, and before the time limited for his doing so has expired, may be raised by the defendant in his Defence, either alone or together with other grounds of defence." (Order XXIV. r. 1.)

"Where any ground of defence arises after the defendant has delivered a Defence, or after the time limited for his doing so has expired, the defendant may within eight days after such ground of defence has arisen, or at any subsequent time by leave of a Court or a judge, deliver a further Defence setting forth the same." (Order XXIV. r. 2.)

"Whenever any defendant in his Defence or in any further Defence as in the last rule mentioned alleges any ground of defence which has arisen after the commencement of the action the plaintiff may deliver a confession of such defence (which confession may be in the Form No. 5, Appendix B., with such variations as circumstances may require), and may thereupon sign judgment for his costs up to the time of the pleading of such defence, unless the Court or a judge shall either before or after the delivery of such confession otherwise order." (Order XXIV. r. 3.)

In olden times when the pleadings were each entered separately on the record, every entry after the first one was called a *continuance*. When the matter of defence arose after writ, but before plea or continuance, it was said to be pleaded "to the further maintenance" of the action. When it arose after plea or continuance, it was called a plea of *puis darrein continuance*—since the last continuance. (See 1 H. & C. 697.)

Former Proceedings.

That the plaintiff brought a previous action and recovered damages against the same defendant for the same cause of action, is a bar to any subsequent action, even though fresh damage has since arisen from the defendant's unlawful act; for the jury in the former action must be taken to have assessed the damages once for all, and the probability or possibility that this subsequent damage would follow should have been submitted to their consideration then. Whether there is not an exception to this rule in the case where damage is essential to the cause of action, was much discussed in *Darley Main Colliery Co.* v. *Mitchell* (11 App. Cas. 127; 55 L. J. Q. B. 529; 54 L. T. 882), and Lord Blackburn unfortunately differed from Lord Bramwell (11 App. Cas. pp. 143, 145). I think, however, after the decision in that case, the better opinion is that a second action will lie for fresh special damage, in cases where special damage is part of the cause of action.

So, too, a previous recovery against another person may be a bar to the present action, if the former defendant was jointly concerned with the present defendant in the very cause of action now sued on. Thus, if A. and B. be in partnership, a previous judgment recovered against A. would be a bar to any action against B. for the same cause of action, even though the judgment obtained in the prior action be not satisfied. (*Brown* v. *Wootton*, Cro. Jac. 73; Yelv. 67; *King* v. *Hoare*, 13 M. & W. 494, 504; *Brinsmead* v. *Harrison*, L. R. 7 C. P. 547; 41 L. J. C. P. 190; 20 W. R. 784; 27 L. T. 99; *Munster* v. *Cox*, 1 Times L. R. 542; *Houston* v. *Sligo*, 29 Ch. D. 448; 52 L. T. 96; *Hammond* v. *Schofield*, (1891) 1 Q. B. 453.) But this is only because they ought to have been sued jointly, and could, even before the Judicature Act, have been so sued. Where two are severally liable, judgment against one is no bar to an action against the other.

So, if the prior action was unsuccessful, this will also be a bar to the action, unless, indeed, the plaintiff was only non-suited on some technical ground, and the judge, in giving judgment of nonsuit, expressly declared that it was a common law nonsuit, and that the plaintiff might bring a second action.

But it must be clear that the cause of action is the same in both cases. As to this, see *Serrao* v. *Noel*, 15 Q. B. D. 549.

The defence of *res judicata* cannot be raised unless it is

specially pleaded in the Defence. (*Ederain* v. *Cohen* (C. A.), 43 Ch. D. 187; 38 W. R. 8, 177; 62 L. T. 17.)

Estoppel.

An estoppel must always* be specially pleaded, unless it appears on the face of the adverse pleading, when it is ground for an objection in point of law. It cannot be pleaded by a stranger to the estoppel. (*Butts* v. *Bilke*, 4 Price, 240.) A plea of estoppel should state the facts on which the party pleading relies as constituting the estoppel, and should also specify the allegations which it is alleged the other party is precluded from proving.† A plea of estoppel must always be drafted with great care and particularity. It is one of those pleas of which it was said in former days that it "must be of certain intent in every particular," *i.e.*, it must meet and exclude by anticipation every possible answer of the adversary.

Plea in Abatement.

There was only one other plea in which certainty was required in every particular. And that was a plea in abatement. The judges were very strict over such a plea, as may be seen in *Digby* v. *Alexander*, 8 Bing. 416.

Formerly the law and practice as to "parties" was of the

---

* It was formerly held that an estoppel by *record* or *deed* must be specially pleaded or it would not be available (*Bowman* v. *Rostron*, 2 A. & E. 295, n.); but that an estoppel *in pais* might be given in evidence without being specially pleaded. (*Freeman* v. *Cooke*, 2 Exch. 654; *Phillips* v. *Im Thurn*, 18 C. B. N. S. 400.) But now it is, I think, clear that the facts which are said to amount to an estoppel are material facts and should be specially pleaded.

† Formerly such a plea always concluded thus:—"Wherefore he prays judgment, if the plaintiff ought to be admitted, against his own acknowledgment, by his deed aforesaid" (or otherwise, according to the matter of the estoppel), "to say that" (stating the allegation to which the estoppel relates). *Veale* v. *Warner*, 1 Wms. Saund. 325.

utmost importance, misjoinder of a plaintiff being ground of nonsuit, while non-joinder of a necessary plaintiff was the subject of a plea in abatement. In actions founded upon a contract, the non-joinder as defendant of a co-contractor was ground for a plea in abatement. But the non-joinder of a necessary co-plaintiff, though it might be objected to by such plea, was even more serious; as the defendant might, if he thought fit, traverse the alleged contract and thus show a variance at the trial; or, where the declaration showed the defect, he might demur. The non-joinder of a defendant in an action of tort never was any ground of objection. A defendant cannot plead in abatement or in bar that another joint wrong-doer has not been made a co-defendant. (*Mitchell* v. *Tarbutt and others*, 5 T. R. 649.) For all persons engaged in a common wrongful act are liable jointly and severally for the consequent damage. (Co. Litt. 232 a; 1 Wms. Saund. 291 f; *Sutton* v. *Clarke*, 6 Taunt. 29.)

But now, by Order XXI. r. 20, "No plea or defence shall be pleaded in abatement." If the defendant considers that the proper parties are not before the Court, his remedy is to take out a summons under Order XIII. r. 12, to add or strike out or substitute a plaintiff or a defendant. If, for instance, the plaintiff sues the defendant alone for a debt due from his firm, he should apply to have his partners joined as co-defendants, if they are still alive and within jurisdiction. And in every case where a plea in abatement in respect of non-joinder could formerly have been pleaded (see *ante*, p. 67), the defendant may (subject to the rules as to one or more persons representing all the parties, such as Order XVI. rr. 9 and 37) take out a summons to add the party who ought to have been joined, the action, where necessary, being in the meantime stayed. (See *Kendall* v. *Hamilton*, 4 App. Cas. 504; 48 L. J. C. P. 705; 28 W. R. 97; 41 L. T. 418; *Sheehan* v. *Gt. E. Rail. Co.*, 16 Ch. D. 59; 50 L. J. Ch. 68; 29 W. R. 69; 43 L. T. 432; *Werder*-

man v. *Société Générale*, 19 Ch. D. 246; 30 W. R. 33; 45 L. T. 514; *Pilley* v. *Robinson*, 20 Q. B. D. 155; 57 L. J. Q. B. 54; 36 W. R. 269; 58 L. T. 110.)

Fraud.

Where fraud is intended to be charged, it must be distinctly charged, and its details specified. General allegations, however strong, are insufficient to amount to an averment of fraud of which any Court ought to take notice. (*Wallingford* v. *Mutual Society*, 5 App. Cas. 697; 50 L. J. Q. B. 49; *Lawrance* v. *Lord Norreys*, 15 App. Cas. 221; 59 L. J. Ch. 681.) Counsel must insist on being fully instructed before placing a plea of fraud on the record. Such a plea should never be pleaded on insufficient material, nor without a marginal note warning the defendant that by adopting such an aggressive line of defence he may double or treble the amount of damages which he may ultimately have to pay.

Justification in Libel and Slander.

This also is a most dangerous plea, and should never be placed on the record without careful consideration of the sufficiency of the evidence by which it is to be supported, for the strictest proof is required (see *Leyman* v. *Latimer*, 3 Ex. D. 15, 352; 47 L. J. Ex. 470; 25 W. R. 751; 26 W. R. 305; 37 L. T. 360, 819); and, if it be not proved, the defendant's persistence in the charge is some evidence of malice, and will always tend to aggravate the damages given against him. The defence cannot be raised without a special plea; and counsel should never draw such a plea without express instructions, and even then should always caution the defendant as to the risk he runs.

Where it appears from the Statement of Claim that the defendant did not make a direct charge himself, but only repeated what A. said, then a general plea that the words are true will be insufficient. (*Duncan* v. *Thwaites*, 3 B. & C. 556.) The defendant must plead and prove not only that A. said so, but in addition that what A. said was true.

Privilege.

Formerly, it was unnecessary specially to plead privilege; this defence was available under the plea of Not Guilty, as it still is in criminal cases. (*Lillie* v. *Price*, 5 A. & E. 645.) But since the Judicature Act, privilege must be specially pleaded, and facts and circumstances must also be stated showing why and how the occasion is privileged. (Order XIX. r. 18; *Spackman* v. *Gibney*, Ex. D. (not reported); *Simmonds* v. *Dunne*, Ir. R. 5 C. L. 358.)

But any plea which wears a doubtful aspect, which may be either a justification, or a mere traverse, or a plea of privilege, will be struck out at chambers as embarrassing. (*Carr* v. *Duckett*, 5 H. & N. 783; 29 L. J. Ex. 468; *Brembridge* v. *Latimer*, 12 W. R. 878; 10 L. T. 816; *O'Keefe* v. *Cardinal Cullen*, Ir. R. 7 C. L. 319.)

Rescission.

This must be specially pleaded. It is a useful plea in an action of breach of promise of marriage.

Tender.

"The defendant, before action, to wit, on March 23rd 1891, tendered and offered to the plaintiff to pay him the sum of £——, which the plaintiff now claims in this action, but the plaintiff refused to accept it. And the defendant now brings the said sum of £—— into Court ready to be paid to the plaintiff." The sum alleged to have been tendered must be brought into Court. (Order XXII. r. 3.) But this is not an ordinary plea of payment into Court. A plea of tender is a defence proper. If the plaintiff take the money out of Court under Order XXII. r. 7 in satisfaction of his claim, he will not be entitled to his costs, as there is a difference between a payment into Court with a mere denial of liability, and a payment into Court with a plea of tender. In the former case, if the money were taken out in satisfaction, the plaintiff would be entitled to his costs; but not in the latter case. (*Griffiths* v. *Ystradyfodwg School Board*, 24 Q. B. D. 307; 59 L. J. Q. B. 116; 38 W. R. 425.) A plea of tender should state that the tender was *before action*, but the omission of these two words is immaterial, if it can be inferred from the dates given that it was before action. (*Ibid.*, 62 L. T. 151.)

Payment into Court.

If the defendant has no case, and the damages claimed are unliquidated, it is sometimes the best plan (*e. g.*, in some actions of breach of promise of marriage) to put in no defence at all, but to let judgment go by default. The damages will then be assessed by a sheriff's jury, who do not, as a rule, take an extravagant view of the case, and less publicity attends a hearing before the sheriff. But in most cases the better plan is, for a defendant who has no defence, to pay money into Court as amends. This he can do at any stage of the action, and the earlier it is done, the better for the defendant. He must give the plaintiff the notice in Form No. 3, Appendix B., referred to in Order XXII. r. 4, and he must either admit or deny liability to the extent of the amount so paid in.

Payment into Court is not strictly a defence; it is rather an attempt at a compromise. In the vast majority of actions, a defendant is allowed, by the express words of Order LII. r. 1, to pay money into Court, while, at the same time, he denies all liability. This, however, is a somewhat doubtful privilege.

The jury regard a payment into Court as a practical admission of liability to the extent of the amount paid in. Hence it is not wise, as a rule, for a defendant, who has any defence on the merits to the whole action, to pay money into Court.

If, however, he decides to do so, he should pay in a good round sum; generally twice as much as the defendant himself thinks the plaintiff is entitled to, will be about the right amount. As a rule it is not worth while to pay a farthing or a shilling into Court, for it is very improbable that plaintiff will accept that sum, and if the jury do not award more than such contemptuous damages, the judge would probably order the plaintiff to pay his own costs, whether that amount had been paid into Court or not.

Payment into Court shall be signified in the Defence, and the claim or cause of action in satisfaction of which such payment is made shall be specified therein. (Order XXII. r. 2.) Unless defendant, on paying money into Court, at the same time expressly denies liability, such payment is considered to admit the plaintiff's claim (Order XXII. r. 1), and the plaintiff can have the money so paid in paid out to him at his request. (*Ibid.* r. 5.) But if defendant has denied liability in the Defence, the plaintiff may either accept the money in full satisfaction of his claim, and have his costs taxed up to date, or he may go on with the action (in which case the money remains in Court), and if the plaintiff recovers less than the sum paid in, he receives the amount he has recovered, but no costs.

The defendant is entitled to pay money into Court generally, even though the plaintiff's claim is liquidated, and consists of several distinct items. He cannot be ordered to deliver particulars, specifying how much he has paid in to each item; he cannot even be compelled to state in respect of which items the payment is made. (*Paraire* v. *Loibl*, (C. A.), 49 L. J. C. P. 481; 43 L. T. 427.) There is only one exception: "in an action on a bond under the statute 8 & 9 Will. III. c. 11, payment into Court shall be admissible to particular breaches only, and not to the whole action." (Order XXII. r. 1.)

If the defendant has, before Defence, paid money into Court under Order XIV., he can now appropriate the whole, or such part as he thinks fit, of such money to the satisfaction of the plaintiff's claim. (Order XXII. r. 11.) A special form of plea is necessary in this case: "The defendant does not admit that he is under any liability to the plaintiff, but he has paid into Court the sum of £——, pursuant to the order of Master Walton, dated May 15th, 1891, and made under Order XIV. And he now appropriates that sum to the satisfaction of the whole of the plaintiff's claim in this action, which he says it is sufficient to satisfy."

Payment into Court in actions of Libel and Slander.

In actions of libel and slander, however, a defendant is not allowed to pay money into Court at all, if he at the same time deny liability. In those actions, if he pays money into Court at all, he must do so "by way of satisfaction, which shall be taken to admit the claim or cause of action in respect of which the payment is made." (Order XXII. r. 1.) I do not know why this exception is made, but it was made in 1883. Hence, now in such actions no defence denying liability can be pleaded if any money is paid into Court.

Where the words are defamatory in their natural and obvious meaning, and the plaintiff by his innuendo puts on them a more defamatory meaning, the defendant may traverse the innuendo and at the same time pay money into Court, as such a traverse is not in that case "a defence denying liability," provided he makes it clear that the money is paid in to the words without the alleged meaning. (*Mackay* v. *Manchester Press Co.*, 54 J. P. 22; 6 Times L. R. 16.) The form of such a plea is given, *post*, p. 159.

Lord Campbell's Act.

The same rule applies where the case falls within sect. 2 of Lord Campbell's Act. Money must be paid into Court by way of amends at the time any plea under that section is delivered, or it will be treated as a nullity. (8 & 9 Vict. c. 75, s. 2.) Hence no defence denying liability can now be joined with such a plea.

It was formerly the law that the defendant's admission of liability under this section was conditional, and not absolute. (See *per* Pollock, C. B., in *Lafone* v. *Smith*, 4 H. & N. at p. 159; and *per* Channell, B., in *Jones* v. *Mackie*, L. R. 3 Ex. at p. 3.) But the portion of the section on which those decisions were based was repealed in 1879, before Order XXII. r. 1, was framed in its present form. It follows, therefore, that a payment into Court, accompanied by a plea under Lord Campbell's Act, is an absolute admission of liability, and that the above cases are no longer law.

Set-Off and Counterclaim.

"A defendant in an action may set-off, or set up, by way of counterclaim against the claims of the plaintiff, any right or claim, whether such set-off or counterclaim sound in damages or not, and such set-off or counterclaim shall have the same effect as a cross-action, so as to enable the Court to pronounce a final judgment in the same action, both on the original and on the cross-claim. But the Court or a judge may, on the application of the plaintiff before trial, if in the opinion of the Court or judge such set-off or counterclaim cannot be conveniently disposed of in the pending action, or ought not to be allowed, refuse permission to the defendant to avail himself thereof." (Order XIX. r. 3.) It is no longer necessary to have recourse to any cross-action.

"Where any defendant seeks to rely upon any grounds as

supporting a right of counterclaim, he shall, in his Statement of Defence, state specifically that he does so by way of counterclaim." (Order XXI. r. 10.)

"If in any case in which the defendant sets up a counterclaim the action of the plaintiff is stayed, discontinued, or dismissed, the counterclaim may, nevertheless, be proceeded with." (Order XXI. r. 16.)

"Where in any action a set-off or counterclaim is established as a defence against the plaintiff's claim, the Court or a judge may, if the balance is in favour of the defendant, give judgment for the defendant for such balance, or may otherwise adjudge to the defendant such relief as he may be entitled to upon the merits of the case." (Order XXI. r. 17.)

There is still a distinction maintained between a set-off and a counterclaim. A set-off is a statutory defence to an action; a counterclaim is a cross-action. In other words, a set-off remains precisely what a set-off always was under the statute 2 Geo. II. c. 22; and every other kind of cross-claim is a counterclaim. A set-off had always to be specially pleaded, and it existed only in respect of mutual debts of a certain definite character. The two debts must be due in the same right and between the same parties. A claim against the estate of a man deceased could not be set-off against a debt due to him in his lifetime. (*Rees* v. *Watts*, 11 Ex. 410.) Again, both debts must be legal debts, and for a liquidated amount. If either debt sounded in damages (even though they could be easily calculated), or was in the nature of a penalty, or was of an equitable character, there was no set-off.

It is perhaps unfortunate that this distinction should be preserved, but it was difficult to avoid it. If a man die insolvent, or if a company be wound up, the creditors only get a dividend on their claims, while the debtors to the estate must pay up their debts in full. If the same man be both a debtor and a creditor he is naturally anxious to set one amount against the other, and pay up or receive the balance only. And this he may do if he has a strict statutory right of set-off, not otherwise. If he has only a counterclaim for the debt due to him from the estate, he must pay up his debt to the estate in full, and prove in the administration or the winding-up for his dividend. (*Newell* v. *National Provincial Bank*, 1 C. P. D. 496; 45 L. J. C. P. 285; 24 W. R. 458; 34 L. T. 533.)

Again, as a set-off is a defence proper to an action, a plaintiff who brings an action and is met by a set-off equal in amount to his claim must pay the defendant his costs of the whole action; for he has failed in the whole action. Whereas if the defendant can plead only a counterclaim for the same amount the plaintiff will recover his costs of the claim, and the defendant only his costs of the counterclaim, which is treated as a cross-action by the defendant against the plaintiff. "Then," as Brett, L. J., says, in *Baines* v. *Bromley* (C. A.), 6 Q. B. D. at p. 695; 50 L. J. Q. B. 465; 29 W. R. 706; 44 L. T. 915, "the proper principle of taxation, if not otherwise ordered, is to take the claim as if it and its issues were an action, and then to take the counterclaim and its issues as if it were an action, and then to give the *allocatur* for costs for the balance in favour of the litigant in whose favour the balance turns." (See *Shrapnel* v. *Laing*, 20 Q. B. D. 334; 57 L. J. Q. B. 195; 36 W. R. 297; 58 L. T. 705; and *Westacott* v. *Bevan and another*, (1891) 1 Q. B. 774.)

Third Parties.

But the defendant's right is not limited to merely setting off his claim against that of the plaintiff. Not only may he by way of counterclaim set up against the plaintiff any claim, and seek any relief which he could have made the ground of a cross-action at law, or suit in equity; he may claim like relief, if only it relate to or be connected with the original subject of the action, against any third person, whether already a party to the action or not, and make him a defendant to the counterclaim along with the plaintiff. Provision is made for bringing in the necessary new parties in rules 11—15 of Order XXI. A second title must be added at the head of the pleading.

Again, there may be some one from whom the defendant, if himself found liable in the action, has a right to demand contribution or indemnity. He may be sued as a surety, and if found liable, may be entitled to contribution from a co-surety. He may be sued upon a contract which he made as agent for another person, and may be entitled to be indemnified by his principal. In such cases it is obviously desirable to bring in the third person against whom the defendant will ultimately have to seek his remedy, so that the decision as to the defendant's liability in the present action shall be binding and conclusive upon him when in a subsequent proceeding the now defendant seeks his remedy against him. This case is also provided for by rr. 48—54 of Order XVI. But the machinery provided by these rules does not work very satisfactorily; and the rights and liabilities of such third person, when brought in, are not very clearly defined. (See *Edison Swan Co.* v. *Holland*, 33 Ch. D. 497; 56 L. J. Ch. 124; 35 W. R. 178; 55 L. T. 587; 41 Ch. D. 28; 58 L. J. Ch. 525; 37 W. R. 699; 61 L. T. 32; *Re Salmon*, 42 Ch. D. 351, 363; 38 W. R. 150; 61 L. T. 146; *Hammond* v. *Bussey*, 20 Q. B. D. 79, 97; 57 L. J. Q. B. 58; *Byrne* v. *Brown*, 22 Q. B. D. 657; 58 L. J. Q. B. 410; 60 L. T. 651.)

Severing Defences.

If counsel is instructed on behalf of more than one defendant then the question arises, should he draw one Defence for all, or should they put in separate Defences? This depends on what their case will be at the trial. If for any reason they ought to be separately represented then, they must sever now; if they join in one Defence they cannot appear by different counsel at the hearing. If their interests are practically identical, this does not matter; but if they occupy different positions, hold different offices, or took different shares in the transaction, they had better sever, otherwise a special defence peculiar to one of them may be lost.

Illustrations.

Action of trespass for false imprisonment against two defendants. Defence that one of them, A., having ground to believe that his horse had been stolen by the plaintiff, gave him in charge to the other defendant, a constable, whereupon the constable and A., in his aid and by his command, laid hands on the plaintiff, &c. This plea was adjudged to be bad as to both the defendants, because it showed no reasonable ground of suspicion: for A. could not justify the arrest without showing such ground; and though the case might be different as to the constable whose duty was to act on the charge and not to deliberate, yet as he had not pleaded separately but had joined in A.'s justification, the plea was bad as to him also.

Hedges v. *Chapman*, 2 Bing. 523.

And see *Hyde* v. *Graham*, 1 H. & C. 593; 32 L. J. Ex. 27.

The editor, printer, and proprietor of a newspaper should, as a rule, put in separate Defences, certainly they should never join in one Defence with the writer of the libel complained of.

Special care is necessary in drafting a Defence. For though a plaintiff may amend his Statement of Claim once without leave, a defendant cannot ever amend his Defence without an order (see Order XXVIII., rr. 2 and 3); and leave to amend will be refused if the defendant only applies for an order at the last moment, *e.g.*, on the day before the trial. (*Kirby* v. *Simpson*, 3 Dowl. 791.)

Time.

Where a Statement of Claim is delivered to a defendant he shall deliver his Defence within ten days from the delivery of the Statement of Claim, or from the time limited for appearance, whichever shall be last, unless such time is extended by the Court or a judge (Order XXI. r. 6), or by consent under Order LXIV. r. 7. There is, as a rule, no difficulty in obtaining one or two extensions for a week or so, unless the case is to be tried at the assizes and the commission day is drawing near. Then the plaintiff will rightly insist upon the defendant consenting to accept short notice of trial, if he require further time to plead. Then, again, a defendant may gain more time by applying for particulars. Merely taking out the summons does not of course operate as a stay or give any extension of time. But if he

succeeds in obtaining an order for particulars, the master will
generally, if asked, extend his time to plead until, say, seven
days after the delivery of the particulars ordered, and make this
extension part of the order. If, however, the order be silent on
the matter, the defendant will have the same length of time for
pleading after the delivery of the particulars that he had at the
return of the summons. (Order XIX. r. 8.) Then again, when
the writ is specially indorsed, the plaintiff may himself extend
the time for Defence by taking out a summons under Order XIV.
For where the plaintiff serves such a summons on the defendant, no Defence should be delivered until the summons is
disposed of, even if the prescribed time for delivering the
Defence will expire before the summons is returnable. (*Hobson*
v. *Monks*, Weekly Notes for 1884, p. 8.)

By Order XXI. r. 8, " Where leave has been given to a
defendant to defend under Order XIV., he shall deliver his
Defence (if any) within such time as shall be limited by the
order giving him leave to defend; or if no time is thereby
limited, then within eight days after the order." (See *G.* v. *II.*,
Weekly Notes for 1883, p. 233; *Egerton* v. *Anderson*, Weekly
Notes for 1884, p. 95.) All these rules as to time are subject
to the provisions of Order LXIV. r. 7, under which an extension of the time for pleading may be granted even after the
time allowed for pleading has expired. If the time expires
and no Defence is delivered, the plaintiff may sign judgment by
default. But if he delays doing this the defendant may put in
a Defence after time, which will prevent judgment being signed;
though defendant will probably be ordered to pay all costs
incurred through his delay. (*Gill* v. *Woodfin*, 25 Ch. D. 707;
53 L. J. Ch. 617; *Graves* v. *Terry*, 9 Q. B. D. 170; 51
L. J. Q. B. 464; *Kennane* v. *Mackey*, 24 L. R. Ir. 495.)

Precedents.

The following precedents may be found useful to the student :—

Defence in an Action of Goods sold and delivered.

1. The plaintiff never sold any goods to this defendant, and this defendant never bought any goods from the plaintiff, and is not indebted to the plaintiff in the sum of 320*l*. 19*s*. 6*d*., or any other sum.

2. This defendant never ordered any goods of the plaintiff, nor were any goods ever delivered by the plaintiff to this defendant at his request, or at all.

3. This defendant never agreed to pay the plaintiff the prices charged for the goods set out in the particulars or any of them, or any other prices.

4. The prices charged by the plaintiff for the said goods are excessive, unreasonable, and exorbitant.

Defence in an Action for Work and Labour done and Materials supplied.

1. The plaintiff never did any of the work or labour, or provided any of the materials, specified in the particulars indorsed on the writ.

2. None of the said work or labour was done, nor were any of the said materials supplied, for or to the defendant at his request.

3. The defendant never agreed to pay the plaintiff the prices charged for the said work labour and materials, or any other prices. The prices charged by the plaintiff are unreasonable and exorbitant.

4. The defendant never agreed to pay the plaintiff any interest on the sum of 217*l*. 3*s*. 4*d*., or on any other sum, and no interest is in any way due to the plaintiff in respect thereof.

Defence to a Claim for Extras.

1. By a contract under seal dated the 9th day of January 1889, and entered into between the plaintiffs of the one part and the defendants of the other part, the plaintiffs agreed to do the work and labour, and to supply the materials therein specified for the defendants for the sum of 2,790*l*.

2. The plaintiffs did the work and labour, and supplied the materials therein specified, and the defendants have paid the plaintiffs the said sum of 2,790*l*. They have also paid to the plaintiffs the sum of £—— for "extras." They thus before action satisfied the plaintiffs' whole claim under the said contract.

3. As to all work labour and materials other than those for which the defendants so paid the plaintiffs before action, the defendants do not admit that the plaintiffs have done or supplied the same, or any part thereof. The defendants never ordered any such work, labour, or materials. No such work and labour has been done and no such materials have been supplied by the plaintiffs for or to the defendants at their request or at all.

4. The defendants never agreed to pay the plaintiffs the prices which they have charged for the said work labour and materials. Such prices are excessive and unreasonable.

5. If, however, the plaintiffs are claiming the sum of 4,169*l*. 0*s*. 8*d*. under the said contract of January 9th 1889 for "extras" within the meaning of the said contract, then the defendants say that the same are not "extras," but were included and paid for in the said fixed sum of 2,790*l*. The following clauses of the said contract are in that case also material:—

[*Set out the clauses on which defendant relies.*]

6. No instructions were ever given in writing by the engineer or any other person duly authorized on behalf of the defendants for any of the work, labour, or materials, the price of which is sought to be recovered in this action. No such instructions in writing stated that any such matter was to be the subject of an extra or varied charge. No claim was made in writing by the plaintiffs in respect of any such work within one week from the execution thereof or before the same became out of view or beyond check or admeasurement.

7. The plaintiffs did not deliver from time to time within one week after the expiration of the month in which the work then claimed for was done, a true or proper or any claim in a form prescribed by the engineer, or in any other form. The engineer has not certified or recommended the amount claimed in this action or any other amount to be paid to the plaintiffs by the defendants. No such certificate has ever been presented to the engineer or to any other duly authorized agent of the defendants. No dispute has yet been referred to or settled by the engineer; nor has he ever given any decision thereon.

Defence to a Claim on a Policy of Life Assurance.

1. In the month of July 1890 Joseph Brown (mentioned in the Statement of Claim and hereinafter called "the assured") was desirous to effect an assurance with the defendant company, and signed and delivered to them a declaration in writing, dated the 5th day of July 1890, which he agreed should be the basis of the contract of assurance which he desired to effect with the defendant company. And on the faith

of the statements contained in the said declaration, the defendant company granted him the policy sued on, No. 24,942. In the said declaration the assured stated that his age next birthday was sixty-nine years.

2. By the said policy, after reciting the facts in the last paragraph mentioned, and that satisfactory evidence of the statement as to age had to be furnished to the directors, the defendant company covenanted to pay the executors, administrators or assigns of the assured, within one calendar month next after satisfactory proof of title, and of the age and death of the assured, shall have been duly furnished to the directors of the defendant company, the sum of 200*l*.

3. No satisfactory proof of the title of the plaintiff or of the age of the assured has ever been furnished to the directors of the defendant company.

4. The defendant company do not admit that the plaintiff is the legal personal representative of the assured.

5. It was a condition of the said policy that all persons making claims thereunder must give satisfactory proof of the time of birth of the person on whose life the assurance shall have been effected, also of their title to the sum assured, with such further information on each point as the directors shall think reasonable. The plaintiff has given no satisfactory proof of the time of birth of the assured or of her title to the sum assured.

6. It was a condition of the said policy that the declaration, referred to in paragraph 1 above, should form the basis of the contract between the assured and the defendant company, and that if the said declaration was not in all respects true, the said policy should be void. The said declaration was not in all respects true. The age of the assured, on his next birthday, was then 71, and not 69 as therein stated; and the said policy is therefore void.

7. The said policy was made on the life of the assured, for the use and benefit of one David Dawson, and not of the assured. But the name of the said David Dawson was not inserted in the said policy, as is required by sect. 2 of the statute 14 Geo. III., c. 48, and the defendant company will therefore object that the said policy is illegal and void.

8. The plaintiff is not the holder of the said policy. She is not entitled to receive the monies, if any, which the defendant company may be liable to pay under the said policy.

Defence in an Action for Fraudulent Representations.

1. Neither defendant ever made any of the representations alleged in the Statement of Claim.

2. No one of the said alleged representations was false in fact; no one of them was false to the knowledge of either of the defendants; no one of

them was made fraudulently or recklessly or without caring whether the same was true or false.

3. The plaintiff was not induced by any of the alleged representations to buy the goodwill, tenancy, and licence of the Duke of York Tavern. The plaintiff ascertained for himself the value and extent of the business done at the said tavern, and the class of customers using the same. He himself examined the books and visited the said tavern before he agreed to purchase the same, and he made the said purchase in reliance upon his own judgment and the result of his own inquiries and investigations, and not upon any statement or representations made by the defendants or either of them.

4. The plaintiff has not suffered the alleged or any damage by reason of any act or default of either of the defendants. The defendants will object that the damage claimed is too remote.

Defence in an Action of Slander.

1. The defendant never spoke or published any of the words set out in paragraph 2 of the Statement of Claim.

2. The defendant never spoke or published the said words with the meaning in the said paragraph alleged. The said words are incapable of the said meaning or of any other defamatory or actionable meaning.

3. The defendant never spoke or published the said words of the plaintiff in relation to his trade, &c. (*Follow the exact words of the Statement of Claim*). The plaintiff is not a ——

4. The defendant will object that the said words are not actionable without proof of special damage, and that none is alleged (*or*, and that the special damage alleged is too remote and is not sufficient in law to sustain the action).

Defence in Slander—Vulgar Abuse.

1. The defendant admits that he spoke and published the words set out in paragraphs 2 & 3 of the Statement of Claim, but denies that he spoke or published them with the meanings in the said paragraphs alleged.

2. The said words are merely vulgar abuse, and were uttered by the defendant in anger, as all who heard the words were well aware; they did not convey, and were not understood to convey, any specific charge or imputation against the plaintiff.

3. The said words are incapable of any of the said meanings, or of any other actionable or defamatory meaning.

4. The defendant will object that the said words (taken either by themselves or with any innuendo of which they are capable) are not actionable without proof of special damage, and that none is alleged.

Defence in an Action of Libel.

1. The defendants are the proprietors of a weekly newspaper called the "Stock Exchange."

2. The defendants admit that they printed and published in their said newspaper the words set out in paragraph 1 of the Statement of Claim, but deny that they did so with any of the meanings in the said paragraph alleged. The said words are incapable of the said alleged meanings or any other defamatory or actionable meaning.

3. The said words without the said alleged meanings are no libel.

4. The said words are part of a fair and accurate report of a judicial proceeding, viz., an action tried before Mr. Justice ——— on ———, in which A. B. was plaintiff and C. D. defendant, and were published by the defendants *bonâ fide* for the information of the public, and in the usual course of the defendants' business and duty as public journalists and without any malice towards the plaintiff, and are therefore privileged.

5. The said words are fair and *bonâ fide* comment on matters of public interest, namely, the said judicial proceeding and the promotion and registration of the J. B. E. Co., and were published by the defendants *bonâ fide* for the benefit of the public and without any malice towards the plaintiff.

6. The said words without the said alleged meanings and according to their natural and ordinary signification are true in substance and in fact.

Defence in an Action of Libel.

1. The defendant is the proprietor of a weekly newspaper called "The ——— Gazette."

2. The defendant admits that he printed and published in his said newspaper the words set out in paragraph 1 of the Statement of Claim, but he denies that he published them with any of the meanings in the said paragraph alleged, or with any defamatory meaning.

3. In so far as the said words consist of allegations of fact, they are true in substance and in fact; in so far as they consist of expressions of opinion they are fair comments made in good faith and without malice upon the said facts, which are matters of public interest.*

---

* This form of pleading was approved by the Divisional Court, in *Lord Penrhyn* v. *The Licensed Victuallers' Mirror,* 7 Times L. R. 1 (Mathew and Grantham, JJ.)

Defence in an Action of Libel—Pleading an Apology and Payment into Court.

1. The defendant admits that she wrote and published the words set out in paragraph 2 of the Statement of Claim. She denies that they bear the meanings alleged in the said paragraph, but she admits that they are libellous in their natural signification, and that they refer to the plaintiff. She has, since the action, tendered to the plaintiff a full apology for her publication of the said words, and has also offered to pay a sum of money to the plaintiff for damages and costs. And the defendant now repeats such apology and expresses her sincere regret for such publication. She unreservedly withdraws all imputation on the plaintiff's character, and brings into Court the sum of 5*l.* 5*s.*, and says that the same, together with such apology, is sufficient to satisfy the plaintiff's claim in this action in respect of the said words without the said alleged meanings, which are denied.

[N.B.—A defendant may deny the innuendo and yet pay money into Court, provided it is made clear that the money is paid into Court, in respect of the words without the innuendo, which is denied. *Mackay* v. *Manchester Press Co.*, 54 J. P. 22; 6 Times L. R. 16.]

Chapter IX.

REPLY, &c.

The plaintiff must deliver his Reply within twenty-one days after the Defence or the last of the Defences shall have been delivered, unless the time be extended by consent or by order. (Order XXIII., r. 1; Order LXIV., r. 8.) Where there is a Counterclaim, he must deliver a "Reply and Defence to Counterclaim" within the same period. (*Rumley* v. *Winn*, 22 Q. B. D. 265; 58 L. J. Q. B. 128.)

"Where a Counterclaim is pleaded, the Reply thereto shall be subject to the rules applicable to Statements of Defence." (Order XXIII., r. 4.) "A plaintiff may, in answer to a Counterclaim, pay money into Court in satisfaction thereof, subject to the like conditions as to costs and otherwise as upon payment into Court by a defendant." (Order XXII., r. 9.) "If, after a Defence has been delivered, any ground of defence arises to any set-off or counterclaim alleged therein by the defendant, it may be raised by the plaintiff in his Reply, either alone or together with any other ground of reply." (Order XXIV., r. 1.) "Where any ground of defence to any set-off or counterclaim arises after Reply, or after the time limited for delivering a Reply has expired, the plaintiff may, within eight days after such ground of defence has arisen, or at any subsequent time, by leave of the Court or a judge, deliver a further Reply setting forth the same." (Order XXIV., r. 2.)

"It shall not be sufficient for a plaintiff in his Reply to deny generally the facts alleged by the defendant in his Counterclaim;

he must deal specifically with each allegation of fact of which he does not admit the truth, except damages." (Order XIX., r. 17.) He may not join issue on a Counterclaim. (*Benbow* v. *Low*, 13 Ch. D. 553; 49 L. J. Ch. 259; *Green* v. *Sevin*, 13 Ch. D. 589; 41 L. T. 724.) He must plead to it as though it were a Statement of Claim. He may even counterclaim to it in respect of any cause of action which has accrued to him *since writ*, provided it arises at the same time and out of the same transaction as the Counterclaim. (*Toke* v. *Andrews*, 8 Q. B. D. 428; 51 L. J. Q. B. 281.) But he cannot do this if such cause of action had arisen before writ; in that case, he must amend his Statement of Claim. (*James* v. *Page*, 85 Law Times Newspaper, 157.)

"Subject to the last preceding rule, the plaintiff by his Reply may join issue upon the Defence, and each party in his pleading (if any) subsequent to Reply may join issue upon the previous pleading. Such joinder of issue shall operate as a denial of every material allegation of facts in the pleading upon which issue is joined, but it may except any facts which the party may be willing to admit, and shall then operate as a denial of the facts not so admitted." (Order XIX., r. 18.)

A joinder of issue runs simply thus: "The plaintiff joins issue with the defendant on his Defence." Some pleaders add, "except in so far as the same consists of admissions;" but this qualification is unnecessary, as an admission by the defendant of a fact alleged in the Statement of Claim is not a "material allegation of fact in the pleading upon which issue is joined." So to a plea of payment into Court, some pleaders reply specially that the sum paid in is insufficient; but a mere joinder of issue will raise that point equally well; as the defendant in his plea always asserts that the amount is sufficient.

But the effect of joining issue is merely to *deny;* it does not confess and avoid. It is simply a comprehensive and compendious *traverse*. "The plaintiff must raise by his pleading all such grounds of reply as, if not raised, would be likely to take the opposite party by surprise, or would raise issues of fact not arising out of the preceding pleading, as, for instance, fraud, Statute of Limitations, release, payment, performance, facts showing illegality, either by statute or common law or Statute of Frauds." (Order XIX., r. 15.) "The Reply is the proper place for meeting the Defence by confession and avoidance." (*Per* James, L. J., in *Hall* v. *Eve*, 4 Ch. D. at p. 345.) "The new form merely enables a party to traverse what he might have traversed before the Act, but does not do away with the necessity of pleading in confession and avoidance." (*Per* Parke, B., in *Glover* v. *Dixon and another*, 9 Ex. at p. 160.)

The plaintiff must therefore be careful not merely to join issue where he ought to allege new facts or to raise an objection in point of law. For a joinder of issue merely contradicts the facts alleged by the defendant. Indeed, it is hardly worth while to deliver a mere joinder of issue, where there is no Counterclaim, for in that case, if no further pleading be delivered, all material statements of fact in the pleading last delivered will be deemed to have been denied and put in issue. (Order XXVII., r. 13.)

Illustrations.

Action of trespass. Defence, that it was defendant's own freehold (this was formerly called the plea of *liberum tenementum*). Reply, a mere joinder of issue. At the trial, the plaintiff was not allowed on these pleadings to give evidence of a lease from defendant's ancestor to himself, as that was a new fact consistent with the plea traversed, and should therefore have been specially pleaded.

5 Hen. VII. 10 a, pl. 2.

To a plea of the Statute of Limitations, plaintiff must specially reply absence beyond seas under the Statute of Anne, if he was so absent; or any acknowledgment that will take the case out of the statute.

See *Forsyth* v. *Bristowe*, 8 Ex. 347, 716; 22 L. J. Ex. 70, 255.

To a declaration in covenant for non-payment of money, defendant pleaded that the cause of action did not accrue within twenty years. Replication that it did accrue within twenty years. Held, under stat.

3 & 4 Will. IV., c. 42, ss. 3, 5, that plaintiff could not, in support of this issue, give evidence of an acknowledgment by letter within the twenty years.

Kempe v. *Gibbon*, 9 Q. B. 609; 16 L. J. Q. B. 120.

Action for money had and received to the use of the plaintiff. Plea of the Statute of Limitations. Reply that the defendant had received the money to the use of the plaintiff within six years. It was proved at the trial that the defendant had fraudulently received the money more than six years ago. Held, that the plaintiff could not on this issue give any evidence to show that the defendant had fraudulently concealed the fact that he had received the money till within six years.

Clark v. *Hougham*, 2 B. & Cr. 149; 3 D. & R. 322.

Such a ground of reply must be specially pleaded, and with great particularity.

Gibbs v. *Guild*, 8 Q. B. D. 296; 9 Q. B. D. 59.

Riddell v. *Earl of Strathmore* (C. A.), 3 Times L. R. 329.

Lawrance v. *Lord Norreys*, 15 App. Cas. 210; 59 L. J. Ch. 681; 38 W. R. 753; 62 L. T. 706.

If the defendant obtained from the plaintiff a release of his cause of action, either fraudulently or by duress, the fraud or duress must be specially pleaded in reply to the plea of release.

To a justification setting out a conviction, or to a plea of a previous action, the plaintiff must reply specially *Nul tiel record*, if it be the fact that there is no such record; or if the conviction be erroneously stated in the Defence (as in *Alexander* v. *N. E. Rail. Co.*, 6 B. & S. 340; 34 L. J. Q. B. 152), the plaintiff may set it out correctly in his Reply. Or to such a conviction the plaintiff may reply a pardon (*Cuddington* v. *Wilkins*, Hob. 67, 81; 2 Hawk. P. C. c. 37, s. 48), or that he had undergone his sentence, which will have the same effect.

Leyman v. *Latimer and others*, 3 Ex. D. 15, 352; 47 L. J. Ex. 470; 26 W. R. 305; 37 L. T. 360, 819; 14 Cox, C. C. 51.

To a plea of the Statute of Frauds, the plaintiff may plead specially a part performance, where such a reply is applicable.

Ungley v. *Ungley*, 5 Ch. D. 887; 46 L. J. Ch. 854; 25 W. R. 733; 37 L. T. 52.

Maddison v. *Alderson*, 8 App. Cas. 467; 52 L. J. Q. B. 737; 31 W. R. 820; 49 L. T. 303; 47 J. P. 821.

Action for specific performance of an agreement to grant a lease. Defence, breaches of contract, which entitled defendants to put an end to agreement, and to refuse to grant any lease. The plaintiff, in his Reply, denied all such breaches, but pleaded also that if any were committed, they were waived, and this Reply was held good. A plaintiff may confess and avoid by his Reply; for it is no part of the Statement of Claim to anticipate

the Defence, and the old rule of pleading still holds, "that you should not leap before you come to the stile." (See *ante*, p. 20.)
Hall v. *Eve* (C. A.), 4 Ch. D. 341, 347; 46 L. J. Ch. 145; 25 W. R. 177; 35 L. T. 926.

A Reply must not refer to an independent document, such as plaintiff's answer to interrogatories, as containing facts on which the pleader relies, without setting out such document itself as part of the Reply. A Reply must not set up new claims. A Reply must not plead mere evidence or argument, or state conclusions of law to be drawn or inferred from the facts pleaded.
Williamson v. *L. & N. W. Rail. Co.*, 12 Ch. D. 787; 49 L. J. Ch. 559; 27 W. R. 724.

Departure.

It is at the stage of reply that the rule against what is called "a departure in pleading" applies for the first time. "No pleading shall, except by way of amendment, raise any new ground of claim, or contain any allegations of fact inconsistent with the previous pleadings of the party pleading the same." (Order XIX. r. 16.)

A departure takes place when in any pleading the party deserts the ground that he took up in his preceding pleading, and resorts to another and a different ground; or, to give Lord Coke's definition, "A departure in pleading is said to be when the second plea containeth matter not pursuant to his former, and which fortifieth not the same; and therefore it is called *decessus*, because he departeth from his former plea." (Co. Litt. 304 a.) This is clearly embarrassing; a Reply is not the proper place in which to raise new claims; to permit this would tend to spin out the pleadings to an intolerable length. The plaintiff must amend his Statement of Claim by adding the new matter, if need be, in the alternative.

Illustrations.

In an action of debt brought on a bond conditioned to perform an award so that the same were delivered to the defendant by a certain time, the defendant pleaded that the arbitrators did not make any award. The plaintiff replied that the arbitrators did make an award to such an effect, and that the same was tendered by the proper time. The defendant rejoined that the award was not so tendered. On demurrer, it was held that the Rejoinder was a departure from the plea in bar; "for, in the plea in bar, the defendant says that the arbitrators made no award, and now, in his Rejoinder, he has implicitly confessed that the arbitrators have made an award, but says that it was not tendered according to the condition, which is a plain departure, for it is one thing not to make an award, and another thing not to tender it when made."

Roberts v. *Mariett*, 2 Wms. Saund. 188.

Claim: That the defendant was trustee of one-half of 500*l*., which he had received as trustee for himself and the plaintiff.

Defence: I only received 311*l*., half of which I pay into Court.

Reply: You ought to have received the full 500*l*., but you wrongfully compromised with the debtor, so I still claim one-half of 500*l*.

Held that this reply violated Order XIX. r. 16, as it was really setting up a new case which should have been set out in the Statement of Claim.

Earp v. *Henderson*, 3 Ch. D. 254; 45 L. J. Ch. 738; 34 L. T. 844.

If this case was intended to decide anything more than this, it is to that extent overruled by

Hall v. *Eve*, 4 Ch. D. 341, *ante*, pp. 163, 164.

Action for the recovery of land with a claim for mesne profits. Defence: "The following letters passed between the defendant and the plaintiff's late father, who was seised in fee of the lands, which amount to a binding agreement for a lease." The plaintiff cannot turn round and say in his Reply: "Oh! very well, then pay me the rent mentioned in those letters." For by his Statement of Claim he treats the defendant as a trespasser; he must abandon that position before he can claim rent from him as his tenant.

A. died in 1833, having devised Blackacre to his younger son, Z., without any words of limitation. On the death of Z., childless and intestate, his elder brother, Y., sued to recover Blackacre from Z.'s stepson, who had got into possession of it. The Statement of Claim alleged that Z. had only an estate for life in Blackacre, the reversion on which was always vested in Y., as heir of the testator.

Defence: that on the true construction of the will, although it was made before the Wills Act, Z. took the fee simple.

Reply: Be it so; Y. is equally heir-at-law of his younger brother, Z., and so entitled to recover. The Master at Chambers held that this Reply was inconsistent with the original claim, that the Statement of Claim must be amended by setting out the precise words of the devise, which had now become material, and that the plaintiff must claim in the alternative (i.) as heir of A. if Z. were but tenant for life; (ii.) as heir of Z. if he were tenant in fee. Costs in cause.

Baker v. *Farmer* (not reported).

Action on a bond conditioned to perform the covenants in an indenture of lease, one of which was, that the lessee at every felling of wood would make a fence. The defendant pleaded that he had not felled any wood, &c. The plaintiff replied that the defendant had felled two acres of wood, but had made no fence. The defendant rejoined that when he felled those two acres, he did make a fence. This was adjudged a jeofail and departure in the Rejoinder.

Anon., 3 Dyer, 253 b.

So, in another action on a bond conditioned to keep the plaintiffs harmless and indemnified from all suits, &c., of one Thomas Cook, the defendants pleaded that they had kept the plaintiffs harmless, &c. The plaintiffs replied that Cook sued them, and so the defendants had not kept them harmless, &c. The defendants rejoined that they had not any notice of the damnification. And the Court held first, that the matter of the Rejoinder was bad, as the plaintiffs were not bound to give notice; and secondly, that the Rejoinder was a departure from the plea in bar, for, in the bar, the defendants plead, that "they have saved harmless the plaintiffs, and in the Rejoinder confess that they have not saved harmless, but allege they had not notice of the damnification; which is a plain departure."

Cutler v. *Southern*, 1 Wms. Saund. 116.

Action against a tenant for rent, brought by the plaintiff who was himself tenant of the premises for a term of years. Defence that plaintiff's term had expired before the rent claimed became due. Counterclaim for money had and received. Reply that defendant wrongfully held over after both his term and the plaintiff's term had expired, and that the plaintiff in consequence had been compelled to pay damages, &c., to the head landlord, which he sought to recover from the defendant. Held a departure.

Duckworth v. *McClelland*, 2 L. R. Ir. 527.
Breslauer v. *Barwick*, 24 W. R. 901; 36 L. T. 52.
Collett v. *Dickinson*, 26 W. R. 403.
Hancock v. *De Niceville*, W. N. (1875) p. 230.

In an action of trespass, the defendant set up that he was entitled to the premises under a lease for 50 years granted to him by the college of R. The plaintiff replied that there was another prior lease of the same premises, which had been assigned to the defendant, and which was unexpired at the time of making the said lease for 50 years; and alleged a proviso in the Act of 31 Hen. VIII. c. 13, avoiding all leases by the colleges to which that Act relates made under such circumstances. The defendant, in his Rejoinder, pleaded another proviso in the statute, which allowed such leases to be good for 21 years if made to the same person, &c., and that by virtue thereof, the demise stated in his plea was available for 21 years at least. The judges held the Rejoinder to be a departure from the plea ; "for in the bar, he pleads a lease of 50 years, and in the Rejoinder he concludes upon a lease for 21 years," &c. And they observed, that " the defendant might have shown the statute and the whole matter at first."

Fulmerston v. *Steward*, Plowd. 102.

But in an action of trespass on the case for illegally taking toll, the plaintiff in his declaration set forth a charter of 26 Hen. VI., discharging him from toll. The defendant pleaded a statute resuming the liberties granted by Hen. VI. The plaintiff replied that by the statute 4 Hen. VII. such liberties were revived; and this was held to be no departure. For the Reply re-established and fortified the claim.

Wood v. *Hawkshead*, Yelv. 13.

So in an action of debt on a bond conditioned to perform covenants, one of which was, that the defendant should account for all sums of money that he should receive, the defendant pleaded performance. The plaintiff replied, that 26*l*. came to his hands, for which he had not accounted. The defendant rejoined that he had accounted for that 26*l*. *modo sequente*, viz., that certain malefactors broke into his countinghouse and stole it, wherewith he acquainted the plaintiff. And it was objected that the Rejoinder was a departure; for fulfilling a covenant to account could not be intended but by actual accounting; whereas the Rejoinder did not show an account, but an excuse for not accounting. But the Court held that showing he was robbed of a sum of money, was giving an account of it, and, therefore, there was no departure.

Vere v. *Smith*, 2 Lev. 5 ; Vent. 121.

A defendant pleaded that a certain condition precedent had not been fulfilled. Can the plaintiff set out in his Reply matter excusing him from fulfilling such condition? Is not this inconsistent with his Statement of Claim in which an averment of the performance or occurrence of all conditions precedent is implied by virtue of Order XIX. r. 14. Strictly, no doubt, such matter of excuse should have been alleged in the plaintiff's previous pleading. (See *ante*, p. 122.) But this is such a harmless and inoffensive departure that only a cantankerous defendant would take objection to it.

New Assignment.

But though no departure was permitted, yet a plaintiff might always "new assign" in his Reply ; in other words, though he might not set up new claims, he might explain and define his original claim, a thing which was often very necessary to do in the days when declarations were worded in very general terms. But now, " no new assignment shall be necessary or used. But everything which was formerly alleged by way of new assignment may hereafter be introduced by amendment of the Statement of Claim, or by way of reply." (Order XXIII. r. 6.)

The words " or by way of reply " were added in 1883, and they practically make nonsense of the rule. For if a plaintiff is now permitted to introduce into his Reply " everything which was formerly alleged by way of new assignment," what is this but new assigning? The former matter is restored to its former place, yet the first clause in the rule forbids its use!

A new assignment was a pleading in the nature of a special reply which explained what the plaintiff's original cause of action really was, whenever it appeared from the Defence that the defendant had misunderstood it, or whenever he pretended to have misunderstood it. Its object was to correct this real or supposed mistake of the defendant, and to show that the defence pleaded was either wholly inapplicable to the causes of action on which the plaintiff was suing, or applied only to part of them. For instance, in an action for repeated trespasses to land the declaration, in former days, usually stated that the defendant on divers days and times before the commencement of the suit broke and entered the plaintiff's close and trod down the soil, &c., without setting forth more specifically in what parts of the close, or on what occasions the defendant trespassed. Now it might be, that the defendant claimed a right of way over a certain part of the close, and in exercise of that right had repeatedly entered and walked over it; and had also entered and trod down the soil, &c., on other occasions and in parts out of the supposed line of way; and the plaintiff, not admitting the right claimed, may have intended to claim damages for both series of trespasses. Yet, from the generality of the declaration, the defendant was entitled to suppose that it referred only to his entering and walking in the line of way. He would therefore in his plea allege, as a complete answer to the whole complaint, that he had a right of way by grant, &c., over the said close. If he did this, and the plaintiff confined himself in his replication to a traverse of that plea, all the defendant would have to do at the trial would be to prove his right of way as alleged; and the plaintiff would have been precluded from giving evidence of any trespasses committed out of the line or track along which the defendant had established his right to pass and repass. The plaintiff's proper course, therefore, was, and still is, both to traverse the plea, and also to new assign by alleging that he brought his action not only for those trespasses which the defendant sought thus to justify but also for others committed on other occasions and in other parts of the close out of the supposed way. This was called a new assignment *extra viam*. Or, of course, if the plaintiff liked to admit the right of way, he would new assign simply without the traverse. (See the forms given in Schedule B. of the 15 & 16 Vict. c. 76, Nos. 55—57; and also *Pratt* v. *Groome*, 15 East, 235; *Oakley* v. *Davis*, 16 East, 82.)

So, whenever the plaintiff wished to state that he was suing for some other cause of action not that admitted by the plea, he was bound to plead by way of new assignment, *e.g.*, for another promise or debt (as in *Heydon* v. *Thompson*, 1 A. & E. 210; *Monkman* v. *Shepherdson*, 11 A. & E. 411; and *Jubb* v. *Ellis*, 3 D. & L. 364); or for an excess in committing an act which the defendant had attempted to justify by his plea (as in *Loweth* v. *Smith*, 12 M. & W. 582; *Worth* v. *Terrington*, 13 M. & W. 781; *Playfair* v. *Musgrove*, 14 M. & W. 239; and *Ash* v. *Dawnay*, 8 Ex. 237). But invariably, under a new assignment, the plaintiff was bound to state and prove a cause of action, which was within the terms of the declaration (*Cheasley* v. *Barnes*, 10 East, 73; *Pugh* v. *Griffith*, 7 A. & E. 827), and of the particulars, if any, delivered by him (Common Law Procedure Act, 1852, s. 87); otherwise he was guilty of a departure. He was not allowed to start any fresh claim in his Reply; all he could do was to point out the exact nature and extent of his original cause of action. In these days when applications for particulars are so frequent it is seldom that any necessity for a new assignment can arise.

Rejoinder, &c.

The defendant's answer to the Reply is called a Rejoinder; but it is seldom more than a joinder of issue, even where a Counter-claim has been pleaded. Further pleadings are possible; there can be a Surrejoinder, a Rebutter, and a Surrebutter; but they are very seldom met with now.

The principle of rule 15 of Order XIX. applies to all these subsequent pleadings. Hence, if the defendant desires to give evidence at the trial of any fresh facts by way of confession and avoidance, in answer to the plaintiff's Reply, he must allege it specially in his Rejoinder. Such, at all events, was the old practice (*per* Bramwell, J. A., in *Hall* v. *Eve*, 4 Ch. D. at p. 347); and as no other provision is made by the Judicature Acts or any rule passed under them, the former practice remains in force by virtue of Order LXXII., r. 2. But if the party pleading desires at this stage to allege any such new matter, he must satisfy the Master that it is necessary and obtain his leave so to plead. For, by Order XXIII., r. 2, "no pleading subsequent to Reply, other than a joinder of issue, shall be pleaded without leave of the Court or a judge, and then shall be pleaded only upon such terms as the Court or judge shall think fit;" "the Court or a judge" meaning in the peculiar language of these rules "a Master or District Registrar."

"Subject to the last preceding rule, every pleading subsequent to Reply shall be delivered within four days after the delivery of the previous pleading, unless the time shall be extended" by order or consent. (Order XXIII., r. 3; Order LXIV., r. 8.)

As soon as any party has joined issue upon the preceding pleading of the opposite party simply without adding any further or other pleading thereto, or has made default as mentioned in Order XXVII., r. 13, the pleadings as between such parties shall be deemed to be closed (Order XXIII., r. 5), and the case proceeds to trial.

Trial without Pleadings.

It is possible but very unusual to go to trial without any pleadings at all. By r. 9 of Order XXXIV.: "When the parties to a cause or matter are agreed as to the questions of fact to be decided between them, they may, after writ issued and before judgment, by consent and order of the Court or a judge, proceed to the trial of any such questions of fact without formal pleadings, and such questions may be stated for trial in an issue in the Form No. 15, in Appendix B., with such variations as circumstances may require, and such issue may be entered for trial and tried in the same manner as any issue joined in an ordinary action, and the proceedings shall be under the control and jurisdiction of the Court or judge, in the same way as the proceedings in an action."

So, too, "the parties to any cause or matter may concur in stating the questions of law arising therein in the form of a special case for the opinion of the Court." (Order XXXIV. r. 1, and see r. 2 of the same Order.) But it is, generally, difficult to induce the parties to concur in any reasonable course. Then, again, the Court or a judge, on any question of fact, may direct an issue to be prepared. (See Order XXXIII. rr. 1, 2.) Such issues take the place of pleadings; they are usually directed to determine whether a particular person was or was not a member of the defendant firm at the time the contract sued on was entered into with that firm, or to determine the liability of a person summoned as a garnishee, or to decide between rival claimants to property taken in execution by the sheriff or in the hands of a stakeholder.

I add a few practical observations on interrogatories and advice on evidence.

Chapter X.

INTERROGATORIES.

In every action, as soon as the Defence is delivered, either party may apply for leave to deliver a string of questions to his opponent who must answer them within ten days. In actions where relief is sought on the ground of fraud or breach of trust, interrogatories may be administered without any order for that purpose (Order XXXI. r. 1). But in order that this privilege may not be abused, the party interrogating must, before delivering the interrogatories to his opponent, pay into the "Security for Costs Account," to abide further order, a sum of money varying with the length of the interrogatories, but never less than £5.

The object of interrogating is twofold; first, to obtain admissions to facilitate the proof of your own case; secondly, to ascertain, so far as you may, the case of your opponent. There is therefore some art required in drawing interrogatories. Think rather of the answer the defendant will probably give you than of the answer which you are instructed he ought to give. The defendant's version of the matter must differ from the plaintiff's version, and your object is to discover precisely where and to what extent they differ. Your questions then should be framed so as in the first place to elicit, if possible, the admission you desire: and at the same time, failing that answer, to get at all events some definite statement sworn to, from which the party interrogated cannot afterwards diverge. Leave him no loophole of escape. If he will not answer the question your way, still at least find out how far he is prepared to go in the opposite direction. To secure this, it is well to ask a long series of short questions, not one long question. Each additional detail should be put in a question by itself.

Illustrations.

Thus, if you are instructed that the plaintiff gave evidence in the Bankruptcy Court, in the presence of a Mr. Henderson, that a certain cheque was in the handwriting of the defendant, it will be of little use to ask merely: "Did you not state on oath, in the Bankruptcy Court, in the presence of J. Henderson, that the said cheque was in the defendant's handwriting?" as the plaintiff will simply answer "No." Nor will it avail to add to the above question the Chancery phrase, "Or, how otherwise?" The only way to discover precisely what it is the plaintiff denies is to split the question up into several—"Were you not examined as a witness in the Bankruptcy Court on the 15th of May, 1880, or some other and what day? Was not a cheque then and there produced to you? Was not the said cheque the one mentioned in paragraph 4 of the Statement of Claim, or some other and what cheque? Did you not state that such cheque was in the handwriting of the defendant? Did you not state so on oath? Did you not state so in the presence of one John Henderson? If nay, in whose handwriting did you state the said cheque to be?"

Here is an interrogatory: "Do you deny that the delay occasioned in the signing of the contract for the sale of the said brewery to the said purchasers arose wholly or in part from the fact that the "tied houses" alleged to be connected with the said brewery were not in your possession or connected with the said brewery?" This should be split up into eight or nine separate questions. As it stands it assumes the existence of numerous facts, each of which may be in dispute. Possibly only one of them may in fact be in dispute, but an interrogatory in this shape will not help you to ascertain which one that is.

What Interrogatories are Admissible.

There are certain rules which determine what interrogatories may be administered and what not:—

1. Interrogatories must be relevant to the matters in issue.

Not every question which could be asked a witness in the box may be put as an interrogatory. (*Per* Martin, B., in *Peppiatt and Wife* v. *Smith*, 33 L. J. Ex. 240; and see the concluding words of Order XXXI., r. 1.) Thus, questions to credit only will not be allowed, although of course they may be asked in cross-examination. (*Allhusen* v. *Labouchere* (C. A.), 3 Q. B. D. 654; 47 L. J. Ch. 819; 27 W. R. 12; 39 L. T. 207.) "We have never allowed interrogatories merely as to the credibility of a party as a witness." (*Per* Cockburn, C. J., in *Labouchere* v. *Shaw*, 41 J. P. 788.) Again, no question need be answered which is not put *bonâ fide* for the purposes of the present action, but with a view to further litigation.

Illustrations.

The publisher of a newspaper must answer the interrogatory: "Was not the passage set out in paragraph 3 of the Statement of Claim intended to apply to the plaintiff?" but he need not answer the further question, "if not, say to whom?"; as, if the passage did not apply to the plaintiff, it is immaterial to whom it referred, so far as the present action is concerned.

Wilton v. *Brignell*, Weekly Notes for 1875, p. 239.

So defendant cannot be asked, "If you did not print the libel, did M'C. & Co., or some other and what firm, print it?"

Pankhurst v. *Wighton & Co.*, 2 Times L. R. 745.

It is however permissible to interrogate as to the names of persons whom you desire to make parties to the present action.

Union Bank of London v. *Manby*, 13 Ch. D. 239; 49 L. J. Ch. 106; 28 W. R. 23; 42 L. T. 393.

Interrogatories asking plaintiff whether similar charges had not been made against him previously in a newspaper, and whether he had contradicted them or taken any notice of them on that occasion, are clearly irrelevant.

Pankhurst v. *Hamilton*, 2 Times L. R. 682.

Prior to the passing of the Law of Libel Amendment Act, 1888, interrogatories were disallowed which asked the plaintiff for particulars of sums already recovered by him in other actions in respect of other publications of the same libel. But now such interrogatories would, it is submitted, be admissible under sect. 6 of that Act.

Tucker v. *Lawson*, 2 Times L. R. 593.

But interrogatories are not, like pleadings, confined to the material facts on which the parties intend to rely; they should be, and generally are, directed to the evidence by which they intend to establish such facts at the trial. (*Att.-Gen.* v. *Gaskill,* 20 Ch. D. 519; 51 L. J. Ch. 870; 30 W. R. 558; 46 L. T. 180.) Either party may interrogate as to any link in the chain of evidence necessary to substantiate his case; the question is relevant as leading up to a matter in issue in the action. How far interrogatories may be addressed to matters which are relevant only in aggravation or diminution of damages, is somewhat doubtful after the recent decision in *Parnell* v. *Walter,* 24 Q. B. D. 441; 59 L. J. Q. B. 125; 38 W. R. 270; 62 L. T. 75. A Master at Chambers has refused to order a defendant to answer interrogatories as to the details of matters which were mentioned only in a notice under Order XXXVI., r. 37.

Illustrations.

Thus, if the defendant denies that he wrote a material document, he may be asked whether other documents produced to him are not in his handwriting, though such other documents have nothing to do with the case, but will only be used for comparison with the libel.

Jones v. *Richards,* 15 Q. B. D. 439; 1 Times L. R. 660.

So, too, a defendant may interrogate as to any fact material to his case upon the issue on a plea of justification.

Marriott v. *Chamberlain* (C. A.), 17 Q. B. D. 154; 55 L. J. Q. B. 448; 34 W. R. 783; 54 L. T. 714.

So if the occasion be privileged, either party may interrogate the other with a view of proving or disproving malice.

Cooper v. *Blackmore and others,* 2 Times L. R. 746.

2. The party interrogating may put his whole case to his opponent if he thinks fit, though it is not always wise to do so; he may also interrogate in full detail as to matters common to the case of both parties; but he is not entitled to obtain more than an outline of his opponent's case. You can compel your adversary to disclose the facts on which he intends to rely, but

not the evidence by which he proposes to prove those facts. You cannot claim to "see his brief" or ask him to name the witnesses he means to call at the trial. You may not ask in whose presence such and such events occurred; but you are entitled to know precisely what is the charge made against you, and what is the case you have to meet. (*Eade and another* v. *Jacobs* (C. A.), 3 Ex. D. 335; 47 L. J. Ex. 74; 26 W. R. 159; 37 L. T. 621; *Johns* v. *James*, 13 Ch. D. 370; *Ashley* v. *Taylor*, 37 L. T. 522; (C. A.) 38 L. T. 44.) And it is no objection that the same information might have been obtained by particulars. In *Gay* v. *Labouchere* (4 Q. B. D. 206; 48 L. J. Q. B. 279; 27 W. R. 413), Cockburn, C. J., asks, "Why should not the plaintiff have this information by means of interrogatories as well as by particulars?" Indeed, there is nothing to prevent a defendant's applying first for particulars and then interrogating the plaintiff as to those particulars afterwards. (But see *Hall* v. *Brice*, 3 Times L. R. 344.)

Illustrations.

A party cannot be asked to name his witnesses. If he relies on an alleged parol agreement or consent, he cannot be compelled to give the names of those who were present on the occasion.
Eade v. *Jacobs* (C. A.), 3 Ex. D. 335; 47 L. J. Ex. 74; 26 W. R. 159; 37 L. T. 621.

But if the party interrogating is in other respects entitled to certain information, he will not be debarred from it merely because supplying it will necessarily disclose the names of persons whom the party interrogated may hereafter wish to call as his witnesses, or otherwise give some clue to his evidence.
Marriott v. *Chamberlain*, 17 Q. B. D. 154; 55 L. J. Q. B. 448; 34 W. R. 783; 54 L. T. 714.
Birch v. *Mather*, 22 Ch. D. 629; 52 L. J. Ch. 292; 31 W. R. 362.
McColla v. *Jones*, 4 Times L. R. 12.

3. But even in interrogating as to your own case, the questions asked must not be "fishing," that is, they must refer to some definite and existing state of circumstances, not be

put merely in the hopes of discovering something which may help the party interrogating to make out some case. They must be confined to matters which there is good ground for believing to have occurred. "Fishing" interrogatories are especially objectionable when their object is to get at something which may support a plea of justification in an action of libel. (*Gourley* v. *Plimsoll*, L. R. 8 C. P. 362; 42 L. J. C. P. 121; 21 W. R. 683; 28 L. T. 598; *Buchanan* v. *Taylor*, W. N. (1876) p. 73.)

Illustration.

Where the plaintiff was charged with having used certain blasphemous phrases, interrogatories were disallowed as "fishing," the object of which was to show that if plaintiff had not said what he was charged with saying, still he had said something very much like it.

Pankhurst v. *Hamilton*, 2 Times L. R. 682.

4. In the Queen's Bench Division, at all events, interrogatories are not allowed as to the contents of written documents, unless it is admitted that such documents have been lost or destroyed. (*Stein* v. *Tabor*, 31 L. T. 444; *Fitzgibbon* v. *Greer*, Ir. R. 9 C. L. 294.) Nor will interrogatories be allowed, the object of which is to contradict a written document. (*Moor* v. *Roberts*, 3 C. B. N. S. 671; 26 L. J. C. P. 246.) But you may ask what has become of a particular document, and continue: "If you state that such document is lost or destroyed, set out the contents of the same to the best of your recollection and belief. If you have a copy, make it an exhibit to your answer." (See *Wolverhampton New Waterworks Co.* v. *Hawksford*, 5 C. B. N. S. 703; 28 L. J. C. P. 198; *Dalrymple* v. *Leslie*, 8 Q. B. D. 5; 51 L. J. Q. B. 61; 30 W. R. 105; 45 L. T. 478.) If, however, the party from whom discovery is sought does not in his affidavit of documents disclose a document which there is good reason for believing was once, at all events, in his possession, then it was said interrogatories might be delivered asking him whether he did not receive a particular document from a certain person

on a given day; whether it is not now in his possession or control; if nay, when did he part with it, and to whom? Was it ever in his possession or control? (*Lethbridge* v. *Cronk*, 44 L. J. C. P. 381; *Jones* v. *Monte Video Gas Co.* (C. A.), 5 Q. B. D. 556; 49 L. J. Q. B. 627; 28 W. R. 758; 42 L. T. 639.) But since those decisions, the Court has expressed the greatest reluctance to going behind the party's affidavit in such a case, and the later decisions leave it very doubtful whether any such interrogatories can ever be administered. See, especially, *Hall* v. *Truman*, 29 Ch. D. 307; 54 L. J. Ch. 717, and *Morris* v. *Edwards*, 15 App. Cas. 309; 60 L. J. Q. B. 292; 63 L. T. 26.

5. Questions which tend to criminate may certainly be asked, unless they are either irrelevant or "fishing," though the party interrogated is not bound to answer them (*post*, p. 183). That the interrogatories will tend to criminate others is no objection, if they be put *bonâ fide* for the purposes of the present action. (*M'Corquodale* v. *Bell*, W. N. (1876) p. 39.) That to answer them would expose the party interrogated, or third persons, to civil actions, was never an objection. (*Tetley* v. *Easton*, 18 C. B. 643; 25 L. J. C. P. 293.)

Interrogatories cannot be administered to an infant plaintiff or defendant (*Mayor* v. *Collins*, 24 Q. B. D. 361; 59 L. J. Q. B. 199); nor in a penal action (*Martin* v. *Treacher*, 16 Q. B. D. 507; 55 L. J. Q. B. 209; *Adams* v. *Batley*, 18 Q. B. D. 625; 56 L. J. Q. B. 393; *Jones* v. *Jones*, 22 Q. B. D. 425; 58 L. J. Q. B. 178; *Hobbs & Co.* v. *Hudson*, 25 Q. B. D. 232; 38 W. R. 682; 63 L. T. 215).

Great care is necessary in applying former decisions as to interrogatories to the present practice. Before the Judicature Act special leave was required to administer interrogatories, and the propriety of any interrogatory proposed to be administered was discussed on the application for leave, which is not the practice now. Then from November 1st, 1875, to October 24th, 1883, either party delivered interrogatories as of right, subject only to this—that if he exhibited interrogatories unreasonably, vexatiously, or at improper length, he might have been ordered to pay the costs of them. Now, again, leave is necessary, which will not be granted except in very exceptional circumstances before the Defence is delivered; and 5l. at least must be paid into Court for the privilege. Then between November 1st, 1875, and November 18th, 1878, the party interrogated was always allowed to apply at chambers to have objectionable interrogatories struck out; this now, as a rule, he may not do; he merely refuses to answer them in his affidavit in answer.

Setting aside Interrogatories.

Interrogatories cannot now be set aside, unless they are, as a whole, "exhibited unreasonably or vexatiously," or unless any one or more of them is or are scandalous. (Order XXXI. r. 7; *Gay* v. *Labouchere*, 4 Q. B. D. 206; 48 L. J. Q. B. 279; 27 W. R. 413.) Any objection to particular interrogatories, or portions of interrogatories, on the ground that they are irrelevant, or "fishing," &c., must be taken in the affidavit in answer, and is no ground for an application to set the interrogatories aside. And both the phrases, "unreasonable or vexatious" and "scandalous," have special meanings. Masters at Chambers, following the dictum of Pollock, B., in *Gay* v. *Labouchere* (4 Q. B. D. 207), construe "unreasonable or vexatious" as referring to the time or stage in the cause at which they are exhibited; in short, that they are "premature." (See *Mercier* v. *Cotton*, 1 Q. B. D. 442; 46 L. J. Q. B. 184; 24 W. R. 566; 35 L. T. 79.) A "scandalous" interrogatory may be defined as an insulting or degrading question, which is irrelevant or impertinent to the matters in issue. "Certainly nothing can be scandalous which is relevant." (*Per* Cotton, L. J., in *Fisher* v. *Owen*, 8 Ch. D. 653.) Questions which tend to criminate are not scandalous, unless they are either irrelevant or "fishing" (*Allhusen* v. *Labouchere*, 3 Q. B. D. 654; 47 L. J. Ch. 819; 27 W. R. 12; 39 L. T. 207), and will not, therefore, be struck out or set aside; the party interrogated must take the objection on oath in his answer. The only case to the contrary, since the Judicature Act came into operation (*Atherley* v. *Harvey*, 2 Q. B. D. 524; 46 L. J. Q. B. 518; 25 W. R. 727; 36 L. T. 551), was decided under a misapprehension of the previous practice in equity, as has been frequently pointed out by learned judges, and is admittedly bad law. (See the remarks of Cotton, L. J., 8 Ch. D. at p. 654.)

And even where the party might have applied to have the interrogatory struck out, he may still take the same objection in his answer. (*Fisher* v. *Owen*, 8 Ch. D. 645; 47 L. J. Ch. 477, 681; 26 W. R. 417, 581; 38 L. T. 252, 577.) He waives nothing by not applying; hence, applications to strike out particular interrogatories are now extremely rare.

Answers to Interrogatories.

The answers must be carefully drawn. The party interrogated may answer guardedly, and make qualified admissions only, so long as both the admission and the qualification are clear and definite. (*Malone* v. *Fitzgerald*, 18 L. R. Ir. 187.) It is quite admissible to answer "Yes" or "No" simply, so long as it is clear how much is thus admitted or denied. So, too, it is quite admissible to say, "I do not know," where the matter is clearly not within the deponent's own knowledge or that of his servants. He is not bound to procure information from others for the purpose of answering. (*Per* Brett, J., in *Phillips* v. *Routh*, L. R. 7 C. P. 287; *Field* v. *Bennett*, 2 Times L. R. 91, 122.) If, however, he "is interrogated about acts which are done in the presence of persons employed by him, their knowledge is his knowledge, and he is bound to answer in respect of that." (*Per* North, J., in *Rasbotham* v. *Shropshire Union Rail. and Canal Co.*, 24 Ch. D. at p. 113; 53 L. J. Ch. 327.) A party to a cause is not excused from answering relevant interrogatories on the ground that they are put as to matters which are not within his own knowledge, if such matters are within the knowledge of his agents or servants, and such knowledge was acquired by them in the ordinary course of their employment. In such a case the party interrogated is bound to obtain the information from such agents or servants, unless he can show that it would be unreasonable to require him to do so. He may be able to satisfy the Master that such agents or servants have now left his employment, or that to answer fully would occasion unreasonable expense or an unreasonable amount of inquiry into detail or the like. (*Bolckow, Vaughan & Co.* v. *Fisher and others*, 10 Q. B. D. 161 ; 52 L. J. Q. B. 12.) If, however, there is nothing to show that the acts referred to were done in the presence of the plaintiff's servants or agents, or that the answer as it stands is not perfectly genuine and fair, the person interrogated cannot be ordered to give any further information.

Illustrations.

Action by the owners of cargo against the owners of a ship for a loss alleged to have arisen from negligence in the navigation of such ship by which she ran ashore and was stranded. Interrogatories as to what was done by those on board with regard to such navigation at the time of the accident. The defendants answered that they were not on board at the time, and had no knowledge or information respecting the matters inquired into, except as appeared by the protest, of which the plaintiffs had had inspection. This answer was held insufficient, as it did not appear that there was any difficulty in the defendants' obtaining the required information from those who were in charge of the ship at the time of the accident.

Bolckow, Vaughan & Co. v. *Fisher and others*, 10 Q. B. D. 161 ; 52 L. J. Q. B. 12; 31 W. R. 235 ; 47 L. T. 724.

Action by owners of water-mills against a canal company for wrongfully diminishing the quantity of water in the river, to the injury of the plaintiffs. The defendants interrogated the plaintiffs, and asked them to give a list of the days between specified dates on which they alleged that the working of their mills was interfered with by the negligence of the defendants. The plaintiffs answered that they were unable to specify the particular days.

Held, that this answer was sufficient, and that the plaintiffs were not bound to state whether they had made inquiries of their agents, servants, and workmen.

Rasbotham v. *Shropshire Union Rail. and Canal Co.*, 24 Ch. D. 110; 53 L. J. Ch. 327; 32 W. R. 117; 48 L. T. 902.

Action for the value of certain missing casks, of which full particulars were given. Interrogatories by the plaintiffs asking whether the defendant company had not received the casks, whether they had lost them, or what had become of them. The information asked for was admittedly contained in the books of the defendant company, or of their agents, Messrs. Pickford & Co. and Chaplain & Horne. The defendant company refused the information, on the ground that it would be a great trouble to search through all these books for many years back, and that such an inquiry would be attended with great expense.

Held, by Lord Coleridge, C. J., and Denman, J. (Grove, J., *dissentiente*), that the defendant company must answer the interrogatories.

Hall v. *L. & N. W. Rail. Co.*, 35 L. T. 848.

Objections to Answer.

Any objection to answering any one or more of several interrogatories should be taken in the affidavit in answer. (Order XXXI. r. 6.) They are usually in the following or some similar form:—

1. "I object to answer the third interrogatory, on the ground that it is irrelevant, and is not put *bonâ fide* for the purposes of this action."

2. "I object to state the evidence by which I intend to establish the facts set out in paragraphs 4, 5, and 6, of my Defence." "I object to name my witnesses." (But see *Marriott* v. *Chamberlain* (C. A.), 17 Q. B. D. 154; 55 L. J. Q. B. 448; 34 W. R. 783; 54 L. T. 714.)

3. "I object to answer the fifth interrogatory on the ground that it is a fishing interrogatory, put for the purpose of making out some case under the defendant's plea of justification."

4. "I object to state the contents of a written document"; or, "the said document when produced will be the best evidence of its own contents." The following answer was held sufficient in *Dalrymple* v. *Leslie* (8 Q. B. D. 5; 51 L. J. Q. B. 61; 30

W. R. 105; 45 L. T. 478) : "I kept no copy and have no copy of the said letter, and I am unable to recollect with exactness what the statements contained therein were."

5. If the person interrogated be a solicitor, it is a sufficient answer to state "I have no personal knowledge of the matter referred to in this interrogatory, and the only information and belief that I have received or have respecting any of such matters has been derived from and is founded on information of a confidential character procured by me as solicitor of the said C., and not otherwise, for the purpose of litigation between the plaintiff and the said C., either pending or threatened by the plaintiff. I claim to be privileged from answering this interrogatory further." (*Procter* v. *Smiles*, 55 L. J. Q. B. 467, 527.) Similarly, a client may refuse to disclose information which he only obtained from his solicitor since action, and which was the result of inquiries instituted by the solicitor for the purposes of the litigation. (*Procter* v. *Raikes and another*, 3 Times L. R. 229.)

6. "In answer to the fifth interrogatory, I say that to answer the said interrogatory would tend to criminate me, wherefore I respectfully decline to answer the same"; or, "wherefore I humbly submit that I am not bound to make any further or other answer to the same." This objection must be stated in clear and unequivocal language. In *Lamb* v. *Munster* (10 Q. B. D. 110; 52 L. J. Q. B. 46; 31 W. R. 117; 47 L. T. 442), it was held sufficient for the defendant to state on oath, "I decline to answer all the interrogatories upon the ground that my answer to them might tend to criminate me." (And see *Jones* v. *Richards*, 15 Q. B. D. 439.)

A fuller form of objection will be found on pp. 187, 188.

PRECEDENTS.

The following precedents may be found of use to the student :—

Interrogatories in an Action for Goods Sold and Delivered to a Farmer, and for Work and Labour done.

1. Is not Mr. J. B. Falding your farm bailiff? Is he not your agent for the management of —— Farm? Is he not authorized to purchase goods, and to order work and labour to be done when the same are necessary for the said farm? If nay, state what his authority and position are.

2. Were not the goods mentioned in the first item indorsed on the writ ordered of the plaintiffs by the said J. B. Falding in the month of September 1876 by word of mouth? If nay, state when and where and of whom the said goods were ordered, and whether verbally or by letter. If verbally, state the terms of the said order. If by letter, identify the document.

3. Were not the said goods delivered to you at the said farm? Have you not seen the said goods, or some and which of them, on your said farm? Have not the said goods, or some and which of them, been used and consumed on the said farm? If nay, state to the best of your knowledge, information, and belief, where each of the said goods now is?

4. Are the prices charged by the plaintiffs for the said goods fair and reasonable? Which of the said prices do you allege to be exorbitant? Specify in each case what sum you would deem a proper and reasonable price.

5. Do you allege that any price was agreed for any and which of the said goods? Which of the prices charged by the plaintiffs do you allege to be in excess of the agreed price? If any, state precisely what price was agreed for each item, and when and where and by whom such agreement was made, and whether verbally or in writing. If verbally, give the substance of it; if in writing, identify the document.

6. Have not the plaintiffs in fact paid the moneys and done the work, and bestowed the attendances set out in their particulars? If nay, state specifically which payments you say were not made, what work you say was not done, and which of the said attendances you say were not bestowed.

7. Were not all such payments made, work done, and attendances bestowed for you at your request, or at the request of the said Mr. Falding, and which? If nay, specify each instance in which you say there was no such request by either of you. Was not Mr. Falding authorized to give such orders on your behalf?

Interrogatories in an Action for Dilapidations.

1. Do you allege that the premises mentioned in the Statement of Claim are now in good and tenantable repair? If nay, set out a full list of all defects of repair which you admit now exist. Do you allege that any and which of such defects existed at the date of the demise of the said premises to you?

2. Is not Mr. A. inspector of nuisances for the borough of T.? Did he not visit and inspect the premises, and when? Did he not report thereon? If yea, identify the document. Is not every statement of fact contained in that report true? If nay, specify every statement therein contained of which you dispute the accuracy, and state what you allege were the true facts in that behalf.

Interrogatories setting up that the Goods were supplied to Defendant as Agent only for others.

1. Were not the goods, the subject-matter of this action, bought of you by X., Y., and Z., or some one or more and which of them? Were not the said goods supplied by you entirely for their use and benefit, and not at all for the use and benefit of the defendant?

2. Were not the said goods supplied for use in or upon certain brick-making works at Swindon? Who was then the owner of the said works, and who was then the occupier? Were you not then aware that the defendant was neither the owner nor occupier of the said brick-making works?

3. Were not the said goods ordered and bought of you, and were you not requested to deliver the same at the said brick-making works by the said X., Y., and Z., or some one or more and which of them, or by some one, and whom, for the use and on the account of one or all of them? If nay, who gave you the said orders, and who requested you to supply the said goods, and when?

4. If you say the defendant gave the said orders, and made the said request, did he not then expressly tell you that he was the servant and agent of the said X., Y., and Z., or some one or more of them, and that he was acting in that capacity in giving the said orders and making the said request, and not otherwise? If nay, for whom did he state that he was acting? Did he not tell you that he was not acting on his own behalf, but for some principal?

5. Did you not know, at the time you received the said orders, that the defendant was then the agent and servant of the said X., Y., and Z., or some one or more of them, and that he was not then acting in his own behalf, but on behalf of some principal?

6. Did you not charge the price of the said goods to the said X., Y.,

and Z., or to some one or more, and which, of them? Did you not give them, or some one or more, and which, of them, credit for the same?

7. Have you not applied to the said X., Y., and Z., or to some one or more, and which, of them, for payment for the same? Did you not prove against the estate of X. for the amount of your claim in this action? Did you not attend and vote at a meeting of his creditors held on July 3rd 1889 or on some other and what day?

8. Did not the said Y. give you a bill of exchange for 60*l*., or some other, and what, amount, as part payment for the said goods, for which you now are suing the defendant? Did not the said Z. give you a bill of exchange for the full amount which you now claim from the defendant? Did you not accept the same in full satisfaction and discharge of your present claim?

Interrogatories in an Action brought against the Editor of a Newspaper who has published an Anonymous Letter signed " A Ratepayer."

1. On what day did you receive the letter signed "A Ratepayer," which is the subject of this action? How long was it after the receipt of the said letter that you published the same in your paper, " The —— Gazette?"

2. Was the said letter sent to you anonymously? Or was there anything, and what, sent with the said letter to show you who wrote it, or from whom it came?

3. Who delivered the said letter at your office? Who received it? Did you yourself see the person who brought it? If nay, who did? How long had the said letter been in your office when you first saw it?

4. Was the said letter delivered at your premises in any envelope or wrapper? Was it still in such envelope or wrapper when you first saw it? If nay, who had opened such envelope or wrapper? Where is such envelope or wrapper now? How was it addressed? What has become of it, and when did you last see it?

5. Was the said letter sent to you by hand, by rail, by post, and which, or how otherwise? Were there any other and what documents or papers with it? If yea, identify the same and state where the same now are and what has become of each of them. From what place did the said letter come? Was there any and what postmark on it?

6. Was any such letter accompanied by any request from any and what person that you would insert it in your paper? Were you ever asked to print the said letter? If yea, state when and by whom, and, if such request was in writing, identify the document. Did you consent or refuse to print it? What reply did you make to such request, if any,

and when and to whom and whether verbally or in writing? If verbal, state what you said. If in writing, identify the document.

7.* Did you know from whom the said letter had come when you first saw it? Do you know now? If yea, state from whom and how and why you knew this. Is it the fact that you published the said letter without knowing who sent it? Did you recognise the handwriting of the said letter or of the address? If yea, state to the best of your knowledge who the writer is, and whether he is or has at any and what time been a ratepayer of St. Saviour's parish?

8. Did you before you published the said letter, make any and what inquiries as to whether the writer thereof was a ratepayer of St. Saviour's parish, or as to who the writer was? If yea, what was the nature and result of such inquiries, and when and how and of whom did you make them?

9. Did you, before you published the said letter take any and what precautions, or make any and what inquiries as to the truth of the statements contained in it, or make any and what inquiry at all with respect to the said letter? Have you ever made any such and what inquiries, and when? And what was the result of such inquiries?

10. Did you at the time that you published the said letter believe that the allegations contained therein, and those made in the article set out in the Statement of Claim, were true? If yea, what were your grounds for such belief?

11. Was the letter received by you altered in any way before insertion in "The —— Gazette?" If yea, specify exactly each such alteration.

12. What number of copies of "The —— Gazette" for the 26th of March, and for the 2nd April were printed and published respectively? How many copies of the issue of the 26th of March circulated in St. Saviour's parish? Was not that a larger number than usual?

Objections to Answer.

As to the first and next succeeding interrogatories up to and including the seventh, I object to answer the same on the grounds that they are,

---

* Interrogatory 7 above is only admissible where the identity of such writer is a fact material to some issue raised in the case. (*Hennessy* v. *Wright* (No. 2), 24 Q. B. D. 445, n.; 36 W. R. 879; *Gibson* v. *Evans*, 23 Q. B. D. 384; 58 L. J. Q. B. 612; 61 L. T. 388.) And Interrogatory 9 is not admissible where the only issue is as to the amount of damages. (*Parnell* v. *Walter and another*, 24 Q. B. D. 441; 59 L. J. Q. B. 125; 38 W. R. 270; 62 L. T. 75.)

and each of them is, irrelevant and immaterial to the issues to be tried in this action, and unreasonable, vexatious, prolix, oppressive, and not put *bonâ fide* for the purposes of this action.

I decline to answer the remainder of the Interrogatories, on the grounds that they are, and each of them is, scandalous and irrelevant, that they are oppressive and unnecessary and have been exhibited unreasonably and vexatiously, that they are not material at the present stage of this action, and do not relate to any matters in question in this action, but are an abuse of the process of the Court and ought not to be allowed.

Chapter XI.

ADVICE ON EVIDENCE.

As soon as notice of trial is given, or in urgent cases even sooner, the papers should be laid before counsel for his advice on evidence. This should always be done by both sides, even in cases apparently simple; else the action may be lost for want of some certificate or other formal piece of proof, as in *Collins* v. *Carnegie* (1 A. & E. 695). Every document in the case should be sent in to counsel, especially the affidavits of documents, the answers to interrogatories, and the draft notices to produce, and to inspect and admit, the various documents in the case. Also some statement as to the oral evidence proposed to be given, if not the full proofs which will afterwards form part of the brief.

Counsel in advising on evidence must consider, first, what are the issues in the case, and which lie on the plaintiff, which on the defendant; and then state *seriatim* how each is to be proved or rebutted. This is, perhaps, the most important piece of work which a junior barrister has to do; success at the trial so much depends on the care with which the case is got up beforehand, and the country solicitor who has perhaps had but little experience in litigious work looks to counsel for advice on every necessary detail. Besides, as the advice on evidence is often copied into, or merged in, the brief, the junior counsel has thus an opportunity of laying his views of the facts and of the law clearly before his leader, of which he is generally glad to avail himself.

Burden of Proof.

The burden of proof lies as a rule upon the party who has in his pleading maintained the *affirmative* of the issue; for a *negative* is in general incapable of proof. Consequently, unless he succeed in proving that affirmative, the jury are to consider the opposite proposition, the negative of the issue, as established. (See *Catherwood* v. *Chabaud*, 1 B. & Cr. 150.) The affirmative is generally maintained by the party who first raises the issue. Thus, the *onus* lies on the defendant, as a rule, to prove all facts which he has pleaded by way of confession and avoidance, such as fraud, performance, release, rescission, accord and satisfaction, &c. But this is not always so. In some cases, though the point has been raised by the defendant in his Defence, the burden of proof is on the plaintiff. Thus, if the defendant has pleaded the Statute of Limitations, the *onus* of proving that his cause of action arose within the period prescribed lies on the plaintiff (*Wilby* v. *Henman*, 2 Cr. & M. 658); for the defendant pleaded in the negative that it did not arise within that time. There are also exceptions to the rule that the burden of proof lies on the party who affirms. For if money has been paid into Court the *onus* lies on the plaintiff of proving that the amount is insufficient, although it was the defendant who pleaded affirmatively that it was sufficient. If the defendant in an action of libel has pleaded a plea under sect. 2 of Lord Campbell's Act, the *onus* lies on him to prove that the libel was inserted without gross negligence. (*Per* Wills, J., in *Peters* v. *Edwards*, 3 Times L. R. 423.) So, too, if the issue be whether A. B. is still living or not, the party asserting the negative, viz., that he is not living, must prove the death; because the presumption is in favour of the continuance of life, till the contrary be shown. (*Wilson* v. *Hodges*, 2 East, 312.) So, upon the issue whether a bill of exchange was accepted for good consideration, the burden of proof lies on the party asserting the negative; the presumption is that such negotiable instruments are given for value. (Order XIX. r. 25.) Other exceptions are noticed in Taylor on Evidence (8th ed.), Vol. I., pp. 343—347.

As a rule, the party on whom the *onus* lies begins at the trial. But there is an exception where the plaintiff claims unliquidated damages. In such cases, the plaintiff is always entitled to begin and prove his damage, even though the burden of proof lies on the defendant. (*Carter* v. *Jones*, 6 C. & P. 64; 1 M. & R. 281; *Mercer* v. *Whall*, 5 Q. B. 447, 462, 463; 14 L. J. Q. B. 267, 272.)

Witnesses.

Having determined what facts his client has to prove at the trial, counsel proceeds to state how they are to be proved, what witnesses must be called, and what documents must be put in on each issue. Do not forget that *primâ facie* proof is often all that is necessary; some letter may contain an admission which will shift the *onus* of proof on to your opponent. You need not prove every fact up to the hilt. For instance, strict proof of the plaintiff's special character is not, as a rule, required. In order to prove that a man holds a public office, it is not necessary to produce his written or sealed appointment thereto. (*Berryman* v. *Wise*, 4 T. R. 366; *Cannell* v. *Curtis*, 2 Bing. N. C. 228; 2 Scott, 379.) It is sufficient to show that he acted in that office, and it will be presumed that he acted legally. Each party should be prepared with evidence not only to prove the issues which lie upon him, but also to rebut his adversary's case. It may be necessary to postpone the trial in order to secure the attendance of witnesses who are ill or absent abroad. (*Turner* v. *Meryweather*, 7 C. B. 251; 18 L. J. C. P. 155; *Brown* v. *Murray*, 4 D. & R. 830; *M'Cauley* v. *Thorpe*, 1 Chit. 685; 5 Madd. 19.) In other cases, it may be necessary to apply for a commission abroad, or for the examination before trial of a witness who is dangerously ill or about to leave the country. (Order XXXVII. r. 5; *Procter* v. *Tyler*, 3 Times L. R. 282.) It is generally necessary to state on affidavit the general nature of the evidence which such witness is expected to give. (*Barry* v. *Barclay*, 15 C. B. N. S. 849.) It is in every way a misfortune not to have the evidence of an important witness given orally in Court. The deposition, when read aloud at the trial, produces but a faint effect; the jury like to see the man, and hear him examined and cross-examined. Moreover, your opponent learns exactly what your case is, and has plenty of time to prepare his answer to it.

Documentary Evidence.

After he has decided what witnesses to call, counsel must next consider what documents will be required, and how, if the originals cannot be produced, they may be proved by secondary evidence. For this purpose he must carefully go through the notice to inspect and admit, and the notice to produce, and advise on their sufficiency. For unless notice has been given to your opponent to produce a document in his possession, you cannot give any secondary evidence of its contents. And unless you give him notice to inspect and admit the documents in your possession, you will have to give strict proof of the handwriting at the trial. If, after notice to admit, your opponent denies his own handwriting, he will probably, even though he succeed on other issues, have to pay the costs of proving this document. But your client, if successful, will not be allowed such costs, unless he served on his opponent notice to admit it, and so gave him the opportunity of saving the expense. (Order XXXII. r. 2.)

Proof of Handwriting.

Anyone who has ever seen the defendant write (even though once only: *Garrells* v. *Alexander*, 4 Esp. 37), can be called to prove his handwriting. So can anyone who has corresponded with the defendant, or seen letters which have arrived in answer to letters addressed to the defendant. Thus, a clerk in a merchant's office, who has corresponded with the defendant on his master's behalf, may be called to prove the defendant's handwriting. (*R.* v. *Slaney*, 5 C. & P. 213.) The usual course is for the plaintiff's counsel merely to ask the witness, "Are you acquainted with the defendant's handwriting?" leaving it to defendant's counsel to cross-examine as to the extent of his acquaintance. Such cross-examination will only weaken the force of his evidence, not destroy its admissibility. (*Eagleton* v. *Kingston*, 8 Ves. 473; *Doe* d. *Mudd* v. *Suckermore*, 5 A. & E. 730.) By sect. 27 of the Common Law Procedure Act, 1854, "comparison of a disputed writing with any writing proved to the satisfaction of the judge to be genuine, shall be permitted to be made by the witnesses; and such writings, and the evidence of witnesses respecting the same, may be submitted to the Court and jury as evidence of the genuineness or otherwise of the writing in dispute." It may be necessary to call some expert in handwriting. But the jury generally receive the evidence of experts with caution. It is well to back it up with evidence of witnesses who have seen the person write. If the suggestion is that the document was written by either party to the suit, and he is present in Court, he may, it seems, be then and there required to write something which the Court and jury may compare with the document in dispute. (*Doe* d. *Devine* v. *Wilson*, 10 Moo. P. C. at p. 530.)

Proof of a Document.

The original document itself must be produced at the trial, if it be possible to obtain it. And if the plaintiff puts it in, the defendant is entitled to have the whole of it read as part of the plaintiff's case. (*Cooke* v. *Hughes*, R. & M. 112.) The original must be carefully traced where it has passed through many hands. (*Fryer* v. *Gathercole*, 4 Ex. 262; 18 L. J. Ex. 389;

Adams v. *Kelly*, Ry. & Moo. 157.) If the original be not produced, it must be satisfactorily accounted for. But where a large number of copies are printed from the same type, or lithographed at the same time by the same process, none of them are copies in the legal sense of the word. They are all counterpart originals, and each is primary evidence of the contents of the rest. (*R.* v. *Watson*, 2 Stark. 129; *Johnson* v. *Hudson and Morgan*, 7 A. & E. 233, n.)

Sometimes a grave difficulty is experienced in putting in evidence a state document, *e.g.*, a letter or memorial sent to a Secretary of State or to some government department. An objection is often raised to production of such documents on grounds of public policy. If this objection appears to the judge to be well founded, no evidence can be given of the contents of such letter or memorial. In *Beatson* v. *Skene* (5 H. & N. 838; 29 L. J. Ex. 430; 6 Jur. N. S. 780; 2 L. T. 378) it was decided that the objection must be taken by the head of the public department of State, who is alone able to judge. The strict rule on the point is that "the Court is entitled to have the pledge and security of the head officer of state to give the reason for the non-production of those documents which it is objected to produce, and to demand that he shall come into the witness-box, and there say that he is the head of the department, and objects to such and such documents being produced, specifying them, on the ground of public policy." But as a rule the judge does not trouble the head of the department to attend in Court but accepts the evidence of a government clerk, who states that the head officer has directed him to take the objection.

Secondary Evidence.

If the original document has been lost or destroyed, secondary evidence may be given of it, except where the objection is taken by the proper officer that the document is an official one which is privileged from production on the ground of public policy.

In that case the same public policy requires that no secondary evidence of its contents shall be given. (*Home* v. *Bentinck*, 2 Brod. & B. 130; *Anderson* v. *Hamilton*, Ib. 156, n.; *Stace* v. *Griffith*, L. R. 2 P. C. 428; 6 Moore, P. C. C. N. S. 18; 20 L. T. 197; *Dawkins* v. *Lord Rokeby* (Ex. Ch.), L. R. 8 Q. B. 255.) The plaintiff is also entitled to give secondary evidence of the contents of the document, if the original is in the defendant's possession and is not produced after notice to produce it has been served on the defendant's solicitor a reasonable time before the trial (*R.* v. *Boucher*, 1 F. & F. 486); and also where it is in the possession of some one beyond the jurisdiction of the Court, who refuses to produce it on request, although informed of the purpose for which it is required. (*Boyle* v. *Wiseman*, 10 Ex. 647; 24 L. J. Ex. 160; *Newton* v. *Chaplin*, 10 C. B. 356; *R.* v. *Llanfaethly*, 2 E. & B. 940; 23 L. J. M. C. 33; *R.* v. *Aickles*, 1 Leach, 330.) As to copies in the possession of the defendant's solicitor, see *Paris* v. *Levy*, 2 F. & F. 73. Where words are written, or a paper placarded, on a wall so that it cannot conveniently be brought into Court, secondary evidence may be given of its contents. (*Per* Lord Abinger in *Mortimer* v. *M'Callan*, 6 M. & W. at p. 68; *Bruce* v. *Nicolopulo*, 11 Ex. at p. 133; 24 L. J. Ex. at p. 324.)

In addition to these provisions of the common law, several statutes have been passed which make copies of registers and other public and official documents admissible in evidence, if duly authenticated, so as to save the necessity for conveying ancient records up and down the country. Such copies are of three kinds—

(i.) Examined copies,
(ii.) Certified copies,
(iii.) Office copies (see Roscoe's Nisi Prius (16th ed.), p. 97);

and counsel must be careful to advise his solicitor to obtain the proper kind of copy required by the particular Act.

For instance, by sect. 24 of the Common Law Procedure Act, 1854, if a witness in any cause be questioned as to whether he has been convicted of any felony or misdemeanour, and if he either denies the fact or refuses to answer, the opposite party may prove such conviction, however irrelevant the fact of such conviction may be to the matter in issue in the cause. (*Ward* v. *Sinfield*, 49 L. J. C. P. 696; 43 L. T. 253.) In former days, this could only be done by producing the original record in Court. Now the right method of proving a conviction at the assizes or quarter sessions, either for this purpose or as evidence under a plea of justification, is by a certificate under the Common Law Procedure Act, 1854, s. 25, containing the substance and effect of the indictment and conviction, but omitting the formal parts. Both this section, however, and sect. 6 of 28 & 29 Vict. c. 18, are confined to convictions for felony or misdemeanour on indictment. Hence, where the conviction was at petty sessions only, it was decided, in *Hartley* v. *Hindmarsh* (L. R. 1 C. P. 553; 35 L. J. M. C. 255; 12 Jur. N. S. 502; 14 W. R. 862; 13 L. T. 795), that either the record itself must be produced, or an examined copy of it. This involves the trouble and expense of having the record duly made up for the purpose. (*Per* Byles, J., L. R. 1 C. P. at p. 556.) But since that decision, the Prevention of Crimes Act, 1871 (34 & 35 Vict. c. 112), has become law, and though the rest of this Act applies entirely to criminal proceedings, yet sect. 18 contains the words, "in any legal proceedings whatever." Hence, certificates under that section are now received without objection in civil as well as criminal proceedings.

All questions as to the admissibility of secondary evidence are for the judge. The objection must be taken at once, and should be decided by the judge then and there. (*Boyle* v. *Wiseman*, 11 Ex. 360; 24 L. J. Ex. 284; 25 L. T. O. S. 203.) Once the copy is admitted, the Court will not afterwards entertain any objection to it. (*Williams* v. *Wilcox*, 8 A. & E. 337.)

Besides such documents as are in themselves primary or secondary evidence for one side or the other, there are documents which may be referred to by a witness in the box, to fix a date or to refresh his memory as to what was said at a particular interview. If the witness committed the words to writing shortly after they were uttered, he may refer to the writing to refresh his memory; but it must be the original memorandum that is referred to, not a fair copy. (*Burton* v. *Plummer*, 2 A. & E. 343.) Be sure and have the original in Court.

The plaintiff may also offer evidence in aggravation, the defendant in mitigation, of damages. (See *ante*, p. 27.) In all actions for libel or slander in which the defendant does not by his Defence assert the truth of the statement complained of, his counsel must consider the advisability of giving a notice under Order XXXVI. r. 37. For by that rule, "the defendant shall not be entitled on the trial to give evidence in chief, with a view to mitigation of damages, as to the circumstances under which the libel or slander was published, or as to the character of the plaintiff, without the leave of the judge, unless seven days at least before the trial he furnishes particulars to the plaintiff of the matters as to which he intends to give evidence." There has been considerable misunderstanding as to the effect of this rule. In the first place, it in no way affects the right of cross-examination. The preceding rule of the same order attempts to do that. In the next place, it in no way alters the substantive rules of evidence, but only the procedure relative thereto. It makes nothing admissible in evidence which was not admissible before. The Divisional Court decided, in *Scott* v. *Sampson* (8 Q. B. D. 491; 51 L. J. Q. B. 380; 30 W. R. 541; 46 L. T. 412), that evidence of rumours before the publication of the libel that the plaintiff had committed the offences charged in it, and evidence of particular facts and circumstances tending to show misconduct on the part of the plaintiff could not be admitted in reduction of damages, but only evidence of his general bad character. This still remains good law. But the Court held further that, assuming such evidence to be in other respects admissible, the particular facts and circumstances must be stated or referred to in the Defence, regarding this as required by Order XIX. r. 4. It is to this latter ruling that Order XXXVI. r. 37 is addressed. The pleading is not the proper place for such allegations, which merely go to reduce the damages. (See *ante*, p. 27.) They are strictly not "material facts." Yet it is only fair to the plaintiff that he should have some notice before the trial that this peculiarly offensive line will be taken by the defendant. Hence the Rule Committee require particulars of such evidence as is otherwise admissible in mitigation of damages to be stated, no longer in the Defence, but in a special notice to be delivered seven days at least before the trial.

Mode and Place of Trial.

Counsel must also consider the advisability of securing a jury, or whether it would be better for his client that the action should be tried by a learned judge alone. If he decides to have a jury, should it be a common or a special jury? (Order XXXVI. r. 7.) Next, should he apply to change the venue? The plaintiff has *primâ facie* the right to fix the place of trial; the defendant must therefore show a distinct preponderance of convenience to oust the plaintiff of his right. Where the defendant resides is quite immaterial. (*Per* Quain, J., 1 Charley, 119; Bitt. 53.) Where the cause of action arose has now but little to do with the question. The defendant must prove that a trial in the place which he prefers will be less expensive and more convenient for the majority of witnesses on both sides. That it will be more convenient for defendant's witnesses is alone no ground for the application. (*Wheatcroft* v. *Mousley*, 11 C. B. 677.) But the defendant will be entitled to have the venue changed if he can show that there is no probability of a fair trial in the place the plaintiff has selected, *e.g.*, if a local newspaper of extensive circulation has published unfair attacks on the defendant with reference to the subject-matter of the action. (*Pybus* v. *Scudamore*, Arn. 464; *Walker* v. *Brogden*, 17 C. B. N. S. 571.) If a plaintiff insists on a place of trial which is not the natural or most convenient one, he may be ordered to pay the additional costs occasioned by trying the action in that place. (*Roberts* v. *Jones*; *Willey* v. *Gt. N. Ry. Co.*, (1891) 2 Q. B. 194.)

PRECEDENTS.

I add one or two precedents.

Advice on Evidence in an Action by the Assignee of a Debt.

This is an action brought by the plaintiffs as assignees of a debt against the executor of the deceased debtor. The defendant refuses to admit either the assignment or notice of the assignment. This is, I presume, only an idle traverse. But, as both facts are denied, they must both be strictly proved; otherwise the present plaintiffs cannot recover. Give the defendant notice to inspect and admit the indenture of July 15th 1889 and our copy of the notice of assignment. Give him also notice to produce the original notice of assignment served on him on August 2nd 1889. If the defendant refuses to admit due service of this notice, it must be proved by the person who posted it, if it went by post, or who delivered it to him personally, if it was delivered by hand. The indenture of the 15th of July, 1889, can be proved either by Curtis himself or by anybody acquainted with his handwriting.

Then comes the main question in the action :—Did the testator at the date of his death owe Curtis £189, the amount assigned by Curtis to the plaintiffs [&c., *deal with the facts and difficulties of this part of the case*]. Curtis himself will be our best witness as to the original transaction, he will prove that the testator ordered him to do the work. He can refresh his memory by referring to the pocket-book in which he took down the testator's order. Be sure and have the original entry in Court and not a clean copy of it.

The plaintiffs' witnesses then will be: Mr. Curtis and his partner, the foreman, &c. (*name them all*). Mr. B. must be served with a *subpœna duces tecum* a copy of his letter to the testator and his original reply. Who is "C. Morgan" who witnessed the testator's signature to his last letter to Curtis? He should be in attendance at the trial, and a proof of his evidence should be taken and inserted in the brief, as it may be necessary to call him, if any attack is made on the genuineness of the letter.

Have in Court [*such and such documents*].

Give full notices to produce and to inspect and admit the correspondence and all relevant documents in the possession of either party. Include in the notice to produce the draft contract (undated), the . . . . and in the notice to admit, Curtis's ledger, &c. (*name the documents*). It would be well to have a copy made of all the more important documents for the use of the judge. Put them in strict order of date and each on a separate page.

Commencement of an Advice on Evidence in an Action of Deceit or Misrepresentation.

In this case the *onus* of proving all the issues lies on the plaintiff; but the defendant must, of course, be prepared with evidence to rebut any *primâ facie* case which the plaintiff may establish.

The plaintiff cannot succeed unless he prove:—

1. That the defendant or some agent of his duly authorized in that behalf made representations to the plaintiff as to some existing fact
2. With the intention of thereby inducing the plaintiff to purchase the defendant's brewery and to enter into the agreement of the 12th November, 1887.
3. That such representations were false in fact
4. To the knowledge of the defendant or of his authorized agent.
5. That such representations induced the plaintiff to buy the defendant's brewery and to enter into the said agreement.
6. That the plaintiff has thereby suffered damage. . . . . . .

Commencement of an Advice on Evidence in an Action of Malicious Prosecution.

In an action for malicious prosecution it is necessary for the plaintiff to prove five things, viz.:—

1. That the defendant preferred criminal (*or* took bankruptcy) proceedings against the plaintiff before a judicial officer.
2. That the defendant acted maliciously.
3. That the defendant acted without reasonable or probable cause.
4. That the proceedings terminated in plaintiff's favour.
5. That plaintiff has suffered in person, reputation, or pocket. (See *per* Bowen, L. J., in *Abrath* v. *N. E. Rail. Co.*, 11 Q. B. D. at p. 455, and *per* Hawkins, J., in *Hicks* v. *Faulkner*, 8 Q. B. D. 167, 175.) . . . . . .

Portion of an Advice on Evidence in an Action of Seduction.

This is an action for damages for the alleged seduction of the plaintiff's daughter by the defendant. It is really an impudent attempt to levy blackmail on the defendant by fathering upon him some other person's twins.

In an action for seduction it is necessary for the plaintiff to prove:—

1. That the girl seduced was the servant of the plaintiff, *both* at the time of the seduction and at the date of the subsequent illness and birth.
2. That the defendant seduced the girl.
3. That the child born was the result of this intercourse.
4. Loss of service, and other damages.

The pleadings put all these questions in issue, and the *onus* of proving each of them lies on the plaintiff.

1. The relationship of master and servant is the gist of the action. The plaintiff must prove that his daughter was acting in some capacity as his servant at the date of the seduction (otherwise there is no *injuria*: *Davies* v. *Williams*, 10 Q. B. 725); and also at the time of her pregnancy and illness (otherwise there would be no *damnum*: *Hedges* v. *Tagg*, L. R. 7 Ex. 283).

The fact that the daughter lived with her parents is not alone sufficient to constitute her their servant (*Hall* v. *Hollander*, 4 B. & C. 660). But "the smallest degree of service will do." (*Per* Abbott, C. J., in *Manvell* v. *Thomson*, 2 C. & P. at p. 304.) And indeed where, as here, the person seduced is the plaintiff's daughter, living in her father's house, under age, but capable of acts of service, the law holds that she owes some service to her father and will therefore presume that such services were in fact rendered. (See *Harris* v. *Butler*, 2 M. & W. at pp. 542, 543; *Rex* v. *Chillesford*, 4 B. & C. at p. 102.) It is sufficient if the plaintiff shows that he had a right to demand his daughter's services. (*Maunder* v. *Venn*, M. & M. 323.) It is clear from the decision in *Rist* v. *Faux* (32 L. J. Q. B. 386), that for the purposes of this action a person can serve two masters, and it is not enough for the defendant to show that the person he seduced was employed elsewhere during the daytime, so long as it appears that she slept at home and assisted in the evening in the household work. . . . . . .

APPENDIX.

PLEADING RULES.

Order XIX.

1. The following rules of pleading shall be used in the High Court of Justice.

2. The plaintiff shall, subject to the provisions of Order XX., and at such time and in such manner as therein prescribed, deliver to the defendant a statement of his claim, and of the relief or remedy to which he claims to be entitled. The defendant shall, subject to the provisions of Order XXI., and at such time and in such manner as therein prescribed, deliver to the plaintiff his defence, set-off, or counter-claim (if any), and the plaintiff shall, subject to the provisions of Order XXIII., and at such time and in such manner as therein prescribed, deliver his reply (if any) to such defence, set-off, or counter-claim. SUCH STATEMENTS SHALL BE AS BRIEF AS THE NATURE OF THE CASE WILL ADMIT, and the taxing officer in adjusting the costs of the action shall at the instance of any party, or may without any request, inquire into any unnecessary prolixity, and order the costs occasioned by such prolixity to be borne by the party chargeable with the same.

3. A defendant in an action may set-off, or set-up, by way of counter-claim against the claims of the plaintiff, any right or claim, whether such set-off or counter-claim sound in damages or not, and such set-off or counter-claim shall have the same effect as a cross action, so as to enable the Court to pronounce a final judgment in the same action, both on the original and on the cross claim. But the Court or a judge may, on the application of the plaintiff before trial, if in the opinion of the Court or judge such set-off or counter-claim cannot be conveniently disposed of in the pending action, or ought not to be allowed, refuse permission to the defendant to avail himself thereof.

4. Every pleading shall contain, and contain only, a statement in a summary form of the material facts on which the party pleading relies for his claim or defence, as the case may be, but not the evidence by which they are to be proved, and shall, when necessary, be divided into paragraphs, numbered consecutively. Dates, sums, and numbers shall be expressed in figures, and not in words. Signature of counsel shall not be necessary; but where pleadings have been settled by counsel or a special pleader, they shall be signed by him, and if not so settled they shall be signed by the solicitor or by the party if he sues or defends in person.

5. The Forms in Appendices C, D, and E, when applicable, and where they are not applicable forms of the like character, as near as may be, shall be used for all pleadings, and where such forms are applicable and sufficient any longer forms shall be deemed prolix, and the costs occasioned by such prolixity shall be disallowed to or borne by the party so using the same, as the case may be.

6. In all cases in which the party pleading relies on any misrepresentation, fraud, breach of trust, wilful default, or undue influence, and in all other cases in which particulars may be necessary beyond such as are exemplified in the forms aforesaid, particulars (with dates and items if necessary) shall be stated in the pleading; provided that, if the particulars be of debt, expenses, or damages, and exceed three folios, the fact must be so stated, with a reference to full particulars already delivered or to be delivered with the pleading.

7. A further and better statement of the nature of the claim or defence, or further and better particulars of any matter stated in any pleading, notice, or written proceeding requiring particulars, may in all cases be ordered, upon such terms, as to costs and otherwise, as may be just.

8. The party at whose instance particulars have been delivered under a judge's order shall, unless the order otherwise provides, have the same length of time for pleading after the delivery of the particulars that he had at the return of the summons. Save as in this Rule provided, an order for particulars shall not, unless the order otherwise provides, operate as a stay of proceedings, or give any extension of time.

9. Every pleading which shall contain less than ten folios (every figure being counted as one word) may be either printed or written,

or partly printed and partly written, and every other pleading, not being a petition or summons, shall be printed.

10. Every pleading or other document required to be delivered to a party, or between parties, shall be delivered in the manner now in use to the solicitor of every party who appears by a solicitor, or to the party if he does not appear by a solicitor, but if no appearance has been entered for any party, then such pleading or document shall be delivered by being filed with the proper officer.

11. Every pleading shall be delivered between parties, and shall be marked on the face with the date of the day on which it is delivered, the reference to the letter and number of the action, the Division to which the judge (if any) to whom the action is assigned belongs, the title of the action, and the description of the pleading, and shall be indorsed with the name and place of business of the solicitor and agent, if any, delivering the same, or the name and address of the party delivering the same if he does not act by a solicitor.

12. Nothing in these Rules contained shall affect the right of any defendant to plead not guilty by statute. And every defence of not guilty by statute shall have the same effect as a plea of not guilty by statute has heretofore had. But if the defendant so plead, he shall not plead any other defence to the same cause of action without the leave of the Court or a judge.

13. EVERY ALLEGATION OF FACT in any pleading, not being a petition or summons, IF NOT DENIED SPECIFICALLY OR BY NECESSARY IMPLICATION, OR STATED TO BE NOT ADMITTED IN THE PLEADING OF THE OPPOSITE PARTY, SHALL BE TAKEN TO BE ADMITTED, except as against an infant, lunatic, or person of unsound mind not so found by inquisition.

14. Any condition precedent, the performance or occurrence of which is intended to be contested, shall be distinctly specified in his pleading by the plaintiff or defendant (as the case may be); and, subject thereto, an averment of the performance or occurrence of all conditions precedent necessary for the case of the plaintiff or defendant shall be implied in his pleading.

15. THE DEFENDANT OR PLAINTIFF (AS THE CASE MAY BE) MUST RAISE BY HIS PLEADING ALL MATTERS WHICH SHOW THE ACTION OR COUNTER-CLAIM NOT TO BE MAINTAINABLE, OR THAT THE TRANSACTION IS EITHER VOID OR VOIDABLE IN POINT OF LAW, AND ALL SUCH GROUNDS OF DEFENCE OR REPLY, AS THE CASE MAY BE, AS IF NOT RAISED WOULD

BE LIKELY TO TAKE THE OPPOSITE PARTY BY SURPRISE, OR WOULD RAISE ISSUES OF FACT NOT ARISING OUT OF THE PRECEDING PLEADINGS, as, for instance, fraud, Statute of Limitations, release, payment, performance, facts showing illegality either by statute or common law, or Statute of Frauds.

16. No pleading, not being a petition or summons, shall, except by way of amendment, raise any new ground of claim or contain any allegation of fact inconsistent with the previous pleadings of the party pleading the same.

17. It shall not be sufficient for a defendant in his statement of defence to deny generally the grounds alleged by the statement of claim, or for a plaintiff in his reply to deny generally the grounds alleged in a defence by way of counter-claim, but EACH PARTY MUST DEAL SPECIFICALLY WITH EACH ALLEGATION OF FACT OF WHICH HE DOES NOT ADMIT THE TRUTH, except damages.

18. Subject to the last preceding Rule, the plaintiff by his reply may join issue upon the defence, and each party in his pleading (if any), subsequent to reply, may join issue upon the previous pleading. Such joinder of issue shall operate as a denial of every material allegation of facts in the pleading upon which issue is joined, but it may except any facts which the party may be willing to admit, and shall then operate as a denial of the facts not so admitted.

19. When a party in any pleading denies an allegation of fact in the previous pleading of the opposite party, HE MUST NOT DO SO EVASIVELY, BUT ANSWER THE POINT OF SUBSTANCE. Thus, if it be alleged that he received a certain sum of money, it shall not be sufficient to deny that he received that particular amount, but he must deny that he received that sum or any part thereof, or else set out how much he received. And if an allegation is made with divers circumstances, it shall not be sufficient to deny it along with those circumstances.

20. When a contract, promise, or agreement is alleged in any pleading, a bare denial of the same by the opposite party shall be construed only as a denial in fact of the express contract, promise, or agreement alleged, or of the matters of fact from which the same may be implied by law, and not as a denial of the legality or sufficiency in law of such contract, promise, or agreement, whether with reference to the Statute of Frauds or otherwise.

21. Wherever the contents of any document are material, it shall

be sufficient in any pleading to state the effect thereof as briefly as possible, without setting out the whole or any part thereof, unless the precise words of the document or any part thereof are material.

22. Wherever it is material to allege malice, fraudulent intention, knowledge, or other condition of the mind of any person, it shall be sufficient to allege the same as a fact without setting out the circumstances from which the same is to be inferred.

23. Wherever it is material to allege notice to any person of any fact, matter, or thing, it shall be sufficient to allege such notice as a fact, unless the form or the precise terms of such notice, or the circumstances from which such notice is to be inferred, be material.

24. Whenever any contract or any relation between any persons is to be implied from a series of letters or conversations, or otherwise from a number of circumstances, it shall be sufficient to allege such contract or relation as a fact, and to refer generally to such letters, conversations, or circumstances without setting them out in detail. And if in such case the person so pleading desires to rely in the alternative upon more contracts or relations than one as to be implied from such circumstances, he may state the same in the alternative.

25. NEITHER PARTY NEED IN ANY PLEADING ALLEGE ANY MATTER OF FACT WHICH THE LAW PRESUMES IN HIS FAVOUR, OR AS TO WHICH THE BURDEN OF PROOF LIES UPON THE OTHER SIDE, unless the same has first been specifically denied: (*e.g.*, consideration for a bill of exchange, where the plaintiff sues only on the bill, and not for the consideration as a substantive ground of claim.)

26. No technical objection shall be raised to any pleading on the ground of any alleged want of form.

27. The Court or a judge may at any stage of the proceedings order to be struck out or amended any matter in any indorsement or pleading which may be unnecessary or scandalous or which may tend to prejudice, embarrass, or delay the fair trial of the action; and may in any such case, if they or he shall think fit, order the costs of the application to be paid as between solicitor and client.

Order XX.

1. The delivery of statements of claim shall be regulated as follows:—

(*a*) Where the writ is specially indorsed under Order III.

Rule 6, no further statement of claim shall be delivered, but the indorsement on the writ shall be deemed to be the statement of claim:

(b) Subject to the provisions of Order XIII. Rule 12, as to filing a statement of claim when there is no appearance, no statement of claim need be delivered unless the defendant at the time of entering appearance, or within eight days thereafter, gives notice in writing to the plaintiff or his solicitor that he requires a statement of claim to be delivered:

(c) If no statement of claim has been delivered and the defendant gives notice requiring the delivery of a statement of claim, the plaintiff shall, unless otherwise ordered by the Court or a judge, deliver it within five weeks from the time of the plaintiff receiving such notice:

(d) The plaintiff may (except as in (a) mentioned) deliver a statement of claim, either with the writ of summons or notice in lieu of writ of summons, or at any time afterwards either before or after appearance, notwithstanding that the defendant may have appeared and not required the delivery of a statement of claim: Provided that in no case where a defendant has appeared shall a statement be delivered more than six weeks after the appearance has been entered unless otherwise ordered by the Court or a judge:

(e) Where the plaintiff delivers a statement of claim without being required to do so, or the defendant unnecessarily requires such statement, the Court or a judge may make such order as to the costs occasioned thereby as shall be just, if it appears that the delivery of a statement of claim was unnecessary or improper.

4. Whenever a statement of claim is delivered the plaintiff may therein alter, modify, or extend his claim without any amendment of the indorsement of the writ.

5. The statement of claim must in all cases in which it is proposed that the trial should be elsewhere than in Middlesex, show the proposed place of trial.

6. Every statement of claim shall state specifically the relief which the plaintiff claims, either simply or in the alternative, and it shall not be necessary to ask for general or other relief, which

may always be given, as the Court or a judge may think just, to the same extent as if it had been asked for. And the same rule shall apply to any counter-claim made, or relief claimed by the defendant, in his defence.

7. Where the plaintiff seeks relief in respect of several distinct claims or causes of complaint founded upon separate and distinct grounds, they shall be stated, as far as may be, separately and distinctly. And the same rule shall apply where the defendant relies upon several distinct grounds of defence, set-off, or counter-claim founded upon separate and distinct facts.

8. In every case in which the cause of action is a stated or settled account, the same shall be alleged with particulars, but in every case in which a statement of account is relied on by way of evidence or admission of any other cause of action which is pleaded, the same shall not be alleged in the pleadings.

Order XXI.

1. In actions for a debt or liquidated demand in money comprised in Order III. rule 6, a mere denial of the debt shall be inadmissible.

2. In actions upon bills of exchange, promissory notes, or cheques, a defence in denial must deny some matter of fact; *e. g.*, the drawing, making, endorsing, accepting, presenting, or notice of dishonour of the bill or note.

3. In actions comprised in Order III. rule 6, classes (A.) and (B.), a defence in denial must deny such matters of fact, from which the liability of the defendant is alleged to arise, as are disputed; *e.g.*, in actions for goods bargained and sold or sold and delivered, the defence must deny the order or contract, the delivery, or the amount claimed; in an action for money had and received, it must deny the receipt of the money, or the existence of those facts which are alleged to make such receipt by the defendant a receipt to the use of the plaintiff.

4. No denial or defence shall be necessary as to damages claimed or their amount; but they shall be deemed to be put in issue in all cases, unless expressly admitted.

5. If either party wishes to deny the right of any other party to claim as executor, or as trustee whether in bankruptcy or otherwise, or in any representative or other alleged capacity, or the alleged

constitution of any partnership firm, he shall deny the same specifically.

6. Where a statement of claim is delivered to a defendant he shall deliver his defence within ten days from the delivery of the statement of claim, or from the time limited for appearance, whichever shall be last, unless such time is extended by the Court or a judge.

7. A defendant who has appeared in an action, and who has neither received nor required the delivery of a statement of claim, must deliver his defence (if any) at any time within ten days after his appearance, unless such time is extended by the Court or a judge.

8. Where leave has been given to a defendant to defend under Order XIV., he shall deliver his defence (if any) within such time as shall be limited by the order giving him leave to defend, or if no time is thereby limited, then within eight days after the order.

9. Where the Court or a judge shall be of opinion that any allegations of fact denied or not admitted by the defence ought to have been admitted, the Court or judge may make such order as shall be just with respect to any extra costs occasioned by their having been denied or not admitted.

10. Where any defendant seeks to rely upon any grounds as supporting a right of counter-claim, he shall, in his statement of defence, state specifically that he does so by way of counter-claim.

11. Where a defendant by his defence sets up any counter-claim which raises questions between himself and the plaintiff along with any other persons, he shall add to the title of his defence a further title similar to the title in a statement of claim setting forth the names of all the persons who, if such counter-claim were to be enforced by cross action, would be defendants to such cross action, and shall deliver his statement of defence to such of them as are parties to the action within the period within which he is required to deliver it to the plaintiff.

12. Where any such person as in the last preceding Rule mentioned is not a party to the action, he shall be summoned to appear by being served with a copy of the defence, and such service shall be regulated by the same rules as are hereinbefore contained with respect to the service of a writ of summons, and every defence so served shall be indorsed in the Form No. 2 in Appendix B., or to the like effect.

13. Any person not a defendant to the action, who is served with a defence and counter-claim as aforesaid, must appear thereto as if he had been served with a writ of summons to appear in an action.

14. Any person named in a defence as a party to a counter-claim thereby made may deliver a reply within the time within which he might deliver a defence if it were a statement of claim.

15. Where a defendant sets up a counter-claim, if the plaintiff or any other person named in manner aforesaid as party to such counter-claim contends that the claim thereby raised ought not to be disposed of by way of counter-claim, but in an independent action, he may at any time before reply apply to the Court or a judge for an order that such counter-claim may be excluded, and the Court or a judge may, on the hearing of such application, make such order as shall be just.

16. If, in any case in which the defendant sets up a counter-claim, the action of the plaintiff is stayed, discontinued, or dismissed, the counter-claim may nevertheless be proceeded with.

17. Where in any action a set-off or counter-claim is established as a defence against the plaintiff's claim, the Court or a judge may, if the balance is in favour of the defendant, give judgment for the defendant for such balance, or may otherwise adjudge to the defendant such relief as he may be entitled to upon the merits of the case.

19. In every case in which a party shall plead the general issue, intending to give the special matter in evidence by virtue of an Act of Parliament, he shall insert in the margin of his pleading the words "by statute," together with the year of the reign in which the Act of Parliament on which he relies was passed, and also the chapter and section of such Act, and shall specify whether such Act is public or otherwise; otherwise such defence shall be taken not to have been pleaded by virtue of any Act of Parliament.

20. No plea or defence shall be pleaded in abatement.

21. No defendant in an action for the recovery of land who is in possession by himself or his tenant need plead his title, unless his defence depends on an equitable estate or right or he claims relief upon any equitable ground against any right or title asserted by the plaintiff. But, except in the cases hereinbefore mentioned, it shall be sufficient to state by way of defence that he is so in possession, and it shall be taken to be implied in such statement that he denies, or does not admit, the allegations of fact contained in the plaintiff's

statement of claim. He may nevertheless rely upon any ground of defence which he can prove except as hereinbefore mentioned.

ORDER XXII.

1. Where any action is brought to recover a debt or damages, any defendant may, before or at the time of delivering his defence, or at any later time by leave of the Court or a judge, pay into Court a sum of money by way of satisfaction, which shall be taken to admit the claim or cause of action in respect of which the payment is made; or he may, with a defence denying liability (except in actions or counter-claims for libel or slander), pay money into Court which shall be subject to the provisions of rule 6 : Provided that in an action on a bond under the statute 8 & 9 Will. III. c. 11, payment into Court shall be admissible to particular breaches only, and not to the whole action.

2. Payment into Court shall be signified in the defence, and the claim or cause of action in satisfaction of which such payment is made shall be specified therein.

3. With a defence setting up a tender before action, the sum of money alleged to have been tendered must be brought into Court.

4. If the defendant pays money into Court before delivering his defence, he shall serve upon the plaintiff a notice specifying both the fact that he has paid in such money, and also the claim or cause of action in respect of which such payment has been made. Such notice shall be in the Form No. 3 in Appendix B., with such variations as circumstances may require.

5. In the following cases of payment into Court under this Order, viz. :—

(*a*) When payment into Court is made before delivery of defence;

(*b*) When the liability of the defendant, in respect of the claim or cause of action in satisfaction of which the payment into Court is made, is not denied in the defence;

(*c*) When payment into Court is made with a defence setting up a tender of the sum paid;

the money paid into Court shall be paid out to the plaintiff on his request, or to his solicitor on the plaintiff's written authority, unless the Court or a judge shall otherwise order.

6. When the liability of the defendant, in respect of the claim or cause of action in satisfaction of which the payment into Court has

ORDER XXII.

been made, is denied in the defence, the following rules shall apply :—

(*a*) The plaintiff may accept, in satisfaction of the claim or cause of action in respect of which the payment into Court has been made, the sum so paid in, in which case he shall be entitled to have the money paid out to him as hereinafter provided, notwithstanding the defendant's denial of liability, whereupon all further proceedings, in respect of such claim or cause of action, except as to costs, shall be stayed ; or the plaintiff may refuse to accept the money in satisfaction and reply accordingly, in which case the money shall remain in Court subject to the provisions hereinafter mentioned :

(*b*) If the plaintiff accepts the money so paid in, he shall, after service of such notice in the Form No. 4 in Appendix B., as is in Rule 7 mentioned, or after delivery of a reply accepting the money, be entitled to have the money paid out to himself on request, or to his solicitor on the plaintiff's written authority, unless the Court or a judge shall otherwise order :

(*c*) If the plaintiff does not accept, in satisfaction of the claim or cause of action in respect of which the payment into Court has been made, the sum so paid in, but proceeds with the action in respect of such claim or cause of action, or any part thereof, the money shall remain in Court and be subject to the order of the Court or a judge, and shall not be paid out of Court except in pursuance of an order. If the plaintiff proceeds with the action in respect of such claim or cause of action, or any part thereof, and recovers less than the amount paid into Court, the amount paid in shall be applied, so far as is necessary, in satisfaction o the plaintiff's claim, and the balance (if any) shall, under such order, be repaid to the defendant. If the defendant succeeds in respect of such claim or cause of action, the whole amount shall, under such order, be repaid to him.

7. The plaintiff, when payment into Court is made before delivery of defence, may within four days after the receipt of notice of such payment, or when such payment is first signified in a defence, may, before reply, accept in satisfaction of the claim or cause of

action in respect of which such payment has been made, the sum so paid in, in which case he shall give notice to the defendant in the Form No. 4 in Appendix B., and shall be at liberty, in case the entire claim or cause of action is thereby satisfied, to tax his costs after the expiration of four days from the service of such notice, unless the Court or a judge shall otherwise order, and in case of non-payment of the costs within forty-eight hours after such taxation, to sign judgment for his costs so taxed.

8. Where money is paid into Court in two or more actions which are consolidated, and the plaintiff proceeds to trial in one, and fails, the money paid in and the costs in all the actions shall be dealt with under this Order in the same manner as in the action tried.

9. A plaintiff may, in answer to a counter-claim, pay money into Court in satisfaction thereof, subject to the like conditions as to costs and otherwise as upon payment into Court by a defendant.

10. Where money is paid into Court in the Queen's Bench Division under the certificate of a Master or Associate, such payment must be expressly authorised in such certificate.

11. Money paid into Court under an order of the Court or a judge or certificate of a Master or Associate shall not be paid out of Court except in pursuance of an order of the Court or a judge: Provided that, where before the delivery of defence money has been paid into Court by the defendant pursuant to an order under the provisions of Order XIV., he may (unless the Court or a judge shall otherwise order), by his pleading, appropriate the whole or any part of such money, and any additional payment, if necessary, to the whole or any specified portion of the plaintiff's claim; and the money so appropriated shall thereupon be deemed to be money paid into Court pursuant to the preceding rules of this Order relating to money paid into Court, and shall be subject in all respects thereto.

Order XXIII.

1. A plaintiff shall deliver his reply, if any, in Admiralty actions within six days, and in other actions within twenty-one days, after the defence or the last of the defences shall have been delivered, unless the time shall be extended by the Court or a judge.

2. No pleading subsequent to reply other than a joinder of issue shall be pleaded without leave of the Court or a judge, and then shall be pleaded only upon such terms as the Court or judge shall think fit.

3. Subject to the last preceding Rule, every pleading subsequent to reply shall be delivered within four days after the delivery of the previous pleading, unless the time shall be extended by the Court or a judge.

4. Where a counter-claim is pleaded, a reply thereto shall be subject to the Rules applicable to statements of defence.

5. As soon as any party has joined issue upon the preceding pleading of the opposite party simply without adding any further or other pleading thereto, or has made default as mentioned in Order XXVII. r. 13, the pleadings as between such parties shall be deemed to be closed.

6. No new assignment shall be necessary or used. But everything which was formerly alleged by way of new assignment may hereafter be introduced by amendment of the statement of claim, or by way of reply.

Order XXIV.

1. Any ground of defence which has arisen after action brought, but before the defendant has delivered his statement of defence, and before the time limited for his doing so has expired, may be raised by the defendant in his statement of defence, either alone or together with other grounds of defence. And if, after a statement of defence has been delivered, any ground of defence arises to any set-off or counter-claim alleged therein by the defendant, it may be raised by the plaintiff in his reply, either alone or together with any other ground of reply.

2. Where any ground of defence arises after the defendant has delivered a statement of defence, or after the time limited for his doing so has expired, the defendant may, and where any ground of defence to any set-off or counter-claim arises after reply, or after the time limited for delivering a reply, has expired, the plaintiff may, within eight days after such ground of defence has arisen, or at any subsequent time by leave of the Court or a judge, deliver a further defence or further reply as the case may be, setting forth the same.

3. Whenever any defendant, in his statement of defence, or in any further statement of defence as in the last Rule mentioned, alleges any ground of defence which has arisen after the commencement of the action, the plaintiff may deliver a confession of such defence (which confession may be in the Form No. 5 in Appendix B.,

with such variations as circumstances may require), and may thereupon sign judgment for his costs up to the time of the pleading of such defence, unless the Court or a judge shall, either before or after the delivery of such confession, otherwise order.

Order XXV.

1. No demurrer shall be allowed.

2. Any party shall be entitled to raise by his pleading any point of law, and any point so raised shall be disposed of by the judge who tries the cause at or after the trial, provided that by consent of the parties, or by order of the Court or a judge on the application of either party, the same may be set down for hearing and disposed of at any time before the trial.

3. If, in the opinion of the Court or a judge, the decision of such point of law substantially disposes of the whole action, or of any distinct cause of action, ground of defence, set-off, counter-claim, or reply therein, the Court or judge may thereupon dismiss the action or make such other order therein as may be just.

4. The Court or a judge may order any pleading to be struck out, on the ground that it discloses no reasonable cause of action or answer, and in any such case or in case of the action or defence being shown by the pleadings to be frivolous or vexatious, the Court or a judge may order the action to be stayed or dismissed, or judgment to be entered accordingly, as may be just.

5. No action or proceeding shall be open to objection, on the ground that a merely declaratory judgment or order is sought thereby, and the Court may make binding declarations of right whether any consequential relief is or could be claimed, or not.

Order XXVII.

13. If the plaintiff does not deliver a reply, or any party does not deliver any subsequent pleading, within the period allowed for that purpose, the pleadings shall be deemed to be closed at the expiration of that period, and all the material statements of fact in the pleading last delivered shall be deemed to have been denied and put in issue.

Order XXVIII.

1. The Court or a judge may, at any stage of the proceedings, allow either party to alter or amend his indorsement, or pleadings,

in such manner and on such terms as may be just, and all such amendments shall be made as may be necessary for the purpose of determining the real questions in controversy between the parties.

2. The plaintiff may, without any leave, amend his statement of claim, whether indorsed on the writ or not, once at any time before the expiration of the time limited for reply and before replying, or, where no defence is delivered, at any time before the expiration of four weeks from the appearance of the defendant who shall have last appeared.

3. A defendant who has set up any counter-claim or set-off may, without any leave, amend such counter-claim or set-off at any time before the expiration of the time allowed him for answering the reply, and before such answer, or in case there be no reply, then at any time before the expiration of twenty-eight days from defence.

4. Where any party has amended his pleading under either of the last two preceding Rules, the opposite party may, within eight days after the delivery to him of the amended pleading, apply to the Court or a judge to disallow the amendment, or any part thereof, and the Court or judge may, if satisfied that the justice of the case requires it, disallow the same, or allow it subject to such terms as to costs or otherwise as may be just.

5. Where any party has amended his pleading under Rules 2 or 3, the opposite party shall plead to the amended pleading, or amend his pleading, within the time he then has to plead, or within eight days from the delivery of the amendment, whichever shall last expire: and in case the opposite party has pleaded before the delivery of the amendment, and does not plead again or amend within the time above mentioned, he shall be deemed to rely on his original pleading in answer to such amendment.

6. In all cases not provided for by the preceding Rules of this Order, application for leave to amend may be made by either party to the Court or a judge, or to the judge at the trial of the action, and such amendment may be allowed upon such terms as to costs or otherwise as may be just.

7. If a party who has obtained an order for leave to amend does not amend accordingly within the time limited for that purpose by the order, or if no time is thereby limited, then within fourteen days from the date of the order, such order to amend shall, on the expiration of such limited time as aforesaid, or of such fourteen days, as

the case may be, become *ipso facto* void, unless the time is extended by the Court or a judge.

8. An indorsement or pleading may be amended by written alterations in the copy which has been delivered, and by additions on paper to be interleaved therewith if necessary, unless the amendments require the insertion of more than 144 words in any one place, or are so numerous or of such a nature that the making them in writing would render the document difficult or inconvenient to read, in either of which cases the amendment must be made by delivering a print of the document as amended.

9. Whenever any indorsement or pleading is amended, the same, when amended, shall be marked with the date of the order, if any, under which the same is so amended, and of the day on which such amendment is made, in manner following, viz.: " Amended day of   pursuant to order of   dated the   of   ."

10. Whenever any indorsement or pleading is amended, such amended document shall be delivered to the opposite party within the time allowed for amending the same.

11. Clerical mistakes in judgments or orders, or errors arising therein from any accidental slip or omission, may at any time be corrected by the Court or a judge on motion or summons without an appeal.

12. The Court or a judge may at any time, and on such terms as to costs or otherwise as the Court or judge may think just, amend any defect or error in any proceedings, and all necessary amendments shall be made for the purpose of determining the real question or issue raised by or depending on the proceedings.

13. The costs of and occasioned by any amendment made pursuant to Rules 2 and 3 of this Order shall be borne by the party making the same, unless the Court or a judge shall otherwise order.

Order XXXI.

1. In any action where relief by way of damages or otherwise is sought on the ground of fraud or breach of trust, the plaintiff may at any time after delivering his statement of claim, and a defendant may, at or after the time of delivering his defence, without any order for that purpose, and in every other cause or matter the plaintiff or defendant may by leave of the Court or a judge, deliver interrogatories in writing for the examination of the opposite

parties, or any one or more of such parties, and such interrogatories when delivered shall have a note at the foot thereof, stating which of such interrogatories each of such persons is required to answer: Provided that no party shall deliver more than one set of interrogatories to the same party without an order for that purpose: Provided also that interrogatories which do not relate to any matters in question in the cause or matter shall be deemed irrelevant, notwithstanding that they might be admissible on the oral cross-examination of a witness.

2. In deciding upon any application for leave to exhibit interrogatories, the Court or judge shall take into account any offer which may be made by the party sought to be interrogated, to deliver particulars, or to make admissions, or to produce documents relating to the matter in question, or any of them.

3. In adjusting the costs of the cause or matter inquiry shall at the instance of any party be made into the propriety of exhibiting such interrogatories, and if it is the opinion of the taxing officer or of the Court or judge, either with or without an application for inquiry, that such interrogatories have been exhibited unreasonably, vexatiously, or at improper length, the costs occasioned by the said interrogatories and the answers thereto shall be paid in any event by the party in fault.

4. Interrogatories shall be in the Form No. 6 in Appendix B., with such variations as circumstances may require.

5. If any party to a cause or matter be a body corporate or a joint stock company, whether incorporated or not, or any other body of persons, empowered by law to sue or be sued, whether in its own name or in the name of any officer or other person, any opposite party may apply for an order allowing him to deliver interrogatories to any member or officer of such corporation, company, or body, and an order may be made accordingly.

6. Any objection to answering any one or more of several interrogatories on the ground that it or they is or are scandalous or irrelevant, or not *bonâ fide* for the purpose of the cause or matter, or that the matters inquired into are not sufficiently material at that stage, or on any other ground, may be taken in the affidavit in answer.

7. Any interrogatories may be set aside on the ground that they have been exhibited unreasonably or vexatiously, or struck out on the ground that they are prolix, oppressive, unnecessary, or scanda-

lous; and any application for this purpose may be made within seven days after service of the interrogatories.

8. Interrogatories shall be answered by affidavit to be filed within ten days, or within such other time as a judge may allow.

9. An affidavit in answer to interrogatories shall, unless otherwise ordered by a judge, if exceeding ten folios, be printed, and shall be in the Form No. 7 in Appendix B., with such variations as circumstances may require.

10. No exceptions shall be taken to any affidavit in answer, but the sufficiency or otherwise of any such affidavit objected to as insufficient shall be determined by the Court or a judge on motion or summons.

11. If any person interrogated omits to answer, or answers insufficiently, the party interrogating may apply to the Court or a judge for an order requiring him to answer, or to answer further, as the case may be. And an order may be made requiring him to answer or answer further, either by affidavit or by *vivâ voce* examination, as the judge may direct.

26. Any party seeking discovery by interrogatories shall, before delivery of interrogatories, pay into Court to a separate account in the action, to be called " Security for Costs Account," to abide further order, the sum of 5*l.*, and, if the number of folios exceeds five, the further sum of 10*s.* for every additional folio. Any party seeking discovery otherwise than by interrogatories shall, before making application for discovery, pay into Court, to a like account, to abide further order, the sum of 5*l.*, and may be ordered further to pay into Court as aforesaid such additional sum as the Court or a judge shall direct. The party seeking discovery shall, with his interrogatories or order for discovery, serve a copy of the receipt for the said payment into Court, and the time for answering or making discovery shall in all cases commence from the date of such service. The party from whom discovery is sought shall not be required to answer or make discovery unless and until the said payment has been made.

27. Unless the Court or a judge shall at or before the trial otherwise order, the amount standing to the credit of the " Security for Costs Account" in any cause or matter, shall, after the cause or matter has been finally disposed of, be paid out to the party by whom the same was paid in on his request, or to his solicitor on such party's written authority, in the event of the costs of the cause

or matter being adjudged to him, but, in the event of the Court or judge ordering him to pay the costs of the cause or matter, the amount in Court shall be subject to a lien for the costs ordered to be paid to any other party.

Order XXXVI.

37. In actions for libel or slander, in which the defendant does not by his defence assert the truth of the statement complained of, the defendant shall not be entitled on the trial to give evidence in chief, with a view to mitigation of damages, as to the circumstances under which the libel or slander was published, or as to the character of the plaintiff, without the leave of the judge, unless seven days at least before the trial he furnishes particulars to the plaintiff of the matters as to which he intends to give evidence.

Order LXX.

1. Non-compliance with any of these Rules, or with any rule of practice for the time being in force, shall not render any proceedings void unless the Court or a judge shall so direct, but such proceedings may be set aside either wholly or in part as irregular, or amended, or otherwise dealt with in such manner and upon such terms as the Court or judge shall think fit.

2. No application to set aside any proceeding for irregularity shall be allowed unless made within reasonable time, nor if the party applying has taken any fresh step after knowledge of the irregularity.

Order LXXII.

2. Where no other provision is made by the Acts or these Rules, the present procedure and practice remain in force.

INDEX.

ABATEMENT,
    plea in, 22, 33, 67, 118, 141, 142.
        abolished, 67, 142, 211.

ABSENCE,
    of witnesses, 191.
    beyond the seas, 162.

ABUSE,
    of process of the Court, 94, 188.
    merely vulgar, precedent of plea in slander, 157.

ACCORD AND SATISFACTION,
    plea of, 90, 138.
    proof of, 190.

ACCOUNT,
    action of, 21, 35, 44.
    indorsement for, 114, 115.
    preliminary order for, 114.
    settled, 35, 209.

ACT OF PARLIAMENT,
    where it makes no alteration in form of pleading, 23, 24, 57.
    public, need not be stated in pleading, 10, 40.
    private, must be stated, 10.
    defence by virtue of, 134, 211.

ACTION,
    forms of, at common law, 116, 117.
    separate causes of, 118, 119.
    discontinuance of, 118 n., 149, 211.
    staying, 142, 149, 152, 211.
    consolidation of, 119, 214.
    cross, 148, 150, 203, 210.
    local and transitory, 46.

ADMINISTRATOR, ADMINISTRATRIX, 22, 75.

ADMISSION,
 by party, should not be pleaded, 34.
 of documents, 78.
 of facts, 77.
 by not denying allegations in pleading, 74—79, 131, 161, 205.
 of liability, on paying money into Court, 145—148, 212.
 judgment on admissions, 78.

ADULTERY,
 particulars of, 99.

ADVICE ON EVIDENCE,
 materials required for preparing, 189.
 points of importance in :—
   burden of proof, 69, 87, 190, 191.
   necessary witnesses, 191, 192.
   proof of material documents, 192—194.
   secondary evidence of documents, 182, 192, 194, 195, 196.
   damages, 118, 125, 197.
   mode and place of trial, 128, 198. And see VENUE.
 PRECEDENTS of, 199—201.

AFFIDAVIT,
 under Order XIV., 107.
 of documents, 189.
 in answer to interrogatories, 189, 220.

AGENCY,
 pleading, 32, 80, 88, 151.
 PRECEDENT of interrogatories where defendant pleads, 185.

AGGRAVATION,
 matter of, may be pleaded, but need not be answered, 26—28, 125.
 interrogatories as to, 175.
 evidence in, 197, 198.

ALLOCATUR, 150.

ALTERNATIVE,
 promises, 122.
 pleading in the, 96, 130, 164.
 performance of condition in the, how pleaded, 122, 124.
 claim for relief in the, 119, 126, 208.

AMBIGUITY,
   of pleadings before 1875 .. 11—13.
   of negative pregnant, 85.

AMENDMENT,
   of parties, 118 n., 142.
   of pleadings, 16, 19, 109, 117, 152, 164, 165, 168, 207, 216—218.
   at trial, 16, 62, 88, 126, 137, 217.

ANCIENT LIGHTS, 34.

ANTICIPATING OPPONENT'S PLEADING, 20, 41, 141, 164.

APPEARANCE,
   to writ, 107, 113, 114, 117, 205, 208.
   by third party to counterclaim, 211.

APPROPRIATION
   of money paid into Court under Order XIV., 147, 214.

ARBITRATION,
   action on award, 10, 11, 119, 164.

ASSAULT AND BATTERY, 20, 49, 85, 89, 120.

ASSIGNMENT,
   new, 167—169.
   of leaseholds, how pleaded, 18, 52, 55, 56.
   of debt, under Judicature Act, 24, 53, 111.
   PRECEDENT of advice on evidence in action by assignee, 199.

ASSIZES, 152.

ASSUMPSIT, 30, 33, 83, 116.

ASSURANCE,
   contract of, 32, 37, 47.
          PRECEDENT of defence in action on, 155.

AUTHORITY,
   pleading, 19, 20, 55, 134, 152.
          of inferior or foreign Court, 58.
   certainty of, 56—59.

AVERMENTS,
   introductory, 37, 120, 121.
   inconsistent, 130.

AVOIDANCE,
   plea in confession and, 89—92. See CONFESSION AND AVOIDANCE.

AVOWRY IN REPLEVIN, 19, 51, 56.

AWARD,
    action on, 10, 11, 119, 164.
    "no award," plea of, 10, 11, 164.

BAD PLEADING,
    specimens of, 64, 75, 77, 79, 120.

BAILIFF,
    assisting in the execution of his duty, 20.

BAILMENT,
    action of, 16.

BANKRUPTCY,
    claim by trustee in, 81, 115, 209.

BAR,
    pleas in, 67, 142, 165.

BEGIN,
    right to, at trial, 78, 191.

BILL OF EXCHANGE, ACTION ON,
    claim in, 22, 107, 110.
    notice of dishonour, when necessary to allege, 17.
    defence to, 10, 91, 132, 209.
    consideration presumed, 190, 207.

BILL OF LADING,
    PRECEDENT of Statement of Claim in action on, 39.

BILL OF SALE, 14.

BOND,
    action on, 13, 17, 21, 30, 75, 82, 84, 86, 164, 166, 167.
        specially indorsed writ in, 108.
        under 8 & 9 Will. III. c. 11...146, 212.

BREACH,
    of contract, 121, 124, 163.
    of covenant, or condition, how assigned, 33, 51, 68, 119, 123, 124.
    of trust, particulars of, must be pleaded, 60, 204.
        interrogatories in action for, 172, 218.
    of promise of marriage, 144, 145.

BURDEN OF PROOF,
    general rule as to, 69, 190.
    shifting, 69, 87, 191.
    how it affects pleading, 22, 40, 42, 207.

BUSINESS,
    of plaintiff, when material, 18, 80, 121.

CASE,
    action on the, 116, 117, 134, 167.
    special, 136, 171.

CERTAINTY,
    of issue, 6, 41.
    of names, 36, 67, 118.
    of numbers, 103, 104.
    of damages, 44, 125.
    of time, 34, 44, 45.
    of place, 45.
    of title, 13, 46—56, 121, 135.
    of authority, 19, 20, 56.
        where defendant justifies under judicial process, 57—59.
    of charges of misconduct, 59—61, 143, 197.
    uncertainty, general observations on, 61.

CHANCERY,
    pleadings, 20, 31.
    mannerisms, 77, 79, 126, 173.

CHANGING VENUE, 129, 198.

CHARACTER,
    in which plaintiff sues, 18, 80, 121.
    representative, must be stated on writ, 106, 113.

CHARTERPARTY, 21.

CHATTELS,
    action for recovery of, 23, 48, 49.

CHEQUE,
    action on, specially indorsed writ in, 107.
        defence to, 10, 132, 209.

CLAIM,
    statement of, 116—129. See STATEMENT OF CLAIM.

CLOSE OF PLEADINGS, 5, 170, 215.

Q 2

COMMENCEMENT,
  of estate in fee simple, need not be shown, 50.
  of particular estates, must be shown, 50, 51, 52, 53.
  except where matter in inducement, 49.
  or in showing title of adversary, 55, 56.
  at trial, 78, 191.

COMMISSION,
  evidence on, 191.
  day, 152.

COMMONER,
  action by, 18, 19, 57.

COMMON LAW,
  and statute law, 23, 25, 57.
  pleading principles of, unnecessary, 10, 20.

COMPROMISE,
  action to enforce, 97.

CONDITIONS PRECEDENT,
  what are, 25.
  averment of performance of, implied in every pleading, 24, 40, 122, 137, 167, 205.
  how contested, 136, 156.
  excuse for non-performance, 122, 167.

CONFESSION,
  of defence arising after writ, 139, 215.

CONFESSION AND AVOIDANCE,
  all matters in, must be specially pleaded, 49, 52, 61, 65, 69, 90, 138.
  meaning and object of, 63, 70, 89.
  plea in, how it differs from a traverse, 64, 67, 91.
  effect of admission alone, 89.
  must be commensurate with the claim, 92.
  other defences may be pleaded with, 130.
  in the reply, 162, 163.
  in the rejoinder, 170.
  burden of proof where there is, 69, 70, 190.

CONSIDERATION,
  when a material fact, 16, 121.
  for negotiable instruments, presumed, 16, 22, 190.

CONSOLIDATING ACTIONS,
  order for, 119.

CONSTABLE,
  assisting, in execution of his duty, 152.
  can plead Not Guilty by Statute, 134.

CONTENTS OF DOCUMENT,
  pleading, 16, 34, 37, 40, 79, 122, 206.
  interrogatories as to, 177, 178.

CONTINUANCE, 4, 139.

CONTRACT,
  under seal, 16, 37, 108, 121, 154.
  actions of, 19, 121—124, 154.
    joinder of parties in, 142.
  particulars of, 98.
  breach of, how averred, 124, 163.
  facts showing insufficiency or illegality of, must be pleaded,
    8, 11, 91, 136, 156, 162, 206.
  rescission of, how pleaded, 13, 144.
  consideration for, material, 16, 121.
  customs affecting, material, 16.
  special, 116, 123, 133.
  limitation of liability under, 16.
  conditions precedent in, 24, 40, 122, 167, 205.
  of assurance, 32, 37, 47, 155.
  of agency, 32, 80, 88, 151, 185.
  bill of lading, 39.
  building, 25.
  of guarantee, 65, 66, 108.
  infant's, for necessaries, 33.
  of partnership, 32, 81, 140, 142, 210.
  of sale, 87.
  of service, 30, 69, 84.
  of suretyship, 17, 151.
  time for performance of, 34, 45.
  implied from documents, &c., 34, 107, 121, 122, 155, 207.

CONTRIBUTION, 151.

CONVERSION,
  claim in action for, 21.
  denial of, in trover, 80.
  denial that goods are plaintiff's, 62.

CONVICTION,
  of a crime, how proved, 196.

COPARCENERS, 51.

COPYHOLD,
  title to, how pleaded, 52, 53.

COPYRIGHT,
  breach of, 87, 121.

CORPORATION,
  common law powers of, 9.
  interrogatories to, how administered, 219.

COSTS,
  matters merely affecting, need not be pleaded, 40.
  claiming, in Chancery Division, 126.
  of particulars, 43, 97, 204.
  of amending pleadings, 16, 95, 96, 133, 207, 217, 218.
  of proving documents, 192.
  of misjoinder of parties, 119.
  on accepting money paid into Court, 145, 146.
  on discontinuing action, 118 n., 139, 216.
  taxation of, where there is a set-off or counterclaim, 150.
  of prolixity, 39, 64, 179, 203, 204.
  incurred vexatiously, 78, 146, 153, 179, 199, 208, 210.
      through undue delay, 153.
  security for, 138, 172, 220.

COUNSEL,
  signature of, to pleading, 6, 204.

COUNT, 4, 12.

COUNTERCLAIM,
  defendant may set up, 1, 130, 148, 203.
  equitable, 130.
  claim for relief in, 209.
  how answered, 160, 161, 162.
  against parties other than plaintiffs, 150, 151, 210, 211.
  balance adjudged to defendant on, 149, 211.
  counterclaim to, 161.
  amending, 217.
  distinction between set-off and, 149.
  principle of taxation where there is, 150.

INDEX.

COURT,
 payment into, 104, 144—147, 160, 190, 212—214.

"COURT OR JUDGE,"
 meaning of, in Rules of the Supreme Court, 170.

COVENANT,
 action on a, 134.
 action of, 116.
 exact words in a, when material, 16, 86, 123.
 to repair, 24, 44, 109, 119, 123.
 assigning breach of, 33, 68, 119, 123, 124.
 performance of, how pleaded, 85, 86, 166, 167.

"CRAVES LEAVE TO REFER," 79.

DAMAGES,
 consequential, 32, 120.
 general, 44, 125.
 special, 44, 73, 125, 133, 140, 157, 200.
  particulars of, 98, 101.
 matters affecting, 26—28, 197, 198.
 notice in mitigation of, 27, 197, 198.
 claim sounding in, 108, 148, 203.
 pleading to, 27, 40, 74, 79, 131, 133, 161, 206, 209.
 writ of enquiry to ascertain, 145.
 recovered in previous action, 139.
 particulars of, 41, 98, 204.
 certainty of, 44, 125.
 liquidated and unliquidated, 78, 108, 109, 191.
 remoteness of, 125, 157.
 accrued since writ, 118, 140.

DATES,
 importance of, 38, 44, 51.

DEATH,
 proof of, 190.

DEBT,
 action of, 116.
 where it lay, 108 n.
 indorsement of writ for, 107, 108.
 claim in, on bond, 13, 17, 21, 30, 75, 82, 84, 86, 164, 166.
 mere denial of, insufficient, 10, 132, 206, 209.
 assignment of a, 23, 53, 111, 199.
 particulars of, 41, 43, 204.

DECLARATION,
  under old pleading, 4.
  count in, 4.
  of right, 128.

DEED,
  how pleaded, 14, 122, 123.
  estoppel by, 141 n.
  when executed in wrong name, 118 n.

DEFEAZANCE, 123.

DEFENCE,
  second step in pleading, 1, 203.
  considerations affecting, 130—159, 168.
  must admit or traverse every material allegation in Statement of Claim, 74, 130.
  may confess and avoid, 89—92, 130.
  may object in point of law, 71, 130.
  may raise several defences, 4, 64, 130.
  may contain inconsistent pleas, 4, 130.
      equitable pleas, 31, 130, 131, 135, 211.
  setting up affirmative case in, 86, 87.
  to actions comprised under Order III. r. 6..10, 132, 209.
  leave for, under Order XIV., 107, 153, 210.
  special defences, 136—148.
  paying money into Court with, 144—148.
  set-off, 148—150.
  counterclaim, 148—150.
  third-party procedure, 150, 151.
  where there are several defendants, 151.
  pleading to damages, 40, 74, 79, 131, 133, 161, 206, 209.
  confession of, 139, 215.
  where defendant has no, 107, 145.
  time for delivering, 113, 152, 153, 210.
  dispensing with, 171.
  amendment of, 152.
  how answered, 160, 161, 162.
  various kinds of. See PLEA.
  PRECEDENTS of, 66, 137, 141 n., 144, 147, 154—159.

DELAY,
  in pleading, 152.
  costs occasioned by, 153.

DEMURRER,
  meaning of term, 63, 64.
  when it was necessary, 72 n., 95, 96.
  instances, of, 121, 142, 165.
  abolished, 71, 216.
  special, 37, 71 n.

DENIAL,
  of liability generally, insufficient, 8, 10, 11, 91, 132, 136, 206.
  by necessary implication, 76, 77, 81.
  must be specific, 74, 79—86, 130—133, 209. And see TRAVERSE.

DEPARTURE,
  defined, 164.
  what amounts to, 165—167.
  in reply, 165, 166, 169.
  in rejoinder, 165, 166.

DEPOSITION, 192.

DETINUE,
  action of, 47, 62, 116.
  pleading Not Guilty in, 80.

DEVISEE,
  action by, 21.

DILATORY PLEAS, 66, 67.

DISCOVERY, 102, 103.

DISHONOUR, notice of, 10, 17, 132, 209.

DISTRESS, 19, 45, 56, 134.

DOCUMENTS,
  contents of, pleading, 16, 34, 37, 40, 79, 122, 206.
      interrogatories as to, 177, 178.
  proof of, 193—196.
  secondary evidence of, 182, 192, 194, 195, 196.
  of State, 194, 195.
  copies of, 195, 196, 197.
  to refresh the memory of a witness, 197.
  affidavit of, 178, 189.
  notice to produce, 189, 192, 195, 199, 200.
  notice to inspect and admit, 189, 192, 199, 200.
  effect of notices, 192.

DONATIO MORTIS CAUSA, 9.

DOWER,
    action of, 117.
    writ of right of, 117.

DURESS, 163.

DUTY,
    pleading a, 8, 9, 68, 121, 134.

EASEMENT, 9, 13, 47, 121.

EJECTMENT, 117.

ENDORSEMENT. See INDORSEMENT.

ENTRY FOR TRIAL, 5.

EQUITABLE,
    defence, 31, 130, 131, 135, 211.
    relief, 48, 127, 135, 211.

EQUITY,
    now administered in Queen's Bench Division, 127.
    conflict between law and, 23.

ESCAPE,
    action against sheriff for, 81, 87.

ESTATE,
    title to, how pleaded, 13, 46—56.
    in fee simple, 29, 50, 51, 52, 54.
    in fee tail, 51, 52, 53.
    for life, 51, 52, 53, 54.
    for years, 29, 48, 49, 51, 52, 53, 55.
    at will, 29, 53.
    in reversion, 51, 52, 54, 55.
    in remainder, 51, 52, 55.
    particular, 48, 51, 53.
    copyhold, 52, 53.
    separate, 19, 111.

ESTOPPEL,
    title by, 54, 111.
    by matter of record, 141 n.
    by deed, 141 n.
    by matter in pais, 141 n.
    pleadings by way of, 141.
    PRECEDENT of plea of, 141 n.

EVASIVE,
  traverse, forbidden, 81—86, 131.
EVIDENCE,
  must not be pleaded, 7, 31—35, 40, 164, 204.
  advice on, 189—201.
  on commission, 191.
  disclosing, 101.
  burden of proof, on whom incumbent, 40, 42, 69, 78, 87.
  secondary, of documents, 182, 192, 194, 195.
    when admissible, 196.
EXECUTOR, EXECUTRIX,
  action against, 22, 106.
  claim by, 81, 106, 209.
  PRECEDENT of Statement of Claim in action by, 38.
EXTRAS,
  PRECEDENT of defence to claim for, 154.
EXTRA VIAM,
  new assignment, 169.

FACTS,
  must now be pleaded, 7.
  in a summary form, 7, 36—41, 203.
  not law, 8—14, 164.
  only material facts, 15—20, 40, 161.
  only those material at this stage, 20, 41, 141, 164.
  no material facts must be omitted, 18, 40, 43.
  evidence must not be pleaded, 7, 31—35, 40, 164, 204.
FACTUM PROBANDUM, FACTA PROBANTIA, 31.
FALSE IMPRISONMENT, 120, 126, 152.
FALSE REPRESENTATION,
  particulars of, 60, 61, 98, 204.
  action for, 44.
    PRECEDENT of defence to, 156.
      of advice on evidence in, 200.
FEE SIMPLE,
  estate in, title to, how pleaded, 50, 51, 52, 54.
FEE TAIL,
  estate in, title to, how pleaded, 51, 52, 53.

FELONY,
  conviction for, how proved, 196.
FORMER PROCEEDINGS, 139, 140.
FORMS OF ACTION, 116, 117.
FRAUD,
  action for, 44.
    interrogatories in, 172, 218.
      PRECEDENT of advice on evidence in, 200.
        of defence in, 156.
  motive of, material, 17, 34.
  how pleaded, 90, 91, 136, 143, 206.
  reply alleging, 162, 163.
  particulars of, 60, 61, 66, 204.
  burden of proof of, 190.
FRAUDS, STATUTE OF, 137. See STATUTE OF FRAUDS.
FREEHOLD, 45, 52, 91, 162.
FURTHER MAINTENANCE,
  pleas to the, 139.

GARNISHEE, 171.
GENERAL DAMAGE, 44, 125.
GENERAL INDORSEMENT, 113—115, 117.
GENERAL ISSUE,
  by statute, 134, 211.
  under former pleading system, 12, 60.
  not allowed in present practice, 132, 134, 211.
  Not Guilty by Statute, 93, 134, 205.
GENERAL PERFORMANCE,
  plea of, not permissible, 82, 86.
GOODS SOLD AND DELIVERED,
  action for, 10, 22, 108, 110, 132, 209.
    PRECEDENT of defence in, 154.
      of interrogatories in, 184.
GUARANTEE,
  action on, specially indorsed writ in, 108.
    PRECEDENT of pleadings in, 65, 66.

HANDWRITING,
   proof of, 173, 187, 192, 193.
HEIR,
   party claiming as, must show how, 14, 51, 53, 54.
   claim against, 56.

ILLEGALITY, 8, 11, 91, 136, 156, 162, 206.

IMMATERIAL,
   issue, 28—30, 73.
   matter, need not be answered, 29.

INCORPOREAL HEREDITAMENTS,
   claim to, 47.

INDEMNITY, 151.

INDORSEMENT,
   on writ, 106—115.
   must show representative capacity of party, 106, 113, 205.
   special, 106.
      when allowed, 107, 108, 109.
      advantage of, 107.
      is a Statement of Claim, 106, 110, 117, 208.
      amending, 109.
      PRECEDENTS of, 111, 112.
   general, 106, 113, 117.
      may be extended in Statement of Claim, 113.
      PRECEDENT of, 113.
   for an account, 106, 114, 115.
      when allowed, 114.
      PRECEDENTS of, 114, 115.

INDUCEMENT,
   matters of, 49.
   defined, 120.

INFANT,
   necessaries, 33.
   admissions by, 74, 205.
   interrogatories cannot be administered to, 178.

INJUNCTION,
   claim for, in action, 17, 113, 128.

INNUENDO, 147, 157, 159.

IN PAIS,
   estoppel, 141 n.

INTENTION,
    sometimes material, 15, 17.
    in actions of defamation, 17, 18.
    how pleaded, 34, 207.

INTEREST,
    in a policy of assurance, extent of, 47.

INTERROGATORIES,
    under former practice, 178.
    when delivered, 102, 135, 172, 179, 218.
    object of, 172.
    to a corporation, how administered, 219.
    to an infant, cannot be administered, 178.
    must be relevant, 173, 174.
    as to matters in aggravation in damages, 175.
    as to names of witnesses, 176, 182.
    "fishing," 176, 177, 182.
    incriminating, 178, 183.
    when they may be set aside, 179, 180, 219.
    affidavit in answer to, 189, 220.
    objecting to answer, 180—183, 187, 219.
    rules affecting, 218—221.
    PRECEDENTS of, 184—188.

IRREGULARITY, 93, 221.

ISSUE,
    definitions of, 2, 3, 4.
    in law, in fact, 3, 171.
    ought to be material, 7, 15—41, 73, 75.
    ought to be certain, 6, 36, 41, 42—62.
    enlarging the, 42, 77.
    affirmative of, must be proved, 69, 190.
    substance of, must be proved, 30, 191.
    issues should not be needlessly multiplied, 64.
    in lieu of pleadings, 171.
    joinder of, 91, 136, 161, 162, 169, 170, 171, 206, 214, 215.

JEOFAIL, 166.

JOINDER,
    of causes of action, 109, 118.
    of parties, 142.
    of issue, 136, 161, 162, 169, 170, 171, 206, 214, 215.
        only traverses, 91, 161.

JOINT,
 tenancy, 51.
 and several liability, 140, 142.
JUDGMENT,
 declaratory, 128, 216.
 pleading authority of, 58, 59.
 by default, 113, 145, 153.
JUDGMENT RECOVERED,
 plea of, 59, 139, 140.
"JUMPING BEFORE YOU COME TO THE STILE," 20, 164.
JURISDICTION,
 pleas to the, 67.
 of inferior or foreign Court, 58.
JURY,
 trial by, 1, 198.
 sheriff's, 145.
JUSTIFICATION,
 pleas in, 57, 69, 70, 152, 163.
  are in confession and avoidance, 89, 90.
 under judicial process, 57—59.
 in libel and slander actions, 60, 89, 92, 143, 158, 177.

LACHES, 44, 90.
LAND,
 action for recovery of. See RECOVERY OF LAND.
LAW,
 decided by Judge or Court, 1, 8.
 matter of, not traversable, 41, 67, 74.
  need not be alleged in pleading, 8—14, 164.
 issue in, 3, 171.
  See PLEADING, OBJECTION IN POINT OF LAW.
LAW AND EQUITY,
 administered together in Supreme Court, 114, 127.
 conflict between, 23.
LEASE,
 action on, 18, 44, 54, 55.
 when pleaded in confession and avoidance, 52, 90, 162, 165.
 specific performance of, 163.

LEAVE TO AMEND AT TRIAL, 16, 62, 88, 126, 137, 217.

LEAVE TO DEFEND, 107, 153, 210.

LIABILITY,
  mere denial of, 8, 10, 11, 91, 132, 136, 206, 209.
  joint, 138.
    and several, 140, 142.
  payment into Court admitting, 145, 212.
    denying, 138, 146, 147, 212.
  proviso limiting, material, 16.

LIBEL,
  precise words of, material, 16, 121.
  action for, 44, 69, 120.
    defence to, 21, 152.
    justifying the words, 60, 89, 143.
      part of the words, 28.
    plea of privilege, 10, 21, 92, 144.
      under Lord Campbell's Act, 148, 190.
    paying money into Court in, 147, 212.
    PRECEDENTS of defences to, 158, 159.
    interrogatories in, 174, 175.
    PRECEDENTS of interrogatories in, 186.
  particulars of, 44, 102.
    in mitigation of damages, under Ord. XXXVI.
      r. 37 .. 27, 197, 221.

LIBERUM TENEMENTUM,
  plea of, when sufficient, 52, 91.
    reply to, 162.

LIEN, 49, 90, 138.

LIMITATIONS, STATUTE OF, 137. See STATUTE OF LIMITATIONS.

LIQUIDATED DEMANDS,
  what are, 108.
  indorsement in case of, 107—112.
  mere denial of debt, inadmissible, 10, 132, 209.
  paying money into Court in action for, 146.

LOCAL,
  and transitory actions, distinction between, 46.

LORD CAMPBELL'S ACT,
  payment into Court under, 148, 190.

LUNATIC, 74, 205.

MALICE,
   pleading, 34, 175, 207.
   justification, evidence of, 143.
MALICIOUS PROSECUTION,
   action for, 104.
      PRECEDENT of advice on evidence in, 200.
MARRIED WOMAN,
   action against, 19, 111.
MATERIAL FACTS,
   must now be pleaded, 7—41, 116, 141 n.
   not law, 8—14, 164.
   unnecessary to plead principles of common law, 10, 20.
   or provisions of public statutes, 10, 40.
   secus, private Acts of Parliament, 10.
   evidence must not be pleaded, 31—35, 40, 164.
   rule where the same legal result is attainable in several ways, 13.
   material facts only must be stated, 15—30, 161.
   all material facts must be stated, 18, 110.
   must be stated with certainty, 36, 42—62, 103, 125, 143.
   must be stated in a summary form, 36—41, 203.
   but only those material at given stage of action, 20, 41, 141, 164.
   effect of omitting material facts, 40, 43.
   unnecessary to plead facts which the law presumes in your favour, 22, 40, 207.
   rule where common law is altered or regulated by statute, 23, 24, 57.
   rule as to matters affecting damages, 26—28, 125, 198, 221.
   substance of pleading to be proved, 30, 191.
   result of pleading immaterial facts, 28—30.
MATERIALITY,
   of issue, 7, 15—41, 73, 75.
   test of, 15.
   how it differs from relevancy, 31.
   of consideration for a contract, 16, 121.
   of remuneration of bailee, 16.
   of precise words of covenant, 16, 122, 207.
         of libel or slander, 16, 121.
   of plaintiff's trade, office, profession, or capacity, 80, 81, 121.
   of custom of the country, 16.
   of limitation of liability under a contract, 16.
   of notice, 15, 17, 25, 34, 53, 111, 207.

MATERIALITY—*continued.*
of intention and motive, 15, 17, 34, 207.
of assignment, 18, 24, 52, 53, 55, 56, 111, 199.
of authority, 18, 19, 56—59.
of averments in other cases, 18, 19, 141.
of admissions in a pleading, 161.
of matters affecting damages, 26—28, 125, 197, 198.
of special damage, 73, 125.

MATTER,
of law, must not be pleaded, 8—14, 164.
    not traversable, 40, 67, 74.
affecting damages, 26—28, 125, 197, 198, 221.
    interrogatories as to, 175.
affecting costs, 40.
of inducement, 49, 120.
in confession and avoidance, 49, 52, 61, 65, 69, 90, 138.
arising after writ, pleading, 138, 139, 160, 161, 215.

MEMORANDUM,
to refresh the memory of a witness, 197, 199.

MESNE PROFITS, 108, 111, 112, 165.

MISCONDUCT, CHARGES OF,
certainty of, 59—61, 143, 197.
are not scandalous, if relevant, 97, 179.
in actions of defamation, where justification is not pleaded, 27, 197, 198.

MISDEMEANOUR,
conviction for, how proved, 196.

MISNOMER,
plea of, abolished, 67, 118.

MISREPRESENTATION,
particulars of, 60, 61, 98, 204.
action for, 44.
    PRECEDENT of defence to, 156.
        of advice on evidence in, 200.

MITIGATION OF DAMAGES,
matter in, 26—28.
notice in, 27, 197, 221.
evidence in, 197, 198.

MONEY COUNT, 116.

MONEY HAD AND RECEIVED,
  defence to action for, 10, 132, 163, 209.

MORTGAGEE IN POSSESSION, 44.

MOTION,
  application by, 95.

MOTIVE,
  sometimes material, 15, 17.
  how pleaded, 34, 207.
  particulars of, 102.

NAMES,
  of persons parties to the suit, 36, 106.
          not parties to the suit, 36, 150, 151.
          mistake in, effect of, 67, 118.

NECESSARIES,
  for infants, how pleaded, 33.

NECESSARY IMPLICATION,
  denial by, 76, 77, 81.

NEGATIVE,
  party asserting, not called on to prove, 190.
  covenants, performance of, how pleaded, 86.
  pregnant, ambiguity of, 85.

NEGLIGENCE,
  action for, 17, 181.
  particulars of, 60.
  contributory, 60, 87.
      plea of, is a plea in confession and avoidance, 90.

NEGOTIABLE INSTRUMENTS,
  consideration for, presumed, 16, 22, 190.

NEVER INDEBTED,
  plea of, 12, 60, 132.

NEW ASSIGNMENT,
  meaning of, 167—169.
  now abolished, 168.
  extra viam, 169.

"NO AWARD,"
  plea of, 10, 11, 164.

Non Damnificatus,
plea of, a negative pregnant, 86.
Non-joinder,
plea of, 142.
Non-suit, 116, 140, 142.
Not Guilty,
plea of, what it put in issue, 9, 144.
  by statute, 93, 205.
  when admissible, 134.
Notice,
of fact, sometimes material, 15, 17, 34, 207.
of dishonour, 10, 17, 132, 209.
in mitigation of damages under Ord. XXXVI. r. 37..27, 197, 221.
of assignment, 24, 53, 111.
of discontinuance, 118 n.
of trial, 152.
to produce documents, 189, 192, 195, 199, 200.
to admit documents, 189, 192, 199, 200.
  effect of notice to produce, &c., 192, 195.
to quit, 108.
under Conveyancing Act, 24.
Nul tiel Record, 163.

Objection,
technical, may not be taken to pleadings, 6, 71, 93, 207.
Objection in Point of Law,
meaning of, 63.
can be raised in any pleading, 8, 63—65, 130, 136.
corresponds to a demurrer, 64, 71.
how it differs from a traverse, 64, 67, 162.
party not compelled to raise, 72.
when advisable to raise, 95, 96.
must be clearly taken, 67, 73.
and only where defect apparent on face of pleading objected to, 68.
argument of, 71, 72, 95, 216.
cannot be traversed, 68.
Office,
held by plaintiff, when material, 18, 80, 121.
Official Referee, 1, 114.
Omnia Præsumuntur Contra Spoliatorem, 23.

ORAL PLEADING, 3, 4.

ORDER III. r. 6,
defence to actions comprised under, 132.

ORDER XIV.,
leave to defend under, 107, 153, 210.

ORDER XXXVI. r. 37,
effect of, explained, 197.
particulars under, 27, 197, 221.

PARDON, 163.

PARTICULAR ESTATE, 48, 51, 53.

PARTICULARITY IN PLEADING,
not greater required than the case will conveniently admit, 42, 43.
less required as to matters more within the knowledge of the opposite party, 55, 56.

PARTICULARS,
applications for, 97—105, 169.
    do not act as a stay, 105, 152, 204.
object and effect of, 97, 100, 103.
under former pleading system, 98.
need not be pleaded to, 40.
unnecessary when account is claimed, 44, 99, 100.
will not be ordered of immaterial allegation, 104.
    of negative allegation, 104.
    of application of money paid into Court, 146.
of matters in mitigation of damages, 27, 197, 221.
of debt, expenses, damages, 41, 43, 98, 204.
of fraud, breach of trust, &c., 60, 163, 204.
of justification, 60.
where writ is specially indorsed, 110, 154.
time for pleading after delivery of, 105, 204.

PARTIES,
adding new, 118 n., 142.
representative character of, to be indorsed on writ, 106, 113.
misnomer of, 67, 118.
third, 150, 151, 210, 211.

PARTNERSHIP,
pleading, 32.
action against one member of, 140, 142.
denying constitution of, 81, 210.

PAYMENT,
> plea of, 90, 132, 136, 137, 162, 206.
> of money into Court, 104, 144—147, 212—214.
>> effect of, 146, 190.
>> with plea of tender, 144, 145, 212.
>> admitting liability, 144, 145, 146, 147, 148, 212.
>> denying liability, 138, 145, 146, 212.
>> in action on bond under 8 & 9 Will. III. c. 11.. 146, 212.
>> under Order XIV., 147, 214.
>> in actions of defamation, 147, 212.
>> under Lord Campbell's Act, 148.
>> with reply, 160.

PEDIGREE,
> facts of, when to be pleaded, 33.

PEERAGE,
> claimant to, must show title, 14.

PENAL ACTION,
> claim in, 108.
> pleading "not guilty" in, 134.
> interrogatories cannot be administered in, 178.

PERFORMANCE,
> pleading, 90, 136, 162, 166, 167, 206.
> general plea of, not permitted, 81, 82, 86.
> proof of, 190.
> part, 163.
> specific, 19, 127, 163.

PERSONAL ACTIONS, 116.

PLACE,
> certainty of, 45, 46.
> of trial, 128, 198. See VENUE.

PLEA,
> definition of the term, 4.
> pleading several defences, 3, 64, 130.
> in abatement, 22, 33, 67, 118, 141, 142, 211.
> of accord and satisfaction, 90, 138, 190.
> in the alternative, 96, 130, 164.
> of authority, 19, 20, 55, 134.
> in bar, or peremptory, 67, 142, 165.
> in confession and avoidance, 63—67, 89—92.
> dilatory, 66, 67.

PLEA—*continued.*
of estoppel, 141, 141 n.
of fraud, 90, 91, 136, 143, 156, 162, 163, 190, 206.
to the further maintenance, 139.
general issue, 12, 60, 132, 211.
of illegality, 8, 11, 91, 136, 156, 162, 206.
to the jurisdiction, 67.
of justification, 60, 69, 70, 89, 90, 92, 143, 152, 158, 163, 177.
of *liberum tenementum*, 52, 91, 162.
of lien, 49, 90, 138.
under Lord Campbell's Act, 148, 190.
of matter arising after writ, 138, 139, 160, 161, 215.
of misnomer, 67, 118.
in mitigation of damages, 27, 28.
of non-joinder, 142.
" never agreed as alleged," 8, 91.
" never indebted," 12, 60, 132.
" no award," 10, 11, 164.
" *non damnificatus*," 86.
" not guilty," 9, 144.
" not guilty by statute," 93, 134, 205.
of payment, 90, 132, 136, 137, 162, 206.
of payment into Court, 104, 144—147, 212—214.
of performance, 90, 136, 162, 166, 167, 190, 206.
of general performance, 81, 82, 86.
of possession, 23, 46—50, 135, 136, 137, 211.
of privilege, 10, 21, 92, 144.
puis darrein continuance, 139.
of release, 66, 90, 136, 162, 163, 190, 206.
of rescission, 13, 144, 190.
of *res judicata*, 139, 140, 163.
of set-off, 148—150.
of Statute of Frauds, 12, 66, 91, 92, 136, 137, 162, 163, 206.
of Statute of Limitations, 14, 44, 66, 90, 136, 137, 162, 163, 190, 206.
in suspension, 67.
of tender, 90, 144, 145, 212.
PRECEDENTS of various pleas, 66, 137, 141 n., 144, 147, 154—159.

PLEADINGS,
definition of the term, 1.
object of, 2, 42, 76.
history of, 3—5.

PLEADINGS—*continued.*
　Statement of Claim, 116—129. And see STATEMENT OF CLAIM.
　　　indorsed on writ, 106—112, 117.
　defence, 130—153. And see DEFENCE.
　set-off and counterclaim, 148—150. And see SET-OFF; COUNTERCLAIM.
　reply, 160—169. And see REPLY.
　declaration, 4, 168.
　counts, 4, 12.
　plea, 4, 168.
　replication, 4, 168.
　rejoinder, 169, 170. And see REJOINDER.
　surrejoinder, rebutter, surrebutter, 2, 170.
　ambiguity of, before 1875...11—13, 98.
　strictness of former system, 116, 117.
　must state material facts, 7—41, 116, 141 n.
　　　and only material facts, 15—30, 161.
　　not law, 8—14, 164.
　　　nor evidence, 31—35, 40, 164.
　　　nor facts which the law presumes in your favour, 22, 40.
　　　nor matters affecting only damages, 26—28, 198.
　　　　or costs, 40.
　　　nor the precise words of documents, 16, 34, 37, 40, 79, 122, 206.
　must state facts with certainty, 36, 42—62, 118, 125, 143.
　　　but in a summary form, 7, 36—41, 203.
　amending own pleading, 16, 62, 88, 109, 117, 152, 164, 165, 168, 207, 216—218.
　amending opponent's pleading, 96.
　striking out opponent's pleading, 94.
　answering opponent's pleading, 63—92.
　　　by way of traverse, 63—69, 74—88, 130—133, 136, 161, 162, 205, 206.
　　　by way of confession and avoidance, 63—67, 69, 70, 89—92, 130, 138.
　　　by way of objection in point of law, 8, 63—65, 67, 68, 71—73, 95, 96, 130, 136, 141, 216.
　third party procedure, 150, 151, 210, 211.
　counsel's signature to, 6, 204.
　marking and delivering, 5, 205.
　filing, 205, 208.
　pleading matter arising during action, 138, 139, 160, 161, 215.
　pleading to damages, 40, 74, 79, 131, 133, 161, 206, 209.
　construed distributively, 61.

PLEADINGS—*continued*.
    technical objections to, may not be taken, 6, 71, 93, 207.
    irregularity in, cured by pleading over, 93, 221.
    new assignment in, 167—169.
    variance in, 104, 123, 142.
    departure in, 164—167, 169, 206.
    unnecessary denials, 78, 210.
    costs of prolix, 39, 64, 203, 204.
    close of, 5, 170, 215.
    trial without, 170, 171.
    particulars of, 97—105. And see PARTICULARS.
    PRECEDENTS of. See PRECEDENTS.

POSSESSION,
    title of, to goods, 23, 47, 48.
        to land, 23, 47, 48, 49, 50, 55, 136, 137.
        in action of replevin, 49 n.
        in cases of incorporeal hereditaments, 47.
    plea of, 23, 46—50, 135, 136, 137, 211.
        includes a plea of Statute of Limitations, 137.

PRECEDENTS,
    Statement of Claim in action for recovery of land, to be indorsed on writ, where there is
        (a) an agreement in writing, 111.
        (b) tenancy at will, 111.
        (c) tenancy determined by notice to quit, 112.
    general indorsement on writ, 113.
    indorsement for an account, 114, 115.
    Statement of Claim by an executor for money lent by his testatrix, 38.
        on a bill of lading, 39.
        in action on a guarantee, 65, 66.
    plea of Statute of Frauds, 137.
        Statute of Limitations, 137.
        tender, 144.
        estoppel, 141 n.
        appropriating money paid into Court under Ord. XIV.
        to items of plaintiff's claim, 147.
    defence in action of goods sold and delivered, 154.
        of work and labour done, and materials supplied, 154.
        for extras, 154.
        for fraudulent representations, 156.
        for slander, 157.
        for libel, 158, 159.

Precedents—*continued*,
    defence in action on policy of life assurance, 155.
                on guarantee, 66.
    reply in action on guarantee, 66.
    interrogatories in action of goods sold and delivered, and work and labour done, 184.
                for dilapidations, 185.
                where defendant pleads agency, 185.
                for libel contained in anonymous letter in a newspaper, 186.
                objections to answer, 182, 187.
    advice on evidence in action by assignee of a debt, 199.
                of deceit, 200.
                for malicious prosecution, 200.
                for seduction, 201.

Prescription, 47, 48.

Presumption,
    of law need not be pleaded, 22, 40, 207.
    of fact, 190, 191.

Private Act of Parliament, 10.

Privilege,
    plea of, 10, 21, 92, 144.
    solicitor's, 183.

Process,
    justification under judicial, 57—59.

Prolixity,
    costs of, 39, 64, 179, 203, 204.

Promissory Note, Action on,
    specially indorsed writ in, 107, 110.
    defence to, 10, 132, 209.

Proof,
    burden of, 69, 87, 190.
    of documents, 182, 192, 193—196.
    of handwriting, 173, 187, 192, 193.
    of conviction, 196.

Public Act of Parliament, 10, 40.

Puis Darrein Continuance,
    plea of, 139.
    pleading substituted for, 138, 139.

QUANTUM MERUIT, 108, 123.

QUARE IMPEDIT, 117.

REAL ACTIONS, 116.

REBUTTER, 2, 170.

RECEIVER, 127.

RECORD,
    what it is, 4, 5.
    entering the proceedings on the, 4, 5, 139.
    estoppel by, 141 n.
    nul tiel record, 163.

RECOVERY OF CHATTELS, ACTION FOR, 23, 48, 49.

RECOVERY OF LAND, ACTION FOR,
    claim in, must show title, 13, 50, 52, 53, 121.
    specially indorsed writ in, 108, 111, 112.
    necessary allegations in, where fee simple is claimed, 50.
                        where any other estate is claimed, 51, 52.
    defence to, pleading possession, 23, 46—50, 135, 136, 137, 211.
               pleading lease in confession and avoidance, 52, 165.
               pleading Statute of Limitations, 137.

REFRESHING MEMORY,
    by memoranda made at the time, 197, 199.

REJOINDER,
    answer to reply, 2, 169.
    may only join issue, unless leave obtained, 170, 214.
    departure in, 166, 206.
    time for delivery of, 170, 215.

RELEASE,
    plea of, 66, 90, 136, 162, 163, 206.
    proof of, 190.

RELIEF,
    claim for, need not be pleaded to, 40, 75.
            may be made against several parties, 119.
            may be in the alternative, 119, 126, 208.
            indorsed on writ, may be extended by Statement of Claim, 113, 117, 208.
            to what extent, 118.

Relief—*continued.*
claim for, in Statement of Claim, 126—128.
equitable, 48, 127, 135, 211.
merely declaratory of right, 128, 216.
injunction, 17, 113, 118.
specific performance, 19, 127, 163.

Remainder, Estate in, 51, 52, 55.

Remoteness of Damage, 125, 157.

Rent, 19, 45, 56, 108, 109, 111, 165, 166.

Replevin,
one of the old personal actions, 116.
possessory title in, 49 n.
avowry of *liberum tenementum* in, 52.
under 11 Geo. II. c. 19, s. 22 .. 56.
defence of seizure for distress of rent in arrear, 19, 45.

Replication, 4, 168.

Reply,
answer to defence, 2.
where there is a counterclaim, 160, 161, 215.
may traverse, by joining issue, 161, 162, 206.
may confess and avoid, 162, 206.
to plea of Statute of Frauds, 163.
     Limitations, 162, 163.
of fraud or duress, 163.
of *nul tiel record*, 163.
of part performance, 163.
of waiver, 163.
time for delivering, 160, 214.
dispensing with, 162, 171, 216.
departure in, 164—167, 206.
new assignment in, 167—169, 215.
pleadings subsequent to, 169, 214, 215.
Precedents of, 66, 161.

Representative Character,
must be indorsed on writ, 106, 113, 205.

Rescission,
of contract, 13, 144.
burden of proof of, 190.

RES JUDICATA, 139, 140, 163.

REVERSION, ESTATE IN, 51, 52, 54, 55.

RIGHT,
    declaration of, 128.

RIGHT OF WAY,
    title to, 13, 47, 121.
    termini of, material, 45, 121.
    trespass *extra viam*, 168, 169.

RIGHT TO BEGIN,
    at trial, 78, 191.

SATISFACTION,
    taking money out of Court in, 145—147.

"SCANDALOUS," 6, 96, 97, 179, 207.

SECONDARY EVIDENCE,
    of documents, 182, 192, 194, 195, 196.

SEDUCTION,
    action for, 80.
        PRECEDENT of advice on evidence in, 201.
    particulars of, 99.

SEPARATE ESTATE, 19, 111.

SET-OFF,
    nature of, 90, 149, 150.
    may be pleaded by defendant with other defences, 130, 148, 203, 209.
    how it differs from a counterclaim, 149.
    costs of, 150.

SEVERAL PLEAS,
    formerly not allowed, 3.
    now allowed, 64, 130.

SEVERING DEFENCES, 151.

SHERIFF,
    action against, for escape, 81, 87.

SHERIFF'S JURY, 145.

SHORT NOTICE OF TRIAL,
    defendant must in some cases accept, 152.

SLANDER,
  action for, 44, 69, 120, 121, 125.
  precise words of, material, 16, 121.
  ironical words, 17.
  denial of words alleged, 81.
  justifying, 60, 92, 143.
    part of, 28.
  defence that the occasion was privileged, 10, 92, 144.
  paying money into Court with defence, 147, 212.
  particulars of, 102.
    in mitigation of damages, 27, 197, 221.
  PRECEDENTS of defences, 157.

SOLICITOR'S
  bill of costs, 109.
  privilege, 183.

SPECIAL CASE, 136, 171.

SPECIAL DAMAGE,
  must be clearly claimed, 44, 125.
  where essential to the cause of action, 73, 125, 133, 140, 200.
  remoteness of, 125, 157.
  particulars of, 101.

SPECIAL DEFENCES, 136—148.

SPECIAL INDORSEMENT,
  on writ, of liquidated demand, 106, 107—112.

SPECIAL REFEREE, 1, 114.

SPECIFIC PERFORMANCE, 19, 127, 163.

STATEMENT OF CLAIM,
  first step in pleading, 1, 203.
  supersedes the writ, 113, 118 n., 128, 208.
  what it should include, 116—129.
  must disclose good cause of action, 18.
  indorsed on writ, 106, 110, 117, 208.
  must not anticipate defence, 20, 41, 163.
  performance of conditions precedent implied in, 24, 40, 122, 167.
  when it should state plaintiff's office, profession, or trade, 18, 80, 121.
  giving credit for money in, 138.
  joinder of causes of action in, 118, 119.
  introductory averments in, 37, 120, 121.

STATEMENT OF CLAIM—*continued*.
　filing, 205, 208.
　amendment of, once without leave, 109, 117, 152, 164, 165, 168, 217.
　alleging damage in, 44, 73, 125, 126.
　relief, claim for, in, 126—128. And see RELIEF.
　should indicate place of trial, 128, 129.
　time of delivering, 117, 118 n., 208.
　particulars of, after delivery of defence, 103.
　in action of tort, 120, 121.
　in action of contract, 121—124.
　dispensing with, 113, 171.
　PRECEDENTS of, 38, 39, 65, 66.
　　to be indorsed on writ, 111, 112.

STATUTE,
　adding to, altering, or regulating common law, 23, 24, 57.
　specially indorsed writ for debt arising on, 108.
　Not Guilty by, 93, 134, 205.

STATUTE OF FRAUDS,
　plaintiff need not allege compliance with, 24.
　plea of, 12, 66, 91, 92, 136, 162, 206.
　　PRECEDENT of, 137.

STATUTE OF LIMITATIONS,
　might not be set up under the general issue, 12.
　plea of, 14, 44, 66, 90, 136, 162, 163, 206.
　　PRECEDENTS of, 137.
　reply to, 61, 66, 162, 163.
　burden of proof when pleaded, 190.

STAYING PROCEEDINGS,
　on adding parties, 142.
　no stay on taking out summons for particulars, 105, 152, 204.
　proceeding with counterclaim on plaintiff, 149, 211.

SUBMISSION TO ARBITRATION, 119.

SUBPŒNA DUCES TECUM, 199.

SUMMONS,
　application by, 95, 142, 152.
　　under Ord. XIV., 107, 109, 110.
　　effect of, on time for pleading, 105, 152, 153, 204.

SURETYSHIP, 17, 151.

SURREBUTTER, 2, 170.

SURREJOINDER, 2, 170.

SUSPENSION,
plea in, 67.

TENANCY,
in common, 51.
joint, 51.
for years, 29, 48, 49, 51—53, 55.
at will, 29, 53.

TENDER, PLEA OF,
confesses and avoids, 90.
money must be brought into Court with, 144, 212.
effect of, 145.
PRECEDENT of, 144.

THIRD PARTIES,
introducing, into action, 150, 151, 210, 211.

TIME,
only required to be stated when material, 34, 45.
certainty of, 44, 45.
further, 98, 105, 152, 214.
for delivery of pleadings, &c., 113, 114, 117, 139, 152, 153, 160,
170, 172, 197, 208, 210, 214, 221.
expiration of, 153.
And see STATUTE OF LIMITATIONS.

TITLE,
should be pleaded, 13, 121.
to right of way, 13, 47.
to peerage, 14.
depending on pedigree, 33.
of seller cannot be disputed by buyer, 22.
certainty of, 46—56.
possession, sufficient title in some cases, 23, 46—50, 135—137,
211.
why sufficient, 46, 49.
in action of replevin, 49 n.

TITLE—*continued.*
  pleading, when party is out of possession, 50—54.
    claiming fee simple, 50.
      any other estate, 51—53.
  by assignment, 18, 25, 52, 53, 55, 56, 111.
  by estoppel, 54, 111.
  to copyhold estate, 52, 53.
  pleading title in another, 18, 54—56.
  claiming declaration of, 128.

TORT, ACTION OF,
  Statement of Claim in, 120, 121.
  pleas in justification in, 90.
  joint tortfeasors, 142.

TRADE,
  of plaintiff, when material, 18, 80, 121.

TRANSITORY AND LOCAL ACTIONS, 46.

TRAVERSE,
  meaning of, 63, 74.
  how it differs from an objection in point of law, 64, 67, 162.
      a plea in confession and avoidance, 64, 91, 161, 162.
  puts the opposite party to proof of substance of his allegation, 67, 69, 91.
  must not be taken on matter of law, 40, 67, 74.
      damages, 27, 40, 74, 79, 133, 209.
      particulars, 40, 74.
      form of relief desired, 40, 75.
  I. material facts, if not traversed, admitted, 74, 75—79, 131, 161, 205.
      difference between denying and not admitting, 76.
      dangers and advantages of admissions, 78.
  II. must be specific, 74, 79—81, 130—133, 209.
  III. must not be evasive, 74, 76, 81—86, 131, 144, 206.
      neither too large nor too narrow, 81—86.
      traversing in words of claim, 81, 82, 84.
          disjunctively, 82, 83.
      mere denial of liability, insufficient, 8, 10, 11, 91, 132, 136, 206, 209.
      ambiguity of negative pregnant, 85.
  setting up affirmative case in addition to, 86—88.

O.   S

TRESPASS,
  traversing plaintiff's claim, effect of, 80.
  action of, 44, 45, 47, 49, 85, 90, 116, 133, 134, 162, 166, 168.
    plea of *liberum tenementum* in, 52, 91, 162.
    pleading a lease in confession and avoidance in, 90, 162, 165.
  to goods, 21, 80.
  on the case, 116, 117, 134, 167.

TRIAL,
  short notice of, 152.
  entry for, 5.
  right to begin at, 78.
  where damages claimed are unliquidated, 191.
  without pleadings, 170, 171.
  mode of, 198.
  place of, 128, 198. See VENUE.

TROVER,
  action of, 116.
    claim in, 47.
    plea of not guilty in, 80.

TRUST,
  claim on a, specially indorsed writ, 108.
  breach of, 60, 172, 204, 218.

TRUSTEE,
  claim by, 81, 115, 209.
    against, 165.

UNDUE INFLUENCE,
  particulars of, must be pleaded, 60, 204.

UNLIQUIDATED DAMAGES, 78, 108, 109, 191.

VARIANCE, 104, 123, 142.

VENUE,
  meaning of, 128 n.
  local, abolished, 46, 128 n.
  under new rules, 46, 128, 129, 198, 208.
  changing, 129, 198, 199.

VERDICT,
  defects cured by, 95.

VIRTUTE CUJUS,
  a, not traversable, 68.

WAIVER,
  plea of, 90.
  reply of, 163.
  of irregularity, 93, 221.

WARRANT,
  pleading authority of, 19, 57, 58.

WAY, RIGHT OF,
  title to, 13, 47, 121.
  termini must be shown, 45, 121.
  trespass *extra viam*, 168.

WILL, TENANCY AT, 29, 53.

WITNESS,
  compelling opponent to call, 78.
  disclosing name of, 101, 176, 182.
  commission to examine, 191.
  deposition of, 192.
  refreshing memory, 197, 199.
  expert, 193.

WORK AND LABOUR DONE,
  particulars of, 99.
  action for, 60, 132.
    PRECEDENT of defence in, 154.
      interrogatories in, 184.

WRIT OF EXECUTION,
  pleading authority of, 57, 58.
  return to, 58.

WRIT OF RIGHT OF DOWER, 117.

WRIT OF SUMMONS,
  indorsements on. See INDORSEMENT.
  appearing to, 107, 113, 114, 117, 208.
  amending, 126.

WRIT OF SUMMONS—*continued.*
    matter arising after, 138, 140.
    time for pleading to specially indorsed, 153.
    relief claimed on, may be extended by Statement of Claim, 113, 117, 118, 208.

WRONG-DOER,
    title of possession, sufficient against, 23, 47.

WRONGFUL DISMISSAL, 109.

YEARS, TENANCY FOR, 29, 48, 49, 51, 52, 53, 55.

December, 1891.

A CATALOGUE
OF
LAW WORKS
PUBLISHED BY
STEVENS AND SONS,
LIMITED,
119 & 120, CHANCERY LANE, LONDON,
(And at 14, Bell Yard, Lincoln's Inn).

Telegraphic Address—"RHODRONS, London."

A Catalogue of Modern Law Works, *together with a complete Chronological List of all the English, Irish, and Scotch Reports, an Alphabetical Table of Abbreviations used in reference to Law Reports and Text Books, and an Index of Subjects corrected to end of* 1890. *Demy 8vo.* (114 *pages), limp binding. Post free,* 6d.

Acts of Parliament.—*Public and Local Acts from an early date may be had of the Publishers of this Catalogue, who have also on sale the largest collection of Private Acts, relating to Estates, Enclosures, Railways, Roads, &c., &c.*

ACCOUNT STAMP DUTY.—Gosset.—*Vide* "Stamp Duty."

ACTION AT LAW.—**Foulkes' Elementary View of the Proceedings in an Action in the Supreme Court, with a Chapter on Matters and Arbitrations.**—(Founded on "SMITH'S ACTION AT LAW.") By W. D. I. FOULKES, Esq., Barrister-at-Law. Third Edition. Demy 12mo. 1884. 7s. 6d.

ADMIRALTY.—**Roscoe's Admiralty Practice.**—A Treatise on the Jurisdiction and Practice of the Admiralty Division of the High Court of Justice, and on Appeals therefrom, with a chapter on the Admiralty Jurisdiction of the Inferior and the Vice-Admiralty Courts. With an Appendix containing Statutes, Rules as to Fees and Costs, Forms, Precedents of Pleadings and Bills of Costs. By E. S. ROSCOE, Esq., Barrister-at-Law. Second Edition. Demy 8vo. 1882. 1l. 4s.

ADVOCACY.—**Harris' Hints on Advocacy.**—Conduct of Cases Civil and Criminal. Classes of Witnesses and Suggestions for Cross-examining them, &c., &c. By RICHARD HARRIS, one of her Majesty's Counsel. Ninth Edition (with a new chapter on "Tactics"). Royal 12mo. 1889. 7s. 6d.

"The work is not merely instructive, it is exceedingly interesting and amusing. . . . . We know of no better mode at present of learning some at least of an advocate's duties than in studying this book and the methods of the most distinguished advocates of the day."—*The Jurist.*

"Full of good sense and just observation. A very complete Manual of the Advocate's art in Trial by Jury."—*Solicitors' Journal.*

"A book at once entertaining and really instructive. . . Deserves to be carefully read by the young barrister whose career is yet before him."—*Law Magazine.*

"We welcome it as an old friend, and strongly recommend it to the would-be advocate."—*Law Student's Journal.*

⁂ All standard Law Works are kept in Stock, in law calf and other bindings.

A

AGRICULTURAL LAW.—Beaumont's Treatise on Agricultural Holdings and the Law of Distress as regulated by the Agricultural Holdings (England) Act, 1883, with Appendix containing Full Text of the Act, and Precedents of Notices and Awards. By JOSEPH BEAUMONT, Esq., Solicitor. Royal 12mo. 1883. 10s. 6d.

Cooke's Treatise on the Law and Practice of Agricultural Tenancies.—New edition, in great part re-written with especial reference to Unexhausted Improvements, with Modern Forms and Precedents. By G. PRIOR GOLDNEY and W. RUSSELL GRIFFITHS, Esqs., Barristers-at-Law. Demy 8vo. 1882. 1l. 1s.

Dixon.—*Vide* "Farm."

Griffiths' Agricultural Holdings (England) Act, 1883, containing an Introduction; a Summary of the Act, with Notes; the complete text of the Act, with Forms, and a specimen of an Award under the Act. By W. RUSSELL GRIFFITHS, Esq., of the Midland Circuit. Demy 8vo. 1883. 5s.

Spencer's Agricultural Holdings (England) Act, 1883, with Explanatory Notes and Forms; together with the Ground Game Act, 1880. Forming a Supplement to "Dixon's Law of the Farm." By AUBREY J. SPENCER, B.A., Barrister-at-Law. Demy 8vo. 1883. 6s.

ALLOTMENTS.—Hall's Allotments Acts, 1887, with the Regulations issued by the Local Government Board, and Introductory Chapters, Notes, and Forms. By T. HALL HALL, Barrister-at-Law. Author of "The Law of Allotments." Royal 12mo. 1888. 7s. 6d.

ANNUAL DIGEST.—Mews'.—*Vide* "Digest."

ANNUAL PRACTICE (THE).— The Annual Practice, 1892. Edited by THOMAS SNOW, Barrister-at-Law; CHARLES BURNEY, a Chief Clerk of the Hon. Mr. Justice Chitty, Editor of "Daniell's Chancery Forms"; and F. A. STRINGER, of the Central Office, 2 vols. Demy 8vo. 25s.

"A book which every practising English lawyer must have."—*Law Quarterly Review.*
"Every member of the bar, in practice, and every London solicitor, at all events, finds the last edition of the Annual Practice a necessity."—*Solicitors' Journal.*

ANNUAL STATUTES.—Lely.—*Vide* "Statutes."

ARBITRATION.—Russell's Treatise on the Power and Duty of an Arbitrator, and the Law of Submissions and Awards; with an Appendix of Forms, and of the Statutes relating to Arbitration. By FRANCIS RUSSELL, Esq., M.A., Barrister-at-Law. Seventh Edition. By the Author and HERBERT RUSSELL, Esq., Barrister-at-Law. Royal 8vo. 1891. 30s.

"Comprehensive, accurate, and practical."—*Solicitors' Journal.*

ARCHITECTS.—Macassey and Strahan.—*Vide* "Civil Engineers."

ARTICLED CLERKS.—Rubinstein and Ward's Articled Clerks' Handbook.—Being a Concise and Practical Guide to all the Steps Necessary for Entering into Articles of Clerkship, passing the Preliminary, Intermediate, Final, and Honours Examinations, obtaining Admission and Certificate to Practise, with Notes of Cases. Third Edit. By J. S. RUBINSTEIN and B. WARD, Solicitors. 12mo. 1881. 4s.

"No articled clerk should be without it."—*Law Times.*

ASSETS, ADMINISTRATION OF.—Eddis' Principles of the Administration of Assets in Payment of Debts.—By ARTHUR SHELLY EDDIS, one of Her Majesty's Counsel. Demy 8vo. 1880. 6s.

AVERAGE.—Hopkins' Hand-Book of Average, to which is added a Chapter on Arbitration.—Fourth Edition. By MANLEY HOPKINS, Esq. Demy 8vo. 1884. 1l. 1s.

* *All standard Law Works are kept in Stock, in law calf and other bindings.*

AVERAGE—*continued.*

Lowndes' Law of General Average.—English and Foreign. Fourth Edition. By RICHARD LOWNDES, Average Adjuster. Author of "The Law of Marine Insurance," &c. Royal 8vo. 1888. 1*l*. 10*s*.

"The book is one which shows a mastery of its subject."—*Solicitors' Journal.*
"It may be confidently asserted that, whether for the purposes of the adjuster or the lawyer, Mr. Lowndes' work presents (in a style which is a model of clear and graceful English) the most complete store of materials relating to the subject in every particular, as well as an excellent exposition of its principles."—*Law Quarterly Review.*

BALLOT.—**Fitzgerald's Ballot Act.**—With an Introduction. Forming a Guide to the Procedure at Parliamentary and Municipal Elections. Second Edition. By GERALD A. R. FITZGERALD, Esq., Barrister-at-Law Fcap. 8vo. 1876. 5*s*. 6*d*.

BANKING.—**Walker's Treatise on Banking Law.**—Second Edition. By J. D. WALKER, Esq., Barrister-at-Law. Demy 8vo. 1885. 15*s*.

BANKRUPTCY.—**Chitty's Index, Vol. I.**—*Vide* "Digests."

Lawrance's Precedents of Deeds of Arrangement between Debtors and their Creditors; including Forms of Resolutions for Compositions and Schemes of Arrangement under the Bankruptcy Acts, 1883 and 1890, with Introductory Chapters, also the Deeds of Arrangement Acts, 1887 and 1890, with Notes. Fourth Edition. By H. ARTHUR SMITH, Esq., Barrister-at-Law. Demy 8vo. 1892.
(*Nearly ready.*) 7*s*. 6*d*.
"Concise, practical, and reliable."—*Law Times.*

Williams' Law and Practice in Bankruptcy.—Comprising the Bankruptcy Acts, 1883 to 1890, the Bankruptcy Rules, 1886, 1890, the Debtors Acts, 1869, 1878, the Bankruptcy (Discharge and Closure) Act, 1887, and the Deeds of Arrangement Act, 1887. By the Hon. Sir ROLAND VAUGHAN WILLIAMS, one of the Justices of Her Majesty's High Court of Justice. Fifth Edition. By EDWARD WM. HANSELL, Esq., Barrister-at-Law. Roy. 8vo. 1891. 25*s*.
"This book will now, if possible, since the appointment of its distinguished author as Bankruptcy Judge, take higher rank as an authority than before."—*Law Journal.*
"Mr. Hansell has done his editorial work with evident care and industry."—*Law Times.*

BILLS OF EXCHANGE.—**Chalmers' Digest of the Law of Bills of Exchange, Promissory Notes, Cheques and Negotiable Securities.** Fourth Edition. By His Honour Judge CHALMERS, Draughtsman of the Bills of Exchange Act, 1882, &c. Demy 8vo. 1891. 18*s*.
"As for the main part of the work, the intimate connection of the author with the subject for so many years is a guarantee of its value and completeness."—*Law Journal.*
"This excellent work is unique. As a statement and explanation of the law, it will be found singularly useful."—*Solicitors' Journal.*

BILLS OF SALE.—**Fithian's Bills of Sale Acts, 1878 and 1882.** With an Introduction and Explanatory Notes, together with an Appendix of Precedents, Rules of Court, Forms, and Statutes. Second Edition. By EDWARD WILLIAM FITHIAN, Esq., Barrister-at-Law. Royal 12mo. 1884. 6*s*.

BOOK-KEEPING.—**Matthew Hale's System of Book-keeping for Solicitors,** containing a List of all Books necessary, with a comprehensive description of their objects and uses for the purpose of Drawing Bills of Costs and the rendering of Cash Accounts to clients; also showing how to ascertain Profits derived from the business; with an Appendix. Demy 8vo. 1884. 5*s*. 6*d*.
"We think this is by far the most sensible, useful, practical little work on solicitors' book-keeping that we have seen."—*Law Students' Journal.*

*** *All standard Law Works are kept in Stock, in law calf and other bindings.*

A 2

BUILDING SOCIETIES.—Wurtzburg on Building Societies.—
The Acts relating to Building Societies, comprising the Act of 1836 and the Building Societies Acts, 1874, 1875, 1877, and 1884, and the Treasury Regulations, 1884; with an Introduction, copious Notes, and Precedents of Rules and Assurances. By E. A. WURTZBURG, Esq., Barrister-at-Law. Royal 12mo. 1886. *7s. 6d.*

"The work presents in brief, clear, and convenient form the whole law relating to Building Societies."

CANALS.—Webster's Law Relating to Canals: Comprising a Treatise on Navigable Rivers and Canals, together with the Procedure and Practice in Private Bill Legislation; with a coloured Map of the existing Canals and Navigations in England and Wales. By ROBERT G. WEBSTER, M.P., Barrister-at-Law. Demy 8vo. 1885. *1l. 1s.*

Street.—*Vide* "Company Law."

CARRIERS.—Carver's Treatise on the Law relating to the Carriage of Goods by Sea.—Second Edition. By THOMAS GILBERT CARVER, Esq., Barrister-at-Law. Royal 8vo. 1891. *1l. 12s.*

"A careful and accurate treatise."—*Law Quarterly Review.*

Macnamara's Law of Carriers.—A Digest of the Law of Carriers of Goods and Passengers by Land and Internal Navigation, including the Railway and Canal Traffic Act, 1888.—By WALTER HENRY MACNAMARA, of the Inner Temple, Barrister-at-Law, Registrar to the Railway Commission. Royal 8vo. 1888. *1l. 8s.*

"Mr. Macnamara seems to have done his work soundly and industriously, and to have produced a book which will be useful to practitioners in a large class of cases."—*Saturday Review,* June 15, 1889.

"A complete epitome of the law relating to carriers of every class."—*Railway Press.*

"We cordially approve of the general plan and execution of this work. . . . The general arrangement of the book is good."—*Solicitors' Journal,* March 9, 1889.

"Should find a place in the library of all railway men. The work is written in a terse, clear style, and is well arranged for speedy reference."—*Railway News,* Dec. 8, 1888.

CHAMBER PRACTICE.—Archibald's Practice at Judges' Chambers and in the District Registries in the Queen's Bench Division, High Court of Justice; with Forms of Summonses and Orders. Second Edition. By W. F. A. ARCHIBALD, Esq., Barrister-at-Law, and P. E. VIZARD, of the Summons and Order Department, Royal Courts of Justice. Royal 12mo. 1886. *15s.*

CHANCERY, *and Vide* "Equity."

Daniell's Chancery Practice.—The Practice of the Chancery Division of the High Court of Justice and on appeal therefrom. Sixth Edit. By L. FIELD, E. C. DUNN, and T. RIBTON, assisted by W. H. UPJOHN, Barristers-at-Law. 2 vols. in 3 parts. Demy 8vo. 1882-84. *6l. 6s.*

Daniell's Forms and Precedents of Proceedings in the Chancery Division of the High Court of Justice and on Appeal therefrom. Fourth Edition. With Summaries of the Rules of the Supreme Court, Practical Notes and References to the Sixth Edition of "Daniell's Chancery Practice." By CHARLES BURNEY, B.A. Oxon., a Chief Clerk of the Hon. Mr. Justice Chitty. Royal 8vo. 1885. *2l. 10s.*

Morgan's Chancery Acts and Orders.—The Statutes, Rules of Court and General Orders relating to the Practice and Jurisdiction of the Chancery Division of the High Court of Justice and the Court of Appeal. With Copious Notes. Sixth Edition. By the Right Hon. GEORGE OSBORNE MORGAN, one of Her Majesty's Counsel, and E. A. WURTZBURG, Barrister-at-Law. Royal 8vo. 1885. *1l. 10s.*

Peel's Chancery Actions.—A Concise Treatise on the Practice and Procedure in Chancery Actions under the Rules of the Supreme Court, 1883. Third Edition. By SYDNEY PEEL, Esq., Barrister-at-Law. Demy 8vo. 1883. *8s. 6d.*

*** *All standard Law Works are kept in Stock, in law calf and other bindings.*

CHARITABLE TRUSTS.—Mitcheson's Charitable Trusts.—The Jurisdiction of the Charity Commission; being the Acts conferring such jurisdiction, 1853—1883, with Introductory Essays and Notes on the Sections. By RICHARD EDMUND MITCHESON, Esq., Barrister-at-Law. Demy 8vo 1887. 18s.
"A very neat and serviceable hand-book of the Law of the Charity Commissioners."—*Law Journal.*

CHARTER PARTIES.—Carver.—*Vide* "Carriers." Wood.—*Vide* "Mercantile Law."

CIVIL ENGINEERS.—Macassey and Strahan's Law relating to Civil Engineers, Architects and Contractors.—Primarily intended for their own use. By L. LIVINGSTON MACASSEY and J. A. STRAHAN, Esqrs., Barristers-at-Law. Demy 8vo. 1890. 10s. 6d.

COAL MINES.—Chisholm's Manual of the Coal Mines Regulation ACT, 1887.—With Introduction, Explanatory and Practical Notes and References to Decisions in England and Scotland, Appendix of Authorized Forms, Particulars as to Examinations for Certificates, &c., and a copious Index. By JOHN C. CHISHOLM, Secretary to the Midland and East Lothian Coalmasters' Association. Demy 8vo. 1888. 7s. 6d.

COLLISIONS.—Marsden's Treatise on the Law of Collisions at Sea.—With an Appendix containing Extracts from the Merchant Shipping Acts, the International Regulations for preventing Collisions at Sea; and local Rules for the same purpose in force in the Thames, the Mersey, and elsewhere. By REGINALD G. MARSDEN, Esq., Barrister-at-Law. Third Edition. By the Author and the Hon. J. W. MANSFIELD, Barrister-at-Law. Demy 8vo. 1891. 1l. 5s.
"Mr. Marsden's work has by this time taken its place as one of the standard books on its subject. It is clear in statement and careful in summarizing the results of decisions."—*Solicitors' Journal,* May 16, 1891.

COMMERCIAL LAW.—The French Code of Commerce and most usual Commercial Laws.—With a Theoretical and Practical Commentary, and a Compendium of the Judicial Organization and of the Course of Procedure before the Tribunals of Commerce; together with the text of the law; the most recent decisions, and a glossary of French judicial terms. By L. GOIRAND, Licencié en droit. Demy 8vo. 1880. 2l. 2s.

COMMON LAW.—Ball's Short Digest of the Common Law; being the Principles of Torts and Contracts. Chiefly founded upon the Works of Addison, with Illustrative Cases, for the use of Students. By W. EDMUND BALL, LL.B., Barrister-at-Law. Demy 8vo. 1880. 16s.

Chitty's Archbold's Practice of the Queen's Bench Division of the High Court of Justice and on Appeal therefrom to the Court of Appeal and House of Lords in Civil Proceedings. Fourteenth Edition. By THOMAS WILLES CHITTY, assisted by J. ST. L. LESLIE, Barristers-at-Law. 2 vols. Demy 8vo. 1885. 3l. 13s. 6d.

Chitty's Forms.—*Vide* "Forms."

Fisher's Digest of Reported Decisions in all the Courts, with a Selection from the Irish; and references to the Statutes, Rules and Orders of Courts from 1756 to 1883. Compiled and arranged by JOHN MEWS, assisted by C. M. CHAPMAN, HARRY H. W. SPARHAM and A. H. TODD, Barristers-at-Law. In 7 vols. Royal 8vo. 1884.
(Published at 12l. 12s.) Reduced to *net* 5l. 5s.

Mews' Consolidated Digest of all the Reports in all the Courts, for the years 1884-88, inclusive. By JOHN MEWS, Barrister-at-Law. Royal 8vo. 1889. (Pub. at 1l. 11s. 6d.) Reduced to *net* 15s.

The Annual Digest for 1889 and 1890. By JOHN MEWS. *Each,* 15s.

*** The above works bring Fisher's Common Law and Chitty's Equity Digests down to end of 1890.

*** *All standard Law Works are kept in Stock, in law calf and other bindings.*

COMMON LAW—*continued.*

Napier's Concise Practice of the Queen's Bench and Chancery Divisions and of the Court of Appeal, with an Appendix of Questions on the Practice, and intended for the use of Students. By T. BATEMAN NAPIER, Esq., Barrister-at-Law. Demy 8vo. 1884. 10s.

Shirley.—*Vide* "Leading Cases."

Smith's Manual of Common Law.—For Practitioners and Students. Comprising the Fundamental Principles, with useful Practical Rules and Decisions. By JOSIAH W. SMITH, B.C.L., Q.C. Tenth Edition. By J. TRUSTRAM, LL.M., Esq., Barrister-at-Law. 12mo. 1887. 14s.

COMMONS AND INCLOSURES.—**Chambers' Digest of the Law relating to Commons and Open Spaces,** including Public Parks and Recreation Grounds. By GEORGE F. CHAMBERS, Esq., Barrister-at-Law. Imperial 8vo. 1877. 6s. 6d.

COMPANY LAW.—**Hamilton's Manual of Company Law:** For Directors and Promoters. Being a Treatise upon the nature of Trading Corporations, the Rights, Duties, and Liabilities of Directors and Promoters (including their Liabilities under the Directors Liability Act, 1890), the Appointment and Removal of Directors, the Powers of Directors, and the Law of Ultra Vires. By WILLIAM FREDERICK HAMILTON, LL.D. (Lond.), assisted by KENNARD GOLDORNE METCALFE, M.A., Esqrs., Barristers-at-Law. Demy 8vo. 1891. 12s. 6d.

"The work is executed throughout with great care and accuracy . . . . may be safely recommended as a most useful manual of the law with which it deals."—*Law Gazette.*

Palmer's Private Companies and Syndicates, their Formation and Advantages; being a Concise Popular Statement of the Mode of Converting a Business into a Private Company, and of establishing and working Private Companies and Syndicates for Miscellaneous Purposes. Ninth Edition. By F. B. PALMER, Esq., Barrister-at-Law. 12mo. 1891. *Net* 1s.

Palmer.—*Vide* "Conveyancing" and "Winding-up."

Palmer's Shareholders' and Directors' Legal Companion.—A Manual of Every-day Law and Practice for Promoters, Shareholders, Directors, Secretaries, Creditors and Solicitors of Companies under the Companies Acts, 1862 to 1890, with Appendix of useful Forms. 12th edit. By F. B. PALMER, Esq., Barrister-at-Law. 12mo. 1892. *Net,* 2s. 6d.

Street's Law relating to Public Statutory Undertakings; comprising Railway Companies, Water, Gas, and Canal Companies, Harbours, Docks, &c., with special reference to Modern Decisions. By J. BAMFIELD STREET, Esq., Barrister-at Law. Demy 8vo. 1890. 10s. 6d.

"This book contains in a small compass a large amount of useful information: its style is clear and its arrangement good."—*Solicitors' Journal,* November 1, 1890.

Thring.—*Vide* "Joint Stocks."

COMPENSATION.—**Cripps' Treatise on the Principles of the Law of Compensation.** Second Edition. By C. A. CRIPPS, Esq., Barrister-at-Law. Demy 8vo. 1884. 16s.

COMPOSITION DEEDS.—**Lawrance.**—*Vide* "Bankruptcy."

CONTINGENT REMAINDERS.—**An Epitome of Fearne on Contingent Remainders and Executory Devises.** Intended for the Use of Students. By W. M. C. Post 8vo. 1878. 6s. 6d.

CONTRACTS.—**Addison on Contracts.** Being a Treatise on the Law of Contracts. 9th Edit. By HORACE SMITH, Esq., Bencher of the Inner Temple, Metropolitan Magistrate, assisted by A. P. PERCEVAL KEEP, Esq., Barrister-at-Law. Royal 8vo. 1892. (*Nearly ready.*) 2l. 10s.

"A satisfactory guide to the vast storehouse of decisions on contract law."—*Sol. Jour.*

⁎⁎ *All standard Law Works are kept in Stock, in law calf and other bindings.*

CONTRACTS—*continued.*

Fry.—*Vide* "Specific Performance."

Leake's Law of Contracts.—Third Edition. By STEPHEN MARTIN LEAKE, Barrister-at-Law. (*In the press.*)

Pollock's Principles of Contract.—Being a Treatise on the General Principles relating to the Validity of Agreements in the Law of England. Fifth Edition, with a new Chapter. By Sir FREDERICK POLLOCK, Bart., Barrister-at-Law, Professor of Common Law in the Inns of Court, &c. Demy 8vo. 1889. 1*l.* 8*s.*

"The reputation of the book stands so high that it is only necessary to announce the publication of the fifth edition, adding that the work has been thoroughly revised."—*Law Journal.*

Smith's Law of Contracts.—Eighth Edition. By V. T. THOMPSON, Esq., Barrister-at-Law. Demy 8vo. 1885. 1*l.* 1*s.*

CONVEYANCING.—**Dart.**—*Vide* "Vendors and Purchasers."

Greenwood's Manual of Conveyancing.—A Manual of the Practice of Conveyancing, showing the present Practice relating to the daily routine of Conveyancing in Solicitors' Offices. To which are added Concise Common Forms and Precedents in Conveyancing. Eighth Edition. Edited by HARRY GREENWOOD, M.A., LL.D., Esq., Barrister-at-Law. Demy 8vo. 1891. 16*s.*

"That this work has reached its eighth edition is sufficient evidence of the fact that it is one of those books which no lawyer's bookshelf should be without. Recent Acts have necessitated several changes which have been carried out, and cases are cited up to date. The book is a complete guide to Conveyancing, and, though the author says that it is intended for students and articled and other clerks, we can fearlessly assert that those who would perhaps consider it an insult to be mistaken for students will find in it very much that is useful. The Table of Precedents could not, we imagine, be made more complete than it is. Where and how the author obtained his information is a perfect puzzle to us, and no conceivable state of affairs seems to have been left unprovided for."—*Law Gazette.*

"We should like to see it placed by his principal in the hands of every articled clerk. One of the most useful practical works we have ever seen."—*Law Students' Journal.*

Morris's Patents Conveyancing.—Being a Collection of Precedents in Conveyancing in relation to Letters Patent for Inventions. Arranged as follows:—Common Forms, Agreements, Assignments, Mortgages, Special Clauses, Licences, Miscellaneous; Statutes, Rules, &c. With Dissertations and Copious Notes on the Law and Practice. By ROBERT MORRIS, M.A., Barrister-at-Law. Royal 8vo. 1887. 1*l.* 5*s.*

"Contains valuable dissertations, and useful notes on the subject with which it deals.... We think it would be difficult to suggest a form which is not to be met with or capable of being prepared from the book before us. To those whose business lies in the direction of letters patent and inventions it will be found of great service.... Mr. Morris' forms seem to us to be well selected, well arranged, and thoroughly practical."—*Law Times.*

Palmer's Company Precedents.—For use in relation to Companies subject to the Companies Acts, 1862 to 1890. Arranged as follows:—Promoters, Prospectus, Agreements, Memoranda and Articles of Association, Resolutions, Notices, Certificates, Private Companies, Power of Attorney, Debentures and Debenture Stock, Petitions, Writs, Pleadings, Judgments and Orders, Reconstruction, Amalgamation, Arrangements, Special Acts, Provisional Orders, Winding-up. With Copious Notes and an Appendix containing the Acts and Rules. Fifth Edition. By FRANCIS BEAUFORT PALMER, assisted by CHARLES MACNAGHTEN, Esqrs., Barristers-at-Law. Royal 8vo. 1891. 1*l.* 16*s.*

"No company lawyer can afford to be without it."—*Law Journal,* April 25, 1891.

"As regards company drafting—as we remarked on a former occasion—it is unrivalled."—*Law Times.*

** *All standard Law Works are kept in Stock, in law calf and other bindings.*

CONVEYANCING—*continued.*
Prideaux's Precedents in Conveyancing—With Dissertations on its Law and Practice. Fourteenth Edition. By FREDERICK PRIDEAUX, late Professor of the Law of Real and Personal Property to the Inns of Court, and JOHN WHITCOMBE, Esqrs., Barristers-at-Law. 2 vols. Royal 8vo. 1889. 3*l*. 10*s*.
"The most useful work out on Conveyancing."—*Law Journal.*
"This work is accurate, concise, clear, and comprehensive in scope, and we know of no treatise upon conveyancing which is so generally useful to the practitioner."—*Law Times.*

Turner's Duties of Solicitor to Client as to Partnership Agreements, Leases, Settlements, and Wills.—By EDWARD F. TURNER, Solicitor, Lecturer on Real Property and Conveyancing, Author of "The Duties of Solicitor to Client as to Sales, Purchases, and Mortgages of Land." (Published by permission of the Council of the Incorporated Law Society.) Demy 8vo. 1884. 10*s*. 6*d*.
"The work has our full approval, and will, we think, be found a valuable addition to the student's library."—*Law Students' Journal.*

CONVICTIONS.—Paley's Law and Practice of Summary Convictions under the Summary Jurisdiction Acts; including Proceedings preliminary and subsequent to Convictions, and the responsibility of convicting Magistrates and their Officers, with Forms. Seventh Edition. By W. H. MACNAMARA, Esq., Barrister-at-Law.
(*In preparation.*)

COPYRIGHT.—Slater's Law relating to Copyright and Trade Marks, treated more particularly with Reference to Infringement; forming a Digest of the more important English and American decisions, together with the Practice of the English Courts, &c. By JOHN HERBERT SLATER, Esq., Barrister-at-Law. 8vo. 1884. 18*s*.

CORONERS.—Jervis on the Office and Duties of Coroners.—The Coroners Act, 1887. With Forms and Precedents. By R. E. MELSHEIMER, Esq., Barrister-at-Law. Being the Fifth Edition of "Jervis on Coroners." Post 8vo. 1888. 10*s*. 6*d*.
"The present edition will hold the place of that occupied by its predecessors, and will continue to be the standard work on the subject."—*Law Times.*

COSTS.—Morgan and Wurtzburg's Treatise on the Law of Costs in the Chancery Division.—Second Edition. With Forms and Precedents. By the Rt. Hon. GEORGE OSBORNE MORGAN, Q.C., and E. A. WURTZBURG, Esq., Barrister-at-Law. Demy 8vo. 1882. 1*l*. 10*s*.

Summerhays and Toogood's Precedents of Bills of Costs in the Chancery, Queen's Bench, Probate, Divorce and Admiralty Divisions of the High Court of Justice; in Conveyancing; the Crown Office; Bankruptcy; Lunacy; Arbitration under the Lands Clauses Consolidation Act; the Mayor's Court, London; the County Courts; the Privy Council; and on Passing Residuary and Succession Accounts; with Scales of Allowances and Court Fees; Rules of Court relating to Costs; Forms of Affidavits of Increase, and of Objections to Taxation. By WM. FRANK SUMMERHAYS, and THORNTON TOOGOOD, Solicitors. Sixth Edition. By THORNTON TOOGOOD, Solicitor. Royal 8vo. 1889. 1*l*. 8*s*.

Summerhays and Toogood's Precedents of Bills of Costs in the County Courts. Royal 8vo. 1889. 5*s*.

Scott's Costs in the High Court of Justice and other Courts. Fourth Edition. By JOHN SCOTT, of the Inner Temple, Esq., Barrister-at-Law. Demy 8vo. 1880. 1*l*. 6*s*.

Webster's Parliamentary Costs.—Private Bills, Election Petitions, Appeals, House of Lords. Fourth Edition. By C. CAVANAGH, Esq., Barrister-at-Law. Post 8vo. 1881. 20*s*.

*** *All standard Law Works are kept in Stock, in law calf and other bindings.*

COUNTY COUNCILS.—Bazalgette and Humphreys, Chambers.
—*Vide* "Local and Municipal Government."

COUNTY COURTS.—Heywood's Annual County Court Practice,
1892.—By His Honour Judge WASHINGTON HEYWOOD. 2 vols.
Demy 8vo. (*Nearly ready*) 25s.

Pitt-Lewis' County Court Practice.—A Complete Practice of the
County Courts, including that in Admiralty and Bankruptcy, embodying the County Courts Act, 1888, and other existing Acts,
Rules, Forms and Costs, with Full Alphabetical Index to Official
Forms, Additional Forms and General Index. Fourth Edition.
With Supplementary Volume containing the NEW WINDING-UP
PRACTICE. By G. PITT-LEWIS, Esq., Q.C., M.P., Recorder of Poole.
3 vols. Demy 8vo. 1890-91. 2*l*. 10*s*.
*** *The Supplement sold separately*. 7*s*. 6*d*.
"A complete practice of the County Courts."—*Law Journal*.
"The present edition of this work fully maintains its reputation as the standard
County Court Practice."—*Solicitors' Journal*.

Pitt-Lewis' County Courts Act, 1888.—With Introduction, Tabular
Indices to consolidated Legislation, Notes, and an Index to the Act.
Second Edition. By GEORGE PITT-LEWIS, Esq., Q.C., Author of "A
Complete Practice of the County Courts." Imperial 8vo. 1889. 5*s*.
*** The above, with THE COUNTY COURT RULES, 1889. Official
copy. *Limp binding*. 10*s*. 6*d*.

Summerhays and Toogood.—*Vide* "Costs."

COVENANTS.—Hamilton's Law of Covenants.—A Concise Treatise
on the Law of Covenants. By G. BALDWIN HAMILTON, of the Inner
Temple, Esq., Barrister-at-Law. Demy 8vo. 1888. 7*s*. 6*d*.
"A handy volume written with clearness, intelligence, and accuracy, and will be
useful to the profession."—*Law Times*.

CRIMINAL LAW.—Archbold's Pleading and Evidence in Criminal
Cases.—With the Statutes, Precedents of Indictments, &c., and the
Evidence necessary to support them. Twentieth Edition. By
WILLIAM BRUCE, Esq., Stipendiary Magistrate for the Borough of
Leeds. Royal 12mo. 1886. 1*l*. 11*s*. 6*d*.

**Mews' Digest of Cases relating to Criminal Law from 1756 to
1883, inclusive.**—By JOHN MEWS, assisted by C. M. CHAPMAN,
HARRY H. W. SPARHAM, and A. H. TODD, Barristers-at-Law. Royal
8vo. 1884. 1*l*. 1*s*.

Phillips' Comparative Criminal Jurisprudence.—Vol. I. Penal
Law. Vol. II. Criminal Procedure. By H. A. D. PHILLIPS, Bengal
Civil Service. 2 vols. Demy 8vo. 1889. 1*l*. 4*s*.

Roscoe's Digest of the Law of Evidence in Criminal Cases.—
Eleventh Edition. By HORACE SMITH and GILBERT GEORGE KENNEDY, Esqrs., Metropolitan Magistrates. Demy 8vo. 1890. 1*l*. 11*s*. 6*d*.
"To the criminal lawyer it is his guide, philosopher and friend. What Roscoe says
most judges will accept without question. . . . Every addition has been made necessary
to make the digest efficient, accurate, and complete"—*Law Times*.

Russell's Treatise on Crimes and Misdemeanors.—Fifth Edition. By SAMUEL PRENTICE, Esq., one of Her Majesty's Counsel,
3 vols. Royal 8vo. 1877. 5*l*. 15*s*. 6*d*.

Shirley's Sketch of the Criminal Law.—By W. S. SHIRLEY, Esq.,
Barrister-at-Law. Second Edition. By CHARLES STEPHEN HUNTER,
Esq., Barrister-at-Law. Demy 8vo. 1889. 7*s*. 6*d*.
As a primary introduction to Criminal Law, it will be found very acceptable to
students."—*Law Students' Journal*.

Shirley.—*Vide* "Leading Cases." **Thring.**—*Vide* "Navy."

*** *All standard Law Works are kept in Stock, in law calf and other bindings.*

DECISIONS OF SIR GEORGE JESSEL.—Peter's Analysis and Digest of the Decisions of Sir George Jessel; with Notes, &c. By APSLEY PETRE PETER, Solicitor. Demy 8vo. 1883. 16s.

DIARY.—Lawyer's Companion (The), Diary, and Law Directory for 1892.—For the use of the Legal Profession, Public Companies, Justices, Merchants, Estate Agents, Auctioneers, &c., &c. Edited by EDWIN LAYMAN, B.A., of the Middle Temple, Esq., Barrister-at-Law; and contains Tables of Costs in the High Court of Judicature and County Court, &c.; Monthly Diary of County, Local Government, and Parish Business; Oaths in Supreme Court; List of Statutes of 1891; Alphabetical Index to the Practical Statutes since 1820; the New Schedule of Stamp Duties; Legal Time, Interest, Discount, Income, Wages and other Tables; Probate, Legacy and Succession Duties; and a variety of matters of practical utility: together with a complete List of the English Bar, and London and Country Solicitors, with date of admission and appointments.
PUBLISHED ANNUALLY. Forty-sixth Issue. 1892. (*Now ready.*)

Issued in the following forms, octavo size, strongly bound in cloth:—
1. Two days on a page, plain . . . . 5s. 0d.
2. The above, INTERLEAVED for ATTENDANCES . . . 7 0
3. Two days on a page, ruled, with or without money columns . 5 6
4. The above, with money columns, INTERLEAVED for ATTENDANCES . 8 0
5. Whole page for each day, plain 7 6
6. The above, INTERLEAVED for ATTENDANCES . . . 9 6
7. Whole page for each day, ruled, with or without money columns 8 6
8. The above, INTERLEAVED for ATTENDANCES . . . 10 6
9. Three days on a page, ruled blue lines, without money columns . 5 0

The Diary contains memoranda of Legal Business throughout the Year.
"Contains all the information which could be looked for in such a work, and gives it in a most convenient form and very completely."—*Solicitors' Journal.*
"The 'Lawyer's Companion and Diary' is a book that ought to be in the possession of every lawyer, and of every man of business."
"The 'Lawyer's Companion' is, indeed, what it is called, for it combines everything required for reference in the lawyer's office."—*Law Times.*
"The practitioner will find in these pages, not only all that he might reasonably expect to find, but a great deal more."—*Law Journal,* December 6, 1890.
"It should be in the hands of all members of both branches of the profession."—*Law Gazette,* November 27, 1890.
"The thousand and one things that one needs constantly to know and yet can never remember, will be found handily arranged for immediate reference."—*Pump Court.*
"This legal Whitaker is a noble work, and no lawyer has any right to want to know anything—except law, which it would not tell him."—*Saturday Review.*

DICTIONARY.—The Pocket Law Lexicon.—Explaining Technical Words, Phrases and Maxims of the English, Scotch and Roman Law, to which is added a complete List of Law Reports, with their Abbreviations. Second Edition, Enlarged. By HENRY G. RAWSON, Esq., Barrister-at-Law. Fcap. 8vo. 1884. 6s. 6d.
"A wonderful little legal Dictionary."—*Indermaur's Law Students' Journal.*
"A very handy, complete, and useful little work."—*Saturday Review.*

Wharton's Law Lexicon.—Forming an Epitome of the Law of England, and containing full Explanations of the Technical Terms and Phrases thereof, both Ancient and Modern; including the various Legal Terms used in Commercial Business. Together with a Translation of the Latin Law Maxims and selected Titles from the Civil, Scotch and Indian Law. Ninth Edition. By J. M. LELY, Esq., Barrister-at-Law. Super-royal 8vo. (*In the press.*)
"On almost every point both student and practitioner can gather information from this invaluable book, which ought to be in every lawyer's office."—*Gibson's Law Notes.*
"One of the first books which every articled clerk and bar student should procure."—*Law Students' Journal.*
"As it now stands the Lexicon contains all it need contain, and to those who value such a work it is made more valuable still."—*Law Times.*

* *All standard Law Works are kept in Stock, in law calf and other bindings.*

DIGESTS.—Chitty's Index to all the Reported Cases decided in the several Courts of Equity in England, the Privy Council, and the House of Lords, with a selection of Irish Cases, on or relating to the Principles, Pleading, and Practice of Equity and Bankruptcy from the earliest period. Fourth Edition. Wholly Revised, Re-classified, and brought down to the End of 1883. By HENRY EDWARD HIRST, Barrister-at-Law. Complete in 9 vols. Roy. 8vo. 1883-89. (Published at 12l. 12s.) *Reduced to net, 5l. 5s.*
*** The volumes sold separately. *Each net, 15s.*

"A work indispensable to every bookcase in Lincoln's Inn."—*Law Quarterly Review.*
"The practitioner can hardly afford to do without such a weapon as Mr. Hirst supplies, because if he does not use it probably his opponent will."—*Law Journal.*
"We think that we owe it to Mr. Hirst to say that on each occasion when a volume of his book comes before us we exert some diligence to try and find an omission in it, and we apply tests which are generally successful with ordinary text-writers, but not so with Mr. Hirst. At present we have not been able to find a flaw in his armour. We conclude, therefore, that he is an unusually accurate and diligent compiler."—*Law Times.*

Dale and Lehmann's Digest of Cases, Overruled, Not Followed, Disapproved, Approved, Distinguished, Commented on and specially considered in the English Courts from the Year 1756 to 1886 inclusive, arranged according to alphabetical order of their subjects; together with Extracts from the Judgments delivered thereon, and a complete Index of the Cases, in which are included all Cases reversed from the year 1856. By CHAS. WM. MITCALFE DALE, and RUDOLF CHAMBERS LEHMANN, assisted by CHAS. H. L. NEISH, and HERBERT H. CHILD, Barristers-at-Law. Royal 8vo. 1887. (Published at 2l. 10s.) *Reduced to net, 25s.*
(*Forms a Supplement to Chitty's Equity Index and Fisher's Common Law Dig.*)
"One of the best works of reference to be found in any library."—*Law Times.*
"The book is divided into two parts, the first consisting of an alphabetical index of the cases contained in the Digest presented in a tabular form, showing at a glance how, where, and by what judges they have been considered. The second portion of the book comprises the Digest itself, and bears marks of the great labour and research bestowed upon it by the compilers."—*Law Journal.*

Fisher's Digest of the Reported Decisions of the Courts of Common Law, Bankruptcy, Probate, Admiralty, and Divorce, together with a Selection from those of the Court of Chancery and Irish Courts from 1756 to 1883 inclusive. Founded on Fisher's Digest. By J. MEWS, assisted by C. M. CHAPMAN, H. H. W. SPARHAM, and A. H. TODD, Barristers-at-Law. 7 vols. Roy. 8vo. 1884. (Published at 12l. 12s.) *Reduced to net, 5l. 5s.*
"To the common lawyer it is, in our opinion, the most useful work he can possess. —*Law Times.*

Mews' Consolidated Digest of all the Reports in all the Courts, for the Years 1884—88 inclusive.—By JOHN MEWS, Barrister-at-Law. Royal 8vo. 1889. (Published at 1l. 11s. 6d.) *Reduced to net, 15s.*
"This work is an indispensable companion to the new edition of Chitty's Digest, which ends with 1883, and also Fisher's Digest ending with the same year. . . . . The work appears to us to be exceedingly well done."—*Solicitors' Journal.*

Or the whole of the above Digests, together 18 Volumes, net £10.

The Annual Digest for 1889 and 1890. By JOHN MEWS. *Each, 15s.*
*** The above Works bring Fisher's Common Law and Chitty's Equity Digests down to end of 1890.

Talbot and Fort's Index of Cases Judicially noticed (1865—1890); being a List of all Cases cited in Judgments reported in the "Law Reports," "Law Journal," "Law Times," and "Weekly Reporter," from Michaelmas Term, 1865 to the end of 1890, with the places where they are so cited.—By GEORGE JOHN TALBOT and HUGH FORT, Barristers-at-Law. Royal 8vo. 1891. 25s.
"Talbot and Fort is forthwith established in our revolving bookcase side by side with 'Dale and Lehmann.'"—*Law Quarterly Review*, July, 1891.

*** *All standard Law Works are kept in Stock, in law calf and other bindings.*

DISCOVERY.—Hare's Treatise on the Discovery of Evidence.— Second Edition. By SHERLOCK HARE, Barrister-at-Law. Post 8vo. 1877. 12s.

Sichel and Chance's Discovery.—The Law relating to Interrogatories, Production, Inspection of Documents, and Discovery, as well in the Superior as in the Inferior Courts, together with an Appendix of the Acts, Forms and Orders. By WALTER S. SICHEL, and WILLIAM CHANCE, Esqrs., Barristers-at-Law. Demy 8vo. 1883. 12s.

DISTRESS.—Oldham and Foster on the Law of Distress.—A Treatise on the Law of Distress, with an Appendix of Forms, Table of Statutes, &c. Second Edition. By ARTHUR OLDHAM and A. LA TROBE FOSTER, Esqrs., Barristers-at-Law. Demy 8vo. 1889. 18s.

"This is a useful book, because it embraces the whole range of the remedy by distress, not merely distress for rent, but also for *damage feasant*, tithes, poor and highway rates and taxes, and many other matters."—*Solicitors' Journal.*

DISTRICT REGISTRIES.—Archibald.—*Vide* "Chamber Practice."

DIVORCE.—Browne and Powles' Law and Practice in Divorce and Matrimonial Causes. Fifth Edition. By L. D. POWLES, Esq., Barrister-at-Law. Demy 8vo. 1889. 1l. 6s.

"The practitioner's standard work on divorce practice."—*Law Quarterly Review.*
"Mr. Powles' edition cites all the necessary information for bringing the book down to date, supplies an excellent index, on which he has spent much pains, and maintains the position which Browne's Divorce Treatise has held for many years."—*Law Journal.*

Winter's Manual of the Law and Practice of Divorce.—By DUNCAN CLERK WINTER, Solicitor. (Reprinted from "The Jurist.") Crown 8vo. 1889. *Net*, 2s. 6d.

DOGS.—Lupton's Law relating to Dogs.—By FREDERICK LUPTON, Solicitor. Royal 12mo. 1888. 5s.

"Within the pages of this work the reader will find every subject connected with the law relating to dogs touched upon, and the information given appears to be both exhaustive and correct."—*Law Times.*

DOMICIL.—Dicey's Le Statut Personnel anglais ou la Loi du Domicile.—Ouvrage traduit et complété d'après les derniers arrêts des Cours de Justice de Londres, et par la comparaison avec le Code Napoléon et les Diverses Législations du Continent. Par EMILE STOCQUART, Avocat à la Cour d'Appel de Bruxelles. 2 Tomes. Demy 8vo. 1887-88. 1l. 4s.

EASEMENTS.—Goddard's Treatise on the Law of Easements.—By JOHN LEYBOURN GODDARD, Esq., Barrister-at-Law. Fourth Edition. Demy 8vo. 1891. 1l. 1s.

"An indispensable part of the lawyer's library."—*Solicitors' Journal.*
"The book is invaluable: where the cases are silent the author has taken pains to ascertain what the law would be if brought into question."—*Law Journal.*
"Nowhere has the subject been treated so exhaustively, and, we may add, so scientifically, as by Mr. Goddard. We recommend it to the most careful study of the law student, as well as to the library of the practitioner."—*Law Times.*

Innes' Digest of the English Law of Easements. Third Edition. By Mr. JUSTICE INNES, lately one of the Judges of Her Majesty's High Court of Judicature, Madras. Royal 12mo. 1884. 6s.

ECCLESIASTICAL LAW.- Phillimore's Ecclesiastical Law of the Church of England. With Supplement. By the Right. Hon. Sir ROBERT PHILLIMORE, D.C.L. 2 vols. 8vo. 1873-76. (Published at 3l. 7s. 6d.) *Reduced to net*, 1l. 10s.

ELECTION IN EQUITY.—Serrell's Equitable Doctrine of Election. By GEORGE SERRELL, M.A., LL.D., Esq., Barrister-at-Law. Royal 12mo. 1891. 7s. 6d.

"The work is well executed, and will be of service to all who desire to master the doctrine of election."—*Law Journal.*

✱✱✱ *All standard Law Works are kept in Stock, in law calf and other bindings.*

ELECTIONS.—Hedderwick's Parliamentary Election Manual: A Practical Handbook on the Law and Conduct of Parliamentary Elections in Great Britain and Ireland, designed for the Instruction and Guidance of Candidates, Election Agents, Sub-Agents, Polling and Counting Agents, Canvassers, Volunteer Assistants, and Members of Political Clubs and Associations. By T. C. H. HEDDERWICK, Esq., Barrister-at-Law. Demy 12mo. 1892. (*Nearly ready.*)

Rogers on Elections.—In two parts.
Part I. REGISTRATION, including the Practice in Registration Appeals; Parliamentary, Municipal, and Local Government; with Appendices of Statutes, Orders in Council, and Forms. Fifteenth Edition. By MAURICE POWELL, of the Inner Temple, Esq., Barrister-at-Law. Royal 12mo. 1890. 1*l.* 1*s.*
"The practitioner will find within these covers everything which he can be expected to know, well arranged and carefully stated."—*Law Times.*

Part II. ELECTIONS AND PETITIONS. Parliamentary and Municipal, with an Appendix of Statutes and Forms. Fifteenth Edition. Incorporating all the Decisions of the Election Judges, with Statutes, and a new and exhaustive Index. By JOHN CORRIE CARTER, and J. S. SANDARS, Esqrs., Barristers-at-Law. Royal 12mo. 1886. 1*l.* 1*s.*
"A very satisfactory treatise on election law . . . . well arranged, and tersely expressed. The completeness and general character of the book as regards the old law are too well known to need description."—*Solicitors' Journal.*

ELECTRIC LIGHTING.—Bazalgette and Humphreys.—*Vide* "Local and Municipal Government."

Cunynghame's Treatise on the Law of Electric Lighting, with the Acts, Rules and Orders, a Model Provisional Order, and Forms. By HENRY CUNYNGHAME, Barrister-at-Law. Royal 8vo. 1883. 12*s.* 6*d.*

EMPLOYERS' LIABILITY.—Firth's Law relating to the Liability of Employers for Injuries suffered by their Servants in the course of their Employment.—By T. W. STAPLEE FIRTH, Solicitor (The Sir Henry James Prize Essay). Demy 8vo. 1890.

EQUITY, and *Vide* **CHANCERY.** *Net* 2*s.* 6*d.*
Chitty's Index.—*Vide* "Digests."
Mews' Digest.—*Vide* "Digests."
Serrell.—*Vide* "Election in Equity."

Seton's Forms of Judgments and Orders in the High Court of Justice and in the Court of Appeal, having especial reference to the Chancery Division, with Practical Notes. Fifth Edition. By CECIL C. M. DALE, Esq., of Lincoln's Inn, Barrister-at-Law, and W. CLOWES, Esq., a Registrar of the Supreme Court of Judicature. In 2 vols. Royal 8vo. Vol. I. 1891. 2*l.*
"We have no fault to find with the treatment of either editor. Seton in its new guise is well up to the character which it has for so many years sustained of being the best book of forms of judgment which is known on the north side of the Strand."—*Law Times.*

Shearwood's Introduction to the Principles of Equity. By JOSEPH A. SHEARWOOD, Author of "A Concise Abridgment of Real and Personal Property," &c., Barrister-at-Law. 8vo. 1885. 6*s.*

Smith's Manual of Equity Jurisprudence.—A Manual of Equity Jurisprudence for Practitioners and Students, founded on the Works of Story, Spence, and other writers, comprising the Fundamental Principles and the points of Equity usually occurring in General Practice. By JOSIAH W. SMITH, Q.C. Fourteenth Edition. By J. TRUSTRAM, LL.M., Esq., Barrister-at-Law. 12mo. 1889. 12*s.* 6*d.*
"Still holds its own as the most popular first book of equity jurisprudence, and one which every student must of necessity read."—*Law Journal.*
"It will be found as useful to the practitioner as to the student."—*Solicitors' Journal.*
"A book that must very nearly be learnt by heart."—*The Jurist.*

_{*} *All standard Law Works are kept in Stock, in law calf and other bindings.*

EQUITY—*continued.*

Smith's Practical Exposition of the Principles of Equity, illustrated by the Leading Decisions thereon. For the use of Students and Practitioners. Second Edition. By H. ARTHUR SMITH, M.A., LL.B., Esq., Barrister-at-Law. Demy 8vo. 1888. 21s.

"This excellent practical exposition of the principles of equity is a work one can well recommend to students either for the bar or the examinations of the Incorporated Law Society. It will also be found equally valuable to the busy practitioner. It contains a mass of information well arranged, and is illustrated by all the leading decisions. All the legislative changes that have occurred since the publication of the first edition have been duly incorporated in the present issue."—*Law Times.*

ESTOPPEL.—Everest and Strode's Law of Estoppel. By LANCELOT FIELDING EVEREST, and EDMUND STRODE, Esqrs., Barristers-at-Law. Demy 8vo. 1884. 18s.

"A useful repository of the case law on the subject."—*Law Journal.*

EXAMINATION GUIDES.—Bedford's Digest of the Preliminary Examination Questions in Latin Grammar, Arithmetic, French Grammar, History and Geography, with the Answers. Second Edition. Demy 8vo. 1882. 18s.

Bedford's Student's Guide to the Ninth Edition of Stephen's New Commentaries on the Laws of England.—Third Edition. Demy 8vo. 1884. 7s. 6d.

Haynes and Nelham's Honours Examination Digest, comprising all the Questions in Conveyancing, Equity, Common Law, Bankruptcy, Probate, Divorce, Admiralty, and Ecclesiastical Law and Practice asked at the Solicitors' Honours Examinations, with Answers thereto. By JOHN F. HAYNES, LL.D., and THOMAS A. NELHAM, Solicitor (Honours). Demy 8vo. 1883. 15s.

"Students going in for honours will find this one to their advantage."—*Law Times.*

Napier's Modern Digest of the Final Examinations; a Modern Digest of the Law necessary to be known for the Final Examination of the Incorporated Law Society, done into Questions and Answers; and a Guide to a Course of Study for that Examination. By T. BATEMAN NAPIER, LL.D., London, of the Inner Temple, Barrister-at-Law. Demy 8vo. 1887. 18s.

"As far as we have tested them we have found the questions very well framed, and the answers to them clear, concise and accurate. If used in the manner that Dr. Napier recommends that it should be used, that is, together with the text-books, there can be little doubt that it will prove of considerable value to students."—*The Jurist.*

Napier & Stephenson's Digest of the Subjects of Probate, Divorce, Bankruptcy, Admiralty, Ecclesiastical and Criminal Law necessary to be known for the Final Examination, done into Questions and Answers. With a Preliminary Chapter on a Course of Study for the above Subjects. By T. BATEMAN NAPIER and RICHARD M. STEPHENSON, Esqrs., Barristers-at-Law. Demy 8vo. 1888. 12s.

"It is concise and clear in its answers, and the questions are based on points, for the most part, material to be known."—*Pump Court.*

Napier & Stephenson's Digest of the Leading Points in the Subject of Criminal Law necessary to be known for Bar and University Law Examinations. Done into Questions and Answers. By T. BATEMAN NAPIER and RICHARD M. STEPHENSON, Esqrs., Barristers-at-Law. Demy 8vo. 1888. 5s.

"We commend the book to candidates for the Bar and University Legal Examinations."—*Pump Court.*

Shearwood's Guide for Candidates for the Professions of Barrister and Solicitor.—Second Edition. By JOSEPH A. SHEARWOOD, Esq., Barrister-at-Law. Demy 8vo. 1887. 6s.

"A practical little book for students."—*Law Quarterly Review.*

*** *All standard Law Works are kept in Stock, in law calf and other bindings.*

EXECUTIONS.—Edwards' Law of Execution upon Judgments and Orders of the Chancery and Queen's Bench Divisions of the High Court of Justice.—By C. Johnston Edwards, of Lincoln's Inn, Esq., Barrister-at-Law. Demy 8vo. 1888. 16s.

"Will be found very useful, especially to solicitors. . . . In addition to the other good points in this book, it contains a copious collection of forms and a good index."—*Solicitors' Journal.*

"Mr Edwards writes briefly and pointedly, and has the merit of beginning in each case at the beginning, without assuming that the reader knows anything. He explains who the sheriff is; what the Queen, in a writ *Elegit*, for example, orders him to do; how he does it; and what consequences ensue. The result is to make the whole treatise satisfactorily clear and easy to apprehend. If the index is good—as it appears to be—practitioners will probably find the book a thoroughly useful one."—*Law Quarterly Review.*

EXECUTORS.—Macaskie's Treatise on the Law of Executors and Administrators, and of the Administration of the Estates of Deceased Persons. With an Appendix of Statutes and Forms. By S. C. MACASKIE, Esq., Barrister-at-Law. 8vo. 1881. 10s. 6d.

Williams' Law of Executors and Administrators.—Ninth Edition. By the Hon. Sir ROLAND VAUGHAN WILLIAMS, a Justice of the High Court. 2 vols. Roy. 8vo. (*In the press.*)

EXTRADITION.—Kirchner's L'Extradition.—Recueil Renfermant in Extenso tous les Traités conclus jusqu'au 1er Janvier, 1883, entre les Nations civilisées, et donnant la solution précise des difficultés qui peuvent surgir dans leur application. Avec une Préface de Mc GEORGES LACHAUD, Avocat à la Cour d'Appel de Paris. Publié sous les auspices de M. C. E. HOWARD VINCENT, Directeur des Affaires Criminelles de la Police Métropolitaine de Londres. Par F. J. KIRCHNER, Attaché à la Direction des Affaires Criminelles. In 1 vol. (1150 pp.). Royal 8vo. 1883. 2l. 2s.

FACTORS ACTS.—Boyd and Pearsons Factors Acts (1823 to 1877). With an Introduction and Explanatory Notes. By HUGH FENWICK BOYD and ARTHUR BEILBY PEARSON, Barristers-at-Law. Royal 12mo. 1884. 6s.

Neish & Carter's Factors Act, 1889: with Commentary and Notes; designed particularly for the use and guidance of Mercantile Men. By CHARLES H. L. NEISH and A. T. CARTER, Esqrs., Barristers-at-Law. Royal 12mo. 1890. 4s.

FARM, LAW OF.—Dixon's Law of the Farm, with a Digest of Cases connected with the Law of the Farm, and including the Agricultural Holdings (England) Act, 1883, and other recent Acts, and the Agricultural Customs of England and Wales. Fifth Edition. By AUBREY J. SPENCER, Esq., Barrister-at-Law. Demy 8vo. (*In the press.*)

"It is impossible not to be struck with the extraordinary research that must have been used in the compilation of such a book as this."—*Law Journal.*

FIXTURES.—Amos and Ferard on the Law of Fixtures and other Property partaking both of a Real and Personal Nature. Third Edition. By C. A. FERARD and W. HOWLAND ROBERTS, Esqrs., Barristers-at-Law. Demy 8vo. 1883. 18s.

"An accurate and well written work."—*Saturday Review.*

FORMS.—Allen.—*Vide* "Pleading."
Archibald.—*Vide* "Chamber Practice."
Bullen and Leake.—*Vide* "Pleading."
Chitty's Forms of Practical Proceedings in the Queen's Bench Division of the High Court of Justice. Twelfth Edition. By T. W. CHITTY, Esq., Barrister-at-Law. Demy 8vo. 1883. 1l. 16s.

"The forms themselves are brief and clear, and the notes accurate and to the point. —*Law Journal.*

*** *All standard Law Works are kept in Stock, in law calf and other bindings.*

FORMS—*continued.*
Daniell's Forms and Precedents of Proceedings in the Chancery Division of the High Court of Justice and on Appeal therefrom.—Fourth Edition, with Summaries of the Rules of the Supreme Court, Practical Notes and References to the Sixth Edition of "Daniell's Chancery Practice." By CHARLES BURNEY, B.A. (Oxon.), a Chief Clerk of the Hon. Mr. Justice Chitty. Royal 8vo. 1885. 2*l*.10*s*.
"Mr. Burney appears to have performed the laborious task before him with great success."—*Law Journal.*
"The standard work on Chancery Procedure."—*Law Quarterly Review.*

FRAUD AND MISREPRESENTATION.—**Moncreiff's Treatise on the Law relating to Fraud and Misrepresentation.**—By the Hon. FREDERICK MONCREIFF, of the Middle Temple, Barrister-at-Law. Demy 8vo. 1891. 21*s*.
"The task which Mr. Moncreiff has undertaken has been handled carefully and with considerable ability, and the work will well repay perusal."—*Solicitors' Journal,* June 6, 1891.
"There is a very full and carefully edited Index, with a large Table of Cases. Altogether the work is an admirable one."—*Law Gazette,* May 21, 1891.

GOODWILL.—**Allan's Law relating to Goodwill.**—By CHARLES E. ALLAN, M.A., LL.B., Esq., Barrister-at-Law. Demy 8vo. 1889. 7*s*. 6*d*.
"A work of much value upon a subject which is by no means easy."—*Solicitors' Journal.*

HIGHWAYS.—**Baker's Law of Highways in England and Wales,** including Bridges and Locomotives. Comprising a succinct Code of the several Provisions under each Head, the Statutes at length in an Appendix; with Notes of Cases, Forms, and copious Index. By THOMAS BAKER, Esq., Barrister-at-Law. Royal 12mo. 1880. 15*s*.
Bazalgette and Humphreys.—*Vide* "**Local and Municipal Government.**"
Chambers' Law relating to Highways and Bridges, being the Statutes in full and brief Notes of 700 Leading Cases. By GEORGE F. CHAMBERS, Esq., Barrister-at-Law. 1878. 7*s*. 6*d*.

HOUSE TAX.—**Ellis' Guide to the House Tax Acts, for the use of the Payer of Inhabited House Duty in England.**—By ARTHUR M. ELLIS, LL.B. (Lond.), Solicitor, Author of "A Guide to the Income Tax Acts." Royal 12mo. 1885. 6*s*.
"We have found the information accurate, complete and very clearly expressed."—*Solicitors' Journal.*

HUSBAND AND WIFE.—**Lush's Law of Husband and Wife;** within the Jurisdiction of the Queen's Bench and Chancery Divisions. By C. MONTAGUE LUSH, Esq., Barrister-at-Law. 8vo. 1884. 20*s*.
"Mr. Lush has one thing to recommend him most strongly, and that is his accuracy."—*Law Magazine.*

INCOME TAX.—**Ellis' Guide to the Income Tax Acts.**—For the use of the English Income Tax Payer. Second Edition. By ARTHUR M. ELLIS, LL.B. (Lond.), Solicitor. Royal 12mo. 1886. 7*s*. 6*d*.
"Contains in a convenient form the law bearing upon the Income Tax."—*Law Times.*

INLAND REVENUE CASES.—**Highmore's Summary Proceedings in Inland Revenue Cases in England and Wales.**—Second Edition. By N. J. HIGHMORE, Esq., Barrister-at-Law, and of the Solicitors' Department, Inland Revenue. Roy. 12mo. 1887. 7*s*. 6*d*.
"Is very complete. Every possible information is given."—*Law Times.*

INSURANCE.—**Arnould on the Law of Marine Insurance.**—Sixth Edition. By DAVID MACLACHLAN, Esq., Barrister-at-Law. 2 vols. Royal 8vo. 1887. 3*l*.
"As a text book, 'Arnould' is now all the practitioner can want."—*Law Times.*
Lowndes' Practical Treatise on the Law of Marine Insurance.—By RICHARD LOWNDES. Author of "The Law of General Average," &c. Second Edition. Demy 8vo. 1885. 12*s*. 6*d*.

*** *All standard Law Works are kept in Stock, in law calf and other bindings.*

INSURANCE—*continued.*

McArthur on the Contract of Marine Insurance.—Second Edition. By CHARLES MCARTHUR, Average Adjuster. Demy 8vo. 1890. 16s.

INTERNATIONAL LAW.—Kent's International Law.—Kent's Commentary on International Law. Edited by J. T. ABDY, LL.D., Judge of County Courts. Second Edition. Crown 8vo. 1878. 10s. 6d.

Nelson's Private International Law.—Selected Cases, Statutes, and Orders illustrative of the Principles of Private International Law as Administered in England, with Commentary. By HORACE NELSON, M.A., B.C.L., Barrister-at-Law. Roy. 8vo. 1889. 21s.

"The notes are full of matter, and avoid the vice of discursiveness, cases being cited for practically every proposition."—*Law Times.*

Wheaton's Elements of International Law; Third English Edition. Edited with Notes and Appendix of Statutes and Treaties. By A. C. BOYD, Esq., Barrister-at-Law. Royal 8vo. 1889. 1l. 10s.

"A handsome and useful edition of a standard work."—*Law Quarterly Review.*
"Wheaton stands too high for criticism, whilst Mr. Boyd's merits as an editor are almost as well established."—*Law Times.*

INTERROGATORIES.—Sichel and Chance.—*Vide* "**Discovery.**"

JOINT STOCKS.—Palmer.—*Vide* "**Company Law,**" "**Conveyancing,**" and "**Winding-up.**"

Thring's Joint Stock Companies' Law.—The Law and Practice of Joint Stock and other Companies, including the Companies Acts, 1862 to 1886, with Notes, Orders, and Rules in Chancery, a Collection of Precedents of Memoranda and Articles of Association, and other Forms required in Making and Administering a Company. Also the Partnership Law Amendment Act, the Life Assurance Companies Acts, and other Acts relating to Companies. By LORD THRING, K.C.B., formerly the Parliamentary Counsel. Fifth Edition. By J. M. RENDEL, Esq., Barrister-at-Law. Royal 8vo. 1889. 1l. 10s.

"The highest authority on the subject."—*The Times.*
"The book has long taken its place among the authoritative expositions of the law of companies. Its very useful forms are a special feature of the book, which will be of great value to practitioners."—*Law Journal.*

JUDGES' CHAMBER PRACTICE.—Archibald.—*Vide* "**Chamber Practice.**"

JUDICATURE ACTS.—Wilson's Practice of the Supreme Court of Judicature : containing the Acts, Orders, Rules, and Regulations relating to the Supreme Court. With Practical Notes. Seventh Edition. By CHARLES BURNEY, a Chief Clerk of the Hon. Mr. Justice Chitty, Editor of "Daniell's Chancery Forms;" M. MUIR MACKENZIE, and C. A. WHITE, Esqrs., Barristers-at-Law. Roy. 8vo. 1888. 1l.

"A thoroughly reliable and most conveniently arranged practice guide."—*Law Times*

JUSTICE OF THE PEACE.—Stone's Practice for Justices of the Peace, Justices' Clerks and Solicitors at Petty and Special Sessions, in Summary matters, and Indictable Offences, with a list of Summary Convictions, and matters not Criminal. With Forms. Ninth Edit. By W. H. MACNAMARA, Esq., Barrister-at-Law. Demy 8vo. 1882. 1l. 5s.

Wigram's Justice's Note Book.—Containing a short account of the Jurisdiction and Duties of Justices, and an Epitome of Criminal Law. By the late W. KNOX WIGRAM, Esq., Barrister-at-Law, J. P. Middlesex and Westminster. Sixth Edit. By ARCHIBALD HENRY BODKIN, Esq., Barrister-at-Law. Royal 12mo. 1892. (*Nearly ready.*)

"The style is clear, and the expression always forcible, and sometimes humorous. The book will repay perusal by many besides those who, as justices, will find it an indispensable companion."—*Law Quarterly Review.*
"We can thoroughly recommend the volume to magistrates."—*Law Times.*

*** *All standard Law Works are kept in Stock, in law calf and other bindings.*

LAND TAX.—Bourdin's Land Tax.—An Exposition of the Land Tax. Third Edition. Including the Recent Judicial Decisions, and the Incidental Changes in the Law effected by the Taxes Management Act, with other Additional Matter. Thoroughly revised and corrected. By SHIRLEY BUNBURY, of the Inland Revenue Department, Assistant Registrar of the Land Tax. Royal 12mo. 1885. 6s.

LANDLORD AND TENANT.—Woodfall's Law of Landlord and Tenant.—With a full Collection of Precedents and Forms of Procedure; containing also a collection of Leading Propositions. Fourteenth Edit. By J. M. LELY, Esq., Barrister-at-Law, Editor of "Chitty's Statutes," "Wharton's Law Lexicon," &c. Roy. 8vo. 1889. 1l. 18s.

"The editor has expended elaborate industry and systematic ability in making the work as perfect as possible."—*Solicitors' Journal.*

Lely and Peck.—*Vide* "Leases."

LANDS CLAUSES ACTS.—Jepson's Lands Clauses Consolidation Acts; with Decisions, Forms, and Table of Costs. By ARTHUR JEPSON, Esq., Barrister-at-Law. Demy 8vo. 1880. 18s.

LAW LIST.—Law List (The).—Comprising the Judges and Officers of the different Courts of Justice, Counsel, Special Pleaders, Conveyancers, Solicitors, Proctors, Notaries, &c., in England and Wales; the Circuits, Judges, Treasurers, Registrars, and High Bailiffs of the County Courts; Metropolitan and Stipendiary Magistrates, Official Receivers under the Bankruptcy Act, Law and Public Officers in England and the Colonies, Foreign Lawyers with their English Agents, Clerks of the Peace, Town Clerks, Coroners, &c., &c., and Commissioners for taking Oaths, Conveyancers Practising in England under Certificates obtained in Scotland. Compiled, so far as relates to Special Pleaders, Conveyancers, Solicitors, Proctors and Notaries, by JOHN SAMUEL PURCELL, C.B., Controller of Stamps, and Registrar of Joint Stock Companies, Somerset House, and Published by the Authority of the Commissioners of Inland Revenue. 1891. (*Published about March 1.*) (*Net cash, 9s.*) 10s. 6d.

LAW QUARTERLY REVIEW.—Edited by Sir FREDERICK POLLOCK, Bart., M.A., LL.D., Corpus Professor of Jurisprudence in the University of Oxford. Vols. I., II., III., IV., V., VI. and VII. Royal 8vo. 1885-91. *Each*, 12s.

☞ *Subscription* 10s. *per annum, post free.* (*Foreign postage* 2s. 6d. *extra.*)

The Review includes:—The discussion of current decisions of importance in the Courts of this country, and (so far as practicable) of the Colonies, the United States, British India, and other British Possessions where the Common Law is administered; the consideration of topics of proposed legislation before Parliament; the treatment of questions of immediate political and social interest in their legal aspect; inquiries into the history and antiquities of our own and other systems of law and legal institutions. Endeavour is also made to take account of the legal science and legislation of Continental States in so far as they bear on general jurisprudence, or may throw light by comparison upon problems of English or American legislation. The current legal literature of our own country receives careful attention; and works of serious importance, both English and foreign, are occasionally discussed at length.

LAWYER'S ANNUAL LIBRARY.—(1) The Annual Practice.—By SNOW, BURNEY, and STRINGER. **(2) The Annual Digest.**—By MEWS. **(3) The Annual Statutes.**—By LELY. **(4) The Annual County Court Practice.**—By His Honour JUDGE HEYWOOD.

The Complete Series, as above, delivered on the day of publication, *net*, 2l. Nos. 1, 2, and 3 only, *net*, 1l. 10s. Nos. 2, 3, and 4 only, *net*, 1l. 10s. (*Carriage extra*, 2s.)

☞ *Subscriptions, payable on or before August 31st in each year. Full prospectus forwarded on application.*

LAWYER'S COMPANION.—*Vide* "Diary."

⁎ *All standard Law Works are kept in Stock, in law calf and other bindings.*

LEADING CASES.—Ball's Leading Cases. *Vide* "Torts."
Haynes' Student's Leading Cases. Being some of the Principal
Decisions of the Courts in Constitutional Law, Common Law, Conveyancing and Equity, Probate, Divorce, and Criminal Law. With
Notes for the use of Students. Second Edition. By JOHN F.
HAYNES, LL.D. Demy 8vo. 1884. 16s.

Shirley's Selection of Leading Cases in the Common Law.
With Notes. By W. SHIRLEY SHIRLEY, Esq., Barrister-at-Law.
Fourth Edition. By RICHARD WATSON, of Lincoln's Inn, Esq.,
Barrister-at-Law. Demy 8vo. 1891. 16s.
"Mr. Watson has made some great improvements in the 4th edition of this well-known book. One great defect of previous editions was the absence of an index of cases; this has now been supplied, and more ample references to reports are given and a more scientific arrangement adopted of the leading cases on Contracts. . . . There is a mass of information in Shirley's Common Law Cases. It is difficult of digestion, perhaps, but this is so in the case of all concentrated information. To a student who will reflect, as well as read, a sound knowledge of common law can be gleaned from Shirley."—*Law Notes*, October, 1891.

Shirley's Selection of Leading Cases in the Criminal Law. With
Notes. By W. S. SHIRLEY, Esq., Barrister-at-Law. 8vo. 1888. 6s.
"Will undoubtedly prove of value to students."- *Law Notes*.

LEASES.—Lely and Peck's Precedents of Leases for Years,
and other Contracts of Tenancy, and Contracts relating thereto;
mainly selected or adapted from existing Collections, including many
additional Forms, with a short Introduction and Notes. By J. M.
LELY and W. A. PECK, Barristers-at-Law. Royal 8vo. 1889. 10s. 6d.
"Varied, well considered, and thoroughly practical . . . while a useful addition to the library of the conveyancing counsel, will be still more useful to conveyancing solicitors and estate agents."—*Law Times*, November 9, 1889.

LEXICON.—*Vide* "Dictionary."

LIBEL AND SLANDER.—Odgers on Libel and Slander.—A
Digest of the Law of Libel and Slander: the Evidence, Procedure
and Practice, both in Civil and Criminal Cases, and Precedents of
Pleadings. Second Edition, with a SUPPLEMENT, bringing the Law
down to June, 1890. By W. BLAKE ODGERS, LL.D., Barrister-at-
Law. Royal 8vo. 1890. 1l. 12s.
"The best modern book on the law of libel."—*Daily News*.

LIBRARIES AND MUSEUMS.—Chambers' Digest of the Law
relating to Public Libraries and Museums, and Literary and
Scientific Institutions: with much Practical Information useful to
Managers, Committees and Officers of all classes of Associations and
Clubs connected with Literature, Science and Art; including Precedents of By-Laws and Regulations, the Statutes in Full, and brief
Notes of Leading Cases. Third Edition. By GEO. F. CHAMBERS, Esq.,
Barrister-at-Law. Roy. 8vo. 1889. 8s. 6d.

LICENSING.—Lely and Foulkes' Licensing Acts, 1828, 1869,
and 1872—1874; with Notes to the Acts, a Summary of the Law,
and an Appendix of Forms. Third Edit. By J. M. LELY and W. D. I.
FOULKES, Esqrs., Barristers-at-Law. Roy. 12mo. 1887. 10s. 6d.
"We do not know of a more compact or useful treatise on the subject."—*Sol. Jour.*

LOCAL AND MUNICIPAL GOVERNMENT.—Bazalgette and
Humphreys' Law relating to County Councils: being the Local
Government Act, 1888, County Electors Act, 1888, the Incorporated
Clauses of the Municipal Corporations Act, 1882, and a compendious
Introduction and Notes; with Analysis of Statutes affecting the same,
Orders in Council, Circulars, and a Copious Index. By C. N. BAZALGETTE and GEORGE HUMPHREYS, Barristers-at-Law, Joint Authors of
"The Law of Local and Municipal Government." Third Edition.
By GEORGE HUMPHREYS, Esq. Royal 8vo. 1889. 7s. 6d.
"The most stately as regards size, and the best in point of type of all the works. There is a good introduction . . . the notes are careful and helpful."—*Solicitors' Journal*.

*** *All standard Law Works are kept in Stock, in law calf and other bindings.*

LOCAL AND MUNICIPAL GOVERNMENT—*continued.*

Bazalgette and Humphreys' Law relating to Local and Municipal Government. Comprising the Statutes relating to Public Health, Municipal Corporations, Highways, Burial, Gas and Water, Public Loans, Compulsory Taking of Lands, Tramways, Electric Lighting, Artizans' Dwellings, &c., Rivers' Pollution, the Clauses Consolidation Acts, and many others, fully annotated with cases up to date, a selection of the Circulars of the Local Government Board, with a Table of upwards of 2,500 Cases, and full Index. With Addenda containing the Judicial Decisions and Legislation relating to Local and Municipal Government since 1885. By C. NORMAN BAZALGETTE and GEORGE HUMPHREYS, Esqrs., Barristers-at-Law. Sup. royal 8vo. 1888. 3*l.* 3*s.*

* *The Addenda may be had separately. Net,* 2*s.* 6*d.*

"The book is thoroughly comprehensive of the law on all points of which it professes to treat."—*Law Journal.*

"The work is one that no local officer should be without; for nothing short of a whole library of statutes, reports, and handbooks could take its place."—*Municipal Review.*

Chambers' Popular Summary of the Law relating to Local Government, forming a complete Guide to the new Act of 1888. Second Edition. By G. F. CHAMBERS, Barrister-at-Law. Imp. 8vo. 1888. (*Or bound in Cloth with copy of Act,* 5*s.* 6*d.*) *Net,* 2*s.* 6*d.*

MAGISTERIAL LAW.—**Shirley's Elementary Treatise on Magisterial Law,** and on the Practice of Magistrates' Courts.—By W. S. SHIRLEY, Esq., Barrister-at-Law. Roy. 12mo. 1881. 6*s.* 6*d.*

Wigram.—*Vide* "Justice of the Peace."

MALICIOUS PROSECUTIONS. — **Stephen's Law relating to Actions for Malicious Prosecutions.**—By HERBERT STEPHEN, LL.M., of the Inner Temple, Barrister-at-Law, part Author of "A Digest of the Criminal Law Procedure." Royal 12mo. 1888. 6*s.*

"A reliable text-book upon the law of malicious prosecution."—*Law Times.*

MARITIME DECISIONS.—**Douglas' Maritime Law Decisions.**—An Alphabetical Reference Index to Recent and Important Maritime Decisions. Compiled by ROBT. R. DOUGLAS. Demy 8vo. 1888. 7*s.* 6*d.*

Marine Insurance.—*Vide* "Insurance."

MARRIAGE.—**Kelly's French Law of Marriage, and the Conflict of Laws that arises therefrom.** By E. KELLY, M.A., of the New York Bar, Licencié en Droit de la Faculté de Paris. Roy. 8vo. 1885. 6*s.*

MARRIAGE SETTLEMENTS.—**Banning's Concise Treatise on the Law of Marriage Settlements;** with an Appendix of Statutes. By H. T. BANNING, Esq., Barrister-at-Law. Demy 8vo. 1884. 15*s.*

MARRIED WOMEN'S PROPERTY.—**Lush's Married Women's Rights and Liabilities in relation to Contracts, Torts, and Trusts.** By MONTAGUE LUSH, Esq., Barrister-at-Law, Author of "The Law of Husband and Wife." Royal 12mo. 1887. 5*s.*

"Well arranged, clearly written, and has a good index."—*Law Times.*

Smith's Married Women's Property Acts, 1882 and 1884, with an Introduction and Critical and Explanatory Notes, together with the Married Women's Property Acts, 1870 and 1874, &c. 2nd Edit. Revised. By H. A. SMITH, Esq., Barrister-at-Law. Roy.12mo. 1884. 6*s.*

MASTER AND SERVANT.—**Macdonell's Law of Master and Servant.** Part I. Common Law. Part II. Statute Law. By JOHN MACDONELL, M.A., Esq., Barrister-at-Law. Demy 8vo. 1883. 1*l.* 5*s.*

"A work which will be of real value to the practitioner."—*Law Times.*

MAYOR'S COURT PRACTICE.—**Candy's Mayor's Court Practice.**—The Jurisdiction, Process, Practice and Mode of Pleading in Ordinary Actions in the Mayor's Court in London. By GEORGE CANDY, Esq., one of Her Majesty's Counsel. Demy 8vo. 1879. 14*s.*

* *All standard Law Works are kept in Stock, in law calf and other bindings.*

MERCANTILE LAW.—Russell's Treatise on Mercantile Agency. Second Edition. 8vo. 1873. 14s.

Smith's Compendium of Mercantile Law.—Tenth Edition. By JOHN MACDONELL, Esq., a Master of the Supreme Court of Judicature, assisted by GEO. HUMPHREYS, Esq., Barrister-at-Law. 2 vols. Royal 8vo. 1890. 2l. 2s.

"Of the greatest value to the mercantile lawyer."—*Law Times*, March 22, 1890.
"We have no hesitation in recommending the work before us to the profession and the public as a reliable guide to the subjects included in it, and as constituting one of the most scientific treatises extant on mercantile law." *Solicitors' Journal*, May 10, 1890.

Tudor's Selection of Leading Cases on Mercantile and Maritime Law.—With Notes. By O. D. TUDOR, Esq., Barrister-at-Law. Third Edition. Royal 8vo. 1884. 2l. 2s.

Wilson's Mercantile Handbook of the Liabilities of Merchant, Shipowner, and Underwriter on Shipments by General Vessels.—By A. WILSON, Solicitor and Notary. Royal 12mo. 1883. 6s.

Wood's Mercantile Agreements.—The Interpretation of Mercantile Agreements: A Summary of the Decisions as to the Meaning of Words and Provisions in Written Agreements for the Sale of Goods, Charter-Parties, Bills of Lading, and Marine Policies. With an Appendix containing a List of Words and Expressions used in, or in connection with, Mercantile Agreements, and a List of Mercantile Usages. By JOHN DENNISTOUN WOOD, Esq., Barrister-at-Law. Royal 8vo. 1886. 18s.

"A book of great use in the interpretation of written mercantile agreements."—*Law Journal*.

MERCHANDISE MARKS ACT.—Payn's Merchandise Marks Act, 1887.—With special reference to the Important Sections and the Customs Regulations and Orders made thereunder, together with the Conventions with Foreign States for Protection of Trade Marks, and Orders in Council, &c. By HOWARD PAYN, Barrister-at-Law, and of the Secretary's Department of the Board of Customs. Royal 12mo. 1888. 3s. 6d.

"Mr. Payn's lucid introduction places the subject very clearly before the reader, and his book must be a safe guide to all who are interested in the act."—*Law Times*, Feb. 1888.

METROPOLIS BUILDING ACTS. — Woolrych's Metropolitan Building Acts, together with such clauses of the Metropolis Management Acts as more particularly relate to the Building Acts, with Notes and Forms. Third Edition. By W. H. MACNAMARA, Esq., Barrister-at-Law. 12mo. 1882. 10s.

MINES.—Rogers' Law relating to Mines, Minerals and Quarries in Great Britain and Ireland, with a Summary of the Laws of Foreign States, &c. Second Edition Enlarged. By His Honor Judge ROGERS. 8vo. 1876. 1l. 11s. 6d.

MORTGAGE.—Coote's Treatise on the Law of Mortgage.—Fifth Edition. Thoroughly revised. By WILLIAM WYLLYS MACKESON, Esq., one of Her Majesty's Counsel, and H. ARTHUR SMITH, Esq., Barrister-at-Law. 2 vols. Royal 8vo. 1884. 3l.

"A complete, terse and practical treatise for the modern lawyer."—*Solicitors' Journal*.

MUNICIPAL CORPORATIONS.—Bazalgette and Humphreys.— *Vide* "Local and Municipal Government."

Lely's Law of Municipal Corporations.—Containing the Municipal Corporation Act, 1882, and the Enactments incorporated therewith. With Notes. By J. M. LELY, Esq., Barrister-at-Law. Demy 8vo. 1882. 15s.

*** *All standard Law Works are kept in Stock, in law calf and other bindings.*

NAVY.—Thring's Criminal Law of the Navy, with an Introductory Chapter on the Early State and Discipline of the Navy, the Rules of Evidence, and an Appendix comprising the Naval Discipline Act and Practical Forms. Second Edition. By THEODORE THRING, Esq., Barrister-at-Law, and C. E. GIFFORD, Assistant-Paymaster, Royal Navy. 12mo. 1877. 12s. 6d.

NEGLIGENCE.—Smith's Treatise on the Law of Negligence. Second Edition. By HORACE SMITH, Esq., Barrister-at-Law, Editor of "Addison on Contracts, and Torts," &c. 8vo. 1884. 12s. 6d.

"Of great value both to the practitioner and student of law."—*Solicitors' Journal.*

NISI PRIUS.—Roscoe's Digest of the Law of Evidence on the Trial of Actions at Nisi Prius.—Sixteenth Edition. By MAURICE POWELL, Esq., Barrister-at-Law. 2 vols. Demy 8vo. 1891. 2l. 10s.

"Continues to be a vast and closely packed storehouse of information on practice at Nisi Prius."—*Law Journal.*

NONCONFORMISTS.—Winslow's Law Relating to Protestant Nonconformists and their Places of Worship; being a Legal Handbook for Nonconformists. By REGINALD WINSLOW, Esq., Barrister-at-Law. Post 8vo. 1886. 6s.

NOTARY.—Brooke's Treatise on the Office and Practice of a Notary of England.—With a full collection of Precedents. Fifth Ed. By G. F. CHAMBERS, Esq., Barrister-at-Law. Demy 8vo. 1890. 1l. 1s.

OATHS.—Stringer's Oaths and Affirmations in Great Britain and Ireland; being a Collection of Statutes, Cases, and Forms, with Notes and Practical Directions for the use of Commissioners for Oaths, and of all Courts of Civil Procedure and Offices attached thereto. [In succession to "Braithwaite's Oaths."] By FRANCIS A. STRINGER, of the Central Office, Supreme Court of Judicature, one of the Editors of the "Annual Practice." Crown 8vo. 1890. 3s. 6d.

"Indispensable to all commissioners."—*Solicitors' Journal*, Jan. 11, 1890.'
"A most excellent little handbook."—*Law Times*, Feb. 1, 1890.

PARISH LAW.—Steer's Parish Law; being a Digest of the Law relating to the Civil and Ecclesiastical Government of Parishes and the Relief of the Poor. Fifth Edition. By W. H. MACNAMARA, Esq., Barrister-at-Law. Demy 8vo. 1887. 18s.

"An exceedingly useful compendium of Parish Law."—*Law Times.*
"A very complete and excellent guide to Parish Law."—*Solicitors' Journal.*
"Every subject that can be considered parochial is, we think, contained in this volume, and the matter is brought down to date. It is a compendium which is really compendious."—*Law Journal*, Jan. 21, 1888.

PARTNERSHIP.—Pollock's Digest of the Law of Partnership; incorporating the Partnership Act, 1890. Fifth Edition. By Sir FREDERICK POLLOCK, Bart., Barrister-at-Law. Author of "Principles of Contract," "The Law of Torts," &c. Demy 8vo. 1890. 8s. 6d.

"What Sir Frederick Pollock has done he has done well, and we are confident this book will be most popular as well as extremely useful."—*Law Times*, Dec. 13, 1890.

Turner.—*Vide* "Conveyancing."

PATENTS.—Aston's (T.) Patents, Designs and Trade Marks Act, 1883, with Notes and Index to the Act, Rules and Forms. By THEODORE ASTON, Q.C. Royal 12mo. 1884. 6s.

Edmunds' Patents, Designs and Trade Marks Acts, 1883 to 1888, Consolidated, with an Index. By LEWIS EDMUNDS, D.Sc., LL.B., Barrister-at-Law. Imp. 8vo. 1889. *Net* 2s. 6d.

*** *All standard Law Works are kept in Stock, in law calf and other bindings.*

PATENTS—*continued.*

Edmunds on Patents.—The Law and Practice of Letters Patent for Inventions; with the Patents Acts and Rules annotated, and the International Convention, a full collection of Statutes, Forms, and Precedents, and an Outline of Foreign and Colonial Patent Laws, &c. By LEWIS EDMUNDS, assisted by A. WOOD RENTON, Esqrs., Barristers-at-Law. Royal 8vo. (992 pp.). 1890. 1*l*. 12*s*.

"We have nothing but commendation for the book. Conceived in a large and comprehensive spirit, it is well and thoroughly carried out. . . . The statement of the existing law is accurate and clear. . . . The book is one to be recommended."—*Solicitors' Journal*, June 14, 1890.

"We have no hesitation in saying that the book is a useful and exhaustive one, and one which could not have been produced without much labour and considerable research. It describes the law of letters patent and its history, including proceedings in the Privy Council, international arrangements, and an abridgment of foreign laws on the subject. It would be difficult to make it more complete, and it is printed on good paper."—*Law Times*, June 21, 1890.

"Taking the book as a whole, it is undoubtedly the most comprehensive book that has yet been written upon the special branch of law, and, having examined it in some detail, we can commend it as answering well to the many tests we have applied."—*Law Journal*, June 21, 1890.

Johnson's Patentees' Manual.—A Treatise on the Law and Practice of Patents for Inventions. With an Appendix of Statutes, Rules, and Foreign and Colonial Patent Laws, International Convention, and Protocol. Sixth Edition. By JAMES JOHNSON, Esq., Barrister-at-Law; and J. HENRY JOHNSON, Solicitor and Patent Agent. Demy 8vo. 1890. 10*s*. 6*d*.

Morris's Patents Conveyancing.—Being a Collection of Precedents in Conveyancing in relation to Letters Patent for Inventions. Arranged as follows:—Common Forms, Agreements, Assignments, Mortgages, Special Clauses, Licences, Miscellaneous; Statutes, Rules, &c. With Dissertations and Copious Notes on the Law and Practice. By ROBERT MORRIS, Esq., Barrister-at-Law. Royal 8vo. 1887. 1*l*. 5*s*.

"Mr. Morris' forms seem to us to be well selected, well arranged, and thoroughly practical."—*Law Times*.

"The dissertations contain a large amount of valuable and accurate information. The Index is satisfactory."—*Solicitors' Journal*.

Munro's Patents, Designs and Trade Marks Act, 1883, with the Rules and Instructions, together with Pleadings, Orders and Precedents. By J. E. CRAWFORD MUNRO, Esq., Barrister-at-Law. Royal 12mo. 1884. 10*s*. 6*d*.

Thompson's Handbook of Patent Law of all Countries.—By WM. P. THOMPSON, Head of the International Patent Office, Liverpool. Eighth Edition. 12mo. 1889. *Net*, 2*s*. 6*d*.

PERPETUITIES.—**Marsden's Rule against Perpetuities.**—A Treatise on Remoteness in Limitation; with a chapter on Accumulation and the Thelluson Act. By REGINALD G. MARSDEN, Esq., Barrister-at Law. Demy 8vo. 1883. 16*s*.

PERSONAL PROPERTY.—**Shearwood's Concise Abridgment of the Law of Personal Property**; showing analytically its Branches and the Titles by which it is held. By J. A. SHEARWOOD, Esq., Barrister-at-Law. 1882. 5*s*. 6*d*.

"Will be acceptable to many students, as giving them, in fact, a ready-made note book."—*Indermaur's Law Students' Journal*.

Smith.—*Vide* "Real Property."

PLEADING.—**Allen's Forms of Indorsements of Writs of Summons, Pleadings, and other Proceedings in the Queen's Bench Division prior to Trial, pursuant to the Rules of the Supreme Court, 1883**; with Introduction, &c. By GEORGE BAUGH ALLEN, Esq., Special Pleader, and WILFRED B. ALLEN, Esq., Barrister-at-Law. Royal 12mo. 1883. 18*s*.

⁎ *All standard Law Works are kept in Stock, in law calf and other bindings.*

PLEADING—*continued.*

Bullen and Leake's Precedents of Pleadings, with Notes and Rules relating to Pleading. Fourth Edition. By THOMAS J. BULLEN, Esq., Special Pleader, and CYRIL DODD, Esq., Barrister-at-Law. Part I. Statements of Claim. Royal 12mo. 1882. 1l. 4s.
Part II. Statements of Defence. By THOMAS J. BULLEN and C. W. CLIFFORD, Esqrs., Barristers-at-Law. Royal 12mo. 1888. 1l. 4s.
"A very large number of precedents are collected together, and the notes are full and clear."—*Law Times.*

Odgers' Principles of Pleading in Civil Actions under the Judicature Acts.—By W. BLAKE ODGERS, M.A., LL.D., Barrister-at-Law, Author of "A Digest of the Law of Libel and Slander." Demy 8vo. 1892. 8s. 6d.

POISONS.—Reports of Trials for Murder by Poisoning; by Prussic Acid, Strychnia, Antimony, Arsenic and Aconitine; including the trials of Tawell, W. Palmer, Dove, Madeline Smith, Dr. Pritchard, Smethurst, and Dr. Lamson. With Chemical Introductions and Notes. By G. LATHAM BROWNE, Esq., Barrister-at-Law, and C. G. STEWART, Senior Assistant in the Laboratory of St. Thomas's Hospital, &c. Demy 8vo. 1883. 12s. 6d.

POWERS.—Farwell on Powers.—A Concise Treatise on Powers. By GEORGE FARWELL, Esq., Barrister-at-Law. 8vo. 1874. 1l. 1s.

PRINTERS, PUBLISHERS, &c.—Powell's Laws specially affecting Printers, Publishers and Newspaper Proprietors. By ARTHUR POWELL, Esq., Barrister-at-Law. Demy 8vo. 1889. 4s.

PROBATE.—Browne's Probate Practice: A Treatise on the Principles and Practice of the Court of Probate, in Contentious and Non-Contentious Business. By L. D. POWLES, Barrister-at-Law. Including Practical Directions to Solicitors for Proceedings in the Registry. By T. W. H. OAKLEY, of the Principal Registry, Somerset House. 8vo. 1881. 1l. 10s.

PROFIT-SHARING PRECEDENTS.—Rawson's Profit-Sharing Precedents, with Notes.—By HENRY G. RAWSON, of the Inner Temple, Esq., Barrister-at-Law. Royal 12mo. 1891. 6s.
"A most interesting and a thoroughly workmanlike book upon a subject which is every day becoming more important. . . . A collection of very serviceable precedents, which employers introducing a system of profit-sharing will do well to study. . . . No collection of precedents has ever been published which is more readable and more interesting than Mr. Rawson's."—*Law Times,* July 18, 1891.

PUBLIC HEALTH.—Bazalgette and Humphreys.—*Vide* "Local and Municipal Government."

Chambers' Digest of the Law relating to Public Health and Local Government.—With Notes of 1,260 leading Cases. The Statutes in full. A Table of Offences and Punishments, and a Copious Index. Eighth Edition (with Supplement corrected to May 21, 1887). Imperial 8vo. 1881. 16s.
Or, the above with the Law relating to Highways and Bridges. 1l.

Smith's Public Health Acts Amendment Act, 1890.—With Introduction, Notes, and References to Cases; also an Appendix, containing all the Material Sections of the Public Health Act, 1875 ; The Public Health (Rating of Orchards) Act, 1890 ; and The Infectious Diseases (Prevention) Act, 1890: and a Copious Index. By BOVILL SMITH, M.A., of the Inner Temple and Western Circuit, Barrister-at-Law. Royal 12mo. 1891. 6s.

PUBLIC MEETINGS.—Chambers' Handbook for Public Meetings, including Hints as to the Summoning and Management of them. Second Edition. By GEORGE F. CHAMBERS, Esq., Barrister-at-Law. Demy 8vo. 1886. *Net,* 2s. 6d.

⁎⁎* *All standard Law Works are kept in Stock, in law calf and other bindings.*

QUARTER SESSIONS.—Archbold.—*Vide* "Criminal Law."
Leeming & Cross's General and Quarter Sessions of the Peace.
—Their Jurisdiction and Practice in other than Criminal matters. Second Edition. By HORATIO LLOYD, Esq., Judge of County Courts, and H. F. THURLOW, Esq., Barrister-at-Law. 8vo. 1876. 1*l.* 1*s.*
Pritchard's Quarter Sessions.—The Jurisdiction, Practice and Procedure of the Quarter Sessions in Criminal, Civil, and Appellate Matters. By THOS. SIRRELL PRITCHARD, Esq., Barrister-at-Law. 8vo. 1875. (Published at 2*l.* 2*s.*) Reduced to *net* 12*s.*

RAILWAYS.—**Browne and Theobald's Law of Railway Companies.**—Being a Collection of the Acts and Orders relating to Railway Companies in England and Ireland, with Notes of all the Cases decided thereon, and Appendix of Bye-Laws and Standing Orders of the House of Commons. Second Edition. By J. H. BALFOUR BROWNE, Esq., one of Her Majesty's Counsel, and H. S. THEOBALD, Esq., Barrister-at-Law. Royal 8vo. 1888. 1*l.* 15*s.*
" Contains in a very concise form the whole law of railways."—*The Times.*
" The learned authors seem to have presented the profession and the public with the most ample information to be found whether they want to know how to start a railway, how to frame its bye-laws, how to work it, how to attack it for injury to person or property, or how to wind it up."—*Law Times.*

RATES AND RATING.—**Castle's Practical Treatise on the Law of Rating.**—Second Edition. By EDWARD JAMES CASTLE, Esq., one of Her Majesty's Counsel. Demy 8vo. 1886. 25*s.*
" A correct, exhaustive, clear and concise view of the law."—*Law Times.*

Chambers' Law relating to Local Rates; with especial reference to the Powers and Duties of Rate-levying Local Authorities, and their Officers; comprising the Statutes in full and a Digest of 718 Cases. Second Edition. By G. F. CHAMBERS, Esq., Barrister-at-Law. Royal 8vo. 1889. 10*s.* 6*d.*
" A complete repertory of the statutes and case law of the subject."—*Law Journal.*

REAL PROPERTY.—**Greenwood's Real Property Statutes;** comprising those passed during the years 1874—1884, inclusive, consolidated with the earlier statutes thereby amended. With copious notes. Second Edition. By HARRY GREENWOOD, assisted by LEES KNOWLES, Esqrs., Barristers-at-Law. Demy 8vo. 1884. 1*l.* 5*s.*

Leake's Elementary Digest of the Law of Property in Land.—Containing: Introduction. Part I. The Sources of the Law.—Part II. Estates in Land. By STEPHEN MARTIN LEAKE, Barrister-at-Law. Demy 8vo. 8vo. 1874. 1*l.* 2*s.*

Leake's Digest of the Law of Property in Land.—Part III. The Law of Uses and Profits of Land. By STEPHEN MARTIN LEAKE, Barrister-at-Law, Author of "A Digest of the Law of Contracts." Demy 8vo. 1888. 1*l.* 2*s.*

Shearwood's Real Property.—A Concise Abridgment of the Law of Real Property and an Introduction to Conveyancing. Designed to facilitate the subject for Students preparing for examination. By JOSEPH A. SHEARWOOD, Esq., Barrister-at-Law. Third Edition. Demy 8vo. 1885. 8*s.* 6*d.*
" We heartily recommend the work to student's for any examination on real property and conveyancing, advising them to read it after a perusal of other works and shortly before going in for the examination."—*Law Student's Journal.*
" A very useful little work, particularly to students just before their examination."—*Gibson's Law Notes.*
" One of the most obvious merits of the book is its good arrangement. The author evidently understands 'the art of putting things.' All important points are so printed as to readily catch the eye."—*Law Times.*

Shelford's Real Property Statutes.—Ninth Edition. By T. H. CARSON, Esq., Barrister-at-Law. (*In preparation.*)

⁎ *All standard Law Works are kept in Stock, in law calf and other bindings.*

REAL PROPERTY—*continued.*

Smith's Real and Personal Property.—A Compendium of the Law of Real and Personal Property, primarily connected with Conveyancing. Designed as a second book for Students, and as a digest of the most useful learning for practitioners. By JOSIAH W. SMITH, B.C.L., Q.C. Sixth Edition. By the AUTHOR and J. TRUSTRAM, LL.M., Barrister-at-Law. 2 vols. Demy 8vo. 1884. 2*l*. 2*s*.

"A book which he (the student) may read over and over again with profit and pleasure."—*Law Times*.
"Will be found of very great service to the practitioner."—*Solicitors' Journal*.
"The book will be found very handy for reference purposes to practitioners, and very useful to the industrious student as covering a great deal of ground."—*Law Notes*.
"A really useful and valuable work on our system of Conveyancing. We think this edition excellently done."—*Law Student's Journal*.

REGISTRATION.—**Rogers.**—*Vide* "**Elections.**"

Coltman's Registration Cases.—Vol. I. (1879—1885). Royal 8vo. Calf. *Net*, 2*l*. 8*s*.

Fox's Registration Cases.—Vol. I., Part I. (1886), *net*, 4*s*. Part II. (1887), *net*, 6*s*. 6*d*. Part III. (1888), *net*, 4*s*. Part IV. (1889), *net*, 4*s*. Part V. (1890), *net*, 5*s*. 6*d*. (In continuation of Coltman.)

RENTS.—**Harrison's Law Relating to Chief Rents and other Rentcharges and Lands as affected thereby,** with a chapter on Restrictive Covenants and a selection of Precedents. By WILLIAM HARRISON, Solicitor. Demy 12mo. 1884. 6*s*.

ROMAN LAW.—**Goodwin's XII. Tables.**—By FREDERICK GOODWIN, LL.D. London. Royal 12mo. 1886. 3*s*. 6*d*.

Greene's Outlines of Roman Law.—Consisting chiefly of an Analysis and Summary of the Institutes. For the use of Students. By T. WHITCOMBE GREENE, Barrister-at-law. Fourth Edition. Foolscap 8vo. 1884. 7*s*. 6*d*.

Ruegg's Student's "Auxilium" to the Institutes of Justinian.—Being a complete synopsis thereof in the form of Question and Answer. By ALFRED HENRY RUEGG, Esq., Barrister-at-Law. Post 8vo. 1879. 5*s*.

SALES.—**Blackburn on Sales.** A Treatise on the Effect of the Contract of Sale on the Legal Rights of Property and Possession in Goods, Wares, and Merchandise. By Lord BLACKBURN. Second Edition. By J. C. GRAHAM, Esq., Barrister-at-Law. Royal 8vo. 1885. 1*l*. 1*s*.

"We have no hesitation in saying that the work has been edited with remarkable ability and success, and if we may hazard a speculation on the cause, we should say that the editor has so diligently studied the excellent methods and work of his author as to have made himself a highly competent workman in the same kind."—*Law Quarterly Review*.

SALES OF LAND.—**Clerke and Humphry's Concise Treatise on the Law relating to Sales of Land.** By AUBREY ST. JOHN CLERKE, and HUGH M. HUMPHRY, Esqrs., Barristers-at-Law. Royal 8vo. 1885. 1*l*. 5*s*.

Webster's Particulars and Conditions of Sale.—The Law relating to Particulars and Conditions of Sale on a Sale of Land. By WM. FREDK. WEBSTER, Esq., Barrister-at-Law. Royal 8vo. 1889. 1*l*. 1*s*.

"Characterized by clearness of arrangement and careful and concise statement; and we think it will be found of much service to the practitioner."—*Solicitors' Journal*.
"A full account of case law, well arranged under convenient headings, together with a few precedents. The book is fit to be of practical service to a practical man."—*Law Quarterly Review*.
"It forms an admirable digest, evidently prepared with great care, and selected and arranged in a manner likely to be of great practical value. Its treatment has the air of thoroughness, and, although it hardly claims originality, it may be credited with utility."—*Law Journal*.
"A complete and accurate representation of the law. Nothing is shirked or slurred over."—*Law Times*.

⁎ *All standard Law Works are kept in Stock, in law calf and other bindings.*

SALVAGE.—Kennedy's Treatise on the Law of Civil Salvage.—By WILLIAM R. KENNEDY, Esq., one of Her Majesty's Counsel. Royal 8vo. 1891. 12s.

"The best work on the law of salvage that has yet appeared. It is a complete exposition of the subject, and as such is accurate and exhaustive, without being prolix, and contains copious reference to the authorities applicable to this branch of law."—*Law Times*, August 8, 1891.

"Mr. Kennedy's work is certainly a valuable contribution to the literature of the subject."—*Law Gazette*, August 6, 1891.

SETTLED ESTATES STATUTES.—Middleton's Settled Estates Statutes, including the Settled Estates Act, 1877, Settled Land Act, 1882, Improvement of Land Act, 1864, and the Settled Estates Act Orders, 1878, with Introduction, Notes and Forms. Third Edition. By JAMES W. MIDDLETON, Esq., Barrister-at-Law. Royal 12mo. 1882. 7s. 6d.

SHERIFF LAW.—Churchill's Law of the Office and Duties of the Sheriff, with the Writs and Forms relating to the Office. 2nd Edit. By CAMERON CHURCHILL, Esq. Demy 8vo. 1882. 1l. 4s.

"A very complete treatise."—*Solicitors' Journal*.

"Under-sheriffs, and lawyers generally, will find this a useful book."—*Law Mag*.

SHIPPING.—Boyd's Merchant Shipping Laws; being a Consolidation of all the Merchant Shipping and Passenger Acts from 1854 to 1876, inclusive, with Notes of all the leading English and American Cases, and an Appendix. By A. C. BOYD, LL.B., Esq., Barrister-at-Law. 8vo. 1876. 1l. 5s.

Foard's Treatise on the Law of Merchant Shipping and Freight. —By J. T. FOARD, Barrister-at-Law. Roy. 8vo. 1880. Hf. cf. 1l. 1s.

SLANDER.—Odgers.—Vide " Libel and Slander."

SOLICITORS.—Cordery's Law relating to Solicitors of the Supreme Court of Judicature. With an Appendix of Statutes and Rules, and Notes on Appointments open to Solicitors, and the Right to Admission to the Colonies. Second Edition. By A. CORDERY, Esq., Barrister-at-Law. Demy 8vo. 1888. 16s.

"The book is very clear, accurate, and practical, and will be found of much value. Without being bulky, it contains in a concise and intelligible form all the matters usually occurring in a solicitor's practice."—*Solicitors' Journal*.

Turner.—Vide " Conveyancing " and " Vendors and Purchasers."

Whiteway's Hints to Solicitors.—Being a Treatise on the Law relating to their Duties as Officers of the High Court of Justice. By A. R. WHITEWAY, M.A., of the Equity Bar and Midland Circuit. Royal 12mo. 1883. 6s.

SPECIFIC PERFORMANCE.—Fry's Treatise on the Specific Performance of Contracts. By the Hon. Sir EDWARD FRY, a Lord Justice of Appeal. Second Edition. By the Author and W. DONALDSON RAWLINS, Esq. Royal 8vo. 1881. 1l. 16s.

STAMP ACTS.—Highmore's Stamp Act, 1891, and the Stamp Duties Management Act, 1891. With an Introduction and Notes, and a copious Index. By NATHANIEL JOSEPH HIGHMORE, of the Middle Temple, Esq., Barrister-at-Law, Assistant-Solicitor of the Inland Revenue. Demy 8vo. 1891. 5s.

"A useful guide to those who desire to understand the present state of the stamp laws."—*Law Journal*, November 7, 1891.

"Thoroughly well done in every respect."—*Law Gazette*, November 5, 1891.

"This edition supplies practising lawyers with all the help that acuteness, sagacity and experience can give to them."—*Justice of the Peace*, October 17, 1891.

STATUTE LAW.—Wilberforce on Statute Law. The Principles which govern the Construction and Operation of Statutes. By E. WILBERFORCE, Esq., Barrister-at-Law. 1881. 18s.

*** *All standard Law Works are kept in Stock, in law calf and other bindings.*

STATUTES, and vide "Acts of Parliament."
Chitty's Collection of Statutes from Magna Charta to 1880.—A Collection of Statutes of Practical Utility, arranged in Alphabetical and Chronological order, with Notes thereon. The Fourth Edition. By J. M. LELY, Esq., Barrister-at-Law. In 6 vols. Royal 8vo. 1880. Published at 12*l*. 12*s*., reduced to *Net* 6*l*. 6*s*.
The following may still be had separately—

44 & 45 Vict.	1881.	8*s*.
46 & 47 Vict.	1883.	14*s*.
47 & 48 Vict.	1884.	10*s*. 6*d*.
48 & 49 Vict.	1885.	12*s*. 6*d*.
50 & 51 Vict.	1887.	10*s*. 6*d*.
51 & 52 Vict.	1888.	12*s*. 6*d*.
51 & 52 Vict.	1888. (Second Session.)	*Net* 2*s*. 6*d*.
52 & 53 Vict.	1889.	10*s*.
53 & 54 Vict.	1890.	15*s*.
54 & 55 Vict.	1891.	12*s*.

"It is needless to enlarge on the value of 'Chitty's Statutes' to both the Bar and to Solicitors, for it is attested by the experience of many years."—*The Times.*

"A very satisfactory edition of a time-honoured and most valuable work, the trusty guide of present, as of former, judges, jurists, and of all others connected with the administration or practice of the law."—*Justice of the Peace.*

"'Chitty' is pre-eminently a friend in need. Those who do not possess a complete set of the Statutes turn to its chronological index when they wish to consult a particular Act of Parliament. Those who wish to know what Acts are in force with reference to a particular subject turn to that head in 'Chitty,' and at once find all the material of which they are in quest. Moreover, they are, at the same time, referred to the most important cases which throw light on the subject."—*Law Journal.*

SUCCESSION.—Potts' Principles of the Law of Succession to Deceased Persons.—By T. RADFORD POTTS, B.C.L., M.A., Barrister-at-Law. Demy 8vo. 1888. 7*s*. 6*d*.

SUMMARY CONVICTIONS.—Paley's Law and Practice of Summary Convictions under the Summary Jurisdiction Acts.—Seventh Edition. By W. H. MACNAMARA, Esq., Barrister-at-Law.
(*In preparation.*)

Wigram.—*Vide* "Justice of the Peace."

SUMMONSES & ORDERS.—Archibald.—*Vide* "Chamber Practice."

TAXES ON SUCCESSION.—Trevor's Taxes on Succession.—A Digest of the Statutes and Cases (including those in Scotland and Ireland) relating to the Probate, Legacy and Succession Duties, with Practical Observations and Official Forms. Fourth Edition. By EVELYN FREETH and R. J. WALLACE, of the Legacy and Succession Duty Office. Royal 12mo. 1881. 12*s*. 6*d*.

TAXPAYERS' GUIDES.—*Vide* "House Tax," "Income Tax," and "Land Tax."

THEATRES AND MUSIC HALLS.—Geary's Law of Theatres and Music Halls, including Contracts and Precedents of Contracts.—By W. N. M. GEARY, J.P. With Historical Introduction. By JAMES WILLIAMS, Esqrs., Barristers-at-Law. 8vo. 1885. 5*s*.

TITHES.—Bolton's Tithe Acts; including the Recent Act for the Limitation and Redemption of Extraordinary Tithe; with an Introduction and Observations and copious Index. By T. H. BOLTON, Solicitor. Royal 12mo. 1886. 6*s*.

Studd's Law of Tithes and Tithe Rent-Charge.—Being a Treatise on the Law of Tithe Rent-Charge, with a sketch of the History and Law of Tithes prior to the Commutation Acts, and including the Tithe Act of 1891, with the Rules thereunder. Second Edition. By EDWARD FAIRFAX STUDD, Esq., Barrister-at-Law. Royal 12mo. 1891. 6*s*.

"This book was originally a good one. Now it is a better one."—*Law Times.*

"This work is thoroughly reliable."—*Solicitors' Journal.*

⁎* *All standard Law Works are kept in Stock, in law calf and other bindings.*

TORTS.—Addison on Torts; being a Treatise on Wrongs and their Remedies. Sixth Edition. By HORACE SMITH, Esq., Bencher of the Inner Temple, Editor of "Addison on Contracts," &c. Royal 8vo. 1887. 1l. 18s.

"Upon a careful perusal of the editor's work, we can say that he has done it excellently."—*Law Quarterly Review.*

"As now presented, this valuable treatise must prove highly acceptable to judges and the profession."—*Law Times.*

"An indispensable addition to every lawyer's library."—*Law Magazine.*

Ball's Leading Cases on the Law of Torts, with Notes. Edited by W. E. BALL, LL.D., Esq., Barrister-at-Law, Author of "Principles of Torts and Contracts." Royal 8vo. 1884. 1l. 1s.

"The notes are extremely, and as far as we have been able to discover uniformly, good. . . There is much intelligent and independent criticism."—*Solicitors' Journal.*

Innes' Principles of the Law of Torts.—By L. C. INNES, lately one of the Judges of the High Court, Madras, Author of "A Digest of the English Law of Easements." Demy 8vo. 1891. 10s. 6d.

"Throughout the work the author is clear in his definitions, and there is no lack of illustrative examples. . . . A welcome addition to the library of the student and the practitioner."—*Law Times.*

Pollock's Law of Torts: a Treatise on the Principles of Obligations arising from Civil Wrongs in the Common Law. Second Edition, to which is added the draft of a Code of Civil Wrongs prepared for the Government of India. By Sir FREDERICK POLLOCK, Bart., Barrister-at-Law. Author of "Principles of Contract," "A Digest of the Law of Partnership," &c. Demy 8vo. 1890. 21s.

"Concise, logically arranged, and accurate."—*Law Times.*

"A book which is well worthy to stand beside the companion volume on 'Contracts.' Unlike so many law-books, especially on this subject, it is no mere digest of cases, but bears the impress of the mind of the writer from beginning to end."—*Law Journal.*

Shearwood's Sketch of the Law of Tort for the Bar and Solicitors Final Examinations. By JOSEPH A. SHEARWOOD, Esq., Barrister-at-Law. Royal 12mo. 1886. 3s.

TRADE MARKS.—Aston.—*Vide* "Patents."

Graham's Designs and Trade Marks.—By JOHN CAMERON GRAHAM, of the Middle Temple, Barrister-at-Law. Demy 8vo. 1889. 6s.

Sebastian on the Law of Trade Marks and their Registration, and matters connected therewith, including a chapter on Goodwill; together with the Patents, Designs and Trade Marks Acts, 1883-8, and the Trade Marks Rules and Instructions thereunder; Forms and Precedents; the Merchandize Marks Act, 1887, and other Statutory Enactments; the United States Statutes, 1870-81, and the Rules and Forms thereunder; and the Treaty with the United States, 1877. Third Edition. By LEWIS BOYD SEBASTIAN, Esq., Barrister-at-Law. Demy 8vo. 1890. 1l. 5s.

"The work stands alone as an authority upon the law of trade-marks and their registration."—*Law Journal,* August 2, 1890.

"It is hardly necessary to tell anyone who has consulted the last edition of this book that it is characterized by mastery of the subject, exemplary industry, and completeness and accuracy of statement. It is rarely we come across a law book which embodies the results of years of careful investigation and practical experience in a branch of law, or that can be unhesitatingly appealed to as a standard authority. This is what can be said of Mr. Sebastian's book."—*Solicitors' Journal,* Nov. 1, 1890.

Sebastian's Digest of Cases of Trade Mark, Trade Name, Trade Secret, Goodwill, &c., decided in the Courts of the United Kingdom, India, the Colonies, and the United States of America. By LEWIS BOYD SEBASTIAN, Esq., Barrister-at-Law. 8vo. 1879. 1l. 1s.

"A digest which will be of very great value to all practitioners who have to advise on matters connected with trade marks."—*Solicitors' Journal.*

⁎ *All standard Law Works are kept in Stock, in law calf and other bindings.*

TRAMWAYS.—Sutton's Tramway Acts of the United Kingdom; with Notes on the Law and Practice, an Introduction, including the Proceedings before the Committees, Decisions of the Referees with respect to Locus Standi, and a Summary of the Principles of Tramway Rating, and an Appendix containing the Standing Orders of Parliament. Rules of the Board of Trade relating to Tramways, &c. Second Edition. By HENRY SUTTON, assisted by ROBERT A. BENNETT, Barristers-at-Law. Demy 8vo. 1883. 15s.

TRUST FUNDS.—Geare's Investment of Trust Funds.—Incorporating the Trustee Act, 1888. By EDWARD ARUNDEL GEARE, Esq., Barrister-at-Law. Second Edition. Including the Trusts Investment Act, 1889. Royal 12mo. 1889. 7s. 6d.

"The work is written in an easy style, it can very well be read by all trustees, whether they are lawyers or not; and if they will take our advice, and invest their money here before they invest other people's elsewhere, they may be spared much trouble in the future."—*The Jurist.*

TRUSTS AND TRUSTEES.—Godefroi's Law Relating to Trusts and Trustees.—Second Edition. By HENRY GODEFROI, of Lincoln's Inn, Esq., Barrister-at-Law. Royal 8vo. 1891. 1l. 12s.

"The second edition of this work which lies before us is a model of what a legal text-book ought to be. It is clear in style and clear in arrangement, and we can have little doubt that it will soon take the foremost place among text-books dealing with trusts. Moreover, it is brought up to date by including in its scope the Trust Investment Act of 1889, and the Settled Land Act, 1890. The chapter on Precatory Trusts in Mr. Godefroi's work seems to us particularly good and clear, and the many judicial decisions as to what expressions are sufficient and what are insufficient to import a trust are marshalled with great care and accuracy."—*Law Times,* April 18, 1891.

Hamilton's Trustee Acts.—Containing the Trustee Act, 1850; the Trustee Extension Act, 1852; and the Trustee Act, 1888; with Supplement of the Lunacy Act, 1890 (53 Vict. c. 5), so far as relates to Vesting Orders. By G. BALDWIN HAMILTON, Esq., Barrister-at-Law, Author of "A Concise Treatise on the Law of Covenants." Demy 8vo. 1890. 6s.

"This is a very useful little book. We have perused it with much care, and have come to the conclusion that it may be safely trusted to us as a guide to the complicated law to which it relates."—*Law Quarterly Review.*

VENDORS AND PURCHASERS.—Dart's Vendors and Purchasers.—A Treatise on the Law and Practice relating to Vendors and Purchasers of Real Estate. By the late J. HENRY DART, Esq., one of the Six Conveyancing Counsel of the High Court of Justice, Chancery Division. Sixth Edition. By WILLIAM BARBER, Esq., one of Her Majesty's Counsel, RICHARD BURDON HALDANE, and WILLIAM ROBERT SHELDON, both of Lincoln's Inn, Esqrs., Barristers-at-Law. 2 vols. Royal 8vo. 1888. 3l. 15s.

"The new edition of Dart is far ahead of all competitors in the breadth of its range, the clearness of its exposition, and the soundness of its law."—*Law Times.*

"The extensive changes and numerous improvements which have been introduced are the result of assiduous labour, combined with critical acumen, sound knowledge, and practical experience."—*Law Quarterly Review.*

Turner's Duties of Solicitor to Client as to Sales, Purchases, and Mortgages of Land.—By EDWARD F. TURNER, Solicitor, Lecturer on Real Property and Conveyancing. Demy 8vo. 1883. 10s. 6d.

See also Conveyancing.—" Turner."

"A careful perusal of these lectures cannot fail to be of great advantage to students, and more particularly, we think, to young practising solicitors."—*Law Times.*

WAR, DECLARATION OF.—Owen's Declaration of War.—A Survey of the Position of Belligerents and Neutrals, with relative considerations of Shipping and Marine Insurance during War. By DOUGLAS OWEN, Barrister-at-Law. Demy 8vo. 1889. 21s.

*** *All standard Law Works are kept in Stock, in law calf and other bindings.*

WATERS.—Musgrave's Dissertation on the Common Law of Waters and its Application to Natural Circumstances other than those of England.—By W. A. B. Musgrave, D.C.L., of the Inner Temple, Barrister-at-Law. Demy 8vo. 1890. *Net*, 2s.

WILLS.—Theobald's Concise Treatise on the Law of Wills.— Third Edition. By H. S. Theobald, Esq., Barrister-at-Law. Royal 8vo. 1885. 1l. 10s.

" A book of great ability and value. It bears on every page traces of care and sound judgment. It is certain to prove of great practical usefulness."—*Solicitors' Journal.*

Weaver's Precedents of Wills.—A Collection of Concise Precedents of Wills, with Introduction, Notes, and an Appendix of Statutes. By Charles Weaver, B.A. Post 8vo. 1882. 5s.

WINDING UP.—Palmer's Winding-up Forms.—A Collection of 580 Forms of Summonses, Affidavits, Orders, Notices and other Forms relating to the Winding-up of Companies. With Notes on the Law and Practice, and an Appendix containing the Acts and Rules. By Francis Beaufort Palmer, Esq., Barrister-at-Law, Author of "Company Precedents," &c. 8vo. 1885. 12s.

Pitt-Lewis' Winding-up Practice.—A Manual of the Practice as to Winding-up in the High Court and in the County Court; being the Companies (Winding-up) Act, 1890, and the Winding-up of Companies and Associations (Part IV. of the Companies Act, 1862), as now amended, with Notes, and the Companies Winding-up Rules, 1890. Forming a Supplement to "A Complete Practice of the County Courts." By G. Pitt-Lewis, Q.C., M.P., Recorder of Poole. Demy 8vo. 1891. 7s. 6d.

"This is a book that we can cordially recommend, and forms a fitting supplement to the aptly-named larger work of the same author."—*Law Gazette*, March 5, 1891.

WRECK INQUIRIES.—Murton's Law and Practice relating to Formal Investigations in the United Kingdom, British Possessions and before Naval Courts into Shipping Casualties and the Incompetency and Misconduct of Ships' Officers. With an Introduction. By Walter Murton, Solicitor to the Board of Trade. Demy 8vo. 1884. 1l. 4s.

WRONGS.—Addison, Ball, Pollock, Shearwood.—*Vide* "Torts."

REPORTS.—The largest Stock in London. Prices on application.

BINDING.—Executed in the best manner at moderate prices and with dispatch.

The Law Reports, Law Journal, and all other Reports, bound to Office Patterns, at Office Prices.

PRIVATE ACTS.—*The Publishers of this Catalogue possess the largest known collection of Private Acts of Parliament (including Public and Local), and can supply single copies commencing from a very early period.*

LICENSED VALUERS for Probate, Partnership, &c.

LIBRARIES PURCHASED OR EXCHANGED.

STEVENS AND SONS, Ld., 119 & 120, CHANCERY LANE, LONDON.

NEW WORKS AND NEW EDITIONS.

Annual County Court Practice, 1892.—By His Honor Judge WASHINGTON HEYWOOD. 2 vols. Demy 8vo. (*Nearly ready.*)

Browne's Probate Practice.—New Edition. By L. D. POWLES, Barrister-at-Law, and T. W. H. OAKLEY, of the Principal Registry, Somerset House. (*In the press.*)

Dixon's Law of the Farm.—Fifth Edition. By AUBREY J. SPENCER, B.A., Esq., Barrister-at-Law. (*In the press.*)

Fry's Treatise on the Specific Performance of Contracts.—By the Right Hon. Sir EDWARD FRY, one of the Lords Justices of Appeal. Third Edition. By the Author and EDWARD PORTSMOUTH FRY, Esq., Barrister-at-Law. (*In the press.*)

Hedderwick's Parliamentary Election Manual.—By THOMAS CHARLES HEDDERWICK, Esq., Barrister-at-Law. (*Nearly ready.*)

Leake's Law of Contracts.—Third Edition. By STEPHEN MARTIN LEAKE, Barrister-at-Law. (*In the press.*)

Paley's Law and Practice of Summary Convictions under the Summary Jurisdiction Acts.—Seventh Edition. By W. H. MACNAMARA, Esq., Barrister-at-Law. (*In preparation.*)

Phillimore's Ecclesiastical Law of the Church of England.—Second Edition. Edited by Sir WALTER GEO. FRANK PHILLIMORE, Bart., D.C.L., Chancellor of the Diocese of Lincoln. (*In preparation.*)

Rogers on Elections: Parliamentary, Municipal, and Local Government; with Appendices of Statutes, Orders in Council, and Forms. Sixteenth Edition. By MAURICE POWELL, of the Inner Temple, Esq., Barrister-at-Law. (*Part I. (Elections) in preparation.*)

Roscoe's Admiralty Practice.—Third Edition. By E. S. ROSCOE and T. LAMBERT MEARS, Esqrs., Barristers-at-Law. (*In preparation.*)

Selwyn's Abridgment of the Law of Nisi Prius.—14th Edition. By W. H. MACNAMARA, Esq., Barrister-at-Law. (*In preparation.*)

Seton's Forms of Judgments and Orders in the High Court of Justice and Courts of Appeal, having especial reference to the Chancery Division, with Practical Notes. Fifth Edition. By CECIL C. M. DALE, Esq., Barrister-at-Law, and W. CLOWES, Esq., one of the Registrars of the Supreme Court. Vol. 2. (*In the press.*)

Shelford's Real Property Statutes.—Ninth Edition. By T. H. CARSON, Esq., Barrister-at-Law. (*In preparation.*)

Theobald and Schuster's Lunacy Act, 1890, with Notes.—By H. S. THEOBALD and E. J. SCHUSTER, Barristers-at-Law. (*In preparation.*)

Warburton's Selection of Leading Cases in the Criminal Law. With Notes.—By HENRY WARBURTON, Esq., Barrister-at-Law. [Founded on "Shirley's Leading Cases."] (*Nearly ready.*)

Wharton's Law Lexicon.—Ninth Edition. By J. M. LELY, Esq., Barrister-at-Law. (*In the press.*)

Wheeler's Privy Council Law: A Synopsis of all the Appeals decided by the Judicial Committee from 1876 to 1891. Together with a Précis of the Cases from the Supreme Court of Canada in which special leave to appeal has been granted or refused. By GEORGE WHEELER, Esq., Barrister-at-Law, and of the Judicial Department of the Privy Council. (*In preparation.*)

Whitehead's Church Law.—Being a Concise Dictionary of Statutes, Canons and Regulations affecting the Clergy and Laity. By BENJAMIN WHITEHEAD, B.A., Esq., Barrister-at-Law. (*In preparation.*)

Wigram's Justice's Note Book.—By the late W. KNOX WIGRAM, Esq., Barrister-at-Law, J.P. Sixth Edition. By ARCHIBALD HENRY BODKIN, Esq., Barrister-at-Law. (*Nearly ready.*)

Williams' Law of Executors and Administrators.—Ninth Edition. By the Hon. Sir ROLAND VAUGHAN WILLIAMS, a Justice of the High Court. 2 vols. Royal 8vo. (*In the press.*)

STEVENS AND SONS, LD., 119 & 120, CHANCERY LANE, LONDON.

www.ingramcontent.com/pod-product-compliance
Lightning Source LLC
Chambersburg PA
CBHW030750230426
43667CB00007B/914